The Story of San Michele

The Story of San Michele

AXEL MUNTHE

The Story of
San Michele

Flamingo
An Imprint of HarperCollins*Publishers*

Flamingo
An Imprint of HarperCollins*Publishers*
77–85 Fulham Palace Road,
Hammersmith, London W6 8JB

www.**fire**and**water**.com

A Flamingo Modern Classic 1995
9 8 7 6

Previously published in paperback by Grafton 1975

First published in Great Britain by John Murray (Publishers) Ltd 1929

Copyright © Axel Munthe 1929

ISBN 0 586 20810 0

Set in Times

Printed and bound in Great Britain by
Omnia Books Limited, Glasgow

CONTENTS

The Story of San Michele

PREFACE TO THE FIRST EDITION

I had rushed over to London from France to see about my naturalization, it looked as if my country was going to be dragged into the war by the side of Germany. Henry James was to be one of my sponsors, he had just been naturalized himself, 'Civis Britannicus sum,' he said in his deep voice. He knew that I had tried to do my bit and that I had failed because I had become too helpless myself to be of any help to others. He knew the fate that awaited me. He laid his hand on my shoulder and asked me what I was going to do with myself? I told him I was about to leave France for good to hide like a deserter in my old tower. It was the only place I was fit for. As he wished me good-bye he reminded me how years ago when he was staying with me at San Michele he had encouraged me to write a book about my island home, which he had called the most beautiful place in the world. Why not write The Story of San Michele now if it came to the worst and my courage began to flag? Who could write about San Michele better than I who had built it with my own hands? Who could describe better than I all these priceless fragments of marbles strewn over the garden where the villa of Tiberius once stood? And the sombre old Emperor himself whose weary foot had trod the very mosaic floor I had brought to light under the vines, what a fascinating study for a man like me who was so interested in psychology! There was nothing like writing a book for a man who wanted to get away from his own misery, nothing like writing a book for a man who could not sleep.

These were his last words, I never saw my friend again.

I returned to my useless solitude in the old tower, humiliated and despondent. While everybody else was offering his life to his country, I spent my days wandering up and down in the dark tower, restless like a caged animal, while the never-ending tidings of suffering and woe were read to me. Now and then of an evening when the relentless light of the day had ceased to torture my eyes, I used to wander up to San Michele in search of news. The flag of the British Red Cross was flying over San Michele where brave and

11

disabled men were nursed back to health by the same sun that had driven me away from my beloved home. Alas for the news! How long was the waiting for those who could do nothing but wait!

But how many of us dare to confess what so many have felt, that the burden of their own grief seemed easier to bear while all men and women around us were in mourning, that the wound in their own flanks seemed almost to heal while the blood was flowing from so many other wounds? Who dared to grumble over his own fate while the fate of the world was at stake? Who dared to whimper over his own pain while all these mutilated men were lying on their stretchers silent with set teeth?

At last the storm abated. All was silent as before in the old tower, I was alone with my fear.

Man was built to carry his own cross, that is why he was given his strong shoulders. A man can stand a lot as long as he can stand himself. He can live without hope, without friends, without books, even without music, as long as he can listen to his own thoughts and to the singing of a bird outside his window and to the far-away voice of the sea. I was told at St. Dunstan's that he can even live without light, but those who told me so were heroes. But a man cannot live without sleep. When I ceased to sleep I began to write this book, all milder remedies having failed. It has been a great success so far as I am concerned. Over and over again I have blessed Henry James for his advice. I have been sleeping much better of late. It has even been a pleasure to me to write this book, I no longer wonder why so many people are taking to writing books in our days. Unfortunately I have been writing The Story of San Michele under peculiar difficulties. I was interrupted at the very beginning by an unexpected visitor who sat down opposite to me at the writing-table and began to talk about himself and his own affairs in the most erratic manner, as if all this nonsense could interest anybody but himself. There was something very irritating and unEnglish in the way he kept on relating his various adventures where he always seemed to turn out to have been the hero – too much Ego in your Cosmos, young man, thought I. He seemed to think he knew everything, antique art, architecture, psychology, Death and Hereafter. Medicine seemed to be his special hobby, he said he was a nerve specialist and boasted of being a pupil of Charcot's as they all do. God help his patients, I said to myself. As he mentioned the name of the master of the Salpêtrière I fancied for a moment that I had seen him before, long, long ago, but I soon dismissed the thought as absurd, for he looked so young and boisterous, and I felt so old and weary. His unceasing swagger, his very youth began to get on my nerves, and to make matters worse it soon dawned upon me that this young gentleman was making mild fun of me the whole time, as young people are apt to do with old people. He even tried to make me believe that it was he and not I who had built San Michele! He said he loved the place and was going to live there for ever. At last I told him to leave me alone and let me go on with my Story of San Michele and my description of my precious marble fragments from the villa of Tiberius.

'Poor old man,' said the young fellow with his patronizing smile, 'you are talking through your hat! I fear you cannot even read your own handwriting! It is not about San Michele and your precious marble fragments from the villa of Tiberius you have been writing the whole time, it is only some fragments of clay from your own broken life that you have brought to light.'

TORRE DI MATBRITA,
    1928.

ABOUT THIS BOOK

PREFACE TO THE 12TH EDITION

Reviewers of this book seem to have found considerable difficulty in attempting to classify The Story of San Michele, and I do not wonder. Some have described the book as an Autobiography, others have called it 'The Memoirs of a Doctor.' As far as I can understand, it is neither the one nor the other. Surely it could not have taken me five hundred pages, to write down the story of my life, even had I not left out its saddest and most eventful chapters. All I can say is that I never meant to write a book about myself: it was, on the contrary, my constant preoccupation the whole time to try to shake off this vague personality. If anyhow this book has turned out to be an Autobiography, I begin to believe that, judging from the sale of it, the simplest way to write a book about oneself consists in trying as hard as one can to think of somebody else. All a man has to do is to sit still in a chair by himself, and look back upon his life with his blind eye. Better still would be to lie down in the grass and not to think at all, only to listen. Soon the distant roar of the world dies away, and the forests and fields begin to sing with clear bird voices, friendly animals come up to tell him their joys and sorrows in sounds and words that he can understand, and when all is silent even the lifeless things around him begin to whisper in their sleep.

To call this book 'The Memoirs of a Doctor,' as some reviewers have done, seems to me even less appropriate. Its boisterous simplicity, its unblushing frankness, its very lucidity fit ill with such a pompous sub-title. Surely a medical man, like every other human being, has the right to laugh at himself now and then to keep up his spirits, maybe even to laugh at his colleagues if he is willing to stand the risk. But he has no right to laugh at his patients. To shed tears with them is even worse, a whimpering doctor is a bad doctor. An old physician should, besides, think twice before sitting down in his arm-chair to write his memoirs. Better keep to himself what he has seen of Life and Death. Better write no memoirs at all, and leave the dead in peace and the living to their illusions.

15

Somebody has called The Story of San Michele a story of Death. Maybe it is so, for Death is seldom out of my thoughts, 'Non nasce in me pensier che non vi sia dentro scolpita la Morte' wrote Michel Angelo to Vasari. I have been wrestling so long with my grim colleague; always defeated, I have seen him slay one by one all those I have tried to save. I have had a few of them in mind in this book as I saw them live, as I saw them suffer, as I saw them lie down to die. It was all that I could do for them. They were all humble people, no marble crosses stand on their graves, many of them were already forgotten long before they died. They are all right now. Old Maria Porta-Lettere who climbed the 777 Phoenician steps for thirty years on her naked feet with my letters, is now carrying the post in Heaven, where dear old Pacciale sits smoking his pipe of peace, still looking out over the infinite sea as he used to do from the pergola of San Michele, and where my friend Arcangelo Fusco, the street-sweeper in Quartier Montparnasse, is still sweeping the star-dust from the golden floor. Down the stately peristyle of lapis-lazuli columns struts briskly little Monsieur Alphonse, the doyen of the Little Sisters of the Poor, in the Pittsburgh millionaire's brand-new frock-coat, solemnly raising his beloved top-hat to every saint he meets, as he used to do to all my friends when he drove down the Corso in my victoria. John, the blue-eyed little boy who never smiled, is now playing lustily with lots of other happy children in the old nursery of the Bambino. He has learnt to smile at last. The whole room is full of flowers, singing birds are flying in and out through the open windows, now and then the Madonna looks in to see that the children have all they want. John's mother, who nursed him so tenderly in Avenue de Villiers, is still down here. I saw her the other day. Poor Flopette, the harlot, looks ten years younger than when I saw her in the night-café on the boulevard; very tidy and neat in her white dress, she is now second housemaid to Mary Magdalene.

In a humble corner of the Elysian Fields is the cemetery of the dogs. All my dead friends are there; their bodies are still where I laid them down under the cypresses by the old Tower, but their faithful hearts have been taken up here. Kind St. Rocco, the little patron-saint of all dogs, is the custodian of the cemetery, and good old Miss Hall is a frequent visitor there. Even the rascal Billy, the drunkard Baboon, who set fire to Il Canonico Don Giacinto's coffin, has been admitted on trial to the last row of graves in the monkey cemetery some way off, after a close scrutiny from St. Peter, who noticed he smelled of whisky and mistook him at first for a human being. Don Giacinto himself, the richest priest in Capri, who had never given a penny to the poor, is still roasting in his coffin; and the ex-butcher of Anacapri, who blinded the quails with a red-hot needle, has had his own eyes stung out by the Devil in person in a fit of professional jealousy.

One reviewer has discovered that 'there is enough material in *The Story of San Michele* to furnish writers of short sensational stories with plots for the rest of their lives.' They are quite welcome to this material for what it is worth. I have no further use for it. Having concentrated my literary efforts during a lifetime on writing prescriptions, I am not likely to try my hand on short sensational stories so late in the day. Would that I had thought of it before, or I should not be where I am to-day! Surely it must be a more comfortable job to sit in an arm-chair and write short sensational stories than to toil through life to collect the material for them, to describe diseases and Death than to fight them, to concoct sinister plots than to be knocked down by them without warning! But why do not these professionals collect their material themselves? They seldom do. Novel writers, who insist on taking their readers to the slums, seldom go there themselves. Specialists on disease and Death can seldom be persuaded to come with you to the hospital where they have just finished off their heroine. Poets and philosophers, who in sonorous verse and prose hail Death as the Deliverer, often grow pale at the very mention of the name of their best friend. It is an old story. Leopardi, the greatest poet of modern Italy, who longed for Death in exquisite rhymes ever since he was a boy, was the first to fly in abject terror from cholera-stricken Naples. Even the great Montaigne, whose calm meditations on Death are enough to make him immortal, bolted like a rabbit when the peste broke out in Bordeaux. Sulky old Schopenhauer, the greatest philosopher of modern times who had made the negation of life the very keystone of his teaching, used to cut short all conversation about Death. The bloodiest war novels were written, I believe, by peaceful citizens well out of the range of the long-distance German guns. Authors who delight in making their readers assist at scenes of sexual orgies are generally very indifferent actors in such scenes. Personally I only know of one exception to this rule, Guy de Maupassant, and I saw him die of it.

I am aware that some of the scenes in this book are laid on the ill-defined borderland between the real and the unreal, the dangerous No Man's Land between fact and fancy where so many writers of memoirs have come to grief and where Goethe himself was apt to lose his bearings in his 'Dichtung und Wahrheit.' I have tried my best by means of a few well-known technical tricks to make at least some of these episodes pass off as 'short sensational stories.' After all, it is

17

only a question of form. It will be a great relief to me if I have suc-ceeded, I do not ask for better than not to be believed. It is bad enough and sad enough anyhow. God knows I have a good deal to answer for as it is. I shall also take it as a compliment, for the greatest writer of short sensational stories I know is Life. But is Life always true?

Life is the same as it always was, unruffled by events, indifferent to the joys and sorrows of man, mute and incomprehensible as the Sphinx. But the stage on which the everlasting tragedy is enacted changes constantly to avoid monotony. The world we lived in yesterday is not the same world as we live in to-day, inexorably it moves on through the infinite towards its doom, and so do we. No man bathes twice in the same river, said Heraclitus. Some of us crawl on our knees, some ride on horseback or in motor-car; others fly past the carrier-pigeon in aeroplanes. There is no need for hurry, we are all sure to reach the journey's end.

No, the world I lived in when I was young is not the same world that I live in to-day, at least it does not seem so to me. Nor do I think it will seem so to those who read this book of rambles in search of adventure in the past. There are no more brigands with a record of eight homicides to offer you to sleep on their mattresses in tumble-down Messina. No more granite sphinxes are crouching under the ruins of Nero's villa in Calabria. The maddened rats in the cholera slums of Naples, who frightened me to death, have long ago retreated in safety to their Roman sewers. You can drive up to Anacapri in a motor-car, and to the top of the Jungfrau in a train, and climb the Matterhorn with rope-ladders. Up in Lapland no pack of hungry wolves, their eyes blazing in the dark like burning coals, is likely to gallop behind your sledge across the frozen lake. The gallant old bear, who barred my way in the lonely Suvla gorge, has long ago departed to the Happy Hunting Fields. The foaming torrent I swam across with Ristin, the Lap girl, is spanned by a railway-bridge. The last stronghold of the terrible Stalo, the Troll, has been pierced by a tunnel. The Little People I heard patter about under the floor of the Lap tent, no more bring food to the sleeping bears in their winter quarters: that is why there are so few bears in Sweden to-day. You are welcome to laugh incredulously at these busy Little People as much as you like, at your own risk and peril. But I refuse to believe that any reader of this book will have the effrontery to deny that it was a real goblin I saw sitting on the table in Forsstugan and pull cauti-ously at my watch-chain. Of course it was a real goblin. Who could it otherwise have been? I tell you I saw him distinctly with both my eyes when I sat up in my bed just as the tallow candle was flickering out.

18

I am told to my surprise that there are people who have never seen a goblin. One cannot help feeling sorry for such people. I am sure there must be something wrong with their eyesight. Old uncle Lars Anders in Forsstugan, six feet six in his sheepskin-coat and wooden shoes, is dead long ago, and so is dear old Mother Kerstin, his wife. But the little goblin I saw sitting cross-legged on the table in the attic over the cow-stall is alive. It is only we who die.

    St. James's Club, 1930

INSTEAD OF A PREFACE

INTRODUCTION TO ILLUSTRATED EDITION

I am in disgrace with my friend John Murray for having backed out at the last moment from writing another preface to this book. I have told him that a man who cannot sleep cannot write a preface or, at least, he ought not to do so. I have also told him that I have nothing to say. To be just to my publisher, I am bound to admit that this last argument is no valid excuse for not writing a preface, nor, for the matter of that, for not writing a whole book. If I were to write a preface, I should begin by asking the reader to explain to me in clear language why The Story of San Michele is a Best Seller in twenty-five tongues. I have asked many readers and reviewers this same question, but so far I have asked in vain. Nobody seems to know more about it than I do, the riddle remains unsolved.

The only attempts at an explanation I have yet come across are that 'This book is unlike any other book I have ever read,' or that 'This man is quite unlike other people I have ever met.' One acute American reviewer has tried to get out of his difficulties by advancing the theory that 'Axel Munthe does not exist.' I admit that this hypothesis has caused me some hard thinking. I warmly recommend it to the benevolent attention of interviewers, photographers, autograph hunters, palmists, agents for film companies and lecturing tours in America, and to hero-worshippers at all costs. I also recommend to them a little known letter of Petrarch's in his Epistolæ Familiares where he observes that the learned men of his age were apt to think little of a man's writings if they had even once seen him. Why all this fuss about me? What would become of me to-day if I had not enough sense of humour left in my old head to see the joke? Alas! it has all come too late. I am too old to be vain, too old to be a Best Seller. Yet another strange adventure on my road through life before the Great Adventure at the journey's end, the strangest of all! Yet another disillusion added to the long list, yet another failure in the grip of success, yet another broken toy from life's withered Christmas tree in the hand of Fortune's spoiled child! Does she then not see, the fickle Goddess, that I am too old to play with toys, too wise to be taken in? Does she not know that I have thrown too many Best Sellers on the floor not to have learnt something about their average weight: that I have found out long ago that the large sale of a book is no safer index for the right estimate of an author than is a large clientèle for the right estimate of a doctor, and that in neither case is it sufficient to rely solely on the testimony of the living? It needs a coming generation of readers and reviewers to fix the value of a book, and then God help us Best Sellers of a day!

I am not a bookwriter and I hope never to become one. The Story of San Michele was the result of an unforeseen accident while I was groping my way in the dusk among the hammers and wheels of my newly acquired Corona, hard at work learning to typewrite; I had been warned it was high time. I was far too busy superintending the acrobatics of my ten clumsy fingers to pay much attention to the whimsical game of hide-and-seek going on at the back of my head between thought and word. 'Ich habe nie über das Denken genacht,' I have never bestowed much thought on thinking, said Goethe. But now and then between the hammer-strokes I could hear the beating of my heart.

But my chief difficulty in writing this book was to keep still where I was, I always seemed to be on the move from place to place. 'My thoughts go to sleep unless they and I wander,' wrote Montaigne. As often as not in the midst of a chapter on something else, I had to rush off to Lapland on a visit to some goblins and trolls or to interview a bear and, in the very next sentence, to take a swim in the Blue Grotto in Capri, to look after poor Jacques, the sick gorilla in Paris, and to roll down the ice-slopes of Mont Blanc between two commas, helping myself off and on to a glass of vino vecchio under the pergola of San Michele. While I was flirting in the moonshine with the fair Countess in her château in Touraine, I managed to mix up the two coffins in the train from Heidelberg and to kiss the nun in the convent of the Sepolte Vive in cholera-stricken Naples before I fell asleep in tumble-down Messina on the mattress of my bosom friend Signor Amedeo, who had murdered eight people and lent me five hundred lire. I had a restless night, for I was back in Avenue de Villiers in my dream, trembling with fear of the terrible Mamsell Agata.

Suddenly in the midst of my wanderings, as I looked up from my typewriter in search of inspiration, I saw to my surprise that the whole room was full of people, street-sweepers and organ-grinders from Quartier Montparnasse and broken-down prostitutes from the outer boulevards in Paris, gravediggers from the Protestant cemetery in Rome, and tottering inmates from the almshouse of the Little Sisters of the Poor, shabby old monks and frati, street-singers, blind beggars, idiots, cripples and all sorts of outcasts from the slums of Naples. Some wiped off a tear, some cracked a joke; it seemed just as in old times. They said they were all dead but better so. They had plenty to eat now and nothing to do the whole day long and could go about wherever they liked as dead people do. So they just wanted to look in for a moment to help me to get on with the book, they were not going to drop an old friend from bygone days of misery and woe. They thought I had far better clear out without further delay from this depressing planet and come along with them to their new quarters. Nothing to worry about, it was quite an easy journey. They had good reasons to believe that a word of recommendation from one of them would prove most useful with the passport authorities, who were besides far more lenient and easygoing than they were supposed to be, as long as you did not carry any money. I said I was greatly relieved to be told this and went on banging my Corona faster than ever. All of a sudden it grew dark as night around me, they all vanished, and I was left alone with my fear. I stretched out my hand and my old dog came and put his head in my lap. I started singing to myself Schubert's 'An die musik' to pretend I was not afraid and began the next chapter of The Story of San Michele.

When at last the long manuscript was read to me, I was reminded of the old Doge in Venice who, when shown Tintoretto's frescoes glorifying his various deeds and victories, asked with unfeigned astonishment if it really was he who had achieved all this. As I am now reading through this rambling narrative to its bitter end for the first time by the critical light of my own eyes, I have an uneasy feeling that I have come out in this book a far better man than I have been in life, and that I ought to warn the reader to try not to believe all the nice things I have been telling about myself with un-English volubility. I am not conscious of having told any deliberate lies to my readers. Where I may have deceived them, I have been deceived myself, deceived by the better man I might have been. But in one respect at least I can say with a clear conscience that I have not deceived my readers – in my love for animals. I have loved them and suffered with them my whole life. I have loved them far more than I have ever loved my fellow-men. All that is best in me I have given to them, and I mean to stand by them to the last and share their fate whatever it may be. If it is true that there is to be no haven of rest for them when their sufferings here are at an end, I, for one, am not going to bargain for any haven for myself. I shall go without fear where they go, and by the side of my brothers and sisters from forests and fields, from skies and seas, lie down to merciful extinction in their mysterious underworld, safe from any further torments inflicted by God or man, safe from any haunting dream of eternity.

The night will be dark for there will be no stars overhead and no hope for a dawn, but I have been in darkness before. It will be lonely to be dead, but it cannot be much more lonely than to be alive.

St. James's Club.   May 15, 1936.

I

Youth

I sprang from the Sorrento sailing-boat on to the little beach. Swarms of boys were playing about among the upturned boats or bathing their shining bronze bodies in the surf, and old fishermen in red Phrygian caps sat mending their nets outside their boat-houses. Opposite the landing-place stood half-a-dozen donkeys with saddles on their backs and bunches of flowers in their bridles, and around them chattered and sang as many girls with the silver spadella stuck through their black tresses and a red handkerchief tied across their shoulders. The little donkey who was to take me up to Capri was called Rosina, and the name of the girl was Gioia. Her black lustrous eyes sparkled with fiery youth, her lips were red like the string of corals round her neck, her strong white teeth glistened like a row of pearls in her merry laughter. She said she was fifteen and I said that I was younger than I had ever been. But Rosina was old, 'è antica,' said Gioia. So I slipped off the saddle and climbed leisurely up the winding path to the village. In front of me danced Gioia on naked feet, a wreath of flowers round her head, like a young Bacchante, and behind me staggered old Rosina in her dainty black shoes, with bent head and drooping ears, deep in thought. I had no time to think, my head was full of rapturous wonder, my heart full of the joy of life, the world was beautiful and I was eighteen. We wound our way through bushes of ginestra and myrtle in full bloom, and here and there among the sweet-scented grass many small flowers I had never seen before in the land of Linnaeus, lifted their graceful heads to look at us as we passed.

'What is the name of this flower?' said I to Gioia. She took the flower from my hand, looked at it lovingly and said: 'Fiore!'

'And what is the name of this one?' She looked at it with the same tender attention and said: 'Fiore!'

'And how do you call this one?'

'Fiore! Bello! Bello!'

She picked a bunch of fragrant myrtle, but would not give it to me. She said the flowers were for S. Costanzo, the patron saint of Capri who was all of solid silver and had done so many miracles,

S. Costanzo, bello! bello!

A long file of girls with tufa stones on their heads slowly advanced towards us in a stately procession like the caryatides from the Erechtheum. One of the girls gave me a friendly smile and put an orange into my hand. She was a sister of Gioia's and even more beautiful, thought I. Yes, they were eight sisters and brothers at home, and two were in Paradiso. Their father was away coral-fishing in 'Barbaria,' look at the beautiful string of corals he had just sent her, 'che bella collana! Bella! Bella!'

'And you also are bella, Gioia, bella, bella!'

'Yes,' said she.

My foot stumbled against a broken column of marble, 'Roba di Timberio!' explained Gioia. 'Timberio cattivo, Timberio mal'occhio, Timberio camorrista!'[1] and she spat on the marble.

'Yes,' said I, my memory fresh from Tacitus and Suetonius, 'Tiberio cattivo!'

We emerged on the high road and reached the Piazza with a couple of sailors standing by the parapet overlooking the Marina, a few drowsy Capriotes seated in front of Don Antonio's osteria, and half-a-dozen priests on the steps leading to the church, gesticulating wildly in animated conversation: 'Moneta! Moneta! Molta moneta; Niente moneta!' Gioia ran up to kiss the hand of Don Giacinto who was her father confessor and un vero santo, though he did not look like one. She went to confession twice a month, how often did I go to confession?

Not at all!

Cattivo! Cattivo!

Would she tell Don Giacinto that I had kissed her cheek under the lemon-trees?

Of course not.

We passed through the village and halted at Punta Tragara.

'I am going to climb to the top of that rock,' said I, pointing to the most precipitous of the three Faraglioni glistening like amethysts at our feet. But Gioia was sure I could not do it. A fisherman who had tried to climb up there in search of sea-gulls' eggs had been hurled back into the sea by an evil spirit, who lived there in the shape of a blue lizard, as blue as the Blue Grotto, to keep watch over a golden treasure hidden there by Timberio himself.

Towering over the friendly little village the sombre outline of

[1] The old emperor who lived the last eleven years of his life on the island of Capri and is still very much alive on the lips of its inhabitants, is always spoken of as Timberio.

26

Monte Solaro stood out against the western sky with its stern crags and inaccessible cliffs.

'I want to climb that mountain at once,' said I.

But Gioia did not like the idea at all. A steep path, seven hundred and seventy-seven steps, cut in the rock by Timberio himself led up the flank of the mountain, and halfway up in a dark cave lived a ferocious werewolf who had already eaten several Cristiani. On the top of the stairs was Anacapri, but only gente di montagna lived there, all very bad people; no forestieri ever went there and she herself had never been there. Much better climb to the Villa Timberio, or the Arco Naturale or the Grotta Matromania!

'No, I had no time, I must climb that mountain at once.'

Back to the Piazza, just as the rusty bells of the old campanile were ringing 12 o'clock to announce that the macaroni was ready. Wouldn't I at least have luncheon first under the big palm-tree of the Albergo Pagano. Tre piatti, vino a volontà, prezzo una lira. No, I had no time, I had to climb the mountain at once. 'Addio, Gioia bella, bella! Addio Rosina!' 'Addio, addio e presto ritorno!' Alas! for the presto ritorno!

'È un pazzo inglese,' were the last words I heard from Gioia's red lips as, driven by my fate, I sprang up the Phoenician steps to Anacapri. Half-way up I overtook an old woman with a huge basket full of oranges on her head. 'Buon giorno, signorino.' She put down her basket and handed me an orange. On the top of the oranges lay a bundle of newspapers and letters tied up in a red handkerchief. It was old Maria Porta-Lettere who carried the post twice a week to Anacapri, later on my life-long friend, I saw her die at the age of ninety-five. She fumbled among the letters, selected the biggest envelope and begged me to tell her if it was not for Nannina la Crapara [1] who was eagerly expecting *la lettera* from her husband in America. No, it was not. Perhaps this one? No, it was for Signora Desdemona Vacca.

'Signora Desdemona Vacca,' repeated old Maria, incredulously. 'Perhaps they mean la moglie dello Scarteluzzo,' [2] she said meditatively. The next letter was for Signor Ulisse Desiderio, 'I think they mean Capolimone,' [3] said old Maria, 'he had a letter just like this a month ago.' The next letter was for Gentilissima Signorina Rosina Mazzarella. This lady seemed more difficult to trace. Was it la Cacciacavallara? [4] or la Zopparella? [5] Or la Capatosta? [6] Or la

[1] 'The Goat-woman.'   [2] 'The wife of the Hunchback.'
[3] 'Lemonhead.'   [4] 'The Cheese-woman.'
[5] 'The lame Woman.'   [6] 'The Hardhead.'

Femmina Antica?[1] Or Rosinella Pane Asciutto?[2] Or perhaps la Fesseria?[3] suggested another woman who had just overtaken us with a huge basket of fish on her head. Yes, it might be for la Fesseria if it was not for la moglie di Pane e Cipolla.[4] But was there no letter for Peppinella 'n'coppo u camposanto[5] or for Mariucella Caparossa[6] or for Giovannina Ammazzacane[7] who were all expecting *la lettera* from America? No, I was sorry there was not. The two newspapers were for Il reverendo parroco Don Antonio di Giuseppe and Il canonico Don Natale di Tommaso, she knew it well, for they were the only newspaper-subscribers in the village. The parroco was a very learned man and it was he who always found out who the letters were for, but to-day he was away in Sorrento on a visit to the Archbishop, and that was why she had asked me to read the envelopes. Old Maria did not know how old she was, but she knew that she had carried the post since she was fifteen when her mother had to give it up. Of course she could not read. When I had told her that I had sailed over that very morning with the post-boat from Sorrento and had had nothing to eat since then, she gave me another orange which I devoured skin and all, and the other woman offered me at once from her basket some frutta di mare which made me frightfully thirsty. Was there an inn in Anacapri? No, but Annarella, la moglie del sagrestano could supply me with excellent goat-cheese and a glass of excellent wine from the vineyard of the priest Don Dionisio, her uncle, un vino meraviglioso. Besides there was La Bella Margherita, of course I knew her by name and that her aunt had married 'un lord inglese.' No, I did not, but I was most anxious to know La Bella Margherita.

We reached at last the top of the seven hundred and seventy-seven steps, and passed through a vaulted gate with the huge iron hinges of its former drawbridge still fastened to the rock. We were in Anacapri. The whole bay of Naples lay at our feet encircled by Ischia, Procida, the pine-clad Posilipo, the glittering white line of Naples, Vesuvius with its rosy cloud of smoke, the Sorrento plain sheltered under Monte Sant'-Angelo and further away the Apennine mountains still covered with snow. Just over our heads, riveted to the steep rock like an eagle's nest, stood a little ruined chapel. Its vaulted roof had fallen in, but huge blocks of masonry shaped into an unknown pattern of symmetrical network, still

[1] 'The Ancient Woman.' [2] 'Stale Bread.'
[3] Not for ears polite. [4] 'The wife of Bread and Onions.'
[5] 'Above the Cemetery.' [6] 'Carrots.'
[7] 'Kill-dog.'

28

supported its crumbling walls.

'Roba di Timberio,' explained old Maria.

'What is the name of the little chapel?' I asked eagerly.

'San Michele.'

'San Michele, San Michele!' echoed in my heart. In the vineyard below the chapel stood an old man digging deep furrows in the soil for the new vines. 'Buon giorno, Mastro Vincenzo!' The vineyard was his and so was the little house close by, he had built it all with his own hands, mostly with stones and bricks of the Roba di Timberio that was strewn all over the garden. Maria Porta-Lettere told him all she knew about me and Mastro Vincenzo invited me to sit down in his garden and have a glass of wine. I looked at the little house and the chapel. My heart began to beat so violently that I could hardly speak.

'I must climb there at once,' said I to Maria Porta-Lettere! But old Maria said I had better come with her first to get something to eat or I would not find anything, and driven by hunger and thirst I reluctantly decided to follow her advice. I waved my hand to Mastro Vincenzo and said I would come back soon. We walked through some empty lanes and stopped in a piazzetta. 'Ecco La Bella Margherita!'

La Bella Margherita put a flask of rose-coloured wine and a bunch of flowers on the table in her garden and announced that the 'macaroni' would be ready in five minutes. She was fair like Titian's Flora, the modelling of her face exquisite, her profile pure Greek. She put an enormous plate of macaroni before me, and sat herself by my side watching me with smiling curiosity. 'Vino del parroco,' she announced proudly, each time she filled my glass. I drank the parroco's health, her health and that of her dark-eyed sister, la bella Giulia, who had joined the party, with a handful of oranges I had watched her picking from a tree in the garden. Their parents were dead and the brother Andrea was a sailor and God knows where he was, but her aunt was living in her own villa in Capri, of course I knew that she had married *un lord inglese*? Yes, of course I knew, but I did not remember her name. 'Lady G——,' said La Bella Margherita proudly. I just remembered in time to drink her health, but after that I did not remember anything except that the sky overhead was blue like a sapphire, that the parroco's wine was red like a ruby, that La Bella Margherita sat by my side with golden hair and smiling lips.

'San Michele!' suddenly rang through my ears. 'San Michele!' echoed deep down in my heart!

29

'Addio, Bella Margherita!' 'Addio e presto ritorno!' Alas for the presto ritorno!

I walked back through the empty lanes, steering as straight as I could for my goal. It was the sacred hour of the siesta, the whole little village was asleep. The piazza, all ablaze with sun, was deserted. The church was closed, only from the half-open door of the municipal school the stentorian voice of the Rev. Canonico Don Natale trumpeted in sleepy monotony through the silence: 'Io mi ammazzo, tu ti amazzi, egli si ammazza, noi ci ammazziamo, voi vi ammazzate, loro si ammazzano,' repeated in rhythmic chorus by a dozen barelegged boys, in a circle on the floor at the feet of their schoolmaster.

Further down the lane stood a stately Roman matron. It was Annarella herself, beckoning me with a friendly waving of the hand to come in. Why had I gone to La Bella Margherita instead of to her? Did I not know that her *cacciacavallo* was the best cheese in all the village? And as for the wine, everybody knew that the parroco's wine was no match for that of the Rev. Don Dionisio. 'Altro che il vino del parroco!' she added with a significant shrug of her strong shoulders. As I sat under her pergola in front of a flask of Don Dionisio's vino bianco it began to dawn upon me that maybe she was right, but I wanted to be fair and had to empty the whole flask before giving my final opinion. But when Gioconda, her smiling daughter, helped me to a second glass from the new flask I had made up my mind. Yes, Don Dionisio's vino bianco was the best! It looked like liquid sunshine, it tasted like the nectar of the Gods, and Gioconda looked like a young Hebe as she filled my empty glass. 'Altro che il vino del parroco! Did I not tell you so,' laughed Annarella. 'È un vino miracoloso!' Miraculous indeed, for suddenly I began to speak fluent Italian with vertiginous volubility amid roars of laughter from mother and daughter. I was beginning to feel very friendly towards Don Dionisio; I liked his name, I liked his wine, I thought I would like to make his acquaintance. Nothing was easier, for he was to preach that evening to 'le Figlie di Maria' in the church.

'He is a very learned man,' said Annarella. He knew by heart the names of all the martyrs and all the saints and had even been to Rome to kiss the hand of the Pope. Had she been to Rome? No. And to Naples? No. She had been to Capri once, it was on her wedding-day, but Gioconda had never been there, Capri was full of 'gente malamente.' I told Annarella I knew of course all about their patron saint, how many miracles he had done and how beautiful he was, all of solid silver. There was an uncomfortable silence.

'Yes, they say their San Costanzo is of solid silver,' ejaculated Annarella with a contemptible shrug of her broad shoulders, 'but who knows, chi lo sa?' As to his miracles you could count them on the top of your fingers, while Sant'Antonio, the patron saint of Anacapri, had already done over a hundred. Altro che San Costanzo! I was at once all for Sant'Antonio, hoping with all my heart for a new miracle of his to bring me back as soon as possible to his enchanting village. Kind Annarella's confidence in the miraculous power of Sant'Antonio was so great that she refused pointblank to accept any money.

'Pagherete un' altra volta, you will pay me another time.'

'Addio Annarella, addio Gioconda!'

'Arrividerla, presto ritorno, Sant'Antonio vi benedica! La Madonna vi accompagni!'

Old Mastro Vincenzo was still hard at work in his vineyard, digging deep furrows in the sweet-scented soil for the new vines. Now and then he picked up a slab of coloured marble or a piece of red stucco and threw it over the wall, 'Roba di Timberio,' said he. I sat down on a broken column of red granite by the side of my new friend. Era molto duro, it was very hard to break, said Mastro Vincenzo. At my feet a chicken was scratching in the earth in search of a worm and before my very nose appeared a coin. I picked it up and recognized at a glance the noble head of Augustus, 'Divus Augustus Pater.' Mastro Vincenzo said it was not worth a *baiocco*, I have it still. He had made the garden all by himself and had planted all the vines and fig-trees with his own hands. Hard work, said Mastro Vincenzo showing me his large horny hands, for the whole ground was full of roba di Timberio, columns, capitals, fragments of statues and teste di cristiani, and he had to dig up and carry away all this rubbish before he could plant his vines. The columns he had split into garden steps and of course he had been able to utilize many of the marbles when he was building his house and the rest he had thrown over the precipice. A piece of real good luck had been when quite unexpectedly he had come upon a large subterranean room just under his house, with red walls just like that piece there under the peach-tree all painted with lots of stark naked cristianai, tutti spogliati, ballando come dei pazzi,[1] with their hands full of flowers and bunches of grapes. It took him several days to scrape off all these paintings and cover the wall with

[1] All naked, dancing like mad people.

31

cement, but this was small labour compared to what it would have meant to blast the rock and build a new cistern, said Mastro Vincenzo with a cunning smile. Now he was getting old and hardly able to look after his vineyard any more, and his son who lived on the mainland with twelve children and three cows wanted him to sell the house and come and live with him. Again my heart began to beat. Was the chapel also his? No, it belonged to nobody and people said it was haunted by ghosts. He himself had seen when he was a boy a tall monk leaning over the parapet, and some sailors coming up the steps late one night had heard bells ringing in the chapel. The reason for this, explained Mastro Vincenzo, was that when Timberio had his palace there he had fatto ammazzare Gesù Cristo, put Jesus Christ to death, and since then his damned soul came back now and then to ask forgiveness from the monks who were buried under the floor in the chapel. People also said that he used to come there in the shape of a big black snake. The monks had been *ammazzati* by a brigand called Barbarossa, who had boarded the island with his ships and carried away into slavery all the women who had taken refuge up there in the castle overhead, that is why it was called Castello Barbarossa. Padre Anselmo, the hermit, who was a learned man, and besides a relation of his, had told him all this and also about the English who had turned the chapel into a fortress and who in their turn had been *ammazzati* by the French.

'Look!' said Mastro Vincenzo, pointing to a heap of bullets near the garden wall and 'look' he added, picking up an English soldier's brass button. The French, he continued, had placed a big gun near the chapel, and had opened fire on the village of Capri held by the English. 'Well done,' he chuckled. 'The Capresi are all bad people.' Then the French had turned the chapel into a powder magazine, that was why it was still called La Polveriera. Now it was nothing but a ruin, but it had proved very useful to him, for he had taken most of his stones for his garden walls from there.

I climbed over the wall and walked up the narrow lane to the chapel. The floor was covered to a man's height with the débris of the fallen vault, the walls were covered with ivy and wild honeysuckle and hundreds of lizards played merrily about among big bushes of myrtle and rosemary, stopping now and then in their game to look at me with lustrous eyes and panting breasts. An owl rose on noiseless wings from a dark corner, and a large snake asleep on the sunlit mosaic floor of the terrace unfolded slowly his black coils and glided back into the chapel with a warning hiss at the intruder. Was it the ghost of the sombre old Emperor still haunting the ruins where his imperial villa once stood?

I looked down at the beautiful island at my feet. How could he live in such a place and be so cruel! thought I. How could his soul be so dark, with such a glorious light on Heaven and Earth! How could he ever leave this place, to retire to that other even more inaccessible villa of his on the eastern cliffs, which still bears his name and where he spent the last three years of his life?

To live in such a place as this, to die in such a place, if ever death could conquer the everlasting joy of such a life! What daring dream had made my heart beat so violently a moment ago when Mastro Vincenzo had told me that he was getting old and tired, and that his son wanted him to sell his house? What wild thoughts had flashed through my boisterous brain when he had said that the chapel belonged to nobody? Why not to me? Why should I not buy Mastro Vincenzo's house, and join the chapel and the house with garlands of vines and avenues of cypresses and columns supporting white loggias, peopled with marble statues of gods and bronzes of emperors and . . . I closed my eyes, lest the beautiful vision should vanish, and gradually realities faded away into the twilight of dreamland.

A tall figure wrapped in a rich mantle stood by my side.

'It shall all be yours,' he said in a melodious voice, waving his hand across the horizon. 'The chapel, the garden, the house, the mountain with its castle, all shall be yours, if you are willing to pay the price!'

'Who are you, phantom from the unseen?'

'I am the immortal spirit of this place. Time has no meaning for me. Two thousand years ago I stood here where we now stand by the side of another man, led here by his destiny as you have been led here by yours. He did not ask for happiness as you do, he only asked for forgetfulness and peace, and he believed he could find it here on this lonely island. I told him the price he would have to pay: the branding of an untarnished name with infamy through all ages.

'He accepted the bargain, he paid the price. For eleven years he lived here surrounded by a few trusty friends, all men of honour and integrity. Twice he started on his way to return to his palace on the Palatine Hill. Twice his courage failed him; Rome never saw him again. He died on his homeward journey in the villa of his friend Lucullus on the promontory over there. His last words were that he should be carried down in his litter to the boat that was to take him to his island home.'

'What is the price you ask of me?'

'The renunciation of your ambition to make yourself a name in your profession, the sacrifice of your future.'

'What then am I to become?'

'A Might-Have-Been, a failure.'

'You take away from me all that is worth living for.'

'You are mistaken, I give you all that is worth living for.'

'Will you at least leave me pity. I cannot live without pity if I am to become a doctor.'

'Yes, I will leave you pity, but you would have fared much better without it.'

'Do you ask for anything more?'

'Before you die, you will have to pay another price as well, a heavy price. But before this price is due, you will have watched for many years from this place the sun set over cloudless days of happiness and the moon rise over starlit nights of dreams.'

'Shall I die here?'

'Beware of searching for the answer to your question; man could not endure life if he was aware of the hour of his death.'

He laid his hand on my shoulder, I felt a slight shiver run through my body. 'I shall be with you once more at this place when the sun has set to-morrow; you may think it over till then.'

'It is no good thinking it over, my holiday is at an end, this very night I have to return to my every day's toil far away from this beautiful land. Besides, I am no good at thinking. I accept the bargain, I will pay the price, be it what it may. But how am I to buy this house, my hands are empty.'

'Your hands are empty but they are strong, your brain is boisterous but clear, your will is sound, you will succeed.'

'How am I to build my house? I know nothing about architecture.'

'I will help you. What style do you want? Why not Gothic? I rather like the Gothic with its subdued light and its haunting mystery.'

'I am going to invent a style of my own, such that not even you shall be able to give it a name. No mediaeval twilight for me! I want my house open to sun and wind and the voice of the sea, like a Greek temple, and light, light, light everywhere!'

'Beware of the light! Beware of the light! Too much light is not good for the eyes of mortal man.'

'I want columns of priceless marble, supporting loggias and arcades, beautiful fragments from past ages strewn all over my

34

garden, the chapel turned into a silent library with cloister stalls round the walls and sweet-sounding bells ringing Ave Maria over each happy day.'

'I do not like bells.'

'And here where we stand with this beautiful island rising like a sphinx out of the sea below our feet, here I want a granite sphinx from the land of the Pharaohs. But where shall I find it all?'

'You stand upon the site of one of Tiberio's villas. Priceless treasures of bygone ages lie buried under the vines, under the chapel, under the house. The old Emperor's foot has trod upon the slabs of coloured marble you saw the old peasant throw over the wall of his garden, the ruined fresco with its dancing fauns and the flower-crowned bacchantes once adorned the walls of his palace. Look,' said he, pointing down to the clear depths of the sea a thousand feet below. 'Didn't your Tacitus tell you at school that when the news of the Emperor's death had reached the island, his palaces were hurled into the sea?'

I wanted to leap down the precipitous cliffs at once and plunge into the sea in search of my columns. 'No need for such a hurry,' he laughed, 'for two thousand years the corals have been spinning their cobwebs round them and the waves have buried them deeper and deeper in the sand, they will wait for you till your time comes.'

'And the sphinx? Where shall I find the sphinx?'

'On a lonely plain, far away from the life of to-day, stood once the sumptuous villa of another Emperor, who had brought the sphinx from the banks of the Nile to adorn his garden. Of the palace nothing remains but a heap of stones, but deep in the bowels of the earth still lies the sphinx. Search and you will find her. It will nearly cost you your life to bring it here, but you will do it.'

'You seem to know the future as well as you know the past.'

'The past and the future are all the same to me. I know everything.'

'I do not envy you your knowledge.'

'Your words are older than your years; where did you get that saying from?'

'From what I have learned on this island to-day, for I have learned that this friendly folk who can neither read nor write are far happier than I, who ever since I was a child have been straining my eyes to gain knowledge. And so have you, I gather from your speech. You are a great scholar, you know your Tacitus by heart.'

'I am a philosopher.'

'You know Latin well?'

'I am a doctor of theology from the university of Jena.'

'Ah! that is why I fancied I detected a slight German twang in your voice. You know Germany?'

'Rather,' he chuckled.

I looked at him attentively. His manners and bearing were those of a gentleman, I noticed for the first time that he carried a sword under his red mantle and there was a harsh sound in his voice I seemed to have heard before.

'Pardon me, sir, I think we have already met in the Auerbach Keller in Leipzig, isn't your name . . . ?' As I spoke the words, the church bells from Capri began to ring Ave Maria. I turned my head to look at him. He was gone.

II

Quartier Latin

Quartier Latin. A student's room in the Hôtel de l'Avenir, piles of books everywhere, on tables, chairs and in heaps on the floor, and on the wall a faded photograph of Capri. Mornings in the wards of La Salpêtrière, Hôtel Dieu and La Pitié, going from bed to bed to read chapter after chapter in the book of human suffering, written with blood and tears. Afternoons in the dissecting rooms and amphitheatres of l'École de Médecine or in the laboratories of the Institut Pasteur, watching in the microscope with wondrous eyes the mystery of the unseen world, the infinitely small beings, arbiters of the life and death of man. Nights of vigil in the Hôtel de l'Avenir, precious nights of toil to master the hard facts, the classical signs of disorder and disease collected and sifted by observers from all lands, so necessary and so insufficient for the making of a doctor. Work, work, work! Summer holidays with empty cafés in Boulevard St. Michel, École de Médecine closed, laboratories and amphitheatres deserted, clinics half-empty. But no holiday for suffering in the hospital wards, no holiday for Death. No holiday in the Hôtel de l'Avenir. No distraction but an occasional stroll under the lime-trees of the Luxembourg Gardens, or a greedily enjoyed hour of leisure in the Louvre Museum. No friends. No dog. Not even a mistress. Henri Murger's 'Vie de Bohême' was gone, but his Mimi was still there, very much so, smilingly strolling down the Boulevard St. Michel on the arm of almost every student, when the hour for the apéritif was approaching, or mending his coat or washing his linen in his garret while he was reading for his exam.

No Mimi for me! Yes, they could afford to take it easy, these happy comrades of mine, to spend their evenings in idle gossip at the tables of their cafés, to laugh, to live, to love. Their subtle Latin brain was far quicker than mine, and they had no faded photograph of Capri on the wall of their garret to spur them on, no columns of precious marble waiting for them under the sand at Palazzo al Mare. Often during the long wakeful nights, as I sat there in the Hôtel de l'Avenir, my head bent over Charcot's 'Maladies du Système Nerveux,' or Trousseaux's 'Clinique de l'Hôtel Dieu,' a terrible thought flashed suddenly through my brain: Mastro Vincenzo is old, fancy if he should die while I am sitting here or sell to somebody else the little house on the cliff, which holds the key to my future home! An ice-cold perspiration burst out on my forehead and my heart stood almost still with fear. I stared at the faded photograph of Capri on the wall, I thought I saw it fade away more and more into dimness, mysterious and sphinx-like, till nothing remained but the outline of a sarcophagus, under which lay buried a dream. . . . Then rubbing my aching eyes, I plunged into my book again with frantic fury, like a race-horse spurred on towards his goal with bleeding flanks. Yes, it became a race, a race for prizes and trophies. My comrades began to bet on me as an easy winner, and even the Master with the head of a Caesar and the eye of an eagle mistook me for a rising man – the only error of diagnosis I ever knew Professor Charcot commit during years of watchful observation of his unerring judgment in the wards of his Salpêtrière or in his consulting-room at Boulevard St. Germain, thronged with patients from all the world. It cost me dearly this mistake of his. It cost me my sleep, and it nearly cost me the sight of my eyes. This question is not settled yet for the matter of that. Such was my faith in the infallibility of Charcot who knew more than any living man about the human brain that for a short time I believed he was right. Spurred by ambition to fulfil his prophecy, insensible to fatigue, to sleep, even to hunger, I strained every fibre of mind and body to breaking-point in an effort to win at all costs. No more walks under the lime trees of the Luxembourg Gardens, no more strolls in the Louvre. From morning till night my lungs filled with the foul air of the hospital wards and the amphitheatres, from night till morning with the smoke of endless cigarettes in my stuffy room at the Hôtel de l'Avenir. Exam after exam in rapid succession, far too rapid, alas, to be of any value, success after success. Work, work, work! I was to take my degree in the spring. Luck in everything my hand touched, never failing, amazing, almost uncanny luck. Already I had learned to know the structure of the marvellous machinery which is the human body, the harmonious working of its cogs and wheels in health, its disorders in disease and its final breaking-down in death. Already I had become familiar with most of the afflictions which chained the sufferers in the wards to their beds. Already I had learned to handle the sharp-edged weapons of surgery, to fight on more equal terms the implacable Foe who, scythe in hand, wandered His rounds in the wards, always ready to slay, always at hand any hour of the day or of the night. In fact He seemed to have taken up His abode there for good in the grim old hospital, which for centuries had sheltered so much suffering and woe. Sometimes He came rushing through the ward, striking right and left, young and old, in blind fury like a madman, throttling one victim with the slow grip of His hand, and tearing away the bandage from the gaping wound of another till his last drop of blood had oozed away. Sometimes He came on tiptoe, silent and still, closing with an almost gentle touch of His finger the eyes of another sufferer, who lay there almost smiling after He had gone. Often, I who was there to hinder His approach did not even know He was coming. Only small children at their mother's breast knew of His presence and started in their sleep with a sharp cry of distress as He passed by. And as often as not one of the old nuns, who had spent a lifetime in the wards, saw Him coming just in time to put a crucifix on the bed. At first, when He stood there, victorious, on one side of the bed and I, helpless, on the other, I used to take little notice of Him. Life was everything to me then, I knew that my mission was at an end when His had begun, and I only used to turn my face away from my sinister colleague in resentment at my defeat. But as I became more familiar with Him, I began to watch Him with increasing attention, and the more I saw of Him, the more I wanted to know Him, to understand Him. I began to realize that He had His share in the work, as well as I had mine, His mission to fulfil just as I had mine, that we were comrades after all, that when the wrestling over a life was over and He had won, it was far better to look each other fearlessly in the face and be friends. Later on, there even came a time when I thought He was my only friend, when I longed for Him and almost loved Him, though He never seemed to take any notice of me. What could He not teach me if I only could learn to read His sombre face! What gaps in my scanty knowledge of human suffering could He not fill, He who alone had read the last missing chapter in my medical handbooks, where everything is explained, the solution offered to every riddle, the answer given to every question!

But how could He be so cruel, He who could be so gentle? How could He take away so much of youth and life with one hand, when He could give so much peace and happiness with the other? Why was the grip of His hand round the throat of one of His victims so slow and the blow He dealt to another so swift? Why did He struggle so long with the life of the little child, while He suffered the life of the old to ebb away in merciful sleep? Was it His mission to punish as well as to slay? Was He the Judge as well as the Executioner? What did He do with those He had slain? Had they ceased to exist or were they only asleep? Whither did He take them? Was He the Supreme Ruler of the Kingdom of Death or was He only a vassal, a mere tool in the hands of a far mightier ruler, the Ruler of Life? He had won to-day, but was His victory to be final? Who would conquer in the end, He or Life?

But was it really so that my mission was at an end when His was to begin? Was I to be an impassive spectator of the last unequal battle, to stand by helpless and insensible, while He was doing His work of destruction? Was I to turn my face away from those eyes who implored my help, long after the power of speech had gone? Was I to loosen my hand from those quivering fingers who clung to mine like a drowning man to a straw? I was defeated, but I was not disarmed, I had still in my hands a powerful weapon. He had His eternal sleeping-draught but I had also mine entrusted to me by benevolent Mother Nature. When He was slow in dealing out His remedy why should not I deal out mine with its merciful power to change anguish into peace, agony into sleep? Was it not my mission to help those to die I could not help to live?

The old nun had told me that I was committing a terrible sin, that Almighty God in His inscrutable wisdom had willed it so, that the more suffering He inflicted at the hour of death, the more forgiving would He be on the Day of Judgment. Even sweet Sœur Philomène had looked at me disapprovingly when, alone among my comrades, I had come with my morphia syringe after the old padre had left the bed with his Last Sacrament.

They were still there in their big white cornets, in all the hospitals of Paris, the gentle, all-sacrificing sisters of St. Vincent de Paul. The crucifix was still hanging on the wall of every ward, the padre still read mass every morning before the little altar in Salle Ste. Claire. The Mother Superior, Ma Mère as they all called her, still went her round from bed to bed every evening after the Ave Maria had rung.

La Laïcisation des Hôpitaux was not yet the burning question of the day, the raucous cry of: 'Away with the priests! away with the crucifix! à la porte les sœurs!' had not yet been raised. Alas! I saw them all go ere long and a pity it was. No doubt they had their faults, these nuns. No doubt they were more familiar with handling their rosaries than the nail-brush, more used to dip their fingers in holy water than in carbolic acid solution, then the all-powerful panacea in our surgical wards, soon to be replaced by another. But their thoughts were so clean, their hearts so pure, they gave their whole life to their work and asked for nothing in return but to be

40

allowed to pray for those under their care. Even their worst enemies have never dared to belittle their all-sacrificing devotion and their all-enduring patience. People used to say that the sisters went about their work with sad sullen faces, their thoughts more occupied with the salvation of the soul than that of the body, with more words of resignation than of hope on their lips. Indeed, they were greatly mistaken. On the contrary, these nuns, young and old, were invariably cheerful and happy, almost gay and full of childish fun and laughter, and it was wonderful to watch the way they knew how to communicate their happiness to others. They were also tolerant. Those who believed and those who did not, were all the same to them. If anything they seemed even more anxious to help the latter, for they felt so sorry for them and showed no signs of resentment even for their curses and blasphemies. To me they were all wonderfully kind and friendly. They well knew that I did not belong to their creed, that I did not go to confession and that I did not make the sign of the cross when I passed before the little altar. At first the Mother Superior had made some timid attempts to convert me to the faith which had made her sacrifice her life for others, but she had soon given it up with a compassionate shaking of her old head. Even the dear old padre had lost all hope of my salvation since I told him I was willing to discuss with him the possibility of a purgatory, but point-blank refused to believe in hell, and that in any case I was determined to give morphia in full dose to the dying when their agony was too cruel and too long. The old padre was a saint, but argumentation was not his strong point and we soon abandoned these controversial questions altogether. He knew the life of all the saints, and it was he who told me for the first time the sweet legend of Ste. Claire, who had given her name to the ward. It was also he who made me behold for the first time the wonderful features of her beloved St. Francis of Assisi, the friend of all humble and forlorn creatures of sky and earth, who was to become my lifelong friend as well. But it was Sœur Philomène, so young and fair in her white robe of novice of Sœur St. Augustin, who taught me most, for she taught me to love her Madonna, whose features she wore. Sweet Sœur Philomène! I saw her die of cholera a couple of years later in Naples. Not even Death dared disfigure her. She went to Heaven just as she was.

The Frère Antoine who came to the hospital every Sunday to play the organ in the little chapel was a particular friend of mine. It was the only chance I had those days to hear any music and I seldom missed being there, I who am so fond of music! Although I could not see the sisters where they sat singing near the altar, I recognized quite well the clear, pure voice of Sœur Philomène. The very day before Christmas Frère Antoine caught a bad chill, and a great secret was whispered from bed to bed in the Salle Ste. Claire that after a long consultation between the Mother Superior and the old padre I had been allowed to replace him at the organ to save the situation.

The only other music I ever heard those days was when poor old Don Gaetano came to play to me twice a week on his worn-out barrel-organ under my balcony in the Hôtel de l'Avenir. The 'Miserere' from the 'Trovatore' was his show-piece, and the melancholy old tune suited him well, both him and his half-frozen little monkey, who crouched on the barrel-organ in her red Garibaldi:

> *Ah che la morte ogn'ora*
> *É tarda nel venir!*

It suited equally well poor old Monsieur Alfredo who wandered about the snow-covered streets in his threadbare frock-coat, with the manuscript of his last tragedy under his arm. Equally well my friends in the Italian poor quarter huddled together round their half-extinguished *braciero* with no money to buy a half-penny worth of charcoal to keep themselves warm. There came days too, when the sad melody seemed just the right accompaniment to my own thoughts as well; when I sat before my books in the Hôtel de l'Avenir with no courage left to face a new day, when everything seemed so black and hopeless and the faded old photograph of Capri so far away. Then I used to throw myself on the bed and close my aching eyes, and soon Sant'Antonio set to work to perform another miracle. Soon I was sailing away from all my worries to the enchanting island of my dreams. Gioconda handed me smilingly a glass of Don Dionisio's wine, and once more the blood began to flow, rich and strong, through my tired brain. The world was beautiful and I was young, ready to fight, sure to win. Mastro Vincenzo, still hard at work amongst his vines, waved his hand at me as I walked up the little lane behind his garden to the chapel. I sat for a while on the terrace and looked down spellbound on the fair island at my feet, just wondering how on earth I should manage to drag up my sphinx of red granite to the top of the cliff. Indeed, it would be a difficult job, but of course I would do it quite easily, all by myself! 'Addio bella Gioconda! Addio e presto ritorno!' Yes, of course I would come back soon, very soon, in my next dream! The new day came and looked hard at the dreamer through the window. I opened my eyes and sprang to my feet, and greeting the new-comer with a smile I sat down again at my table, book in hand. Then came spring and dropped the first twig of chestnut flowers on my balcony from the budding trees of the avenue. It was the signal. I went up for my exam and left the Hôtel de l'Avenir with the hard-won diploma in my pocket, the youngest M.D. ever created in France.

III

Avenue de Villiers

Avenue de Villiers. Dr. Munthe from 2 till 3. Door-bell ringing
and messages coming day and night with urgent letters and calls.
Telephone, that deadly weapon in the hands of idle women, not
yet started on its nerve-racking campaign against every hour of
well-earned rest. Consultation-room rapidly filling up with
patients of all sorts and descriptions, mostly nervous cases, the fair
sex in the majority. Many were ill, seriously ill. I listened gravely
to what they had to say and examined them as carefully as I
could, quite sure I could help them, whatever was the matter. Of
these cases I do not feel inclined to speak here. A day may come
when I may have something to say about them. Many were not ill
at all, and might never have become so, had they not consulted
me. Many imagined they were ill. They had the longest tale to tell,
talked about their grandmother, their aunt or mother-in-law, or
produced from their pockets a little paper and began to read out an
interminable list of symptoms and complaints – le malade au petit
papier, as Charcot used to say. All this was new to me, who had no
experience outside the hospitals, where there was no time for any
nonsense, and I made many blunders. Later on, when I began to
know more of human nature, I learned to handle these patients a
little better, but we never got on very well together. They seemed
quite upset when I told them that they looked rather well and their
complexion was good, but they rallied rapidly when I added that
their tongue looked rather bad – as seemed generally to be the case.
My diagnosis, in most of these cases, was over-eating, too many
cakes or sweets during the day or too heavy dinners at night. It
was probably the most correct diagnosis I ever made in those days,
but it met with no success. Nobody wanted to hear anything more
about it, nobody liked it. What they all liked was appendicitis.
Appendicitis was just then much in demand among better-class
people on the lookout for a complaint. All the nervous ladies had
got it on the brain if not in the abdomen, thrived on it beautifully,
and so did their medical advisers. So I drifted gradually into
appendicitis and treated a great number of such cases with varied

success. But when the rumour began to circulate that the American surgeons had started on a campaign to cut out every appendix in the United States, my cases of appendicitis began to fall off in an alarming way. Consternation:

'Take away the appendix! my appendix!' said the fashionable ladies, clinging desperately to their *processus vermicularis*, like a mother to her infant. 'What shall I do without it!'

'Take away their appendices, my appendices!' said the doctors, consulting gloomily the list of their patients. 'I never heard such nonsense! Why, there is nothing wrong with their appendices, I ought to know, I who have to examine them twice a week. I am dead against it!'

It soon became evident that appendicitis was on its last legs, and that a new complaint had to be discovered to meet the general demand. The Faculty was up to the mark, a new disease was dumped on the market, a new word was coined, a gold coin indeed, COLITIS! It was a neat complaint, safe from the surgeon's knife, always at hand when wanted, suitable to everybody's taste. Nobody knew when it came, nobody knew when it went away. I knew that several of my far-sighted colleagues had already tried it on their patients with great success, but so far my luck had been against me.[1]

One of my last cases of appendicitis was, I think, the Countess who came to consult me, on the recommendation of Charcot, as she said. He used to send me patients now and then and I was of course most anxious to do my very best for her, even had she not been as pretty as she was. She looked at the young oracle with ill-concealed disappointment in her large languid eyes, and said she wished to speak to 'Monsieur le Docteur lui-même' and not to his assistant, a first greeting I was accustomed to from a new patient. At first she did not know if she had appendicitis, nor did Monsieur le Docteur lui-même, but soon she was sure that she had it, and I that she had not. When I told her so with unwise abruptness she became very agitated. Professor Charcot had told her I was sure to find out what was the matter with her and that I would help her, and instead of that . . . she burst into tears and I felt very sorry for her.

'What is the matter with me?' she sobbed, stretching out her two

[1] Colitis, as this word is used now, was not known in those days. Many sins have been committed both by doctors and patients in the name of colitis during the early stage of its brilliant career. Even to-day there is not seldom something vague and unsatisfactory about this diagnosis.

empty hands towards me with a gesture of despair.

'I will tell you if you promise to be calm.'

She ceased to cry instantly. Wiping the last tears from her big eyes she said bravely:

'I can stand anything, I have already stood so much, don't be afraid, I am not going to cry any more. What is the matter with me?'

'Colitis.'

Her eyes grew even larger than before, though I would have thought that to be impossible.

'Colitis! That is exactly what I always thought! I am sure you are right! Tell me what is colitis?' I took good care to avoid that question, for I did not know it myself, nor did anybody else in those days. But I told her it lasted long and was difficult to cure, and I was right there. The Countess smiled amiably at me. And her husband who said it was nothing but nerves! She said there was no time to lose and wanted to begin the cure at once, so it was arranged she should come to Avenue de Villiers twice a week. She returned the very next day, and even I who was already getting accustomed to sudden changes in my patients could not help being struck by her cheerful appearance and bright face, so much so that I asked her how old she was.

She was just twenty-five. She only came to ask me if colitis was catching.

Yes, very. The word was hardly out of my mouth before I discovered that this young person was far cleverer than I.

Wouldn't I tell the Count it was safer they shouldn't sleep in the same room?

I assured her it was not at all safer, that although I had not the honour to know Monsieur le Comte, I felt sure he would not catch it. It was only catching with impressionable and highly-strung people like herself.

Surely I would not call her highly-strung, she objected, her big eyes wandering restlessly round the room? . . .

Yes, decidedly.

Could I not cure her of that?

No.

My dearest Ann,

Fancy, my dear, I have got colitis! I am so glad . . . so glad you recommended me this Suédois, or was it Charcot? In any case I told him it was Charcot, to make sure he would give me

46

more time and attention. You are right, he is very clever, though he does not look like it. I am already recommending him to all my friends, I am sure he can do any amount of good to my sister-in-law who is still on her back after her nasty fall at your cotillon, I am sure she has got colitis! Sorry, my dear, we shall not meet at Joséphine's dinner to-morrow, I have already written to her I have got colitis, and can't possibly come. I wish she could put it off till after to-morrow.

Your loving JULIETTE.

P.S. It just struck me that the Suédois ought to have a look at your mother-in-law, who is so worried about her deafness, of course I know the Marquise doesn't want to see any more doctors, and who does! but could it not be arranged that he saw her in some sort of unofficial way? I would not at all be surprised if the root of it all was colitis.

P.P.S. I would not mind asking the doctor to dinner here one day if you could persuade the Marquise to dine here, en petit comité, of course. Do you know he discovered I had colitis only by looking at me through his spectacles? Besides, I want my husband to make his acquaintance, though he does not like doctors more than does your mother-in-law. I am sure he will like this one.

A week later I had the unexpected honour to be invited to dinner at the Countess' hôtel in Faubourg St. Germain, and to sit next to the Dowager Marquise, respectfully watching her with my eagle eye while she devoured an enormous plate of pâté de foie gras in majestic aloofness. She never said a word to me, and my timid attempts to open a conversation came to a standstill when I discovered that she was stone-deaf. After dinner Monsieur le Comte took me to the smoking-room. He was a most polite little man, very fat, with a placid, almost shy face, at least twice the age of his wife, every inch a gentleman. Offering me a cigarette, he said with great effusion:

'I cannot thank you enough for having cured my wife of appendicitis – the very word is hateful to me. I frankly confess I have taken a great dislike to doctors. I have seen so many of them and so far none seems to have been able to do my wife any good, though I must add she never gave any of them a fair chance before she was off to another. I had better warn you, I am sure it will be the same with you.'

'I am not so sure of that.'

'So much the better. She has evidently great confidence in you, which is a strong point in your favour.'

'It is everything.'

'As far as I am concerned, I frankly admit not having taken to you very kindly at first, but now, since we have met I am anxious to correct my first impression and,' he added politely, 'I believe we are en bonne voie. A propos, what is colitis?'

I got out of my difficulties by his adding good-humouredly:

'Whatever it may be, it cannot be worse than appendicitis, and, depend upon it, I shall soon know as much about it as you do.'

He did not ask for much. I liked so much his frank, polite manners that I ventured to put him a question in return.

'No,' he answered with a slight embarrassment in his voice, 'I wish to God we had! We have now been married for five years and so far no sign of it. I wish to God we had! You know, I was born in this old house and so was my father, and my country-seat in Touraine has belonged to us for three centuries, I am the last of my family, and it is very hard, and . . . can nothing be done for these confounded nerves? Have you nothing to suggest?'

'I am sure this enervating air of Paris is not good for the Countess, why don't you go for a change to your castle in Touraine?'

His whole face lit up:

'You are my man,' said the Count, stretching his hands towards me, 'I do not ask for better! I have my shooting there, and my big estate to look after, I love to be there, but it bores the Countess to death and of course it is rather lonely for her who likes to see her friends every day and go to parties or to the theatre every night. But how she can have the strength to go on like this from month to month, she who says she is always tired, is more than I can understand. It would kill me outright. Now she says she must remain in Paris to have her colitis attended to, it was appendicitis before. But I do not want you to think her selfish, on the contrary she is always thinking of me and even wants me to go to the Château Rameaux alone, she knows how happy I am there. But how can I leave her alone in Paris? She is so young and inexperienced.'

'How old is the Countess?'

'Only twenty-nine. She looks even younger.'

'Yes. She looks almost like a young girl.'

He was silent a moment. 'A propos, when are you going to take your holiday?'

'I have not had a holiday for three years.'

'So much the more reason for taking one this year. Are you a good shot?'

'I do not kill animals if I can help it. Why did you ask me this question?'

'Because we have excellent shooting at Château Rameaux and I am sure a week's thorough rest would do you any amount of good. That is at least what my wife says, she says you are awfully overworked and you look it besides.'

'You are very kind, Monsieur le Comte, but I am all right, there is nothing the matter with me except that I cannot sleep.'

'Sleep! I wish I could give you some of mine! I have more than I need of it, and to spare. Do you know, I have hardly time to put my head on the pillow before I am fast asleep and nothing can wake me up. My wife is an early riser, but never once have I heard her get up, and my valet, who brings me my coffee at nine, has to shake me before I wake up. I pity you indeed. A propos, I suppose you do not know of any remedy against snoring?'

It was a clear case. We joined the ladies in the drawing-room. I was made to sit down by the side of the venerable Marquise for the unofficial consultation so skilfully arranged by the Countess. After another attempt to open a conversation with the old lady, I roared into her ear-trumpet that she had not got colitis, but that I was sure she she would get it if she did not give up her pâté de foie gras.

'I told you so,' whispered the Countess, 'isn't he clever?'

The Marquise wished to know at once all the symptoms of colitis and smiled cheerfully at me while I dripped the subtle poison down the ear-trumpet. When I stood up to go, I had lost my voice, but found a new patient.

A week later an elegant coupé stopped at the Avenue de Villiers and a footman rushed upstairs with a hurriedly scribbled note from the Countess to come at once to the Marquise who had been taken ill in the night with evident symptoms of colitis. I had made my entrée in Paris society.

Colitis spread like wildfire all over Paris. My waiting-room was soon so full of people that I had to arrange my dining-room as a sort of extra waiting-room. It was always a mystery to me how all these people could have time and patience to sit and wait there so long, often for hours. The Countess came regularly twice a week, but occasionally she felt seedy and had to come on extra days as well. It was evident that colitis suited her far better than appendicitis, her face had lost its languid pallor and her big eyes sparkled with youth.

49

One day, as I was coming out of the hôtel of the Marquise, she was leaving for the country. I had been there to bid her good-bye. I found the Countess standing by my carriage in friendly conversation with Tom, who was sitting on a huge parcel, half-hidden under the carriage-rug. The Countess was on her way to the Magasins du Louvre to buy a little present for the Marquise for her birthday to-morrow, and did not know in the least what to give her. I suggested a dog.

'A dog! What a capital idea!' She remembered that when as a child she was taken to see the Marquise, she always found her with a pug on her lap, a pug who was so fat that he could hardly walk and who snored so terribly that one could hear him all over the house. Her aunt had been in tears for weeks when he died. A capital idea indeed. We walked down the street to the corner of Rue Cambon, where was the shop of a well-known dog-dealer. There, amongst half-a-dozen mongrels of all sorts and descriptions sat the very dog I wanted, an aristocratic little pug, who snored desperately at us to draw our attention to his sad plight and implored us with his blood-shot eyes to take him away from this mixed society into which he had been thrown by sheer misfortune and by no fault of his. He nearly suffocated with emotion when he realized his luck and was put into a cab and sent to the hôtel in Faubourg St. Germain. The Countess was going anyhow to the Magasins du Louvre to try on a new hat. She said she wanted to go on foot. Then she said she wanted a cab and I volunteered to take her there in my carriage. She hesitated a moment – what will people say if they see me driving about in his carriage? – and then accepted with bonne grâce. But was it not out of my way to drive her to the Louvre; not in the least, for I had nothing to do just then. What is in that parcel, asked the Countess with feminine curiosity. I was just going to tell her another lie when Tom, his mission as sole guardian of the precious parcel being at an end, jumped to his usual place on the seat by my side. The parcel split open and the head of a doll popped out.

'Why on earth do you drive about with dolls, who are they for?'
'For the children.'

She did not know I had any children and seemed almost offended at my reticence about my private affairs. How many children had I got? About a dozen. There was no way of getting out of it, the whole secret had to come out.

'Come along with me,' I said boldly, 'and on the way back I will take you to see my friend Jack, the gorilla in the Jardin des Plantes.

It is just on our way.' The Countess was evidently in her very best mood that day and up to anything, she said she was delighted. After passing Gare Montparnasse she began to lose her bearings and soon she did not know at all where she was. We drove through some sombre, evil-smelling slums. Dozens of ragged children were playing about in the gutter, choked with filth and refuse of all sorts, and almost before every door sat a woman with a baby at her breast and other small children at her side, huddled around the brazier.

'Is this Paris?' asked the Countess with an almost frightened look in her eyes.

Yes, this is Paris, la Ville Lumière! And this is l'Impasse Rousselle, I added, as we stopped before a blind alley, damp and dark like the bottom of a well. Salvatore's wife was sitting on the family's only chair with Petruccio, her child of sorrow, on her lap, stirring the polenta for the family dinner, eagerly watched by Petruccio's two eldest sisters, while the youngest child was crawling about on the floor in pursuit of a kitten. I told Salvatore's wife I had brought a kind lady who wanted to give the children a present. I understood by her shyness it was the first time the Countess had ever entered the house of the very poor. She blushed scarlet as she handed the first doll to Petruccio's mother, for Petruccio himself could not hold anything in his withered hand, he had been paralysed ever since he was born. Petruccio showed no sign of being pleased, for his brain was as numb as his limbs, but his mother was sure that he liked the doll very much. His two sisters received each a doll in their turn and ran away in delight to hide themselves behind the bed to play at little mothers. When did I think Salvatore would come out of the hospital? It was now nearly six weeks since he had fallen from the scaffold and broken his leg. Yes, I had just seen him at the Hôpital Lariboisière, he was doing pretty well and I hoped he would come out soon. How was she getting on with her new landlord? Thank God, very well, he was very kind, he had even promised to put in a fireplace for next winter. And wasn't it nice of him to have opened that little window under the ceiling, didn't I remember how dark the room was before?

'Look how bright and cheerful it is here now, siamo in Paradiso,' said Salvatore's wife. Was it true what Arcangelo Fusco told her that I had said to the old landlord, the day he had turned her out in the street and seized all her belongings, that the hour would come when God would punish him for his cruelty to all of us poor people and that I had cursed him so terribly that he had to hang himself a couple of hours later? Yes, it was quite true and I did not regret what I had done. As we were going away, my friend Arcangelo Fusco, who shared the room with the Salvatore family, was just returning from his day's work, his big broom on his shoulder. His profession was to fare la scopa – in those days most of the street-sweepers in Paris were Italians. I was glad to introduce him to the Countess, it was the least I could do for him in return for the invaluable service he had done to me when he had gone with me to the police-station to corroborate my evidence concerning the death of the old landlord. God knows in what awkward entanglements I might have been involved had it not been for Arcangelo Fusco. Even so, it was a close shave. I was very nearly arrested for murder.[1] Arcangelo Fusco, who had a rose tucked over his ear, Italian fashion, presented his flower with southern gallantry to the Countess who looked as if she had never received a more graceful tribute to her fair youth. It was too late to go to the Jardin des Plantes, so I drove the Countess straight to her hôtel. She was very silent, so I tried to cheer her up by telling her the funny story about the kind lady who had by accident read a little paper of mine about dolls in 'Blackwood's Magazine' and had taken to making dolls by the dozen for the poor children I was speaking about. Hadn't she noticed how beautifully some of the dolls were dressed up? Yes, she had noticed it. Was the lady pretty? Yes, very. Was she in Paris? No, I had had to stop her making more dolls, as I had ended by having more dolls than patients, and I had sent the lady to St. Moritz for a change of air. On saying good-bye to the Countess before her hôtel I expressed my regrets that there had been no time to visit the gorilla in the Jardin des Plantes, but I hoped that anyhow she had not been sorry to have come with me.

'I am not sorry, I am so grateful, but, but, but . . . I am so ashamed,' she sobbed as she sprang in through the gate of her hôtel.

[1] I have related this strange story elsewhere.

IV

A Fashionable Doctor

I had a standing invitation to dine at the hôtel in Faubourg St. Germain every Sunday. The Count had long ago withdrawn his objections to doctors, in fact he was charming to me. Family dinner, only M. l'Abbé and occasionally the cousin of the Countess, the Vicomte Maurice, who treated me with an almost insolent nonchalance. I disliked him from the first time I saw him, and I soon discovered I was not the only one. It was evident that the Count and he had very little to say to each other. The Abbé was a priest of the old school and a man of the world who knew far more of life and human nature than I did. He was at first very reserved towards me and often, when I noticed his shrewd eyes fixed on me, I felt as if he knew more about colitis than I did. I felt almost ashamed before this old man and would have liked to talk openly to him and lay my cards on the table. But I never had the chance, I never had an opportunity of seeing him alone. One day, as I entered my dining-room to snatch a rapid luncheon before beginning my consultation, I was surprised to find him there waiting for me. He said he had come of his own accord, in his quality of an old friend of the family, and wished I should not mention his visit.

'You have been remarkably successful with the Countess,' he began, 'and we are all very grateful to you. I must also compliment you about the Marquise. I have just come from her, I am her confessor, and I must say I am astonished to see how much better she is in every way. But it is about the Count that I have come to speak to you to-day, I am greatly worried about him, I am sure il file un mauvais coton. He hardly ever leaves the house, spends most of his days in his room smoking his big cigars, he sleeps for hours after luncheon and I often find him any time of the day asleep in his armchair with his cigar in his mouth. In the country he is quite a different man, he takes his morning-ride every day after Mass, is active and bright and takes much interest in the management of his big estates. His only wish is to go to his château in Touraine and if the Countess cannot be persuaded to leave Paris, as I fear is the case, I have reluctantly come to the conclusion that he should go alone. He has great confidence in you and if you tell him it is necessary for his health to leave Paris, he will do so. This is precisely what I have come to ask you to do.'

'I am sorry, M. l'Abbé, but I cannot.'

He looked at me with undisguised surprise, almost suspicion.

'May I ask you the reason for your refusal?'

'The Countess cannot leave Paris now and it is only natural that she should accompany the Count.'

'Why cannot she be treated for her colitis in the country, there is a very good and safe doctor at the Castle who has often looked after her before, when she suffered from appendicitis.'

'With what result?'

He did not answer.

'May I in return,' I said, 'ask you this question? Suppose the Countess could be suddenly cured of her colitis, could you make her leave Paris?'

'Honestly speaking, no. But why this supposition, since I understand that this disease is of long duration and difficult to cure?'

'I could cure the Countess of her colitis in a day.'

He looked at me stupefied.

'And why, in the name of All the Saints, don't you? You are incurring a tremendous responsibility.'

'I am not afraid of responsibility, I would not be here if I were. Now let us speak openly. Yes, I could cure the Countess in a day, she no more has colitis than you or I, nor has she ever had appendicitis. It is all in her head, in her nerves. If I took away her colitis from her too rapidly, she might lose her mental balance altogether, or take to something far worse, say, morphia, or a lover. Whether I shall be able to be of any use to the Countess remains to be seen. To order the Countess to leave Paris now would be a psychological error. She would probably refuse and, once having dared to disobey me, her confidence in me would be at an end. Give me a fortnight and she will leave Paris by her own wish – or at least she will think so. It is all a question of tactics. To make the Count go alone would be an error of another order, and you, M. l'Abbé, know this as well as I do.'

He looked at me attentively but said nothing.

'Now as to the Marquise. You were kind enough to compliment me for what I have done for her and I accept the compliment. Medically speaking I have done nothing nor could anybody else do anything. Deaf people suffer considerably from their enforced

54

isolation from others, specially those who have no mental resources of their own, and they are in the majority. To distract their attention from their misfortune is the only thing one can do for them. The Marquise's thoughts are occupied with colitis instead of with deafness and you have yourself seen with what result. I myself am beginning to have quite enough of colitis, and now since the Marquise is going to the country, I am replacing it with a lapdog, more suitable to country life.'

As he was going away, the Abbé turned in the door and looked at me attentively.

'How old are you?'

'Twenty-six.'

'Vous irez loin, mon fils! Vous irez loin!'

'Yes,' thought I. 'I am going far, far away, away from this humiliating life of humbug and deceit, from all these artificial people, back to the enchanting island, back to old Maria Porta-Lettere, to Mastro Vincenzo and to Gioconda, to clean my soul in the little white house high up on the top of the cliff. How much longer am I going to waste my time in this horrible town? When is Sant'Antonio going to work his new miracle?'

On my table lay a letter of good-bye, not good-bye, but au revoir, from the Marquise, full of gratitude and praise. It contained a big bank-note. I looked at the faded photograph of Capri in the corner of my room and put the money in my pocket. What has become of all the money I made in those days of prosperity and luck? I was supposed to save it all for Mastro Vincenzo's house, but the fact remains, I never had any money to save. Wages of sin? Maybe, but if so, the whole faculty ought to have gone bankrupt, for we were all in the same boat, the professors as well as my colleagues, with the same sort of clientèle as I. Luckily for me I had other patients as well, plenty of them and enough to save me from becoming a charlatan altogether. There were in those days far fewer specialists than now. I was supposed to know everything, even surgery. It took me two years to realize that I was not fit to be a surgeon, I fear it took my patients less time. Although I was supposed to be a nerve-doctor, I did everything a doctor can be asked to do, even obstetrics, and God helped mother and child. In fact it was surprising how well the great majority of my patients resisted the treatment. When Napoleon's eagle eye flashed down the list of officers proposed for promotion to generals, he used to scribble in the margin of a name: 'Is he lucky?' I had luck, amazing, almost uncanny luck with everything I laid my hands on, with every patient I saw. I was not a good doctor, my studies had been too rapid, my hospital training too short, but there is not the slightest doubt that I was a successful doctor. What is the secret of success? To inspire confidence. What is confidence? Where does it come from, from the head or from the heart? Does it derive from the upper strata of our mentality or is it a mighty tree of knowledge of good and evil with roots springing from the very depths of our being? Through what channels does it communicate with others? Is it visible in the eye, is it audible in the spoken word? I do not know, I only know that it cannot be acquired by book-reading, nor by the bedside of our patients. It is a magic gift granted by birthright to one man and denied to another. The doctor who possesses this gift can almost raise the dead. The doctor who does not possess it will have to submit to the calling-in of a colleague for consultation in a case of measles. I soon discovered that this invaluable gift had been granted to me by no merit of mine. I discovered it in the nick of time, for I was beginning to become conceited and very pleased with myself. It made me understand how little I knew and made me turn more and more to Mother Nature, the wise old nurse, for advice and help. It might even have made me become a good doctor in the end, had I stuck to my hospital work and to my poor patients. But I lost all my chances, for I became a fashionable doctor instead. If you come across a fashionable doctor, watch him carefully at a safe distance before handing yourself over to him. He may be a good doctor, but in very many cases he is not. First, because as a rule he is far too busy to listen with patience to your long story. Secondly, because he is inevitably liable to become a snob, if he is not one already, to let the Countess pass in before you, to examine the liver of the Count with more attention than that of his valet, to go to the garden-party at the British Embassy instead of to your last-born whose whooping-cough is getting worse. Thirdly, unless his heart is very sound he will soon show unmistakable signs of precocious hardening of that organ; he will become indifferent and insensible to the suffering of others, like the pleasure-seeking people around him. You cannot be a good doctor without pity.

Often, when a long day's work was over, I, who have always been interested in psychology, used to ask myself why all these silly people sat and waited for me for hours in my consulting-room. Why did they all obey me, why could I so often make them feel better, even by a mere touch of my hand? Why, even after the power of speech had gone and the terror of death was staring out of their eyes, did they become so peaceful and still when I laid my hand on their forehead? Why did the lunatics in the Asile St. Anne, foaming with rage and screaming like wild animals, become calm and docile when I loosened their strait-jackets and held their hand in mine? It was a common trick of mine, all the warders knew it and many of my comrades and even the professor used to say of me: *Ce garçon-là a le diable au corps*! I have always had a sneaking liking for lunatics, I used to wander about quite unconcerned in the Salle des Agités as among friends. I had been warned more than once that it would end badly, but of course I knew better. One day, one of my best friends hit me on the back of the head with a hammer he had got hold of in some inexplicable way, and I was carried unconscious to the infirmary. It was a terrible blow, my friend was an ex-blacksmith who knew his business. They thought at first I had a fracture of the skull. Not I! It was only a commotion cérébrale and my misadventure brought me a flattering compliment from the chef de clinique: 'Ce sacré Suédois a le crâne d'un ours, faut voir s'il n'a pas cassé le marteau!'

'After all it may be in the head and not in the hand,' said I to myself when my mental machinery set to work after a standstill of forty-eight hours. As I lay there in the infirmary a whole week with an ice-bag on my 'head of a bear' and no visitors or books to keep me company, I began to think hard on the subject, and not even the blacksmith's hammer could make me abandon my theory that it was all in the hand.

Why could I put my hand between the bars of the black panther's cage in Ménagerie Pezon and, if nobody came near to irritate him, make the big cat roll over on his back, purring amiably at me, with my hand between his paws and yawning at me with his big mouth wide open? Why could I lance the abscess in Léonie's foot and pull out the splinter of wood that had made the big lioness tramp about restlessly on three legs for a week in agonizing pain? The local anaesthetic had proved a failure, and poor Léonie moaned like a child when I pressed the pus out of her paw. Only when I disinfected the wound she got somewhat impatient, but there was no wrath in the subdued thunder of her voice, only disappointment that she was not allowed to lick it herself with her sharp tongue. When the operation was over and I was leaving the menagerie with the baby baboon under my arm M. Pezon had presented to me as my fee, the famous lion-tamer said to me:

'Monsieur le Docteur, vous avez manqué votre profession, vous auriez du être dompteur d'animaux!'

And Ivan, the big Polar Bear at the Jardin des Plantes, did he not clamber out of his tub of water as soon as he saw me, to come to the bars of his prison and standing erect on his hind legs put his black nose just in front of mine and take the fish from my hand in the most friendly manner? The keeper said he did it with nobody else, no doubt he looked upon me as a sort of compatriot. Don't say it was the fish and not the hand, for when I had nothing to offer him he still stood there in the same position as long as I had time to remain, looking steadfastly at me with his shining black eyes under their white eyelashes and sniffing at my hand. Of course we spoke in Swedish, with a sort of Polar accent I picked up from him. I am sure he understood every word I said when I told him in a low monotonous voice how sorry I was for him and that when I was a boy I had seen two of his kinsmen swimming close to our boat amongst floating ice-blocks in the land of our birth.

And poor Jacques, the famous gorilla of the Zoo, so far the only one of his tribe who had been taken prisoner and brought to the sunless land of his enemies! Didn't he confidentially put his horny hand in mine as soon as he saw me? Didn't he like me to pat him gently on his back? He would sit quite still for minutes holding on to my hand without saying anything. Often he would look at the palm of my hand with great attention as if he knew something about palmistry, bend my fingers one after another as if to see how the joints were working, then he would drop my hand and look with the same attention at his own hand with a chuckle, as if to say that he saw no great difference between the two; and he was quite right there. Most of the time he used to sit quite still fingering a straw, in the corner of the cage where his visitors could not see him, seldom using the swing provided for him in the clumsy hope that he might take it for the swinging branch of the sycamore-tree where he used to take his siesta in the days of his freedom. He used to sleep on a low couch made of bamboo, like the *sêrir* of the Arabs, but he was an early riser and I never saw him in bed until he was taken ill. He had been taught by his keeper to eat his midday-meal seated before a low table, a napkin stuck under his chin. He had even been provided with a knife and fork of hard wood, but had never taken to them, he much preferred to eat with his fingers, as did our forefathers up till a couple of hundred years ago and still does the majority of the human race. But he drank his milk with great gusto out of his own cup and also his morning coffee with much sugar in it. It is true that he blew his nose with his fingers, but so did Petrarch's Laura, Mary Queen of Scots, and Le Roi Soleil. Poor Jack! Our friendship lasted to the end. He had been ailing ever since Christmas, his complexion became ashy grey, his cheeks hollow and his eyes sank deeper and deeper into their sockets. He became restless and fretful, was losing flesh rapidly, and soon a dry ominous cough set in. I took his temperature several times but had to be very careful for, like children, he was apt to break the thermometer to see what was moving inside. One day as he sat on my lap holding on to my hand, he had a violent fit of coughing which brought on a slight haemorrhage of the lungs. The sight of the blood terrified him, as is the case with most people. I often noticed during the war how even the bravest Tommies who looked quite unconcerned at their gaping wounds could grow pale at the sight of a few drops of fresh blood. He lost more and more his appetite and could only with great difficulty be coaxed to eat a banana or a fig. One morning I found him lying on his bed with the blanket pulled over his head, just as my patients in the Salle Ste. Claire used to lie, when they were tired to death and sick of everything. He must have heard me coming for he stretched out his hand from under the blanket and got hold of mine. I didn't want to disturb him and sat there for a long while with his hand in mine, listening to his heavy irregular respiration and to the phlegm rattling in his throat. Presently a sharp fit of coughing shook his whole body. He sat up in his bed and put his two hands to his temples in a gesture of despair. The whole expression of his face had changed. He had cast off his animal disguise and become a dying human being. So near had he come to me that he was deprived of the only privilege our Mighty God has granted to the animals in compensation for the sufferings man inflicts upon them – that of an easy death. His agony was terrible, he died slowly strangled by the same Executioner I had so often seen at work in Salle Ste. Claire. I recognized him well by the slow grip of his hand.

And after? What became of my poor friend Jack? I know well that his emaciated body went to the Anatomical Institution and that his skeleton, with its large brain-pan, still stands erect in the Musée Dupuytren. But is that all?

V

Patients

I missed very much my Sunday dinners in Faubourg St. Germain. About a fortnight after my interview with the Abbé the Countess, with her impulsive nature, had suddenly felt the need of a change of air and decided to accompany the Count to their château in Touraine. It came as a surprise to us all, only the Abbé must have had some inkling of it, for I noticed a merry twinkling in his shrewd old eye the last Sunday I dined there. The Countess was kind enough to send me a weekly report to say how she was getting on and I also heard now and then from the Abbé. Everything was going on well. The Count had his ride every morning, never slept during the day and smoked much less. The Countess had taken up her music again, occupied herself diligently with the poor of the village and never complained about her colitis. The Abbé also gave me good news about the Marquise, whose country-seat was a short hour's drive from the château. She was doing very well. Instead of sitting in her arm-chair in mournful seclusion the whole day, worrying about her deafness, she now took a long walk twice a day in the garden for the sake of her beloved Loulou who was getting too fat and greatly in need of exercise.

'He is a horrible little brute,' wrote the Abbé, 'who sits in her lap and snarls and growls at everybody; he has even bitten the maid twice. Everybody hates him, but the Marquise adores him and fusses about him the whole day. Yesterday in the midst of the confession he was suddenly sick all over her beautiful tea-gown and his mistress was in such a state of alarm that I had to interrupt the function. Now the Marquise wants me to ask you if you think it might possibly develop into colitis and asks you to be so kind as to prescribe something for him, she says she feels sure you will understand his case better than anybody.'

The Marquise was not far from the truth there, for I was already then beginning to be known as a good dog-doctor, though I had not reached the eminent position I occupied later in my life, when I became a consulting dog-doctor famous among all dog-lovers of my clientèle. I am aware that the opinions as to my skill as a doctor to my fellow-creatures have been somewhat divided, but I dare to maintain that my reputation as a reliable dog-doctor has never been seriously challenged. I am not conceited enough to wish to deny that this may partly depend upon the absence of jalousie de métier I met with in the exercise of this branch of my profession – I got plenty of it in the other branches, I can assure you.

To become a good dog-doctor it is necessary to love dogs, but it is also necessary to understand them – the same as with us, with the difference that it is easier to understand a dog than a man and easier to love him. Never forget that the mentality of one dog is totally different from that of another. The sharp wit that sparkles in the quick eye of a fox-terrier, for instance, reflects a mental activity totally different from the serene wisdom which shines in the calm eye of a St. Bernard or an old sheep-dog. The intelligence of dogs is proverbial, but there is a great difference of degree, already apparent in the puppies as soon as they open their eyes. There are even stupid dogs, though the percentage is much smaller than in man. On the whole it is easy to understand the dog and to learn to read his thoughts. The dog cannot dissimulate, cannot deceive, cannot lie because he cannot speak. The dog is a saint. He is straightforward and honest by nature. If in exceptional cases there appear in a dog some stigmas of hereditary sin traceable to his wild ancestors, who had to rely on cunning in their fight for existence, these stigmas will disappear when his experience has taught him that he can rely upon straight and just dealings from us. If these stigmas should remain in a dog who is well treated, these cases are extremely rare, this dog is not normal, he is suffering from moral insanity and should be given a painless death. A dog gladly admits the superiority of his master over himself, accepts his judgment as final, but, contrary to what many dog-lovers believe, he does not consider himself as a slave. His submission is voluntary and he expects his own small rights to be respected. He looks upon his master as his king, almost as his god, he expects his god to be severe if need be, but he expects him to be just. He knows that his god can read his thoughts and he knows it is no good to try to conceal them. Can he read the thoughts of his god? Most certainly he can. The Society for Psychical Research may say what they like, but telepathy between man and man has so far not been proved. But telepathy between dog and man has been proved over and over again. The dog can read his master's thoughts, can understand his varying moods, and foretell his decisions. He knows by instinct when he is not wanted, lies quite still for hours when his king is hard at work, as kings often are, or at least ought to be. But when his king is sad and worried he knows that his time has come and he creeps up and lays his head on his lap. Don't worry! Never mind if they all abandon you, I am here to replace all your friends and to fight all your enemies! Come along and let us go for a walk and forget all about it!

It is strange and very pathetic to watch the behaviour of a dog when his master is ill. The dog warned by his infallible instinct is afraid of disease, afraid of death. A dog accustomed for years to sleep on his master's bed is reluctant to remain there when his master is ill. Even in the rare exceptions to this rule, he leaves his master at the approach of death, hiding in a corner of the room and whining pitifully. It has even happened to me to be warned by the behaviour of a dog of the approach of death. What does he know about death? At least as much as we do, probably a good deal more. As I write this I am reminded of a poor woman in Anacapri, a stranger to the village, slowly dying of consumption, so slowly that one after another of the few *comari* who used to go and see her had got tired of her and left her to her fate. Her only friend was a mongrel dog, who, an exception to the rule I have just mentioned, never left his place at the foot of her bed. It was besides the only place to lie on, except on the damp earthen floor of the wretched hole the poor woman lived and died in. One day, as I happened to pass by, I found Don Salvatore there, the only one of the twelve priests of our little village who took the slightest interest in the poor and the sick. Don Salvatore asked me if I did not think the time had come to bring her the Last Sacraments. The woman looked about as usual, her pulse was not worse, she even told us she had felt a little better these last days – la miglioria della morte, said Don Salvatore. I had often marvelled at the amazing tenacity with which she clung to life and I told the priest she might quite well last for another week or two. So we agreed to wait with the Last Sacraments. Just as we were leaving the room the dog jumped down from the bed with a howl of distress and crouched in the corner of the room whining pitifully. I could see no change in the woman's looks, but noticed with surprise that her pulse was now almost imperceptible. She made a desperate effort to say something, but I could not understand at first what she meant. She looked at me with wide-open eyes and raised her emaciated arm several times pointing to the dog. This time I understood and I believe she also understood me when I bent over her and said I would take care of the dog. She nodded contentedly, her eyes closed and the peace of death spread over her face. She drew a deep breath, a few drops of blood oozed out between her lips and it was all over. The immediate cause of this woman's death was evidently an internal haemorrhage. How did the dog know before I knew? When they came in the evening to take her away the dog followed his mistress to the camposanto, the only mourner. Next day old Pacciale, the grave-digger, already then my special friend, told me that the dog was still lying on her grave. It rained torrents the whole day and the following night, but in the morning the dog was still there. In the evening I sent Pacciale with a leash to try to coax him away and take him to San Michele, but the dog growled savagely at him and refused to move. On the third day I went to the cemetery myself and succeeded with great difficulty in making him follow me home, he knew me besides quite well. There were eight dogs in San Michele in those days and I felt very uneasy as to the reception awaiting the newcomer. But all went well, thanks to Billy, the baboon, for he, for some inexplicable reason, at first sight took a great fancy to the stranger, who, once recovered from his stupefaction, soon became his inseparable friend. All my dogs hated and feared the huge monkey who ruled supreme in the garden of San Michele and soon even Barbarossa, the fierce Maremma dog, ceased to growl at the newcomer. He lived there happily for two years and is buried there under the ivy with my other dogs.

A dog can be taught to do almost anything with friendly encouragement, patience and a biscuit when he has learned his lesson with right good will. Never lose your temper or use violence of any sort. Corporal punishment inflicted on an intelligent dog is an indignity which reflects upon his master. It is besides a psychological error. This being said, let me add that naughty puppies as well as very small children before the age of reason, but not after, are quite welcome to a little spanking now and then when too recalcitrant to learn the fundamental rules of good manners. Personally, I have never taught my dogs any sort of tricks, although I admit that many dogs, their lesson once learned, take great pleasure in showing off their tricks. To perform in a circus is quite another matter and a degradation to an intelligent dog. Anyhow these performing dogs are as a rule well looked after on account of the money they bring in and are infinitely better off than their wretched wild comrades in the menagerie. When a dog is ill, he will submit to almost anything, even a painful operation, if it is explained to him in a kind but firm voice that it must be done and why it must be done. Never coax a sick dog to eat, he often does so only to oblige you, even if his instinct warns him to abstain from food, which is as often as not his salvation. Don't worry, dogs, like very small children, can be without food for several days without further inconvenience. A dog can stand pain with great courage, but of course he likes you to tell him how sorry you are for him. Maybe it will be a comfort to some dog-lovers to be told that I do believe that on the whole their sensitiveness to pain is less acute than we think. Never disturb a sick dog when not absolutely necessary. As often as not your untimely interference only distracts nature in her effort to assist him to get well. All animals wish to be left alone when they are ill and also when they are about to die. Alas! the life of a dog is so short and there are none of us who have not been in mourning for a lost friend. Your first impulse and your first words after you have laid him to rest under a tree in the park, are that you never, never wish to have another dog; no other dog could ever replace him, no other dog could ever be to you what he has been. You are mistaken. It is not *a* dog we love, it is *the* dog. They are all more or less the same, they are all ready to love you and be loved by you. They are all representatives of the most lovable and, morally speaking, most perfect creation of God. If you loved your dead friend in the right way, you cannot do without another. Alas! he also will have to part from you, for those beloved by the gods die young. Remember when his time comes what I am going to tell you now. Do not send him to the lethal chamber or ask your kindhearted doctor to see that he is given a painless death under an anaesthetic. It is not a painless death, it is a distressing death. Dogs often resist the deadly effect of these gases and drugs in the most heartrending way. The dose which would kill a full-grown man often leaves a dog alive for long minutes of mental and bodily suffering. I have been present several times at these massacres in lethal chambers and I have myself killed many dogs under anaesthetics, and I know what I am talking about. I shall never do it again. Ask any man you can trust, who is fond of dogs, this condition is necessary, to take your old dog in the park, to give him a bone and while he is eating it to shoot him with a revolver through the ear. It is an instantaneous and painless death, life is extinguished like the candle you blow out. Many of my old dogs have died so by my own hand. They all lie buried under the cypresses in Materita and over their graves stands an antique marble column. There also lies another dog, for twelve years the faithful friend of a gracious lady who, although she has to be the mother of a whole country, my own country, has enough room left in her heart to bring a bunch of flowers to his grave every time she comes to Capri.

Fate has willed that the most lovable of all animals should be the bearer of the most terrible of all diseases – hydrophobia. I witnessed at the Institut Pasteur the early stages of the long-drawn battle between science and the dreaded foe and I also witnessed the final victory. It was dearly won. Hecatombs of dogs had to be sacrificed and maybe some human lives as well. I used to visit the doomed animals and give them what little comfort I could, but it became so painful to me that for some time I gave up going to the Institut Pasteur altogether. Still I never doubted it was right, that what was done had to be done. I was present at many failures, saw many people die both before and after treatment with the new method. Pasteur was violently attacked not only by all sorts of ignorant and well-meaning dog-lovers but also by many of his own colleagues, he was even accused of having caused the death of several of his patients with his serum. He himself went on his way undaunted by failure, but those who saw him in those days knew well how much he suffered from the tortures he had to inflict upon the dogs, for he was himself a great lover of dogs. He was the most kind-hearted of men. I once heard him say that he could never have the courage to shoot a bird. Everything that could possibly be done to minimize the sufferings of the laboratory dogs was done, even the keeper of the kennel at Villeneuve de l'Étang, an ex-gendarme called Pernier, had been chosen for his post by Pasteur himself because he was known as a great lover of dogs. These kennels contained sixty dogs inoculated with serum and regularly taken to the kennels in the old Lycée Rollin for bite tests. In these kennels were kept forty rabid dogs. The handling of these dogs, all foaming with rage, was a very dangerous affair, and I often marvelled at the courage displayed by everybody. Pasteur himself was absolutely fearless. Anxious to secure a sample of saliva straight from the jaws of a rabid dog, I once saw him with the glass tube held between his lips draw a few drops of the deadly saliva from the mouth of a rabid bull-dog, held on the table by two assistants, their hands protected by leather gloves. Most of these laboratory dogs were homeless stray dogs picked up by the police in the streets of Paris, but many of them looked as if they had seen better days. Here they suffered and died in obscurity, Unknown Soldiers in the battle of the human mind against disease and death. Close by, at La Bagatelle, in the elegant dog-cemetery founded by Sir Richard Wallace, lay buried hundreds of lap-dogs and drawing-room dogs, with the records of their useless and luxurious lives inscribed by loving hands on the marble crosses over their graves.

Then came the terrible episode of the six Russian peasants bitten by a pack of mad wolves and sent to the Institut Pasteur at the expense of the Tsar. They were all horribly mauled in the face and hands and their chances from the outset were almost nil. Moreover it was known even then that hydrophobia in wolves was far more dangerous than in dogs, and that those bitten in the face were almost certain to die. Pasteur knew this better than anybody, and, hadn't he been the man he was, he would no doubt have declined to take them in hand. They were placed in a separate ward in the Hôtel Dieu in the charge of Professor Tillaux, the most eminent and the most humane surgeon in Paris in those days and a staunch supporter and great friend of Pasteur's. Pasteur came himself every morning with Tillaux to inoculate them, watching them anxiously from day to day. Nobody could understand a word they said. One afternoon, it was on the ninth day, I was trying to pour a drop of milk down the lacerated throat of one of the moujiks, a giant whose whole face had almost been torn away, when suddenly something wild and uncanny flashed in his eyes, the muscles of the jaws contracted and opened spasmodically with a snapping sound and a ghastly cry I had never heard before either from man or animal rang out from his foaming mouth. He made a violent effort to spring out of bed and nearly knocked me down, as I tried to hold him back. His arms, strong as the paws of a bear, closed on me in a clasp, holding me tight as in a vice. I felt the foul breath from his foaming mouth close to mine and the poisonous saliva dripping down my face. I gripped at his throat, the bandage slipped off his ghastly wound and as I drew back my hands from his snapping jaws, they were red with blood. A convulsive trembling passed over his whole body, his arms relaxed their grasp and fell back inert at his side. I staggered to the door in search of the strongest disinfectant I could get hold of. In the corridor sat Sœur Marthe, drinking her afternoon coffee. She looked at me terrified, and I gulped down her cup of coffee just as I was going to faint. By God's mercy there was not a scratch on my face nor hands. Sœur Marthe was a great friend of mine. She kept her word; so far as I know, the secret never leaked out. I had good reason to keep it secret, strict orders had been given not to approach any of these men unless it was absolutely necessary, and if so, only with the hands protected by thick gloves. I told it later to the Professor himself, he was quite rightly very angry with me, but he had a sneaking weakness for me and he soon forgave me, as he had so often done before for many

66

shortcomings.

'Sacré Suédois,' he muttered, 'tu es aussi enragé que le moujik!' In the evening the moujik, tied hand and foot to the iron bars of the bed, was carried to a separate pavilion isolated from the others. I went to see him next morning with Sœur Marthe. The room was semi-dark. The bandage covered his whole face and I could see nothing but his eyes. I shall never forget the expression of those eyes, they used to haunt me for years afterwards. His breathing was short and irregular, with intervals like the Cheyne-Stokes respiration – the well-known precursory symptom of death. He talked with vertiginous rapidity in a hoarse voice, now and then interrupted by a wild cry of distress or a hooting moan which made me shudder. I listened for a while to the rush of unknown words half-drowned in the flow of saliva, and soon I thought I distinguished one same word repeated incessantly, with an almost desperate accent:

'Crestitsa! Crestitsa! Crestitsa!' I looked attentively at his eyes, kind, humble, imploring eyes.

'He is conscious,' I whispered to Sœur Marthe, 'he wants something. I wish I knew what it is. Listen!'

'Crestitsa! Crestitsa! Crestitsa!' he called out incessantly.

'Run and fetch a crucifix,' I said to the nun.

We laid the crucifix on the bed. The flow of words ceased instantly. He lay there quite silent, his eyes fixed on the crucifix. His breathing grew fainter and fainter. Suddenly the muscles of his giant body stiffened in a last violent contraction, and the heart stood still.

The next day another moujik showed unmistakable signs of hydrophobia, and soon another, and three days later they were all raving mad. Their screams and howls could be heard all over the Hôtel Dieu, people said even below in Place Nôtre Dame. The whole hospital was in emotion. Nobody wanted to go near the ward, even the courageous sisters fled in terror. I can see now the white face of Pasteur as he passed in silence from bed to bed, looking at the doomed men with infinite compassion in his eyes. He sank down on a chair, his head between his hands. Accustomed as I was to see him every day, I had not noticed till then how ill and worn he looked, though I knew from an almost imperceptible hesitation in his speech and a slight embarrassment in the grip of his hand that he had already then received the first warning of the fate that was to overtake him ere long. Tillaux, who had been sent for in the midst of an operation, rushed into the ward, his apron stained with blood. He went up to Pasteur and laid his hand on his shoulder. The two men looked at each other in silence. The kind blue eyes of the great surgeon, who had seen so much horror and suffering, glanced round the ward and his face grew white like a sheet.

'I cannot stand it,' he said in a broken voice and sprang out of the room.

The same evening a consultation took place between these two men. They are few who knew the decision they arrived at, but it was the only right one and an honour to them both. The next morning all was silent in the ward. During the night the doomed men had been helped to a painless death.

The impression in Paris was enormous. All the newspapers were full of the most ghastly descriptions of the death of the Russian moujiks and for days nobody spoke of anything else.

Late one night the following week a well-known Norwegian animal painter came rushing to Avenue de Villiers in a state of fearful agitation. He had been bitten in the hand by his beloved dog, an enormous bull-dog, most ferocious-looking, but hitherto most amiable and a great friend of mine – his portrait painted by his master had besides been in the Salon the year before. We drove at once to the studio in Avenue des Termes. The dog was locked up in the bedroom and his master wanted me to shoot him at once, he said he had not the courage to do it himself. The dog was running to and fro, now and then hiding under the bed with a savage growl. The room was so dark that I put the key in my pocket and decided to wait till next morning. I disinfected and dressed the wound and gave the Norwegian a sleeping-draught for the night. I watched the dog attentively the next morning and decided to postpone shooting him till the following day as I was not quite certain he really had hydrophobia, notwithstanding all the appearances. Errors of diagnosis in the early stages of rabies are very common. Even the classical symptom which has given its name to the dreaded disease – hydrophobia means horror of water – is not to be relied upon. The rabid dog does not abhor water. I have often seen a rabid dog drink with avidity from a bowl of water I had put in his cage. It is only with human beings affected with rabies that this symptom holds good. A great number, if not the majority of dogs killed, suspected of hydrophobia, are suffering from other relatively harmless diseases. But even if this can be proved by post-mortem examination – not one in a dozen of ordinary doctors and vets is competent to do it – it is as a rule most difficult to convince the person who has been bitten by the dog. The dread of the terrible disease remains, and to be haunted by the fear of hydrophobia is as dangerous as the disease itself. The right thing to do is to have the suspected dog safely locked up and provided with food and drink. If he is alive after ten days it is certain that it is not rabies and all is well.

Next morning when I watched the dog through the half-open door he wagged his stump of a tail and looked at me with a quite friendly expression in his blood-shot eyes. But just as I stretched out my hand to pat him, he retired under the bed with a growl. I did not know what to think. Anyhow I told his master I did not believe he was rabid. He would not hear of it and again begged me to shoot the dog at once. I refused and said I wanted to wait another day. His master had spent the night walking to and fro in the studio and on the table lay a medical handbook with the symptoms of hydrophobia in man and dog marked with a pencil. I threw the book in the fire. His neighbour, a Russian sculptor, who had promised me to remain with him the whole day, told me in the evening he had refused all food and drink, was constantly wiping saliva from his lips and talked about nothing but hydrophobia. I insisted upon his drinking a cup of coffee. He looked at me desperately and said he could not swallow and as I handed him the cup I was horrified to see the muscles of his jaw stiffen with a convulsive cramp, his whole body began to tremble and he sank down in his chair with a terrible cry of distress. I gave him a strong injection of morphia and told him I was so sure that the dog was all right that I was willing to go into the room again, but I don't believe I would have had the courage to do it. The morphia began to act and I left him half-asleep in his chair. When I returned late at night, the Russian sculptor told me that the whole house had been in an uproar, that the landlord had sent the concierge to say that the dog must be killed at once and that he had just shot him through the window. The dog had crawled to the door, where he had finished him off with another bullet. He was lying there still in a pool of blood. His master was sitting in his chair staring straight before him without saying a word. I did not like the look in his eyes, I took his revolver from the table and put it in my pocket, there was still one bullet left. I lit the candle and asked the Russian sculptor to help me to carry the dead dog down to my carriage, I wanted to take him straight to the Institut Pasteur for a post-mortem. There was a large pool of blood near the door, the dog was not there.

'Shut the door,' shouted the sculptor behind me as the dog sprang at me from under the bed with a horrible growl, his wide-open mouth streaming with blood. The candlestick dropped from my hand, I fired at random in the dark and the dog fell dead at my very feet. We put him in my carriage and I drove to the Institut Pasteur. Doctor Roux, Pasteur's right-hand man, and later on his successor, saying it looked very bad indeed, promised to make a post-mortem immediately and to let me know as soon as possible. When I came to Avenue des Termes next day, I found the Russian standing outside the studio door. He had spent the night with his friend, who had been walking up and down the whole time in great agitation, till at last he had fallen asleep in his chair an hour ago. The Russian had gone to his own room to wash and on coming back a moment ago had found the studio door locked from the inside.

'Listen,' he said, as if to excuse himself for having disobeyed the orders not to leave him a second, 'it is all right, he is still asleep, don't you hear his snoring?'

'Help me to break open the door,' I shouted, 'it is not snoring, it is the stertorous breathing of . . .'

The door gave way and we rushed in the studio. He was lying on the couch breathing heavily, a revolver still clutched in his hand. He had shot himself through the eye. We carried him to my carriage. I drove full speed to the Hôpital Beaujon where he was operated on at once by Professor Labbé. The revolver he had shot himself with was of smaller calibre than the one I had taken from him, the bullet was extracted. He was still unconscious when I left. The same evening I received a letter from Doctor Roux that the result of the post-mortem examination was negative, the dog had not had hydrophobia. I drove at once to the Hôpital Beaujon. The Norwegian was delirious – *prognosis pessima*, said the famous surgeon. On the third day brain-fever set in. He did not die, he left the hospital a month later, blind. The last I heard of him was that he was in a lunatic asylum in Norway.

My own rôle in this lamentable affair was not satisfactory. I did my best, but it was not enough. If it had happened a couple of years later, this man would not have shot himself. I would have known how to master his fear, and would have been the stronger of the two as I have been in later years more than once, when I have stayed a hand clutching a revolver in fear of life.

When will the anti-vivisectionists realize that when they are asking for total prohibition of experiments on living animals they are asking for what it is impossible to grant them? Pasteur's vaccination against rabies has reduced the mortality in this terrible disease to a minimum and Behring's anti-diphtheric serum saves the lives of over a hundred thousand children every year. Are not these two facts alone sufficient to make these well-meaning lovers of animals understand that discoverers of new worlds like Pasteur, of new remedies against hitherto incurable diseases like Koch, Ehrlich and Behring must be left to pursue their researches unhampered by restrictions and undisturbed by interference from outsiders. Those to be left a free hand are besides so few that they can be counted on one's fingers. For the rest no doubt most severe restrictions should be insisted upon, perhaps even total prohibition. But I go further. One of the most weighty arguments against several of these experiments on living animals is that their practical value is much reduced, owing to the fundamental difference from a pathological and physiological point of view between the bodies of men and the bodies of animals. But why should these experiments be limited to the bodies of animals, why should they not be carried out on the living body of man as well? Why should not the born criminals, the chronic evil-doers, condemned to waste their remaining life in prison, useless and often dangerous to others and to themselves, why should not these inveterate offenders against our laws be offered a reduction of their penal servitude if they were willing to submit under anæsthetics to certain experiments on their living bodies for the benefit of mankind? If the judge, before putting on the black cap, had in his power to offer the murderer the alternative between the gallows and penal servitude for so and so many years, I have little doubt there would be no lack of candidates. Why should not Doctor Woronoff, the practical value of his invention be it what it may, be allowed to open up an enlisting office in the prisons for those willing to enroll themselves as substitutes for his wretched monkeys? Why do not these well-meaning lovers of animals begin by concentrating their efforts on putting a stop to the exhibition of wild animals in circuses and menageries? As long as this scandal is tolerated by our laws there is little chance for us to be looked upon as civilized by a future generation. If you want to realize what a set of barbarians we really are, you have only to enter the tent of a travelling menagerie. The cruel wild beast is not behind the bars of the cage, he stands in front of it.

A propos of monkeys and menageries I venture with due modesty to pride myself on having been in the days of my strength a good monkey-doctor as well. This is an extremely difficult speciality, hampered by all sorts of unexpected complications and pitfalls, and where great rapidity of judgment and profound knowledge of human nature are essential conditions for success. It is sheer nonsense to say that as with children the chief difficulty lies in the fact that the patient cannot speak. Monkeys can speak quite well if they choose to. The chief difficulty is that they are far too clever for our slow brains. You can deceive a human patient – deception, alas, forms a necessary part of our profession, the truth is so often too sad to be told. You can deceive a dog who believes blindly everything you say, but you cannot deceive a monkey, for he sees through you at once. The monkey can deceive you whenever he chooses and he loves to do it, often for sheer fun. My friend Jules, the aged baboon in the Jardin des Plantes, puts his hands on his tummy with the most pitiful air of dejection, and shows me his tongue – it is much easier to make a monkey show you his tongue than a small child – says he has completely lost his appetite and has only eaten my apple to oblige me. Before I have time to open my mouth to say how sorry I am, he has snatched my last banana from me, eaten it, and thrown the skin at me from the top of the cage.

'Kindly look at this red spot on my back,' says Edward. 'I thought at first it was only a flea-bite, but now it burns like a blister. I cannot stand it any longer, cannot you give me something to take away the pain ? – no, not there, higher up, come closer, I know you are somewhat shortsighted, let me show you the exact spot ?' The same instant he sits in his trapeze grinning maliciously at me through my spectacles before breaking them to pieces to be presented as souvenirs to admiring comrades. Monkeys love to make fun of us. But the slightest suspicion that we are making fun of them irritates them profoundly. You must never laugh at a monkey, he cannot stand it. Their whole nervous system is extraordinarily sensitive. A sudden fright can bring them almost into hysterics, convulsions are not very rare amongst them, I have even attended a monkey who suffered from epilepsy. An unexpected noise can make them turn pale. They blush very easily, not from modesty, for God knows they are not modest, but from anger. To observe this phenomenon, however, you must not look only at the monkey's face, he often blushes in another, unexpected place. Why their Maker, for reasons of His own, should have chosen this very place for such a rich and sensitive carnation, such a prodigal display of vivid colours, crimson, blue and orange, remains a mystery to our uneducated eyes. Many startled spectators do not even hesitate to pronounce it at first sight to be very ugly. But we must not forget that opinions as to what is beautiful or not are much at variance in different ages and countries. The Greeks, arbiters of beauty if there ever were any, painted the hair of their Aphrodite blue, how do you like blue hair? Amongst the monkeys themselves this rich carnation is evidently a sign of beauty, irresistible to the ladies' eye, and the happy possessor of such a glow of colours a posteriori is often seen with uplifted tail turning his back upon the spectators in order to be admired. The monkeys are excellent mothers, but you must never attempt to have anything to do with their children, for like the Arab women folk and even Neapolitan women, they believe that you have got the evil eye. The stronger sex is somewhat inclined to flirtation and terrible 'drames passionnels' are constantly enacted in the big monkey-house at the Zoo, where even the tiniest little ouistiti becomes an infuriated Othello, ready to fight the biggest baboon. The ladies watch the tournament with sympathetic side-glances at their various champions and with furious quarrels amongst themselves. Imprisoned monkeys, as long as they are in company, live on the whole a supportable life. They are so busy in finding out all that is going on inside and outside their cage, so full of intrigue and gossip that they have hardly time to be unhappy. The life of an imprisoned big ape, gorilla, chimpanzee, or orang-outang, is of course the life of a martyr, pure and simple. They all fall into profound hypochondria if tuberculosis is too slow to kill them. Consumption is, as everybody knows, the cause of the death of most imprisoned monkeys, big and small. The symptoms, evolution and ending of the disease are exactly the same as with us. It is not the cold air, but the lack of air that starts the disease. Most of the monkeys stand the cold surprisingly well, if provided with ample accommodation for exercise and snug sleeping-quarters for the night, shared with a rabbit as bed companion for the sake of the warmth. As soon as autumn begins, ever vigilant Mother Nature who watches over the monkeys as well as over us, sets to work to provide their shivering bodies with extra fur-coats, suitable for northern winters. This applies to most tropical animals imprisoned in northern climates, who would all live much longer if allowed to live in the open air. Most Zoological Gardens seem to ignore this fact. Perhaps it is better so. Whether the prolongation of the lives of these unhappy animals is a thing to be desired I leave to you to ponder over. My answer is in the negative. Death is more merciful than we are.

VI

Château Rameaux

Paris in summer-time is a very pleasant place for those who belong to the Paris qui s'amuse, but if you happen to belong to the Paris qui travaille, it becomes another matter. Especially so if you have to cope with an epidemic of typhoid at the Villette among the hundreds of Scandinavian workmen, and an epidemic of diphtheria in the Quartier Montparnasse among your Italian friends and their innumerable children. Indeed, there was no lack of Scandinavian children either in the Villette; and the few families who hadn't got any seemed to have chosen this very time to bring them to the world, as often as not with no other assistance, sage-femme included, than myself. Most of the children too small to catch typhoid started scarlet fever and the rest whooping-cough. Of course there was no money to pay for a French doctor, so it fell upon me to look after them as well as I could. It was no joke, there were over thirty cases of typhoid among the Scandinavian workmen in the Villette alone. Anyhow I managed to go to the Swedish church in Boulevard Ornano every Sunday to please my friend the Swedish chaplain, who said it was to set a good example to others. The congregation had dwindled down to half its usual number, the other half was in bed or nursing somebody in bed. The chaplain was on his legs from morning till night, assisting and helping the sick and the poor, a more kind-hearted man I have never set eyes on, and he was penniless too. The only reward he ever got was that he brought the infection to his own home. The two eldest of his eight children caught typhoid, five had scarlet fever, and his last born swallowed a two-franc piece and nearly died of intestinal occlusion. Then the Swedish Consul, a most peaceful and quiet little man, suddenly became a raving lunatic, and, for the matter of that, nearly killed me; but I will tell you this story another time.

Up in Quartier Montparnasse it was a far more serious business, although in many ways it seemed almost easier work to me. I am ashamed to say that I got on much better with these poor Italians than with my own compatriots, who were often difficult to handle, sullen, dissatisfied and rather exacting and selfish. The Italians on the other hand, who had brought nothing with them from their own country but their small means, their all-enduring patience and cheerfulness and their charming manners, were always satisfied and grateful and extraordinarily helpful to each other. When diphtheria broke out in the Salvatore family, Arcangelo Fusco, the street-sweeper, stopped work at once and became a most devoted nurse to them all. All three little girls caught diphtheria, the eldest girl died and the following day the worn-out mother caught the terrible disease. Only the child of sorrow, Petruccio, the helpless idiot, was spared by the inscrutable will of God Almighty. The whole Impasse Rousselle became infected, there was diphtheria in every house and not a family without several small children. Both the hospitals for children were over-crowded. Even had there been a vacant bed the chances of getting admission for these foreign children would have been next to none. So they had to be attended by Arcangelo Fusco and myself, and those we had no time to see, and they were many, had to live or die as best they could. No doctor who has gone through the ordeal of fighting single-handed an epidemic of diphtheria amongst the very poor with no means of disinfection either for others or for himself, can think of such an experience without a shudder, however callous he may be. I had to sit there for hours, painting and scraping the throat of one child after another, there was not much more to be done in those days. And then when it was no longer possible to detach the poisonous membranes obstructing the air passages, when the child became livid and on the point of suffocation and the urgent indication for tracheotomy presented itself, with lightning rapidity! Must I operate at once, with not even a table to put the child on, on this low bed or on its mother's lap, by the light of this wretched oil-lamp and no other assistant than a street-sweeper? Can't I wait till to-morrow and try to get hold of somebody who is more of a surgeon than I am? Can I wait, dare I wait? Alas! I have waited till to-morrow when it was too late and seen the child die before my eyes. I have also operated at once and no doubt saved the life of a child, but I have also operated at once and seen the child die under my knife. My case was even worse than that of many other doctors in a similar plight, for I was myself in deadly fear of diphtheria, a fear I have never been able to overcome. But Arcangelo Fusco was not afraid. He knew the danger as well as I did, for he had seen the terrible infection spreading from one to another, but he had never a single thought for his own safety, he only thought of the others.

When all was over, I was complimented right and left, even by the *Assistance Publique*, but nobody ever said a word to Arcangelo Fusco who had sold his Sunday clothes to pay the undertaker who took away the body of the little girl.

Yes, there came a time when all was over, when Arcangelo Fusco returned to his street-sweeping and I to my fashionable patients. While I had been spending my days at the Villette and Montparnasse, the Parisians had been hard at work packing their trunks and departing to their châteaux or their favourite seaside watering-places. The Boulevards were in the hands of pleasure-seeking foreigners who had crowded to Paris from all parts of the civilized and uncivilized world to spend their surplus money. Many were sitting in my waiting-room, impatiently reading their Baedekers, always insisting on passing in first, seldom asking for anything more than a pick-me-up, from a man much more in need of it than they were. Others, comfortably established on their chaises-longues in their smartest tea-gowns, dernière création Worth, sent for me from their fashionable hotels at the most awkward hours of the day and the night, expecting me to 'fix them up' for the Bal Masqué de l'Opéra to-morrow. They did not send for me twice and I was not surprised.

What a waste of time! thought I as I walked home, dragging my tired legs along the burning asphalt of the Boulevards under the dust-covered chestnut-trees gasping with drooping leaves for a breath of fresh air.

'I know what is the matter with you and me,' said I to the chest-nut-trees, 'we need a change of air, to get out of the atmosphere of the big city. But how are we to get away from this inferno, you with your aching roots imprisoned under the asphalt and with that iron ring around your feet, and I with all these rich Americans in my waiting-room and lots of other patients in their beds? And if I were to go away, who would look after the monkeys in the Jardin des Plantes? Who would cheer up the panting Polar Bear, now that his worst time was about to come? He won't understand a single word other kind people may say to him, he who only understands Swedish! And what about Quartier Montparnasse? Montparnasse!' I shuddered as the word flew through my brain, I saw the livid face of a child in the dim light of a little oil-lamp, I saw the blood oozing from the cut I had just made in the child's throat, and I heard the cry of terror from the heart of the mother. What would the Countess say? ... The Countess! No, there was decidedly something wrong with me, it was high time to look after my own nerves instead of the nerves of others, if such things could be seen and heard on the Boulevard Malesherbes. And what the devil had I to do with the Countess? She was getting on splendidly in her château in Touraine, according to Monsieur l'Abbé's last letter, and I was getting on splendidly in Paris, the most beautiful city in the world. All I was in need of was a little sleep. But what would the Count say if I wrote him a letter to-night that I gladly accepted his kind invitation and was starting to-morrow? If I could only sleep to-night! Why shouldn't I take myself one of those excellent sleeping-draughts I used to concoct for my patients, a strong sleeping-draught that would send me to sleep for twenty-four hours and make me forget everything, Montparnasse, the château in Touraine, the Countess and all the rest? I lay down on my bed without taking off my clothes, I was so tired. But I did not take the sleeping-draught, les cuisiniers n'ont pas faim, as they say in Paris. On entering my consulting-room next morning, I found a letter on the table. It was from Monsieur l'Abbé with a P.S. in the handwriting of the Count:

'You said you liked the song of the skylark the best. He is singing still, but it will not be for long, so you had better come soon.'

The skylark! And I who had not heard any other birds for two years but the sparrows in the Tuileries Gardens!

*   *   *

The horses which took me from the station were beautiful, the château dating from the time of Richelieu, in its vast park of secular lime-trees, was beautiful, the Louis XVI furniture in my sumptuous room was beautiful, the big St. Bernard dog who followed me upstairs was beautiful – everything was beautiful. So was the Countess in her simple white frock with a single La France rose in her waistband. I thought her eyes had grown bigger than ever. The Count was altogether another man, with his rosy cheeks and wide-awake eyes. His charming welcome took away at once my shyness, I was still a barbarian from Ultima Thule, I had never been in such sumptuous surroundings before. M. l'Abbé greeted me as an old friend. The Count said there was just time for a stroll in the garden before tea, or would I prefer to have a look at the stables? I was given a basket full of carrots to give one to each of a dozen magnificent horses who stood there in their well-groomed coats aligned in their boxes of polished oak.

'You had better give him an extra carrot to make friends at once,' said the Count. 'He belongs to you as long as you are here, and this is your groom,' he added, pointing to an English boy who lifted his hand to his cap to salute me.

Yes, the Countess was wonderfully well, said the Count as we strolled back through the garden. She hardly ever spoke about her colitis, went to visit her poor in the village every morning and was discussing with the village doctor the turning of an old farm into an infirmary for sick children. On her birthday all the poor children of the village had been invited to the Castle for coffee and cake and before they left she had presented a doll to every child. Wasn't it a charming idea of hers?

'If she speaks to you about her dolls, don't forget to say something nice to her.'

'No, I won't forget, je ne demande pas mieux.'

Tea was served under the big lime-tree in front of the house.

'Here is a friend of yours, my dear Ann,' said the Countess to the lady sitting by her side, as we walked up to the table. 'I am sorry to say he seems to prefer the company of horses to ours; so far he hasn't had time to say a single word to me, but has been talking half-an-hour to the horses in the stables.'

'And they seemed to have liked the conversation immensely,' laughed the Count, 'even my old hunter, you know how ill-tempered he is with strangers, put his nose to the doctor's face and sniffed at him in the most friendly manner.'

The Baroness Ann said she was glad to see me and gave me excellent news about her mother-in-law, the Marquise Douairière.

'She even thinks she can hear better, but of that I am not sure, for she cannot hear Loulou's snoring and gets quite angry when my husband says he can hear it down in the smoking-room. Anyhow, her beloved Loulou has been a blessing to us all, she could never stand being alone before and it was so fatiguing to talk to her the whole time through her ear-trumpet. Now she sits quite alone for hours with her Loulou on her lap and if you could see her cantering about in the garden every morning to exercise Loulou, you would hardly believe your eyes, she who never left her arm-chair. I remember how you said that she must walk a little every day and how angry you looked when she said she hadn't got the strength. It is indeed a marvellous change. Of course you say it is all the nasty medicine you have given her, but I say it is Loulou, bless him, he is welcome to snore as much as he likes!'

'Look at Leo,' said the Count, changing the conversation, 'look at him with his head on the doctor's lap, as if he had known him ever since he was born. He has even forgotten to come and beg for his biscuit.'

'What is the matter with you, Leo?' said the Countess. 'You had better look out, old boy, or the doctor will hypnotize you. He has been working with Charcot at the Salpêtrière and he can make people do anything he likes only by looking at them. Why don't you make Leo speak Swedish with you?'

'Certainly not, there is no language so sympathetic to my ears as his silence. I am not a hypnotizer, I am only a great lover of animals, and all animals understand this at once and love you in return.'

'I suppose you are just trying to mesmerize that squirrel on the branch over your head,' said the Baroness, 'you have been sitting staring at him the whole time without paying the slightest attention to us. Why don't you make him climb down from his tree and come and sit on your lap beside Leo?'

'If you will give me a nut and all go away, I think I can make him come down and take it out of my hand.'

'You are polite, Monsieur le Suédois,' laughed the Countess, 'come along, Ann dear, he wants us all to go away and leave him alone with his squirrel.'

'Don't make fun of me, I am the last to wish you to go away, I am so glad to see you again.'

'Vous êtes très galant, Monsieur le Docteur, it is the first compliment you have ever paid me, and I like compliments.'

'I am not a doctor here, I am your guest.'

'And cannot your doctor pay you a compliment?'

'Not if the patient looks like you and the doctor is under the age of your father, not even if he wants to badly.'

'Well, all I can say is that if ever you wanted to, you have jolly well resisted the temptation. You have bullied me almost every time I have seen you. The first time I set eyes on you, you were so rude to me that I nearly went away, don't you remember? Ann dear, do you know what he said to me? He looked sternly at me and said with his most atrocious Swedish accent: "Madame la Comtesse, you are more in need of discipline than of drugs!" Discipline! Is that the way a Swedish doctor speaks to a young lady the first time she comes to consult him?'

'I am not a Swedish doctor, I have taken my degree in Paris.'

'Well, I have consulted dozens of Paris doctors, but no one has ever dared to speak to me about disicipline.'

79

'That is the very reason why you have been obliged to consult so many.'

'Do you know what he said to my mother-in-law?' rejoined the Baroness. 'He said in a very angry voice that if she didn't obey him, he would go away and never come back, even if she had colitis! I heard it myself from the drawing-room and when I rushed in I thought the Marquise was going to have a fit. You know I am recommending you to all my friends, but don't take it amiss if I tell you that you Swedes are much too rough-handed for us Latin people. I have been told by more than one of your patients that your bed-side manners are deplorable. We are not accustomed to be ordered about like school-children.'

'Why don't you try to be a little more amiable?' smiled the Countess enjoying the fun immensely.

'I will try.'

'Tell us a story,' said the Baroness, as we were sitting in the drawing-room after dinner. 'You doctors come across so many odd people and are mixed up in so many strange situations. You know more of real life than anybody else, I am sure you have a lot to tell us if you want to.'

'Perhaps you are right, but we are not supposed to talk about our patients, and as to real life, I am afraid I am too young to know much about it.'

'Tell us at least what you do know,' insisted the Baroness.

'I know that life is beautiful, but I also know that we often make a mess of it and turn it into a silly farce or a heart-rending tragedy, or both, so much so that one ends by not knowing whether to cry or to laugh. It is easier to cry, but far better to laugh, so long as one doesn't laugh aloud.'

'Tell us an animal story,' said the Countess to help me on to safer ground. 'They say your country is full of bears, tell us something about them, tell us a Bear-story!'

'There was once a lady who lived in an old manor-house on the border of a big forest, high up in the North. This lady had a pet bear she was very fond of. It had been found in the forest half-dead of hunger, so small and helpless that it had to be brought up on the bottle by the lady and the old cook. This was several years ago and now it had grown up to a big bear, so big and strong that he could have slain a cow and carried it away between his two paws if he had wanted to. But he did not want to, he was a most amiable bear

80

who did not dream of harming anybody, man or beast. He used to sit outside his kennel and look with his small intelligent eyes most amicably at the cattle grazing in the field near by. The three shaggy mountain ponies in the stable knew him well and did not mind in the least when he shuffled into the stable with his mistress. The children used to ride on his back and had more than once been found asleep in his kennel between his two paws. The three Lapland dogs loved to play all sorts of games with him, pull his ears and his stump of a tail and tease him in every way, but he did not mind it in the least. He had never tasted meat, he ate the same food as the dogs and often out of the same plate, bread, porridge, potatoes, cabbages, turnips. He had a fine appetite, but his friend the cook saw to it that he got his fill. Bears are vegetarians if they have a chance, fruit is what they like the best. In the autumn he used to sit and look with wistful eyes at the ripening apples in the orchard and in his young days he had been sometimes unable to resist the temptation to climb the tree and help himself to a handful of them. Bears look clumsy and slow in their movements, but try a bear with an apple-tree and you will soon find out that he can easily beat any school-boy at that game. Now he had learnt that it was against the law, but he kept his small eyes wide-open for any apples that fell to the ground. There had also been some difficulties about the beehives; he had been punished for this by being put on the chain for two days with a bleeding nose and he had never done it again. Otherwise he was never put on the chain except for the night and quite rightly so, for a bear, like a dog, is apt to get somewhat ill-tempered if kept on the chain, and no wonder. He was also put on the chain on Sundays when his mistress went to spend the afternoon with her married sister who lived in a solitary house on the other side of the mountain-lake, a good hour's walk through the dense forest. It was not supposed to be good for him to wander about in the forest with all its temptations, it was better to be on the safe side. He was also a bad sailor and had once taken such a fright at a sudden gust of wind that he had upset the boat and he and his mistress had had to swim to the shore. Now he knew quite well what it meant when his mistress put him on the chain on Sundays, with a friendly tap on his head and the promise of an apple on her return if he had been good during her absence. He was sorry but resigned, like a good dog when his mistress tells him he cannot come with her for a walk. One Sunday when the lady had chained him up as usual and was about half-way through the forest, she suddenly thought she heard the cracking of a tree-branch on the winding foot-path behind her. She looked back and was horrified to see the bear coming along full-speed. Bears look as if they move along quite slowly but they shuffle along much faster than a trotting horse. In a minute he had joined her, panting and sniffing, to take up his usual place, dog-fashion, at her heels. The lady was very angry, she was already late for luncheon, there was no time to take him back home, she did not want him to come with her, and it was besides very naughty of him to have disobeyed her and broken away from his chain. She ordered him in her severest voice to go back at once, menacing him with her parasol. He stopped a moment and looked at her with his cunning eyes, but did not want to go back and kept on sniffing at her. When the lady saw that he had even lost his new collar, she got still more angry and hit him on the nose with her parasol so hard that it broke in two. He stopped again, shook his head and opened his big mouth several times as if he wanted to say something. Then he turned round and began to shuffle back the way he had come, stopping now and then to look at the lady till at last she lost sight of him. When the lady came home in the evening, he was sitting in his usual place outside his kennel looking very sorry for himself. The lady was still very angry and went up to him and began to scold him most severely and said he would have no apple and no supper and that he would have to be chained for two days as well. The old cook who loved the bear as if he had been her son rushed out from the kitchen very angry.

'"What are you scolding him for, missus!" said the cook, "he has been as good as gold the whole day, bless him! He has been sitting here quite still on his haunches as meek as an angel, looking the whole time towards the gate for you to come back."

'It was another bear.'

The clock in the tower struck eleven.

'Time to go to bed,' said the Count. 'I have ordered our horses for seven o'clock to-morrow morning.'

'Sleep well and pleasant dreams,' said the Countess as I went up to my room.

I did not sleep much, but I dreamt a lot.

Leo scratched at my door at six next morning and punctually at seven the Count and I rode down the avenue of splendid old lime-trees leading to the woods. Soon we were in a real forest of elms and beeches with here and there a magnificent oak. The woods were silent, only now and then we heard the rhythmic tapping of the wood-pecker or the cooing of a wild pigeon, the sharp cry of a nuthatch or the deep alto of a blackbird singing the last strophes of his ballad. Soon we emerged on a vast open stretch of fields and meadows in full sunlight. There he was, the beloved skylark, quivering on invisible wings high up in the sky, pouring out his very heart to heaven and earth with thrills of the joy of life. I looked at the little bird and blessed him again as I had so often done before in the frozen North when as a child I used to sit and watch with grateful eyes the grey little messenger of summer, sure at last that the long winter was over.

'It is his last concert,' said the Count. 'His time is up, he will soon have to set to work to help to feed his children and there will be no more time for singing and skylarking. You are right, he is the greatest artist of them all, he sings from his very heart.'

'To think that there are men capable of killing this harmless little songster! You have only to go to Les Halles to find them in hundreds and hundreds for sale to other men who have the stomach to eat them. Their voices fill the whole sky overhead with gladness but their poor little dead bodies are so small that a child can clasp them in the palm of his hand, and yet we eat them with gluttony as though there was nothing else to eat. We shudder at the very word of cannibalism and we hang the savage who wants to indulge in this habit of his ancestors, but the murdering and eating of little birds remains unpunished.'

'You are an idealist, my dear doctor.'

'No, they call it sentimentality and only sneer at it. Let them sneer as much as they like, I do not care. But mark my words! The time will come when they will cease to sneer, when they will understand that the animal world was placed by the Creator under our protection, and not at our mercy: that animals have as much right to live as we have, and that our right to take their lives is strictly limited to our right of defence and our right of existence. The time will come when the mere pleasure of killing will die out in man. As long as it is there, man has no claim to call himself civilized, he is a mere barbarian, a missing link between his wild ancestors who slew each other with stone axes for a piece of raw flesh and the man of the future. The necessity of killing wild animals is indisputable, but their executioners, the proud hunters of to-day, will sink down to the same level as the butchers of domestic animals.'

'Perhaps you are right,' said the Count, looking up in the sky once more as we turned our horses and rode back to the Castle.

While we were at luncheon, a valet brought the Countess a telegram which she handed to the Count who read it without saying a word.

'I think you have already met my cousin Maurice,' said the Countess. 'He will be here for dinner if he can catch the four o'clock train, he is in garrison in Tours.'

Yes, the Vicomte Maurice was with us for dinner, very much so. He was a tall, handsome young fellow with a narrow, sloping forehead, enormous ears, a cruel jaw and a moustache à la général de Galliffet.

'Quel plaisir inattendu, Monsieur le Suèdois, to meet you here, very unexpected I am sure!' This time he condescended to give me his hand, a small, flabby hand with a particularly unpleasant grip which facilitated my classification of the man. Remained only to hear him laugh and he lost no time to offer me this opportunity. His loud monotonous giggle echoed through the room during the whole of dinner. He began at once to tell the Countess a very risky story of the misadventure which had just happened to one of his comrades who had found his mistress in the bed of his orderly. Monsieur l'Abbé was beginning to look very uncomfortable when the Count cut him short by telling his wife across the table about our morning ride, that the wheat was in excellent condition, the clover abundant and that we heard a belated skylark singing his last concert.

'Nonsense,' said the Vicomte. 'There are still plenty of them on the wing, I shot one yesterday and a finer shot I never made, the little beast did not look bigger than a butterfly.'

I got red in my face to the roots of my hair, but the Abbé stopped me in time by putting his hand on my knee.

'You are a brute, Maurice,' said the Countess, 'to kill a skylark.'

'And why shouldn't I shoot a skylark? There are plenty of them and they are besides an excellent target for practising, I know of none better unless it be a swallow. You know, my dear Juliette, I am the crack shot of my regiment and unless I keep on practising I shall soon get rusty. Luckily there are any amount of swallows round our barracks, hundreds and hundreds are nesting under the eaves of the stables, they are busy feeding their young just now and darting to and fro the whole time just before my window. It is great fun, I have a go at them every morning without even leaving my room. Yesterday I made a bet of a thousand francs with Gaston

84

that I would drop six out of ten and, would you believe it, I dropped eight! I know nothing better for daily practice than swallows. I always say it ought to be made compulsory in all Écoles de Tir.' He stopped a moment carefully counting the drops he was pouring in his wine-glass from a little bottle of medicine.

'Now, Juliette dear, don't be silly, come along with me to Paris to-morrow, you need a little spree after having been here all alone for weeks in this out-of-the-way place. It will be a splendid sight, the finest tournament there has ever been, all the best shots of France will be there, and as sure as my name is Maurice, you will see the gold medal offered by the President of the Republic handed over to your cousin. We will have a jolly dinner at the Café Anglais and then I will take you to the Palais Royal to see "Une nuit de noces." It is a most charming play, very rigolo indeed, I have seen it already four times but I should love to see it again with you at my side. The bed stands in the middle of the stage with the lover hidden under it and the bridegroom who is an old . . .'

The Count, visibly annoyed, made a sign to his wife and we stood up from the table.

'I could never kill a skylark,' said the Count drily.

'No, my dear Robert,' roared the Vicomte, 'I know you couldn't, you would miss it!'

I went up to my room almost in tears with suppressed rage and shame of having suppressed it. While I was packing my bag, the Abbé entered the room. I begged him to tell the Count I had been summoned to Paris and was obliged to take the midnight train.

'I never want to set my eyes upon this confounded brute any more or I will smash his insolent monocle out of his empty head!'

'You had better not attempt anything of the sort or he would kill you outright. It is quite true he is a famous shot, I do not know how many duels he has fought, he is always quarrelling with people, he has a very nasty tongue. All I ask of you is to keep your nerves in hand for thirty-six hours. He is going away to-morrow night for the tournament in Paris, and let me tell you, entre nous, that I shall be as glad to see him go as you are.'

'Why?'

The Abbé remained silent.

'Well, Monsieur l'Abbé, I will tell you why. Because he is in love with his cousin and you dislike and distrust him.'

'Since you have guessed the truth, and God knows how, I had better tell you, he wanted to marry her, but she refused him.

Luckily she doesn't like him.'

'But she fears him, which is almost worse.'

'The Count dislikes very much his friendship with the Countess and that is why he didn't want her to remain alone in Paris where he was always taking her out to parties and theatres.'

'I do not believe he is going away to-morrow.'

'He is sure to go, he is much too keen on getting his Gold Medal as he very likely will, it is quite true he is a crack shot.'

'I wish I was, I would like to shoot down this brute to avenge the swallows. Do you know anything about his parents? I guess there is something wrong there.'

'His mother was a German Countess and very beautiful, he gets his good looks from her, but I understand it was a very unhappy marriage. His father was a heavy drinker and was known as an irascible and queer man. He got almost mad in the end. There are people who say he committed suicide.'

'I earnestly hope his son will follow his example, the sooner the better. As to being mad, he is not far from it.'

'You are right, it is true that the Vicomte is very odd in many ways. For instance he, who as you can see is as strong as a horse, is always fussing about his health and in constant fear of catching all sorts of illnesses. Last time he was staying here, the son of the gardener caught typhoid and he left at once. He is always taking drugs, you may have noticed he even helped himself to some medicine during dinner.'

'Yes, it was the only moment he held his tongue.'

'He is always consulting new doctors, it is unfortunate that he does not like you, otherwise I am sure you would get a new patient ... What on earth are you laughing at?'

'I am laughing at something very funny that has just passed through my head. There is nothing better than a good laugh for a man who is angry! You saw in what a state I was when you came into my room. You will be glad to hear that I am all right again now and in the best of tempers. I have changed my mind, I am not going away to-night. Do let us go down and join the others in the smoking-room. I promise you to be on my very best behaviour.'

The Vicomte, red in the face, was standing in front of the big mirror nervously twitching his moustache à la général de Galliffet. The Count was sitting near the window reading his 'Figaro.'

'Quel plaisir inattendu to meet you here, Monsieur le Suédois!' giggled the Vicomte, screwing in his monocle as if to see better how much I would stand. 'I hope no new case of colitis has brought you here.'

'No, not so far, but one never knows.'

'I understand you specialize in colitis, what a pity nobody else seems to know anything about this most interesting disease, you evidently keep it all to yourself. Will you oblige me by telling me what is colitis? Is it catching?'

'No, not in the ordinary sense of the word.'

'Is it dangerous?'

'No, not if taken in hand immediately, and properly attended to.'

'By you, I suppose?'

'I am not a doctor here, the Count has been kind enough to invite me here as his guest.'

'Really! But what will happen to all your patients in Paris while you are away?'

'I suppose they will recover.'

'I am sure they will,' roared the Vicomte.

I had to go and sit down beside the Abbé and get hold of a paper to steady myself. The Vicomte looked nervously at the clock over the mantelpiece.

'I am going up to fetch Juliette for a stroll in the park, it is a pity to remain indoors in this beautiful moonlight.'

'My wife has gone to bed,' said the Count drily from his chair, 'she was not feeling very well.'

'Why the devil didn't you tell me?' retorted the Vicomte angrily, helping himself to another glass of brandy and soda.

The Abbé was reading the 'Journal des Débats,' but I noticed that his sly old eye never stopped watching us.

'Any news, Monsieur l'Abbé?'

'I was just reading about the tournament of "La Société du Tir de France" the day after to-morrow and that the President has offered a gold medal to the winner.'

'I will bet you a thousand francs that it will be mine,' shouted the Vicomte, banging his fist on his broad chest, 'unless there is a railway smash on the Paris night-express to-morrow or,' he added with a malicious grin at me, 'unless I get colitis!'

'Stop that brandy, Maurice,' said the Count from his corner, 'you have had more than is good for you, tu es saoûl comme un Polonais!'

'Cheer up, Doctor Colitis,' giggled the Vicomte, 'don't look so dejected. Have a brandy and soda, there may still be a chance for you! I am sorry I cannot oblige you, but why don't you have a go at the Abbé who is always complaining about his liver and his digestion. Monsieur l'Abbé, won't you oblige Doctor Colitis, can't you see he is longing to have a look at your tongue?'

The Abbé kept reading his 'Journal des Débats' in silence.

'You won't! And what about you, Robert? You looked sulky enough during dinner. Why don't you show your tongue to the Suédois? I am sure you have got colitis! Won't you oblige the doctor? No? Well, Doctor Colitis, you have no luck. But to put you in better spirits I will show you mine, have a good look at it.'

He put out his tongue to me with a diabolical grin. He looked like one of the gargoyles of Notre Dame.

I stood up and examined his tongue attentively.

'You have a very nasty tongue,' said I gravely, after a moment's silence, 'a very nasty tongue!' He turned round immediately to examine his tongue in the mirror – the ugly, coated tongue of the inveterate smoker. I took his hand and felt his pulse, slashed to fever speed by a bottle of champagne and three brandies and sodas.

'Your pulse is very quick,' said I.

I put my hand on his sloping forehead.

'Any headache?'

'No.'

'You will have it when you wake up to-morrow morning, no doubt.'

The Abbé dropped his 'Journal des Débats.'

'Unbutton your trousers,' I said sternly.

He obeyed automatically, docile like a lamb.

I gave him a rapid tap over his diaphragm, which started a hiccup.

'Ah!' said I. Looking him fixedly in the eyes, I said slowly: 'Thank you, that is enough.'

The Count dropped his 'Figaro.'

The Abbé raised his arms to Heaven, his mouth wide open.

The Vicomte stood speechless before me.

'Button your trousers,' I commanded, 'and have a brandy and soda, you will need it.' He buttoned his trousers mechanically and gulped down the brandy and soda I handed him.

'To your health, Monsieur le Vicomte,' said I, raising my glass to my lips, 'to your health!'

He wiped the perspiration from his forehead and turned again to look at his tongue in the mirror. He made a desperate effort to laugh, which however did not succeed.

'Do you mean to say that, do you think, do you mean to say . . .'

'I do not mean to say anything, I have not said anything, I am not your doctor.'

'But what am I to do?' he stammered.

'You are to go to bed, the sooner the better, or you will have to be carried there.' I went to the mantelpiece and rang the bell.

'Take the Vicomte to his room,' I said to the footman, 'and tell his valet to put him to bed at once.'

Leaning heavily on the arm of the footman, the Vicomte reeled to the door.

I went for a beautiful ride next morning all by myself, and there was the lark again high up in the sky, singing his morning hymn to the sun.

'I have avenged the murder of your brothers,' said I to the skylark. 'We will see about the swallows later on.'

While I was sitting in my room having breakfast with Leo, there was a knock at the door and in came a timid-looking little man who saluted me most politely. It was the village doctor who said he had come to pay his respects to his Paris colleague. I was much flattered and begged him to sit down and have a cigarette. He told me about some interesting cases he had had of late, the conversation began to languish and he stood up to go.

'By-the-by, I was sent for last night to Vicomte Maurice and have just called on him again.'

I said I was sorry to hear the Vicomte was unwell, but hoped it was nothing serious, I had the pleasure to see him last night at dinner in splendid health and spirits.

'I don't know,' said the Doctor, 'the case is somewhat obscure, I think it is safer to postpone a definite opinion.'

'You are a wise man, mon cher confrère, of course you keep him in bed?'

'Of course. It is unfortunate the Vicomte was to leave for Paris to-day, but that is of course out of the question.'

'Of course. Is he lucid?'

'Fairly so.'

'As much as can be expected from him I suppose?'

'To tell you the truth I took it at first for a simple embarras gastrique, but he woke up with a violent headache and now a persistent hiccup has set in. He looks wretched, he himself is convinced he has got colitis. I confess I have never attended a case of colitis, I wanted to give him a dose of castor-oil, he has a very nasty tongue, but if colitis is anything like appendicitis, I suppose it is better to beware of the castor-oil. What do you think? He is feeling his pulse the whole time when he is not looking at his tongue. Strange to say he feels very hungry, he was furious when I did not allow him his breakfast.'

'You were quite right, you had better be firm and keep on the safe side, nothing but water for the next forty-eight hours.'

'Quite so.'

'It is not for me to give you any advice, it is clear you know your business, but I do not share your hesitation about the castor-oil. If I were you, I would give him a stiff dose, no good mincing it, three table-spoonfuls would do him a lot of good.'

'Did you really mean to say three table-spoonfuls?'

'Yes, at least, and above all no food whatsoever, only water.'

'Quite so.'

I liked the village doctor very much and we parted great friends.

In the afternoon the Countess drove me to pay my respects to the Marquise Douairière. A beautiful drive through shadowy lanes full of bird-twitter and humming insects. The Countess had got tired of teasing me, but she was in excellent spirits and seemed not to worry in the least about the sudden illness of her cousin. The Marquise was going on splendidly, she said, but had been terribly upset a week ago by the sudden disappearance of Loulou, the whole household had been on their legs during the night in search of him. The Marquise had not closed her eyes and was still prostrated in her bed when Loulou had turned up in the afternoon with an ear split in two and an eye nearly out of its socket. His mistress had wired at once for the vet from Tours, and Loulou was all right again. Loulou and I were formally intrdouced to each other by the Marquise. Had I ever seen such a beautiful dog? No, never.

'Why,' snored Loulou reproachfully at me, 'you who pretend to be a great lover of dogs, you don't mean to say you don't recognize me? Don't you remember when you took me out of that dreadful dog-shop in . . .'

Anxious to change the conversation, I invited Loulou to sniff at my hand. He stopped short, began to sniff attentively each finger in turn.

'Yes, of course I can smell quite distinctly your own particular smell. I remember it quite well since I smelt it last time in the dog-shop; in fact, I rather like your smell. . . . Ah!' He sniffed eagerly. 'By St. Rocco, the patron saint of all dogs, I smell a bone, a big bone! Where is the bone? Why didn't you give it to me? These silly people never give me a bone, they imagine it is bad for a little dog, aren't they fools! To whom did you give the bone?' He jumped in one bound on to my lap, sniffing furiously. 'Well, I never! Another dog! And only the head of a dog! A big dog! An enormous dog, with the saliva dripping down the corner of his mouth! Can it be a St. Bernard! I am a small dog and I suffer somewhat from asthma, but my heart is in the right place, I am not afraid, and you had better tell this big elephant of yours to mind his own business and not come near me or my mistress or I will eat him alive!' He sniffed contemptuously. 'Spratt's biscuits! So that is what you had for dinner last night, you big vulgar brute, the very smell of those disgusting hard cakes they forced me to eat in the dog-shop, makes me feel quite sick! No Spratt's biscuits for me, thank you! I prefer Albert biscuits and ginger nuts or a big slice of that almond cake on the table. Spratt's biscuits!' He crawled back on the lap of his mistress as fast as his fat little legs allowed him.

'Do come back before you return to Paris,' said the kind Marquise.

'Yes, do come back,' snored Loulou, 'you are not such a bad sort after all! I say,' signalled Loulou to me as I stood up to go, 'it is full moon to-morrow, I am feeling very restless and wouldn't mind a little spree.' He blinked cunningly at me. 'Do you happen to know if there are any small pug-ladies in the neighbourhood? Don't tell my mistress, she understands nothing about this sort of thing. . . . I say, never mind the size, any size will do if it comes to the worst!'

Yes, Loulou was right, it was full moon. I do not like the moon. The mysterious stranger has taken too much sleep out of my eyes and whispered too many dreams into my ears. There is no mystery about the sun, the radiant god of the day who brought life and light to our dark world and still watches over us with his shining eye, long after all the other gods, those seated on the banks of the Nile, those of Olympus and those of Walhalla have vanished into gloom. But nobody knows anything about the moon, the pale night-wanderer amongst the stars, who keeps staring at us from afar with her sleepless, cold glittering eyes and her mocking smile.

The Count did not mind the moon, as long as he was allowed to sit in peace in his smoking-room with his after-dinner cigar and his 'Figaro.' The Countess loved the moon. She loved its mysterious twilight, she loved its haunting dreams. She loved to lie silent in the boat and look up at the stars while I rowed her slowly across the shining lake. She loved to wander about under the old lime-trees in the park, now flooded with silvery light, now shaded in a darkness so deep that she had to take my arm to find the way. She loved to sit on a lonely bench and stare with her big eyes into the silent night. Now and then she spoke, but not often, and I liked her silence just as much as her words.

'Why don't you like the moon?'

'I don't know. I believe I am afraid of it.'

'What are you afraid of?'

'I don't know. It is so light that I can see your eyes like two luminous stars and yet it is so dark that I fear I might lose my way. I am a stranger in this land of dreams.'

'Give me your hand and I will show you the way. I thought your hand was so strong, why does it tremble so? Yes, you are right, it is only a dream, don't speak or it will fly away! Listen! do you hear, it is the nightingale.'

'No, it is the garden warbler.'

'I am sure it is the nightingale, don't speak! Listen! Listen!'

Juliette sang with her tender voice, caressing like the night wind among the leaves:

> *Non, non, ce n'est pas le jour,*
> *Ce n'est pas l'alouette,*
> *Dont les chants ont frappé ton oreille inquiète,*
> *C'est le rossignol*
> *Messager de l'amour.'*

'Don't speak! Don't speak!'

An owl hooted its sinister warning from the tree over our heads. She sprang up with a cry of fear. We walked back in silence.

'Good night,' said the Countess as she left me in the hall. 'Tomorrow is full moon. Á demain.'

Leo slept in my room, it was a great secret and we both felt rather guilty about it.

'Where have you been and why are you so pale?' asked Leo as we crept stealthily upstairs. 'All the lights in the Castle are out and all the dogs in the village are silent. It must be very late.'

'I have been far away in a strange land full of mystery and dreams, I nearly lost my way.'

'I was just dropping off to sleep in my kennel when the owl woke me up in time to sneak into the hall when you came.'

'It also woke me up just in time, Leo dear, do you like the owl?'

'No,' said Leo, 'I prefer a young pheasant, I have just eaten one, I saw him running in the moonlight before my very nose. I know it is against the law, but I could not resist the temptation. You won't give me away to the gamekeeper, will you?'

'No, my friend, and you won't give me away to the butler that we came home so late?'

'Of course not.'

'Leo, are you at least sorry that you stole that young pheasant?'

'I am trying to be sorry.'

'But it is not easy,' said I.

'No,' muttered Leo, licking his lips.

'Leo, you are a thief, and you are not the only one here, and you are a bad watch-dog! You who are here to keep thieves away, why don't you rouse your master at once with that big voice of yours instead of sitting here looking at me with such friendly eyes?'

'I can't help it. I like you.'

'Leo, my friend, it is all the fault of the drowsy night-watchman up there in the sky! Why didn't he turn his bull's-eye lantern on every dark corner of the park where there is a bench under an old lime-tree instead of pulling his nightcap of clouds over his bald old head and dozing off to sleep, handing over his job as a night-watchman to his friend the owl? Or did he only pretend he was asleep and keep watching us the whole time from the corner of his wicked eye, the sly old sinner, decrepit old Don Juan, strutting about among the stars like le vieux marcheur on the boulevards, too worn out himself to make love but enjoying still to watch others making fools of themselves.'

'Some people pretend the moon is a beautiful young lady,' said Leo.

'Don't believe it, my friend! The moon is a dried-up old spinster spying from afar with treacherous eyes the immortal tragedy of mortal love.'

'The moon is a ghost,' said Leo.

'A ghost? Who told you that?'

'An ancestor of mine heard it ages ago in the pass of St. Bernard from an old bear who had heard it from Atta Troll, who had heard it from the Great Bear himself who rules over all bears. Why, they are all afraid of the moon up there in the sky. No wonder we dogs are afraid of it and bark at it, when even the brilliant Sirius, the Dog star who rules over all dogs, turns pale when it creeps out of its grave and lifts its sinister face out of the darkness. Down here on our earth do you think you are the only one who cannot sleep when the moon is up! Why, all wild animals and all creeping and crawling things in forests and fields leave their lairs and wander about in fear of its malicious rays. Indeed, you must have been looking hard at somebody else to-night in the park or surely you would have seen that it was a ghost that was watching you the whole time. It likes to creep under the lime-trees in an old park, to haunt the ruins of a castle or a church, to roam about an old cemetery and bend over every grave to read the name of the dead. It loves to sit and stare for hours with steel-grey eyes on the desolation of the snowfields which cover the dead earth like a shroud, or to peep in through a bedroom window to frighten the sleeper with a sinister dream.'

'Enough, Leo, don't let us talk any more about the moon, or we shall not sleep a wink to-night, it makes me feel quite creepy! Kiss me good night, my friend, and let us go to bed.'

'But you will close the shutters, won't you!' said Leo.

'Yes, I always do when there is a moon.'

While we were having our breakfast next morning, I told Leo that I had to go back to Paris at once, it was safest so, because it was full moon to-day and I was twenty-six and his mistress was twenty-five – or was it twenty-nine? Leo had seen me pack my bag and every dog knows what that means. I went down to Monsieur l'Abbé and told him the usual lie that I was summoned to an important consultation and had to leave the Castle by the morning train. He said he was very sorry. The Count who was just getting into the saddle for his morning ride also said he was sorry, and of course it was out of the question to disturb the Countess at so early an hour. I was besides to come back very soon.

As I drove to the station I met my friend the village doctor returning in his dog-cart from his morning visit to the Vicomte. The patient was feeling very low and was yelling for food, but the doctor had been firm in his refusal to take the responsibility of allowing anything but water. The poultice on the stomach and the ice-bag on the head had been kept going the whole night greatly interfering with the patient's sleep. Had I anything to suggest?

No, I felt sure he was in excellent hands. Maybe, if the condition remained stationary, he might try for a change to put the ice-bag on the stomach and the poultice on the head.

How long did I think, if no complications set in, that the patient ought to be kept in bed?

'At least for another week, till the moon has gone.'

The day had been long. I was glad to be back in Avenue de Villiers. I went straight to bed. I did not feel very well, I wondered if I had not got a bit of fever, but doctors never understand if they have fever or not. I fell asleep at once, so tired did I feel. I do not know how long I had been sleeping when suddenly I became aware that I was not alone in the room. I opened my eyes and saw a livid face at the window staring at me with white hollow eyes – for once I had forgotten to close the shutters. Slowly and silently something crept into the room and stretched a long white arm like the tentacle of an enormous octopus, across the floor towards the bed.

'So you want to go back to the Château after all!' it chuckled with its toothless mouth and bloodless lips. 'It was nice and cosy last night under the lime-trees, wasn't it, with me as Best Man and choruses of nightingales singing around you? Nightingales in August! Indeed you must have been far away in a very distant land, you two! And now you want to get back there to-night, don't you? Well, put on your clothes and climb on this white moonbeam of mine you were polite enough to call the arm of an octopus and I will put you back under the lime-trees in less than a minute, my light travels as fast as your dreams.'

'I am not dreaming any more, I am wide awake and I do not want to go back, ghost of Mephisto!'

'So you are dreaming that you are awake, are you! And you have not yet exhausted your vocabulary of silly abuse! Ghost of Mephisto! You have already called me vieux marcheur, Don Juan and a spying old spinster! Yes, I did spy on you last night in the park and I should like to know which of us two was made up as Don Juan, unless you wish me to call you Romeo? By Jupiter, you don't look like him! Blind Fool is your right name, fool who cannot even see what that beast of a dog of yours could see, that I have no age, no sex, no life, that I am a ghost.'

'The ghost of what?'

'The ghost of a dead world. Beware of ghosts! You had better stop your insults, or I will strike you blind with a flash of my subtle rays far more deadly to the eye of man than the golden arrow of the sun-god himself. It is my last word to you, blasphemous dreamer! Dawn is already approaching from the eastern sky, I have to go back to my grave or I shall not see my way. I am old and tired. Do you think it is easy work to have to wander about from night till morning when everything else is at rest? You call me sinister and sombre, do you think it is easy to be cheerful when you have to live in a grave, if you can call that living, as some of you mortals do? You will go to your grave yourself one day and so will the earth you are standing upon now, doomed to death like yourself.'

I looked at the ghost and saw for the first time how old and weary it looked and I would have felt almost sorry for it had not its threat to strike me blind roused my anger once more.

'Clear out from here, gloomy old Undertaker,' I shouted, 'there is no chance of a job for you here, I am full of life!'

'Do you know,' it chuckled, creeping on the bed and putting its long white arm on my shoulder, 'do you know why you put that fool of a Vicomte to bed with an ice-bag on his stomach? To avenge the swallows? I know better. You are a humbug, Othello. It was to prevent him from strolling about in the moonlight with the ...'

'Draw in that claw of yours, venomous old spider, or I shall spring out of bed and close with you.'

I made a violent effort to rouse my sleeping limbs, and I woke dripping with perspiration.

The room was filled with soft silvery light. Suddenly the scales fell from my bewitched eyes and through the open window I saw the full moon, beautiful and serene, looking down upon me from a cloudless sky.

Virginal goddess Luna! can you hear me through the stillness of the night? You look so mild, but you look so sad, can you understand sorrow? Can you forgive? Can you heal wounds with the balsam of your pure light? Can you teach forgetfulness? Come, sweet sister, and sit down by my side, I am so weary! Lay your cool hand on my burning forehead to put my unruly thoughts to rest! Whisper in my ear what I am to do and where I am to go to forget the song of the Sirens!

I went up to the window and stood a long while watching the Queen of the Night treading her path among the stars. I knew them well from many a sleepless night and one by one I called them by their names: the flaming Sirius, Castor and Pollux, beloved by the ancient mariners, Arcturus, Aldebaran, Capella, Vega, Cassiopeia! What was the name of that luminous star just over my head beckoning to me with its steady, true light? I knew it well. Many a night had I steered my boat over angry seas, guided by its light, many a day had it shown me the way across snowfields and forests in the land of my birth – Stella Polaris, the Pole Star!

This is the way, follow my light and you will be safe!

*　　*　　*

Le docteur sera absent pendant un mois. Prière s'adresser à Dr. Norstrom. Boulevard Haussmann. 66.

VII

Lapland

The sun had already gone down behind Vassojarvi but the day was still bright with flame-coloured light slowly deepening into orange and ruby. A golden mist descended over the blue mountains sparkling with patches of purple snow and bright yellow silver birches, glistening with the first hoar-frost.

The day's work was over. The men were returning to the camp with their lassos swung over their shoulders, the women with their huge birch bowls of fresh milk. The herd of a thousand reindeer surrounded by their outposts of vigilant dogs stood collected round the camp, safe for the night from wolf and lynx. The incessant calling of the calves and the crepitating clatter of the hoofs gradually died away: all was silent but for the occasional barking of a dog, the sharp cry of a nightjar or the loud hooting of an eagle owl from the far-away mountains. I sat in the place of honour by the side of Turi himself in the smoke-filled tent. Ellekare, his wife, threw a slice of reindeer's cheese in the kettle suspended over the fire and handed us in turn, the men first and then the women and children, our plate of thick soup which we ate in silence. What remained in the kettle was divided amongst the dogs off duty who one by one had crept in and lain down by the fire. Then we drank each in turn our cup of excellent coffee from the two cups of the household and they all took their short pipes from their leather pouches and began to smoke with great gusto. The men pulled off their reindeer shoes and spread the tufts of carex grass to dry before the fire, Lapps wear no socks. Again I admired the perfect shape of their small feet with their elastic insteps and strong, protruding heels. Some of the women took their sleeping babies from their cradles of birch-bark, filled with soft moss and suspended from the tent-poles, to give them the breast. Others explored the heads of their half-grown children lying flat in their laps.

'I am sorry you are leaving us so soon,' said old Turi, 'it has been a good stay, I like you.'

Turi spoke good Swedish, he had even many years ago been to Luleå to lay the grievances of the Lapps against the new settlers before the governor of the province who was a staunch defender of their lost cause and besides an uncle of mine. Turi was a mighty man, undisputed ruler over his camp of five *Kåtor*, containing his five married sons, their wives and children, all hard at work from morning till night to attend to his herd of a thousand reindeer.

'We will have to break camp soon ourselves,' Turi went on, 'I am sure we shall have an early winter. The snow will soon be too hard under the birch-trees for the reindeer to get at the moss, we shall have to move down to the pine-forest before the month is over. I can hear by the way the dogs are barking that they are already smelling the wolf. Didn't you say you saw the trail of the old bear when you crossed the Sulmö gorge yesterday?' he asked a young Lapp who had just entered the tent and huddled down by the fire.

Yes, he had seen it and plenty of trails of wolves as well.

I said I was delighted to hear there were still bears about, I had been told there were so few of them left in this neighbourhood. Turi said I was quite right. This was an old bear who had been living there for years, he was often seen shuffling about in the gorge. Three times they had ringed him when he was asleep in the winter but he had always managed to escape, he was a very cunning old bear. Turi had even had a shot at him, he had only shaken his head and looked at him with his cunning eyes, he knew quite well that no ordinary bullet could kill him. Only a silver bullet, cast on a Saturday night near the cemetery, could kill him, for he was befriended by the Uldra.

'The Uldra?'

Yes, didn't I know the Uldra, the Little People who lived under the earth? When the bear went to sleep in the winter the Uldra brought him food in the night, of course no animal could sleep the whole winter without food, chuckled Turi. It was the law of the bear that he should not kill a man. If he broke the law the Uldra did not bring him any food and he could not go to sleep in the winter. The bear was not cunning and treacherous like the wolf. The bear had twelve men's strength and one man's cunning. The wolf had twelve men's cunning and one man's strength. The bear liked clean fighting. If he met a man and the man went up to him and said: 'Come let us have a fight, I am not afraid of you,' the bear only knocked him down and scrambled away without doing him any harm. The bear never attacked a woman, all she had to do was to show him that she was a woman and not a man.

I asked Turi if he had ever seen the Uldra.

No, he had not, but his wife had seen them and the children saw

99

them often. But he had heard them moving about underground. The Uldra moved about during night, they slept during the day for they could not see anything when it was daylight. Sometimes when it happened that the Lapps put up their tents just over a place where the Uldra were living, the Uldra gave them warning that they must put up their tents further away. The Uldra were quite friendly as long as you left them alone. If you disturbed them they strewed a powder on the moss which killed the reindeer by the dozen. It had even happened that they carried away a Lapp baby and put one of their own babies in the cradle instead. Their babies had their faces all covered with black hair and long pointed teeth in their mouths. Some people said you should beat their child with a rod of burning birch branches until its mother could not stand its screaming any longer and brought you back your own baby and took away hers. Other people said you should treat their child as your own, the Uldra mother would then feel grateful to you and give you back your child. As Turi spoke a lively discussion as to which of the two methods was the best was going on amongst the women hugging their own babies with uneasy eyes. The wolf was the worst enemy of the Lapps. He dared not attack a herd of reindeer, he stood quite still to let the wind carry his smell to them. As soon as the reindeer smelt the wolf they all dispersed in fear, then the wolf came up and killed them one by one, often a dozen in a single night. God had created all the animals except the wolf, who was begotten by the devil. If a man had the blood of another man upon him the devil often turned him into a wolf if he had not confessed his sin. The wolf could put to sleep the Lapps who were watching the herd at night simply by looking at them through the darkness with his glowing eyes. You could not kill a wolf with an ordinary bullet unless you had carried it in your pocket on two Sundays in church. The best way was to overtake him on your skis on the soft snow and hit him with your staff on the top of his nose. He would then roll over and die at once. Turi himself had killed dozens of wolves in this way, only once had he missed his blow and the wolf had bitten him in the leg, he showed me the ugly scar as he spoke. Last winter a Lapp had been bitten by a wolf just as he was rolling over to die, the Lapp had lost so much blood that he had fallen asleep in the snow, they had found him the following day frozen to death by the side of the dead wolf. Then there was the wolverine who springs to the throat of the reindeer just by the big vein and hangs on for miles till the reindeer has lost so much blood that he falls down dead. There was also the eagle who carried away in his claws the new-born calves if they were left alone for a moment by their mothers. Then there was the lynx who crept up stealthily as a cat to jump at a reindeer who had gone astray from the herd and lost its way.

Turi said he could never understand how the Lapps had managed to keep their herds together in old times before they had associated themselves with the dog. In former days the dog used to hunt the reindeer in company of the wolf. But the dog who is the cleverest of all animals had soon found out that it would suit him better to work with the Lapps instead of with the wolves. So the dog offered to enter into the service of the Lapps on condition that he should be treated as a friend as long as he lived and that when he was about to die he should be hanged. That is why even to-day the Lapps always hanged their dogs when they were too old to work, even the new-born puppies who had to be destroyed for want of food were always hanged. The dogs had lost the power of speech when it was given to man but they could understand every word you said to them. In former days all animals could speak and so could the flowers, the trees and the stones and all lifeless things who were all created by the same God who had created man. Therefore man should be kind to all animals, and treat all lifeless things as if they could still hear and understand. On the day of the Last Judgment the animals would be called in first by God to give evidence against the dead man. Only after the animals had had their say would his fellow creatures be called in as witnesses.

I asked Turi if there were any *stalo* in the neighbourhood, I had heard so much about them in my childhood, I would give anything to meet one of those big ogres.

'God forbid,' said Turi uneasily. 'You know the river you are to ford to-morrow is still called the Stalo river after the old ogre who lived there in former days with his witch of a wife. They had only one eye between them, so they were always quarrelling and fighting who was to have the eye to see with. They always ate their own children, but they ate many Lapp children as well when they had a chance. Stalo said he liked the Lapp babies better, his own children tasted too much of sulphur. Once when they were driving across the lake in a sledge drawn by twelve wolves they began to quarrel about their eye as usual, and Stalo got so angry that he knocked a hole in the bottom of the lake and all the fishes got out of the lake and not one of them has ever come back again. That is why it is still called the Siva lake, you will row across it to-morrow and you will see for yourself that there is not a single fish left.'

I asked Turi what happened when the Lapps were taken ill and how they could get on without seeing the doctor. He said they were very seldom ill and specially not during the winter, except in very severe winters when it happened not so seldom that the newborn baby was frozen to death. The doctor came to see them twice a year by order of the king and Turi thought that was about enough. He had to ride on horseback across the marshes for two days, it took him another day to cross the mountain on foot and last time he forded the river he was nearly drowned. Luckily there were many healers amongst them who could cure most of their ailments much better than the king's doctor. The healers were befriended by the Uldra who had taught them their art. Some of these healers could take away the pain simply by laying their hand on the aching spot. What helped for most ailments was bleeding and rubbing. Mercury and sulphur was also very good and so was a teaspoonful of snuff in a cup of coffee. Two frogs cooked in milk for two hours was very good against the cough, a big toad was still better when you could lay your hands on one. The toads came from the clouds, when the clouds were low the toads fell down in hundreds on the snow. You could not explain it otherwise for you would find them on the most desolate snow-fields where there was no trace of any living thing. Ten lice boiled in milk with plenty of salt and taken on an empty stomach was certain to cure jaundice, a very common complaint among the Lapps in the spring. Dog bites were cured by rubbing the wound with the blood of the same dog. To rub the sore place with a little lamb's wool would take away the pain at once, for Jesus Christ had often spoken of the lamb. When somebody was going to die you were always warned beforehand by a raven or a crow who came and sat down upon the tent-pole. You must not speak or utter a sound lest you might frighten away Life and the dying man might be doomed to live between two worlds for a week. If you got the smell of a dead person in your nostrils you might die yourself.

I asked Turi if there was any of these healers in the neighbourhood; I would like very much to speak to him.

No, the nearest was an old Lapp called Mirko who lived on the other side of the mountain, he was very old, Turi had known him since he was a boy. He was a marvellous healer, much befriended by the Uldra. All animals came up to him without fear, no animal would ever harm him for the animals recognize at once those who are befriended by the Uldra. He could take away your pain by a mere touch of his hand. You could always recognize a healer by the shape of his hand. If you put a wing-shot bird in the hand of a healer the bird would sit quite still because he understood he was a healer.

I put forth my hand to Turi who had no idea I was a doctor. He looked at it attentively without saying a word, bent the fingers one after another most carefully, measured the span between the thumb and the first finger and muttered something to his wife who in her turn took my hand in her brown little claw of a bird with an uneasy glance in her small, almond-shaped eyes.

'Did your mother tell you you were born with a caul? Why didn't she give you the breast? Who gave you the breast? What tongue did your nurse speak? Did she ever put the blood of a raven in your milk? Did she hang the claw of a wolf round your neck? Did she ever make you touch the skull of a dead man when you were a child? Did you ever see the Uldra? Have you ever heard the bells of their white reindeer far away in the forest?

'He is a healer, he is a healer,' said Turi's wife with a quick, uneasy glance at my face.

'He is befriended by the Uldra,' they all repeated with an almost frightened expression in their eyes.

I felt almost frightened myself as I drew back my hand.

Turi said it was time to go to sleep, the day had been long, I was to start at daybreak. We all lay down round the smouldering fire. Soon all was dark in the smoke-filled tent. All I could see was the Pole Star shining down upon me through the smoke-hole of the tent. I felt in my sleep the warm weight of a dog over my breast and the soft touch of his nose in my hand.

We were all on our legs at daybreak, the whole camp was astir to see me off. I distributed among my friends my much appreciated little presents of tobacco and sweets, and they all wished me Godspeed. If all went well I was to arrive the next day at Forsstugan, the nearest human habitation in the wilderness of marshes, torrents, lakes and forests which was the home of the homeless Lapps. Ristin, Turi's sixteen-year-old granddaughter, was to be my guide. She knew a few words of Swedish, she had been once before to Forsstugan, she was to push on from there to the nearest church-village to join the Lapp school once more.

Ristin walked in front of me in her long white reindeer tunic and red woollen cap. Round her waist she wore a broad leather belt, embroidered with blue and yellow thread and studded with buckles and squares of solid silver. Suspended from her belt hung her knife, her tobacco pouch and her mug. I also noticed a small axe for cutting wood stuck under the belt. She wore leggings of soft, white reindeer-skin, fastened to her wide skin-breeches. Her small feet were stuck in dainty, white reindeer shoes neatly trimmed with blue thread. On her back she carried her *laukos*, a knapsack of birch-bark containing her various belongings and our provisions. It was twice as big as my own rucksack, but she did not seem to mind it in the least. She moved down on the steep slope with the rapid, noiseless step of an animal, jumped, swift as a rabbit, over a fallen tree-trunk or a pool of water. Now and then she sprang, agile as a goat, on to a steep rock, looking round in all directions. At the foot of the hill we came upon a broad stream, I had hardly time to wonder how we were to get across before she was in the water up to her hips, there was nothing for me to do but to follow her in the ice-cold water. I soon got warm again as we ascended the steep opposite slope at an amazing speed. She hardly ever spoke and it mattered little, for I had the greatest difficulty to understand what she said. Her Swedish was as bad as my Laplandish. We sat down on the soft moss to an excellent meal of rye biscuits, fresh butter and cheese, smoked reindeer's tongue and delicious cool water from the mountain brook in Ristin's mug. We lit our pipes and tried again to understand each other's speech.

'Do you know the name of that bird?' said I.

'Lahol,' smiled Ristin, recognizing at once the soft, flute-like whistle of the dotterel, which shares its solitude with the Lapps and is much beloved by them.

From a willow-bush came the wonderful song of the bluethroat.

'Jilow! Jilow!' laughed Ristin.

The Lapps say that the bluethroat has a bell in his throat and that he can sing one hundred different songs. High over our heads hung a black cross riveted to the blue sky. It was the royal eagle, surveying on motionless wings his desolate kingdom. From the mountain lake came the weird call of the loon.

'Ro, ro, raik,' repeated Ristin faithfully. She said it meant: 'fine weather to-day, fine weather to-day!' When the loon said: 'Var luk, var luk, luk, luk,' it meant: 'it is going to rain again, it is going to rain again, again,' Ristin informed me.

I lay there stretched out full length on the soft moss, smoking my pipe and watching Ristin carefully arranging her belongings in her laukos. A small blue woollen shawl, an extra pair of neat, little reindeer shoes, a pair of beautiful embroidered red gloves to wear in church, a Bible. Again I was struck with the refined shape of her small hands, common to all Lapps. I asked her what was in the little box cut out of a birch-root? As I could not understand a word of her long explanation in her mixed tongue of Swedish, Finnish and Laplandish I sat up and opened the box. It contained what looked like a handful of earth. What was she going to do with it?

Again she tried her best to explain, again I failed to understand her. She shook her head impatiently, I am sure she thought I was very stupid. Suddenly she stretched herself full length on the moss and lay quite still and stiff with closed eyes. Then she sat up and scratched the moss for a handful of earth which she handed me with a very serious face. Now I understood what was in the birch-root box. It contained a little earth from the grave in the wilderness where a Lapp had been buried last winter under the snow. Ristin was to take it to the priest who was to read the Lord's prayer over it and sprinkle it over the churchyard.

We shouldered our knapsacks and set off again. As we descended the slope, the aspect of the landscape changed more and more. We wandered over immense tundras covered with carex grass and here and there patches of bright yellow clusters of cloudberries which we picked and ate as we passed along. The solitary dwarf-birches, the *betula nana* of the heights, grew into groves of silver birches, intermixed with aspen and ash and thickets of willow-elder, bird-cherry and wild currant. Soon we entered a dense forest of stately fir-trees. A couple of hours later we were walking through a deep gorge walled in by steep, moss-covered rocks. The sky over our heads was still bright with evening sun but it was already almost dark in the ravine. Ristin glanced uneasily around her, it was evident that she was in a hurry to get out of the gorge before night-fall. Suddenly she stood still. I heard the crashing of a broken tree-branch and I saw something dark looming in front of me at a distance of less than fifty yards.

'Run,' whispered Ristin, white in the face, her little hand grasping the axe in her belt.

I was quite willing to run had I been able to do so. As it was, I stood still, riveted to the spot by a violent cramp in the calf of my legs. I could now see him quite well. He was standing knee-deep in a thicket of bilberries, a twig full of his favourite berries was sticking out of his big mouth, we had evidently interrupted him in the midst of his supper. He was of uncommonly large size, by the shabby look of his coat evidently a very old bear, no doubt the same bear Turi had told me about.

'Run,' I whispered in my turn to Ristin with the gallant intention of behaving like a man and covering her retreat. The moral value of this intention was however diminished by the fact that I was still completely unable to move. Ristin did not run. Instead of running away she made me witness an unforgettable scene, enough to repay a journey from Paris to Lapland. You are quite welcome to disbelieve what I am going to tell you, it matters little to me. Ristin, one hand on her axe, advanced a few steps towards the bear. With her other hand raising her tunic, she pointed out the wide leather breeches which are worn by the Lapp women. The bear dropped his bilberry twig, sniffed loudly a couple of times and shuffled off among the thick firs.

'He likes bilberries better than me,' said Ristin as we set off again as fast as we could.

Ristin told me that when her mother had brought her back from the Lapp school in the spring, they had come upon the old bear almost at the same place in the midst of the gorge and that he had scrambled away as soon as her mother had shown him she was a woman.

Soon we emerged from the gorge and wandered through the darkening forest on a carpet of silvery grey moss, soft as velvet and interwoven with bunches of Linnaea and Pyrola. It was neither light nor dark, it was the wonderful twilight of the northern summer night. How Ristin could find her way through the trackless forest was incomprehensible to my stupid brain. All of a sudden we came upon our friend the brook again, I had just time to bend down to kiss his night-cool face as he rushed past us. Ristin announced it was time for supper. With incredible rapidity she chopped some wood with her axe and lit the camp fire between two boulders. We ate our supper, smoked our pipes and were soon fast asleep, our rucksacks under our heads. I was awakened by Ristin presenting me her red cap full of bilberries, no wonder the old bear liked bilberries, I never had a better breakfast. On we went. Hallo! there was our friend the brook again joyously dancing along over hillocks and stones and singing in our ears that we had better come along with him down to the mountain lake. So we did lest he should lose his way in the gloom. Now and then we lost sight of him but we heard him singing to himself the whole time. Now and then he stopped to wait for us by a steep rock or a fallen tree to rush away again faster than ever to make up for lost time. A moment later there was no longer any fear he might lose his way in the gloom for the night had already fled on swift goblin feet deeper into the forest. A flame of golden light quivered in the tree-tops.

'Piavi!' said Ristin, 'the sun is rising!'

Through the mist of the valley at our feet a mountain lake opened its eyelid.

I approached the lake with uneasy forebodings of another ice-cold bath. Luckily I was mistaken. Ristin stopped short before a small *eka*, a flat-bottomed boat, half-hidden under a fallen fir-tree. It belonged to nobody and to everybody, it was used by the Lapps on their rare visits to the nearest church-village to exchange their reindeer-skins for coffee, sugar and tobacco, the three luxuries of their lives. The water of the lake was cobalt blue, even more beautiful than the sapphire blue of the Blue Grotto in Capri. It was so transparent that I thought I almost could see the hole the terrible Stalo had knocked in its bottom. Half across the lake we met two stately travellers swimming side by side, their superb antlers high out of the water. Luckily they mistook me for a Lapp so we could come up so close to them that I could see their soft beautiful eyes looking fearlessly at us. There is something very strange about the eyes of the elk as about those of the reindeer, they always seem to be looking straight at your own eyes at whatever angle you see them. We climbed rapidly the steep opposite shore and wandered once more over an immense marshy plain with nothing to guide us but the sun. My attempts to explain to Ristin the use of my pocket compass had met with so little success that I had given up looking at it myself, putting my trust in Ristin's instinct of a half-tame animal. It was evident that she was in a great hurry, ere long I had the impression that she was not sure of our way. Now and then she set off as fast as she could in one direction, stopped short to sniff the wind with quivering nostrils, then she darted off in another direction to repeat the same manoeuvre. Now and then she bent down to smell the ground like a dog.

'*Rog*,' she said suddenly pointing to a low cloud moving towards us with extraordinary rapidity across the marshes.

Fog indeed! In a minute we were enveloped in a thick mist as impenetrable as a November fog in London. We had to hold each other by the hand not to lose sight of one another. We struggled on for another hour or two knee deep in the ice-cold water. At last Ristin said she had lost our direction, we must wait till the fog was over. How long might it last?

She did not know, perhaps a day and a night, perhaps an hour, it all depended upon the wind. It was one of the worst experiences I have ever gone through. I knew quite well that with our scanty equipment the encounter with a fog on the immense swamps was far more dangerous than the encounter with a bear in the forest. I also knew that there was nothing to do but to wait where we were. We sat for hours on our knapsacks, the fog sticking to our skin as a sheet of ice-cold water. My misery was complete when I was going to light my pipe and found my waistcoat pocket full of water. While I was still staring dejectedly at my soaked match-box, Ristin had already struck fire with her tinder-box and lit her pipe. Another defeat for civilization was when I wanted to put on a pair of dry socks and discovered that my waterproof knapsack of best London make was soaked through and through and that all Ristin's belongings in her home-made laukos of birch-bark were dry as hay. We were just then waiting for the water to boil for a well-needed cup of coffee when a sudden gush of wind blew out the flame of my little spirit lamp. Ristin was off in an instant in the direction of the wind and back again to order me to put on my rucksack at once. In less than a minute a strong steady wind was blowing straight in our faces and the curtain of mist lifted rapidly over our heads. Deep below in the valley at our very feet we saw a huge river glistening in the sun like a sword. Along the opposite shore stretched out a dark pine forest as far as the eye could see. Ristin lifted her hand and pointed to a thin column of smoke rising over the tree-tops.

'Forsstugan,' said Ristin.

She sprang down the slope and without a moment's hesitation she plunged into the river up to her shoulders and I after her. Soon we lost our footing and swam across the river as the elks had swum across the forest lake. After half-an-hour's walk through the forest on the other side of the river we reached a clearing evidently made by the hand of man. A huge Lapland dog came rushing towards us full-speed barking fiercely. After much sniffing at us he was overjoyed to see us and proceeded to lead the way with a friendly wagging of his tail.

*　　*　　*

In front of his red-painted house stood Lars Anders of Forsstugan in his long sheep-skin coat, six feet six in his wooden shoes.

'Good day in the forest!' said Lars Anders. 'Where dost thou come from? Why didst thou not let the Lapp child swim alone across the river to fetch my boat? Put another log on the fire, Kerstin,' he called out to his wife inside the house. 'He has swum the river with a Lapp child, they must dry their clothes.'

Ristin and I sat down on the low bench before the fire.

'He is wet as an otter,' said Mother Kerstin, helping me to pull off

108

my stockings, my knickerbockers, my sweater and my flannel shirt from my dripping body and hanging them to dry on the rope across the ceiling. Ristin had already taken off her reindeer coat, her leggings, her breeches and her woollen vest, shirt she had none. There we sat, side by side on the wooden bench before the blazing fire, stark naked as our Creator had made us. The two old folk thought it was all right so, and so it was.

An hour later I was inspecting my new quarters in Uncle Lars' long black Sunday coat of home-spun cloth and wooden shoes while Ristin sat by the oven in the kitchen where Mother Kerstin was hard at work baking the bread. The stranger who had come there yesterday with a Finn Lapp had eaten up all the bread in the house. Their son was away cutting timber on the other side of the lake, I was to sleep in his little room over the cow-stable. They hoped I would not mind the smell of the cows. Not in the least, I rather liked it. Uncle Lars said he was going to the herbre to fetch a sheep-skin to put over my bed, he was sure I would need it for the nights were already cold. The herbre stood on four poles of stout timber, a man's height over the ground, as a protection against four-footed visitors and the deep snow of the winter. The store-room was full of clothes and furs neatly hung on the antlers nailed to the walls. Uncle Lars' fur coat of wolf's skin, his wife's winter furs, half-a-dozen wolf-skins. On the floor lay a sledge rug of splendid bear-skin. On another peg hung Mother Kerstin's wedding dress, her gaily coloured silk bodice beautifully embroidered with silver thread, her long green woollen skirt, her tippet of squirrel-skin, her bonnet trimmed with old lace, her red leather belt with buckles of solid silver. As we climbed down the ladder of the herbre I told Uncle Lars he had forgotten to lock the door. He said it did not matter, wolves, foxes and weasels would not carry off their clothes, there were no eatables in the herbre. After a stroll in the forest I sat down under the big fir by the kitchen door to a splendid supper: Lapland trout, the best in the world, home-made bread just out of the oven, fresh cheese and home-brewed ale. I wanted Ristin to share my supper, it was evidently against etiquette, she was to have her supper in the kitchen with the grandchildren. The two old folk were sitting by my side watching me while I was eating.

'Hast thou seen the King?'

No, I had not, I had not come by Stockholm, I had come straight from another land, from another town many times bigger than Stockholm.

Uncle Lars did not know there was a town bigger than Stockholm.

I told Mother Kerstin how much I had admired her beautiful wedding dress. She smiled and said her mother had worn it at her own wedding, God knows how many years ago.

'But surely you don't leave the herbre open at night?' I asked.

'Why not?' said Uncle Lars. 'There is nothing to eat in the herbre, I told you the wolves and foxes are not likely to carry away our clothes.'

'But somebody else might carry them away, the herbre stands all by itself in the wood, hundreds of yards away from your house. That bear-skin rug alone is worth a lot of money, any antiquarian in Stockholm would be glad to pay several hundred riksdaler for your wife's wedding dress.'

The two old folk looked at me with evident surprise.

'But didn't you hear me tell you that I had shot that bear myself and all the wolves as well? Don't you understand that it is my wife's wedding dress and that she got it from her own mother? Don't you understand it all belongs to us as long as we are alive, and when we die, it goes to our son? Who would carry it away? What do you mean?'

Uncle Lars and Mother Kerstin looked at me, they seemed almost vexed at my question. Suddenly Lars Anders scratched his head with a cunning expression in his old eyes.

'Now I understand what he means,' he chuckled to his wife, 'he means those people they call thieves!'

I asked Lars Anders about the Siva lake, whether it was true what Turi had told me that the big Stalo had knocked a hole in its bottom and made all the fishes escape. Yes, it was quite true, there was not a single fish in the lake while all the other mountain lakes were full of them, but if the mischief had been done by a Stalo he could not say. The Lapps were superstitious and ignorant. They were not even Christians, nobody knew where they came from, they spoke a language unlike any other tongue in the whole world.

Were there any Giants or Trolls about on this side of the river?

'There certainly were in former days,' said Uncle Lars. When he was a boy he had heard a lot about the big Troll who lived in the mountain over there. The Troll was very rich, he had hundreds of ugly dwarfs who kept watch over his gold under the mountain and thousands of cattle, all snow-white with bells of silver round their necks. Now since the King had begun to blast the rocks for iron ore and started building a railway he had not heard anything more about the Troll. There was of course still the *Skogsrå*, the forest witch, who was always trying to allure people deeper into the

woods where they would miss their way. Sometimes she called with
the voice of a bird, sometimes with the soft voice of a woman.
Many people said she was a real woman very wicked and very
beautiful. If you met her in the forest, you must run away at once, if
you turned your head to look at her a single time you were lost.
You must never sit down under a tree in the forest when the moon
is full. She would then come and sit down by your side and throw
her arms round you like a woman does when she wants a man to
love her. All she wanted to do was to suck the blood out of your
heart.

'Had she very large, dark eyes?' I asked uneasily.

Lars Anders did not know, he had never seen her, but his wife's
brother had met her one moonlit night in the woods. He had lost
his sleep, he had never been right in the head ever since.

Were there any Goblins in this neighbourhood?

Yes, there were plenty of Little People sneaking about in the
dusk. There was one little goblin living in the cow-stable, the grand-
children had often seen him. He was quite harmless as long as he
was left in peace and had his bowl of porridge put out for him in its
usual corner. It would not do to scoff at him. Once a railway
engineer who was to build the bridge over the river had spent the
night in the Forsstugan. He got drunk and spat in the bowl of
porridge and said he would be damned if there was any such thing
as a goblin. When he drove back in the evening across the frozen
lake his horse slipped and fell on the ice and was torn to pieces by a
pack of wolves. He was found in the morning by some people
returning from church, sitting in the sledge, frozen to death. He had
shot two of the wolves with his gun and had it not been for the gun
they would have eaten him as well.

How far was it from Forsstugan to the nearest habitation?

'Eight hours' ride across the forest on a good pony.'

'I heard the sound of bells when I was strolling about in the woods
an hour ago, there must be plenty of cattle round here.'

Lars Anders spat the snuff from his mouth and said abruptly that
I was mistaken, there were no cattle in the woods, nearer than a
hundred miles, his own four cows were in the stable.

I repeated to Lars Anders that I was sure I had heard the bells far
away in the forest, I had even noticed how beautifully they sounded
as if of silver.

Lars Anders and Mother Kerstin glanced uneasily at each other
but nobody spoke. I bade them good night and went to my room
over the cow-stable. The forest stood silent and dark outside the

window. I lit the tallow candle on the table and lay down on the sheep-skin tired and sleepy after my long wanderings. I listened for a while to the munching of the cows in their sleep. I thought I heard the hooting of an owl far away in the woods. I looked at the tallow candle burning dimly on the table, it did my eyes good to look at it, I had never seen a tallow candle since I was a child in my old home. I thought I saw through my closing eyelids a little boy plodding in the deep snow on a dark winter morning on his way to school with a bundle of books in a strap on his back and just such a tallow candle in his hand. For each boy had to bring his own candle to be lit on his own desk in the schoolroom. Some boys brought a thick candle, some brought a thin candle, as thin as the one now burning on the table. I was a rich boy, on my desk burnt a thick candle. On the desk next to mine burnt the thinnest candle in the whole class, for the mother of the boy who sat next to me was very poor. But I was plucked in my exam at Christmas and he passed his exam at the top of us all for he had more light in his brain.

I thought I heard something rattle on the table. I must have slept for a while, for the tallow candle was just flickering out. But I could see quite distinctly a little man as big as the palm of my hand sitting cross-legged on the table carefully pulling at my watch-chain and bending his grey old head on one side to listen to the ticking of my repeater. He was so interested that he did not notice that I was sitting up in my bed and looking at him. Suddenly he caught sight of me, dropped the watch-chain, glided down the leg of the table, sailor fashion, and sprang towards the door as fast as his tiny legs could carry him.

'Don't be afraid, little goblin,' said I, 'it is only me. Don't run away, and I will show you what is inside that gold box you were so interested in. It can ring a bell as they do in church on Sundays.'

He stopped short and looked at me with his small, kind eyes.

'I cannot make it out,' said the goblin, 'I thought I smelt a child in this room or I would never have come in, and you look like a big man. Well, I never . . .' he exclaimed, hoisting himself up on the chair by the bed. 'Well, I never heard of such good luck as to find you here in this far-away place. You are just the same child as when I saw you last time in the nursery of your old home or you could never have seen me to-night sitting on the table. Don't you recognize me? It was I who came to your nursery every night when the whole house was asleep to put things straight for you and smooth away all your worries of the day. It was to me you always brought a slice of your birthday cake and all those walnuts, raisins and sweets from the Christmas tree, and you never forgot to bring me my bowl of porridge. Why did you ever leave your old home in the midst of the big forest? You were always smiling then, why do you look so sad now?'

'Because I have no rest in my head, I cannot stay anywhere, I cannot forget, I cannot sleep.'

'That is like your father. How often have I not watched him wandering up and down in his room the whole night!'

'Tell me something about my father, I remember so little of him.'

'Your father was a strange man, sombre and silent. He was kind to all the poor and to all animals, but he seemed often hard to those around him. He used to flog you a lot, but it is true you were a difficult child. You obeyed nobody, you did not seem to care for either your father or your mother or your sister or your brother or for anybody. Yes, I think you cared for your nurse, don't you remember her, Lena? Nobody else liked her, everybody was afraid of her. She had been taken on as your nurse for sheer necessity as your mother could not give you the breast. Nobody knew where she came from. Her skin was dark like the skin of the Lapp child who brought you here yesterday, but she was very tall. She used to sing to you in an unknown tongue while she gave you the breast, she kept on giving you the breast till you were two years old. Nobody, not even your mother, dared to go near her, she growled like an angry she-wolf if anybody wanted to take you from her arms. At last she was sent away but she returned in the night and tried to steal you. Your mother got so frightened that she had to take her back. She brought you all sorts of animals to play with, bats, hedgehogs, squirrels, rats, snakes, owls and ravens. I once saw her with my own eyes cutting the throat of a raven and putting some drops of his blood in your milk. One day when you were four years old the sheriff came with two country policemen and carried her away, handcuffed. I heard it had something to do with her own child. The whole house was delighted, but you were delirious for several days. Most of your troubles had to do with your animals. Your room was full of all sorts of animals, you even slept with them in your bed. Don't you remember how mercilessly you were flogged for lying on eggs? Every bird's egg you could get hold of you used to try to hatch out in your bed. Of course a small child cannot keep awake, every morning your bed was all in a mess with smashed eggs and every morning you were flogged for it but nothing helped. Don't you remember the evening your parents came home late from a house-party and found your sister in her

113

nightgown sitting on the table under an umbrella screaming with terror? All your animals had escaped from your room, a bat had caught her claw in your sister's hair, all your snakes, toads and rats were crawling about on the floor and in your own bed they found a whole litter of mice. Your father gave you a tremendous thrashing, you stole out of the house at daybreak after breaking into the pantry in the night to fill your knapsack with what eatables you could lay hands on, and smashing your sister's money-box and stealing all her savings – you never had any savings of your own. The whole day and the whole night all the servants were hunting for you in vain. At last your father who had galloped off to the village to speak to the police found you fast asleep in the snow by the roadside, your dog had barked as he rode past. I overheard your father's hunter telling the other horses in the stable how your father lifted you up in the saddle without saying a word and rode home with you and locked you up in a dark room on bread and water for two days and nights. On the third day you were taken to your father's room, he asked you why you had stolen out of the house? You said you were misunderstood by everybody in the house and wanted to emigrate to America. He asked you if you were sorry you had bitten him in the hand, you said no. The next day you were sent to school in the town and were only allowed to return home for the Christmas holidays. On Christmas day you all drove to church for the morning service at four o'clock. A whole pack of wolves galloped behind the sledge as you drove across the frozen lake, the winter was very severe and the wolves were very hungry. The church was all ablaze with light with two big Christmas trees before the High Altar. The whole congregation stood up to sing 'Hail, happy morn.' When they had finished the hymn you told your father you were sorry you had bitten him in the hand and he patted you on the head. On the way back across the lake you tried to jump from the sledge, you said you wanted to follow the trails of the wolves to see where they had gone. In the afternoon you were missing again, everybody was searching for you in vain the whole night. The gamekeeper found you in the morning in the forest asleep under a big fir. There were trails of wolves all round the tree, the gamekeeper said it was a miracle you had not been eaten by the wolves. But the worst of all happened during your summer holidays when the housemaid found a human skull under your bed, a skull with a tuft of red hair still hanging on to the back of the head. The whole house was in commotion. Your mother fainted and your father gave you the severest thrashing you had

114

ever had so far and you were again locked up in a dark room on water and bread. It was discovered that the night before you had ridden on your pony to the village churchyard, had broken into the charnel house and stolen the skull from a heap of bones deposited in the cellar. The parson who had been the headmaster of a boys' school told your father that it was an unheard-of thing that a boy of ten should have committed such an atrocious sin against God and man. Your mother, who was a very pious woman, never got over it. She seemed almost afraid of you, and she was not the only one. She said she could not understand that she could have given birth to such a monster. Your father said that surely you had not been begotten by him but by the devil himself. The old housekeeper said it was all the fault of your nurse who had bewitched you by putting something in your milk and had hung the claw of a wolf round your neck.'

'But is all this really true what you have told me about my childhood? I must have been a strange child indeed!'

'What I have told you is true, every word of it,' answered the goblin. 'What you may tell to others I am not responsible for. You always seem to mix up reality with dreams, as all children do.'

'But I am not a child, I shall be twenty-seven next month.'

'Of course you are a big child or you could not have seen me, only children can see us goblins.'

'And how old are you, little man?'

'Six hundred years. I happen to know because I was born the same year as the old fir-tree outside your nursery window where the big owl had its nest. Your father always said it was the oldest tree in the whole forest. Don't you remember the big owl, don't you remember how it used to sit and blink at you through the window with its round eyes?'

'Are you married?'

'No. I am single,' said the goblin. 'And you?'

'Not so far, but . . .'

'Don't! My father always told us that marriage was a very risky undertaking, and that it was a wise saying that one could not be too careful in the choice of one's mother-in-law.'

'Six hundred years old! Really? You do not look it! I would never have believed it by the way you slid down the leg of the table and ran across the floor when you caught sight of me sitting up in bed.'

'My legs are all right, thank you, only my eyes are getting somewhat tired. I can hardly see anything in the daytime. I have also strange noises in my ears ever since you big people began that dreadful blasting in the mountains around us. Some goblins say you want to rob the Trolls of their gold and iron, others say it is to make a hole for that huge, yellow snake with the two black stripes on his back who is wriggling his way over fields and forests and across the rivers, his mouth foaming with smoke and fire. We are all afraid of him, all the animals in the forests and fields, all the birds in the sky, all the fishes in rivers and lakes, even the Trolls under the mountains are flying north in terror of his approach. What will become of us poor goblins? What will become of all the children when we are no more in the nurseries to put them to sleep with our fairy tales and keep watch over their dreams? Who will look after the horses in the stable, who will see to it that they do not fall on the slippery ice and break their legs? Who will wake the cows and help them to look after their new-born calves? I tell you times are hard, there is something wrong with your world, there is no peace anywhere. All this incessant rattle and noise is getting on my nerves. I dare not stay with you any longer. The owls are already getting sleepy, all the creeping things in the forest are going to bed, the squirrels are already crunching their fir-cones, the cock will soon crow, the terrible blasting across the lake will soon begin again. I tell you I cannot stand it any longer. It is my last night here, I have to leave you. I have to work my way up to Kebnekajse before the sun rises.'

'Kebnekajse! Kebnekajse is hundreds of miles further north, how on earth are you going to get there with your short little legs?'

'I dare say a crane or a wild goose will give me a lift, they are all collecting there now for the long flight to the land where there is no winter. If it comes to the worst I shall ride part of the way on the back of a bear or a wolf, they are all friends to us goblins. I must go.'

'Don't go away, stay with me a little longer and I will show you what is inside that gold box you were so interested in.'

'What do you keep in the gold box? Is it an animal? I thought I heard the beating of its heart inside the box.'

'It is the beating of the heart of Time you heard.'

'What is Time?' asked the goblin.

'I cannot tell you, nor can anybody else tell you what Time means. They say it is made up of three different things, the past, the present and the future.'

'Do you always carry it about with you in that gold box?'

'Yes, it never rests, it never sleeps, it never ceases to repeat the

116

same word in my ears.'

'Do you understand what it says?'

'Alas! only too well. It tells me every second, every minute, every hour of the day and of the night that I am getting older, and that I am going to die. Tell me, little man, before you go, are you afraid of Death?'

'Afraid of what?'

'Afraid of the day when the beating of your heart will cease, the cogs and wheels of the whole machinery fall to pieces, your thoughts stand still, your life flicker out like the light of that dim tallow candle on the table.'

'Who has put all that nonsense in your head? Don't listen to the voice inside the gold box with its silly past, present and future, don't you understand that it all means the same thing! Don't you understand that somebody is making fun of you inside that gold box! If I were you, I would throw your uncanny gold box in the river and drown the evil spirit locked up in it. Don't believe a word of what it tells you, it is nothing but lies! You will always remain a child, you will never grow old, you will never die. You just lie down and get to sleep for a while! The sun will soon rise again over the fir-tops, the new day will soon look in through the window, you will soon see much clearer than you ever saw by the light of that tallow candle.

'I must be off. Good-bye to you, dreamer, and well met!'

'Well met, little goblin!'

He glided down from the chair by my bed and clattered away towards the door in his little wooden shoes. As he was fumbling in his pocket for his latch-key he suddenly burst into such a roar of laughter that he had to hold his stomach with his two hands.

'Death!' he chuckled. 'Well, I never! It beats anything I have ever heard before! What shortsighted fools are they not, these big monkeys, compared with us small goblins. Death! By Robin Goodfellow, I never heard such nonsense!'

When I woke and looked out through the window the ground was white with fresh snow. High overhead I heard the beating of wings and the call of a flock of wild geese. Godspeed, little goblin!

I sat down to my breakfast, a bowl of porridge, milk fresh from the cow and a cup of excellent coffee. Uncle Lars told me he had been up twice in the night, the Lapland dog had been growling uneasily the whole time as if he saw or heard something. He himself had thought he saw the dark form of what might have been a wolf sneaking about outside the house. Once he had thought he heard the sound of voices from the cow-stable, he was quite relieved when he heard it was me talking in my sleep. The hens had been cackling and restless the whole night.

'Do you see that?' said Uncle Lars, pointing to a trail in the fresh snow leading up to my window. 'There must have been at least three of them. I have lived here for over thirty years and I have never seen the trail of a wolf so near the house. Do you see that?' he said, pointing to another trail in the snow as big as the footstep of a man. 'I thought I was dreaming when I saw it first. As sure as my name is Lars Anders the bear has been here to-night and this is the trail of her cub. It is ten years since I shot a bear in this forest. Do you hear that chattering in the big fir by the cow-stable? There must be a couple of dozen of them, I never saw so many squirrels in one tree in my whole life. Did you hear the hooting of the owl in the forest and the calling of the loon from the lake the whole night? Did you hear the nightjar spinning round the house at daybreak? I cannot make it out, as a rule the whole forest is silent as a grave after dark. Why have all these animals come here this night? Neither Kerstin nor I have slept a wink. Kerstin thinks it is the Lapp child who has bewitched the house, but she says she had been baptized in Rukne last summer. But one never knows with these Lapps, they are all full of witchcraft and devil's tricks. Anyhow I sent her off at daybreak, she is swift on foot, she will be at the Lapp school in Rukne before sunset. When are you going?'

I said I was in no hurry, I would like to remain a couple of days, I liked the Forsstugan very much.

Uncle Lars said his son was to return from his timber-cutting in the evening, there would be no room for me to sleep in. I said I did not mind sleeping in the barn, I liked the smell of hay. Neither Uncle Lars nor Mother Kerstin seemed to cherish the idea. I could not help feeling as if they wanted to get rid of me, they hardly spoke a word to me, they almost seemed afraid of me.

I asked Uncle Lars about the stranger who had come to Forsstugan two days ago and who had eaten all the bread. He could not speak a word of Swedish, said Lars Anders, the Finn Lapp who was carrying his fishing tackle and rods said they had lost their way. They were half dead of hunger when they came, they had eaten up everything in the house. Uncle Lars showed me the coin he had insisted on giving to the grandchildren, was it possible that it was real gold?

It was an English sovereign. On the floor by the window lay a

'Times' addressed to Sir John Scott. I opened it and read in huge letters:

TERRIBLE OUTBREAK OF CHOLERA IN NAPLES; OVER A THOUSAND CASES A DAY.

One hour later Pelle, Uncle Lars' grandson, stood in front of the house with the shaggy little Norwegian pony. Uncle Lars was dumbfounded when I wanted to pay him at least for the provisions in my rucksack, he said he had never heard such a thing. He said I had nothing to worry about, Pelle knew the direction quite well. It was quite an easy and comfortable journey this time of the year. Eight hours' ride through the forest to Rukne, three hours downstream in Liss Jocum's boat, six hours on foot across the mountain to the church-village, two hours across the lake to Losso Jarvi, from there eight hours' easy drive to the new railway station. No passenger trains as yet but the engineer would be sure to let me stand on the locomotive for two hundred miles till I could catch the goods train.

Uncle Lars was quite right, it was an easy and comfortable journey, at least it seemed so to me then. What would it have seemed to me to-day? Equally easy and comfortable was the journey across Central Europe in the wretched trains of those days with hardly any sleep. Lapland to Naples, look at the map!

VIII

Naples

If anybody would care to know about my stay in Naples, he must look it up in 'Letters from a Mourning City' if he can get hold of a copy, which is not probable, for the little book is long ago out of print and forgotten. I have just been reading myself with considerable interest these 'Letters from Naples' as they were called in the Swedish original. I could not write such a book to-day to save my life. There is plenty of boyish boisterousness in these letters, there is also plenty of self-consciousness, not to say conceit. I was evidently rather pleased with myself for having rushed from Lapland to Naples at the moment when everybody else had left it. There is a good deal of swaggering as to how I went about night and day in the infected poor quarters, covered with lice, feeding on rotten fruit, sleeping in a filthy locanda. All this is quite true, I have nothing to retract, my description of Naples in cholera time is exact as I saw it with the eyes of an enthusiast.

But the description of myself is far less exact. I had the cheek to put in writing that I was not afraid of the cholera, not afraid of Death. I told a lie. I was horribly afraid of both from the first till the last. I described in the first letter how, half-faint from the stench of carbolic acid in the empty train I stepped out on the deserted Piazza late in the evening, how I passed in the streets long convoys of carts and omnibuses filled with corpses on the way to the cholera cemetery, how I spent the whole night amongst the dying in the wretched fondaci of the slums. But there is no description of how a couple of hours after my arrival I was back once more in the station eagerly inquiring for the first train for Rome, for Calabria, for the Abruzzi, for anywhere, the further the better, only to get out of this hell. Had there been a train there would have been no 'Letters from a Mourning City'. As it was, there was no train till noon the next day, the communications with the infected city having been almost cut off. There was nothing to do but to have a swim at Santa Lucia at sunrise and to return to the slums with a cool head but still trembling with fear. In the afternoon my offer to serve on the staff of the cholera hospital of Santa Maddalena was accepted. Two days later I vanished from the hospital having discovered that the right place for me was not among the dying in the hospital, but among the dying in the slums.

How much easier it would have been for them and for me, thought I, if only their agony was not so long, so terrible! There they were lying for hours, for days in stadium algidum, cold as corpses, with wide-open eyes and wide-open mouths, to all appearances dead and yet still alive. Did they feel anything, did they understand anything? So much the better for the few who could still swallow the teaspoonful of laudanum one of the volunteers of the Croce Bianca rushed in to pour into their mouths. It might at least finish them off before the soldiers and the half-drunk beccamorti came at night to throw them all in a heap in the immense pit on the Camposanto dei Colerosi. How many were thrown there alive? Hundreds, I should say. They all looked exactly alike, I myself was often unable to say if they were dead or alive. There was no time to lose, there were dozens of them in every slum, the orders were strict, they all had to be buried in the night.

As the epidemic approached its climax I had no longer any reason for complaining that their agony was so long. Soon they began to fall down in the streets as if struck by lightning, to be picked up by the police and driven to the cholera hospital to die there a few hours later. The cabby who drove me in the morning in tearing spirits to the convict prison of Granatello, near Portici and was to take me back to Naples, was lying dead in his cab when I came to look for him in the evening. Nobody wanted to have anything to do with him in Portici, nobody wanted to help me to get him out of the cab. I had to climb on to the box and drive him back to Naples myself. Nobody wanted to have anything to do with him there either, it ended by my having to drive him to the cholera cemetery before I could get rid of him.

Often when I returned in the evening to the locanda, I was so tired that I threw myself on the bed as I was, without undressing, without even washing myself. What was the good of washing in this filthy water, what was the good of disinfecting myself when everybody and everything around me was infected, the food I ate, the water I drank, the bed I slept in, the very air I breathed! Often I was too frightened to go to bed, too frightened to be alone. I had to rush out into the street again, to spend the remainder of the night in one of the churches. Santa Maria del Carmine was my favourite night-quarter, the best sleep I have ever had I had on a bench in the left-side aisle of that old church. There were plenty of churches to sleep

121

in when I dared not go home. All the hundreds of churches and chapels of Naples were open the whole night, ablaze with votive candles and thronged with people. All their hundreds of Madonnas and saints were hard at work night and day to visit the dying in their respective quarters. Woe to them if they ventured to appear in the quarter of one of their rivals! Even the venerable Madonna della Colera who had saved the city in the terrible epidemic of 1834, had been hissed a few days before at Bianchi Nuovi.

But it was not only of the cholera I was afraid. I was also terrified from first to last of the rats. They seemed just as much at home in the fondaci, bassi and sotterranei of the slums as the wretched human beings who lived and died there. To be just, they were on the whole inoffensive and well-behaved rats, at least with the living, attending to their business of scavengers, handed over to them alone since the time of the Romans, the only members of the community who were sure to get their fill. They were as tame as cats and almost as big. Once I came upon an old woman, nothing but skin and bones, almost naked, lying on a rotten straw-mattress in a semi-dark sort of grotto. I was told she was the 'vavama,' the grandmother. She was paralysed and totally blind, she had been lying there for years. On the filthy floor of the cave sat on their haunches half-a-dozen enormous rats in a circle round their unmentionable morning meal. They looked quite placidly at me, without moving an inch. The old woman stretched out her skeleton arm and screamed in a hoarse voice: 'Pane! pane!'

But when the sanitary commission started on its vain attempt to disinfect the sewers, the situation changed, my fear grew into terror. Millions of rats who had been living unmolested in the sewers since the time of the Romans, invaded the lower part of the town. Intoxicated by the sulphur fumes and the carbolic acid, they rushed about the slums like mad dogs. They did not look like any rats I had ever seen before, they were quite bald with extraordinarily long red tails, fierce blood-shot eyes and pointed black teeth as long as the teeth of a ferret. If you hit them with your stick, they would turn round and hang on to the stick like a bull-dog. Never in my life have I been so afraid of any animal as I was of these mad rats, for I am sure they were mad. The whole Basso Porto quarter was in terror. Over one hundred severely bitten men, women and children were taken to the Pellegrini hospital the very first day of the invasion. Several small children were literally eaten up. I shall never forget a night in a fondaco in Vicolo della Duchessa. The room, the cave is the better word, was almost dark, only lit up by the little oil-lamp before the Madonna. The father had been dead for two days but the body was still lying there under a heap of rags, the family having succeeded in hiding him from the police in search of the dead to be taken to the cemetery, a common practice in the slums. I was sitting on the floor by the side of the daughter, beating off the rats with my stick. She was already quite cold, she was still conscious. I could hear the whole time the rats crunching at the body of the father. At last it made me so nervous that I had to put him upright in the corner like a grandfather clock. Soon the rats began again eating ravenously his feet and legs. I could not stand it any longer. Faint with fear I rushed away.

The Farmacia di San Gennaro was also a favourite haunt of mine when I was afraid to be alone. It was open night and day. Don Bartolo was always on his legs concocting his various mixtures and miraculous remedies from his row of seventeenth-century Faenza jars with Latin inscriptions of drugs, mostly unknown to me. A couple of large glass bottles with snakes and a foetus in alcohol adorned the sideboard. By the shrine of San Gennaro, the patron saint of Naples, burned the sacred lamp and among the cobwebs in the ceiling hung an embalmed cat with two heads. The speciality of the Farmacia was Don Bartolo's famous anti-cholerical mixture, labelled with a picture of San Gennaro on one side and a skull on the other with the words 'Morte alla coléra' underneath. Its composition was a family secret handed down from father to son ever since the epidemic of 1834 when, in collaboration with San Gennaro, it had saved the city. Another speciality of the Farmacia was a mysterious bottle labelled with a heart pierced by Cupid's arrow, a filtro d'amore. Its composition also was a family secret, it was much in demand, I understood. Don Bartolo's clients seemed chiefly drawn from the many convents and churches round his street. There were always a couple of priests, monks or frati sitting on the chairs before the counter in animated discussion about the events of the day, the last miracles performed by this or that saint, and the efficacy of the various Madonnas, la Madonna del Carmine, la Madonna dell' Aiuto, la Madonna della Buona Morte, la Madonna della Coléra, l'Addolorata, la Madonna Egiziaca. Seldom, very seldom, I heard the name of God mentioned, the name of His Son never. I once ventured to express my surprise to a shabby old Frate who was a particular friend of mine over this omission of Christ in their discussions. The old Frate made no secret of his private opinion that Christ owed his reputation solely to His having the Madonna for His Mother. As far as he knew, Christ had never saved anybody from the cholera. His Blessed Mother had cried her eyes out for Him. What had He done for Her in return? 'Woman,' He said, 'what have I to do with Thee?'

'Perciò ha finito male, that's why He came to a bad end.'

As Saturday approached the names of the various saints and Madonnas dropped more and more from the conversation. On Friday night the Farmacia was full of people gesticulating wildly in animated discussion about their chances for the Banco di Lotto of to-morrow.

Trentaquattro, sessantanove, quarantatre, diciasette!

Don Antonio had dreamt his aunt had died suddenly and left him five thousand lire, sudden death – 49, money – 70! Don Onorato had consulted the hunchback in Via Forcella, he was sure of his terno – 9, 39, 20! Don Bartolo's cat had had seven kittens in the night – numbers 7, 16, 64! Don Dionisio had just read in the 'Pungolo' that a camorrista had stabbed a barber at Immacolatella. Barber – 21, knife – 41! Don Pasquale had got his numbers from the custodian of the cemetery who had heard them distinctly from a grave – il morto che parla – 48!

It was at the Farmacia di San Gennaro I first made the acquaintance of Doctor Villari. I had been told by Don Bartolo that he had come to Naples two years ago as an assistant to old Doctor Rispù, the well-known doctor of all the convents and congregations in the quarter, who at his death had handed over his large practice to his young assistant. I was always glad to meet my colleague, I took a great liking to him from the very first. He was a singularly handsome man with nice, quiet manners, very unlike the ordinary type of Neapolitan. He came from the Abruzzi. It was through him I first heard of the convent of the Sepolte Vive, the grim old building in the corner of the street with its small Gothic windows and huge massive iron gates, sombre and silent like a grave. Was it true that the nuns entered through these gates wrapped in the shroud of the dead and laid in a coffin, and that they could never get out as long as they were alive?

Yes, it was quite true, the nuns had no communication with the outer world. He himself during his rare professional visits to the convent was preceded by an old nun ringing a bell to warn the nuns to shut themselves up in their cells.

Was it true what I had heard from Padre Anselmo, their confessor, that the cloister garden was full of antique marbles?

Yes, he had noticed lots of fragments lying about, he had been

124

told that the convent stood on the ruins of a Greek temple.

My colleague seemed to like to talk to me, he said he had no friends in Naples, like all his countrymen he hated and despised the Neapolitans. What he had witnessed since the outbreak of the cholera made him loathe them more than ever. It was difficult not to believe that it was the punishment of God that had fallen on their rotten city. Sodom and Gomorrah were nothing compared to Naples. Did I not see what was going on in the poor quarters, in the streets, in the infected houses, even in the churches while they were praying to one saint and cursing another? A frenzy of lust was sweeping all over Naples, immorality and vice everywhere in the very face of Death. Assaults on women had become so frequent that no decent woman dared to leave her house.

He did not seem to be afraid of the cholera, he said he felt quite safe under the protection of the Madonna. How I envied him his faith! He showed me the two medallions his wife had hung round his neck the day the cholera broke out, one was a Madonna del Carmine, the other was Santa Lucia, the patron saint of his wife, his wife's name was Lucia. She had worn the little medallion ever since she was a child. I said I knew Santa Lucia well, I knew she was the patron saint of the eyes. I had often wished to light a candle before her shrine, I who had lived for years in fear of losing my sight. He said he would tell his wife to remember me in her prayers to Santa Lucia, who had lost her own eyes but had restored the light to so many others. He told me that from the moment he left his house in the morning, his wife was sitting by the window looking out for his return. She had nobody but him in the world, she had married him against the wish of her parents, he had wanted to send her away from the infected city but she had refused to leave him. I asked him if he was not afraid of death. He said not for himself but for the sake of his wife. If only death from cholera was not so hideous! Better to be taken at once to the cemetery than to be seen by eyes that loved you!

'I am sure you will be all right,' I said, 'you have at least somebody who prays for you, I have nobody.'

A shadow passed over his handsome face.

'Promise me if . . .'

'Don't let us talk about death,' I interrupted him with a shudder.

The little Osteria dell'Allegria behind Piazza Mercato was a favourite resting-place of mine. The food was abominable but the wine was excellent, six sous the litre, I had plenty of it. I often spent half of the night there when I dared not go home. Cesare, the night-waiter, soon became a great friend of mine. After the third case of cholera in my locanda it ended by my moving into an empty room in the house he lived in. My new quarters were as dirty as the locanda, but Cesare was right, it was much better to be 'in compagnia.' His wife was dead, but Mariuccia, his daughter, was alive, very much so. She believed she was fifteen, but she was already in full bloom, black-eyed and red-lipped, she looked like the little Venus of the Capitol Museum. She washed my linen, cooked my macaroni, and made up my bed when she did not forget it. She had never seen a forestiere before. She was always coming into my room with a bunch of grapes, a slice of water-melon or a plate of figs. When she had nothing else to offer me she took the red rose from her black curls and handed it to me with her enchanting smile of a siren and a sparkling question in her eyes, whether I would not like to have her red lips as well? The whole day she was singing from the kitchen in her strong, shrill voice:

'Amore! Amore!'

In the night I heard her tossing about in her bed on the other side of the partition wall. She said she could not go to sleep, she said she was afraid to be alone at night, she was afraid to dormire sola. Was I not afraid to dormire solo?

'Dormite, signorino?' she whispered from her bed.

No, I did not sleep, I was wide awake, I did not like to dormire solo more than she did.

What new fear was making my heart beat so tumultuously and making the blood rush through my veins with fever speed? Why, when sitting half-asleep in the side aisle of Santa Maria del Carmine, had I not noticed before all these beautiful girls in their black mantillas kneeling on the marble floor by my side and smiling at me on the sly in the midst of their prayers and incantations? How could I have passed every day for weeks in front of the fruttivendola in the street corner without stopping to chat with Nannina, her beautiful daughter, with the same colour on her cheeks as the peaches she was selling? Why had I not discovered before that the fioraia in Piazza Mercato had the same enchanting smile as Botticelli's Primavera? How could I have spent so many evenings in the Osteria dell'Allegria unaware that it was not the vino di Gragnano but the sparkle in Carmela's eyes that went to my head? How was it possible that I had only heard the groans of the dying and the tolling of the church-bells when from every street sounded laughter and love-songs, when under every portico stood a girl whispering to her amoroso?

'O Mari', O Mari', quanto sonno ho perso pez te.
Fammi dormire
Abbracciato un poco con te,'

sang a youth under Mariuccia's window.

'O Carmé! O Carmé!' sang another outside the Osteria.

'Vorrei baciare'i tuoi capelli neri,'

rang out from Piazza Mercato.

'Vorrei baciare i tuoi capelli neri,'

echoed in my ears as I lay in my bed listening to the respiration of Mariuccia asleep on the other side of the partition wall.

What had happened to me? Was I bewitched by a strega? Had one of these girls poured some drops of Don Bartolo's filtro d'amore in my wine? What had happened to all these people around me? Were they all drunk with the new wine or had they gone mad with lust in the very face of Death?

Morto la coléra, evviva la gioia!

I was sitting at my usual table in the Osteria half-asleep before my bottle of wine. It was already past midnight, I thought I had better wait where I was, to return home with Cesare when he had finished his job. A boy ran up to my table and handed me a piece of paper.

'Come,' was scribbled on the paper in almost illegible letters.

Five minutes later we stopped before the huge iron gates of the convent of the Sepolte Vive. I was let in by an old nun who preceded me across the cloister garden ringing a bell. We passed along an immense, deserted corridor, another nun held up a lantern to my face and opened the door to a dimly-lit room. Doctor Villari was lying on a mattress on the floor. I hardly recognized him at first. Padre Anselmo was just giving him the Last Sacraments. He was already in stadium algidum, his body was quite cold but I could see by his eyes that he was still conscious. I looked at his face with a shudder, it was not my friend I looked at, it was Death, terrible, repulsive Death. He raised his hands several times pointing at me, his ghastly face twitching under a desperate effort to speak. From his grimacing lips came distinctly the word: 'specchio!' A nun brought after some delay a little mirror, I held it before his half-closed eyes. He shook his head several times, it was the last sign of life he gave, an hour later the heart stood still.

The cart stood before the gate to take away the bodies of the two nuns who had died during the day. I knew it rested with me whether he was to be taken away at the same time or left where he was till the next evening. They would have believed me had I said he was still alive, he looked exactly the same as when I had come. I said nothing. Two hours later his body was thrown with hundreds of other bodies in the common grave in the cholera cemetery. I had understood why he had raised his hand and pointed at me and why he had shaken his head when I had held the mirror before his eyes. He did not want his wife to see what he had seen in the mirror, and he wanted me to go and tell her when all was over.

As I stood before his house I saw the white face of a woman, almost a child, in the window. She reeled back with terror in her eyes as I opened the door.

'You are the foreign doctor he has told me so much about, he has not come back, I have been standing in the window the whole night. Where is he?'

She threw a shawl over her shoulders and rushed to the door.

'Take me to him at once, I must see him at once!'

I held her back, I said I must speak to her first. I told her he had been taken ill in the convent of the Sepolte Vive, the whole place was infected, she could not go there, she must think of the child she was going to give birth to.

'Help me downstairs, help me downstairs! I must go to him at once, why don't you help me?' she sobbed.

Suddenly she gave a piercing scream and sank down on the chair on the point of fainting.

'It is not true, he is not dead, why don't you speak, you are a liar, he cannot be dead without my seeing him.'

She sprang to the door once more.

'I must see him, I must see him!'

Once more I held her back.

'You cannot see him, he is no longer there, he is . . . .'

She sprang at me like a wounded animal.

'You had no right to have him taken away before I had seen him,' she screamed, mad with rage. 'He was the light of my eyes, you have taken the light from my eyes! You are a liar, a murderer! Holy Lucia, take the light from his eyes as he has taken the light from my eyes! Sting out his eyes as you stung out your own eyes!'

An old woman rushed into the room and sprang at me with uplifted hands as if she wanted to scratch my face.

'Holy Lucia, take the sight away from him! Blind him!' she screamed at the top of her voice.

'Potess' essere ciecato, potess' essere ciecato,' she was still shouting from the landing as I reeled down the stairs.

The terrible curse, the most terrible that ever could have been hurled against me, was ringing in my ears the whole night. I dared not go home, I was afraid of the dark. I spent the remainder of the night in Santa Maria del Carmine, I thought the day would never come.

When I staggered into the Farmacia di San Gennaro in the morning for my usual pick-me-up, another of Don Bartolo's specialities of extraordinary efficacy, Padre Anselmo had just left a message for me to come to the convent at once.

The whole convent was in commotion, there had been three fresh cases of cholera. Padre Anselmo told me that after a long conversation between the Abbess and himself, it had been decided to ask me to replace my dead colleague, no other doctor being available. Panic-stricken nuns were running to and fro through the corridors, others were praying and singing incantations in the chapel. The three nuns were lying on their straw mattresses in their cells. One of them died in the evening. In the morning, the old nun who had been assisting me was struck down in her turn. She was replaced by a young nun I had already noticed during my first visit, indeed it was difficult not to notice her, for she was very young and strikingly beautiful. She never said a word to me. She did not even answer when I asked her what was her name, but I found out from Padre Anselmo that she was Suora Ursula. Later in the day I asked to speak to the Abbess and was taken by Suora Ursula to her cell. The old Abbess looked at me with her cold, penetrating eyes, severe and scrutinizing as those of a judge. Her face was rigid and lifeless as if cut in marble, her thin lips looked as if they had never parted in a smile. I told her the whole convent was infected, the sanitary conditions were appalling, the water in the garden well was polluted, the whole place must be evacuated or they would all die of cholera.

She answered it was impossible, it was against the rules of their order, no nun, once inside their convent, had ever left it alive. They all had to remain where they were, they were in the hands of the Madonna and of San Gennaro.

Except for a rapid visit to the Farmacia for a steadily increased dose of Don Bartolo's miraculous pick-me-up, I never left the convent for several unforgettable days of terror. I had to tell Padre Anselmo I must have some wine, and soon I had plenty of it, probably too much. Sleep I had next to none, I did not seem to need any sleep. I do not even believe I could have slept had I had the chance, fear and innumerable cups of black coffee had roused my whole mental machinery into an extraordinary state of excitement which took away all fatigue. My only relaxation was when I could steal into the cloister garden where I sat smoking endless cigarettes on the old marble bench under the cypresses. Fragments of antique marbles were lying all over the garden, even the well-head was made out of what had once been a cippo, a Roman altar. It is now in the courtyard of San Michele. At my very feet lay a mutilated fawn of rosso antico and half-hidden amongst the cypresses stood a little Eros still erect on his column of African marble. A couple of times I had found Suora Ursula sitting on the bench, she said she had to come out for a breath of fresh air or she would faint from the strench all over the building. Once she brought me a cup of coffee and stood in front of me waiting for the cup while I drank my coffee as slowly as possible to make her stand there a little longer. It seemed to me as if she had become a little less shy, as if she did not mind that I was so slow in handing back my empty cup to her. It seemed a rest to my tired eyes to look at her. It soon became a joy, for she was very beautiful. Did she understand what my eyes said to her but my lips dared not say, that I was young and she was fair? There were moments when I almost thought she did.

I asked her why she had come here to bury her young life in the grave of the Sepolte Vive. Did she not know that outside this place of terror and death the world was as beautiful as before, that life was full of joy and not only of sorrow?

'Do you know who is this boy?' I said, pointing to the little Eros under the cypresses.

She thought it was an angelo.

No, it is a god, the greatest of all gods and perhaps the oldest of all gods. He ruled over Olympus and he still rules over our world to-day.

'Your convent stands on the ruins of an antique temple, its very walls had crumbled to dust destroyed by time and man. This little boy alone has remained where he stood with the quiver of arrows in his hand, ready to raise his bow. He is indestructible because he is immortal. The ancients called him Eros, he is the god of Love.'

As I spoke the blasphemous word the bell from the chapel called the nuns to their evening prayer. She crossed herself and hurried out of the garden.

A moment later another nun came rushing to take me to the

Abbess, she had fainted in the chapel, they had just carried her to her cell. The Abbess looked at me with her terrible eyes. She raised her hand and pointed to the Crucifix on the wall, they brought her the Last Sacraments. She never rallied, she never spoke, the action of the heart grew weaker and weaker, she was sinking rapidly. She lay there the whole day, the Crucifix on her breast, her rosary in her hands, her eyes closed, her body slowly growing cold. Once or twice I thought I heard a faint beating of the heart, soon I heard nothing. I looked at the rigid, cruel face of the old Abbess which even death had not been able to soften. It was almost a relief to me that her eyes were closed for ever, there was something in those eyes that had frightened me. I looked at the young nun by my side.

'I cannot stay here any longer,' I said, 'I have not slept since I came here, my head is swimming, I am not myself, I do not know what I am doing, I am afraid of myself, I am afraid of you, I am afraid of . . .'

I had not time to finish the word, she had not time to draw back, my arms had closed round her, I felt the tumultuous beating of her heart against my heart.

'Pietà!' she murmured.

Suddenly she pointed towards the bed and sprang out of the room with a cry of terror. The eyes of the old Abbess were looking straight at me, wide-open, terrible, menacing. I bent over her, I thought I heard a faint fluttering of the heart. Was she dead or alive? Could those terrible eyes see, had they seen? Would those lips ever speak again? I dared not look at those eyes, I pulled the sheet over her face and sprang from the cell, from the Sepolte Vive, never to return there any more.

The next day I fainted in Strada Piliero. When I regained consciousness I was lying in a cab with a terrified policeman sitting on the seat opposite me. We were on our way to Santa Maddalena, the cholera hospital.

I have described elsewhere how that drive ended, how three weeks later my stay in Naples ended with a glorious sail across the bay in Sorrento's best sailing-boat together with a dozen stranded Capri fishermen, how we lay a whole unforgettable day off the Marina of Capri unable to land on account of the quarantine.

I took good care not to describe in 'The Letters from a Mourning City' what happened in the convent of the Sepolte Vive. I have never dared to tell it to anybody, not even to my faithful friend Doctor Norstrom, who was keeping a catalogue of most of the shortcomings of my youth. The memory of my disgraceful conduct haunted me for years. The more I thought of it, the more incomprehensible it seemed to me. What had happened to me? What unknown force had been at work to make me lose the control over my senses, strong, but so far less strong than my head? I was no newcomer to Naples, I had chattered and laughed with those fiery girls of the south before. I had danced the tarantella with them many a summer evening in Capri. I may have stolen a kiss or two from them if it came to the worst, but I had always remained the captain of the ship, quite capable of suppressing any sign of insubordination of the crew. In my student days in Quartier Latin I had fallen almost in love with Soeur Philomène, the beautiful young sister in Salle Ste. Claire, all I had dared to do had been to stretch out my hand timidly to bid her good-bye the day I was leaving the hospital for good, and she did not even take it. Now in Naples I had wanted to throw my arms round every girl I set eyes on, and no doubt I would have done it had I not fainted in Strada Piliero the day I had kissed a nun at the death-bed of an Abbess!

In looking back upon my Naples days after a lapse of so many years I can no more excuse my conduct to-day than I could then, but maybe I can to a certain extent explain it.

I have not been watching during all these years the battle between Life and Death without getting to know something of the two combatants. When I first saw Death at work in the hospital wards it was a mere wrestling match between the two, a mere child's play compared with what I saw later. I saw Him at Naples killing more than a thousand people a day before my very eyes. I saw Him at Messina burying over one hundred thousand men, women and children under the falling houses in a single minute. Later on I saw Him at Verdun, His arms red with blood to the elbows, slaughtering four hundred thousand men, and mowing down the flower of a whole army on the plains of Flanders and of the Somme. It is only since I have seen Him operating on a large scale that I have begun to understand something of the tactics of the warfare. It is a fascinating study, full of mystery and contradictions. It all seems at first a bewildering chaos, a blind meaningless slaughter full of confusion and blunders. At one moment Life, brandishing a new weapon in its hand, advances victoriously, only to retire the next moment, defeated by triumphant Death. It is not so. The battle is regulated in its minutest details by an immutable law of equilibrium between Life and Death. Wherever this equilibrium is upset by some accidental cause, be it pestilence, earthquake or war, vigilant Nature sets to work at once to readjust the balance, to call forth new beings to take the place of the fallen. Compelled by the irresistible force of a Natural Law, men and women fall in each other's arms, blind-folded by lust, unaware that it is Death who presides over their mating, his aphrodisiac in one hand, his narcotic in the other. Death, the giver of Life, the slayer of Life, the beginning and the end.

IX

Back to Paris

I had been away three months instead of one. I felt sure that many
of my patients would stick to my friend Doctor Norstrom, who
had been looking after them during my absence. I was mistaken,
they all came back to me, some better, some worse, all speaking
very kindly of my colleague but equally kindly of me. I should not
have minded in the least if they had stuck to him, I had my hands
full in any case and I knew that his practice was dwindling away
more and more, that he had even had to move from Boulevard
Haussmann to a more modest apartment in Rue Pigalle. Norstrom
had always been a loyal friend, had helped me out of many scrapes
in the beginning of my career when I was still dabbling in surgery,
always ready to share the responsibility for my many blunders. I
well remember, for instance, the case of Baron B. I think I had better tell you this story to make you understand what sort of man my
friend was. Baron B., one of the oldest members of the Swedish
colony, always in indifferent health, had been attended by Norstrom for years. One day Norstrom with his fatal timidity suggested
that I should be called in in consultation. The Baron took a great
liking to me. A new doctor is always believed to be a good doctor
until he has been proved the contrary. Norstrom wanted an
immediate operation, I was against it. The Baron wrote to me he
was getting tired of Norstrom's gloomy face, and asked me to take
him in hand. Of course I refused, but Norstrom insisted upon
retiring and my taking over the case. The Baron's general condition
improved rapidly, I was congratulated on all sides. A month later
it became clear to me that Norstrom was right in his diagnosis, but
that it was now too late for an operation, that the man was
doomed. I wrote to his nephew in Stockholm to come out to bring
him home to die in his own country. It was with the greatest difficulty I succeeded in persuading the old gentleman. He did not
want to leave me; I was the only doctor who understood his case. A
couple of months later his nephew wrote to me that his uncle had
left me in his will a very valuable gold repeater in remembrance of
what I had done for him. I often make it strike the hour to remind

me what sort of stuff the reputation of a doctor is made of.

Of late the position between Norstrom and me had somewhat changed. I was more and more called in consultation by his patients, much too often. I had just seen one of them die rather unexpectedly that very afternoon, the worse luck for Norstrom as the patient was one of the best-known members of the colony. Norstrom was very much upset about it, I took him to dine with me at Café de la Régence to cheer him up a little.

'I wish you could explain to me the secret of your success and of my failure,' said Norstrom, looking gloomily at me across the bottle of St. Julien.

'It is above all a question of luck,' said I. 'There is also a temperamental difference between you and me which enables me to seize Fortune by her hair while you sit still and let her fly past, your hands in your pockets. I am convinced that you know more than I do about the human body in health and disease; it is just possible that although you are twice my age, I know more than you do about the human mind. Why did you tell the Russian professor I handed over to you that he had angina pectoris, why did you explain to him all the symptoms of his fatal disease?'

'He insisted upon knowing the truth, I had to tell him or he would not have obeyed me.'

'I did not tell him anything of the sort, he obeyed me anyhow. He told you a lie when he told you he wanted to know everything and that he was not afraid of death. Nobody wants to know how ill he is, everybody is afraid of death and for good reason. This man now is far worse. His existence is paralysed by fear, it is all your fault.'

'You are always talking about nerves and mind as if our body was made of nothing else. The cause of angina pectoris is arteriosclerosis of the coronary arteries.'

'Ask Professor Huchard what happened in his clinic last week while he was demonstrating to us a case of angina pectoris! The woman suddenly started a terrible attack which the Professor himself thought would be fatal. I asked his permission to try to stop it with mental treatment, he said it was useless but he consented. I laid my hand on her forehead, and told her it would pass off immediately, a minute later the terror went out of her eyes, she drew a deep breath and said she felt all right. Of course you say it was a case of pseudo-angina, fausse angine de poitrine; I can prove you the contrary. Four days later she had another to all appearance quite similar attack, she died in less than five minutes. You are always trying to explain to your patients what you cannot even

135

explain to yourself. You forget that it is all a question of faith not of knowledge, like the faith in God. The Catholic Church never explains anything and remains the strongest power in the world; the Protestant Church tries to explain everything and is crumbling to pieces. The less your patients know the truth, the better for them. It was never meant that the working of the organs of our body should be watched by the mind, to make your patients think about their illness is to tamper with the laws of Nature. Tell them that they must do so and so, take such and such a remedy in order to get better, and that if they don't mean to obey you, they must go to somebody else. Do not call on them except when they are in absolute need of you, do not talk too much to them or they will soon find you out and how little we know. Doctors, like royalties, should keep aloof as much as possible, or their prestige will suffer, we all look our best in a somewhat subdued light. Look at the doctor's own family, who always prefer to consult somebody else! I am actually attending, on the sly, the wife of one of the most celebrated physicians in Paris, not later than to-day she showed me his last prescription to ask me if it would do her any good.'

'You are always having women around you. I wish women would like me as much as they seem to like you, even my old cook is in love with you since you cured her of shingles.'

'I wish to goodness they did not like me, I would gladly hand over all these neurotic females to you. I know that I owe them to a considerable extent my reputation as a so-called fashionable doctor, but let me tell you they are a great nuisance, often even a danger. You say you want women to like you, well don't tell them so, don't make too much of them, don't let them order you about as they please. Women, though they do not seem to know it themselves, like far better to obey than to be obeyed. They pretend to be our equals, but they know jolly well themselves that they are not – luckily for them, for if they were our equals we should like them far less. I think on the whole much better of women than of men, but I do not tell it to them. They have far more courage, they face disease and death much better than we do, they have more pity and less vanity. Their instinct is on the whole a safer guide through their life than our intelligence, they do not make fools of themselves as often as we do. Love means to a woman far more than it means to a man, it means everything. It is less a question of senses than man generally understands. A woman can fall in love with an ugly man, even an old man if he rouses her imagination. A man cannot fall in love with a woman unless she rouses his sexual instinct, which,

136

contrary to Nature's intention, survives in modern man his sexual power. There is therefore no age limit for falling in love, Richelieu was irresistible at the age of eighty when he could hardly stand on his legs, and Goethe was seventy when he lost his head for Ulrike von Levetzow.

'Love itself is short-lived like the flower. With man it dies its natural death in marriage, with woman it often survives to the last transformed in a purely maternal tenderness for the fallen hero of her dreams. Women cannot understand that man is by nature polygamous. He may be tamed to enforced submission to our recent code of social morals, but his indestructible instinct is only dormant. He remains the same animal his Creator made him, ready to carry on business as usual, regardless of undue delay.

'Women are not less intelligent than men, perhaps they are as a rule more intelligent. But their intelligence is of a different order. There is no getting over the fact that the weight of the man's brain is superior to that of the woman's. The cerebral convolutions already visible in the new-born child are quite different in the two brains. The anatomical differences become even more striking when you compare the occipital lobe of the two brains, it is precisely on account of the pseudo-atrophy of this lobe in the brain of the woman that Husche attributes to it such great psychical importance. The law of differentiation between the sexes is an immutable law of Nature which runs through the whole creation to become more and more accentuated the higher the types are developed. We are told that it can all be explained by the fact that we have kept all culture as a sex monopoly to ourselves, that the women have never had a fair chance. Haven't they? Even in Athens the situation of the women was not inferior to that of the men, every branch of the culture was at their disposition. The Ionic and Doric races always recognized their freedom, it was even too great with the Lacedaemonians. During the whole Roman Empire, four hundred years of high culture, the women enjoyed a great deal of freedom. It is enough to remember that they disposed entirely of their own property. During the Middle Ages the instruction of the women was far superior to that of men. The knights knew better how to handle the sword than the pen, the monks were learned but there were plenty of nunneries as well, with equal opportunities to learn for their inmates. Look at our own profession, where the women are no new-comers! There were already women professors at the school of Salerno, Louise Bourgeois physician to Marie de' Medici the wife of Henry IV wrote a bad

137

book on midwifery, Marguerite la Marche was sage-femme en chef at the Hôtel Dieu in 1677, Madame La Chapelle and Madame Boivin wrote endless books on women's diseases, all very poor stuff. During the seventeenth and eighteenth centuries there were plenty of women professors in the famous Italian universities, Bologna, Pavia, Ferrara, Naples. They never did anything to advance their special science. It is just because obstetrics and gynecology were left in the hands of women that these two branches of our profession remained for so long at a hopeless standstill. The advance only began when they were taken in hand by men. Even to-day no woman when her life or the life of her child is in danger will stick to a doctor of her own sex.

'Look at music! All the ladies of the Renaissance played the lute and later on the harpsichord, the harp, the clavecin. For a century all better-class girls have been hard at work at their pianos but so far I know of no first-class piece of music composed by a woman, nor do I know a woman who can play to my liking the *Adagio Sostenuto* of Beethoven's Op. 106. There is hardly a young lady who does not go in for painting, but as far as I know no gallery in Europe contains a picture of the first rank signed by a woman except perhaps Rosa Bonheur, who had to shave her chin and who dressed as a man.

'One of the greatest poets of old times was a woman. Of the wreath of flowers round the enchantress-brow all that remains are a few petals of roses, fragrant with eternal spring. What immortal joy and what immortal sadness does not echo in our ears in this far-away siren-song from the shore of Hellas! Beautiful Sappho, shall I ever hear your voice again? Who knows if you are not singing still in some lost fragment of the anthology, safe under the lava of Herculaneum!'

'I do not want to hear anything more about your Sappho,' growled Norstrom, 'what I know of her and her worshippers is more than enough for me. I do not want to hear anything more about women. You have had more wine than is good for you, you have been talking a lot of nonsense, let us go home!'

Half-way down the Boulevard my friend wanted a bock, so we sat down at a table outside a café.

'Bonsoir, chéri,' said the lady at the next table to my friend. 'Won't you stand me a bock, I have had no supper.' Norstrom told her in an angry voice to leave him alone.

'Bonsoir, Chloe,' said I. 'How is Flopette?'

'She is doing the back streets, she is no good on the Boulevard till after midnight.'

As she spoke Flopette appeared and sat down by the side of her comrade-in-arms.

'You have been drinking again, Flopette,' said I, 'do you want to go to the devil altogether?'

'Yes,' she answered in a hoarse voice, 'it cannot be worse than here.'

'You are not very particular about your acquaintances,' growled Norstrom, looking horrified at the two prostitutes.

'I have had worse acquaintances than these two,' said I. 'I am besides their medical adviser. They both have syphilis, absinthe will do the rest, they will end in St. Lazare or in the gutter ere long. At least they do not pretend to be anything but what they are. Do not forget that what they are, they have to thank a man for, and that another man is standing on the street corner opposite to take from them the money we give them. They are not so bad as you think, these prostitutes, they remain women to the last, with all their faults but also with some of their virtues surviving their collapse. Strange to say, they are even capable of falling in love, in the highest significance of the word, and a more pathetic sight you never saw. I have had a prostitute in love with me, she became timid and shy as a young girl, she could even blush under her coating of rouge. Even this loathsome creature at the next table might have been a nice woman had she had a chance. Let me tell you her story.

'Do you remember,' said I as we strolled down the Boulevard arm in arm, 'do you remember the girls' school in Passy kept by the Sœurs Ste. Thérèse where you took me last year to see a Swedish girl who died of typhoid fever? There was another case in the same school shortly afterwards attended by me, a very beautiful French girl about fifteen. One evening as I was leaving the school I was accosted in the usual way by a woman patrolling the trottoir opposite. As I told her roughly to leave me alone, she implored me in a humble voice to let her say a few words to me. She had been watching me coming out of the school every day for a week, she had not had the courage to speak to me as it was still daylight. She addressed me as Monsieur le Docteur and asked in a trembling voice how was the young girl with typhoid fever, was it dangerous?

'"I must see her before she dies," she sobbed, the tears rolling down her painted cheeks, "I must see her, I am her mother." The nuns did not know, the child had been put there when she was three years old, the money was paid through the bank. She herself had never seen the child since then except when watching her from the street corner every Thursday when the girls were taken out for their afternoon walk. I said I was very worried about the child, that I would let her know if she got worse. She did not want to give me her address, she begged me to let her wait for me in the street every evening for news. For a week I found her there trembling with anxiety. I had to tell her the child was getting worse, I knew well it was out of the question to make this wretched prostitute see her dying child, all I could do was to promise her to let her know when the end was near, whereupon she consented at last to give me her address. Late the next evening I drove to her address in a street of evil repute, behind the Opéra Comique. The cabman smiled significantly at me and suggested he should come back to fetch me in an hour. I said a quarter of an hour would do. After a rapid scrutiny by the matron of the establishment, I was admitted to the presence of a dozen half-naked ladies in short tunics of red, yellow or green muslin. Would I make my choice? I said my choice was made, I wanted Mademoiselle Flopette. The matron was very sorry, Mademoiselle Flopette had not yet come down, she had of late been very negligent of her duties, she was still dressing in her bedroom. I asked to be taken there at once. It was twenty francs payable in advance and a souvenir *à discretion* to Flopette if I was satisfied with her, which I was sure to be, she was une fille charmante, prête à tout and very *rigolo*. Would I like a bottle of champagne taken up to her room?

'Flopette was sitting before her mirror hard at work to cover her face with rouge. She sprang from her chair, snatched a shawl to hide her appalling full undress uniform and stared at me with a face of a clown, with patches of rouge on her cheeks, one eye black with kohl, the other red with tears.

'"No, she is not dead, but she is very bad. The nun who is on night duty is worn out, I have told her I would bring one of my nurses for to-night. Scrape off that horrible paint from your face, straighten out your hair with oil or vaseline or whatever you like, take off your dreadful muslin gown and put on the nurse's uniform you will find in this parcel. I have just borrowed it from one of my nurses, I think it will do, you are about the same size. I shall come back and fetch you in half-an-hour." She stared speechless at me as I went downstairs.

'"Already," said the matron looking very surprised. I told her I wanted Mademoiselle Flopette to spend the night with me, I was coming back to fetch her. As I drove up before the house half-an-hour later Flopette appeared in the open door in the long cloak of a nurse surrounded by all the ladies in their muslin uniforms of Nothing-at-all.

'"Aren't you lucky, old girl," they giggled in chorus, "to be taken to the Bal Masqué the last night of carnival, you look very chic and quite respectable, I wish your monsieur would take us all!"

'"Amusez-vous, mes enfants," smiled the matron, accompanying Flopette to my cab, "it is fifty francs payable in advance."'

'There was not much nursing to be done. The child was sinking rapidly, she was quite unconscious, it was evident that the end was near. The mother sat the whole night by the bed-side staring through her tears at her dying child.

'"Kiss her good-bye," said I as the agony set in, "it is all right, she is quite unconscious."

'She bent over the child but suddenly she drew back.

'"I dare not kiss her," she sobbed, "you know I am rotten all over."'

'The next time I saw Flopette she was blind drunk. A week later she threw herself into the Seine. She was dragged out alive, I tried to get her admitted to St. Lazare, but there was no bed available. A month later she drank a bottle of laudanum, she was already half-dead when I came, I have never forgiven myself for pumping the poison out of her stomach. She was clutching in her hand the little shoe of a small child, and in the shoe was a lock of hair. Then she took to absinthe, as reliable a poison as any, though, alas, slow to kill. Anyhow she will soon be in the gutter, a safer place to drown herself in than is the Seine.'

We stopped before Norstrom's house, Rue Pigalle.

'Good night,' said my friend. 'Thank you for a pleasant evening.'

'The same to you,' said I.

141

X

The Corpse-Conductor

Perhaps the less said the better about the journey I made to Sweden in the summer of that year. Norstrom, the placid recorder of most of the adventures of my youth, said that so far it was the worst story I had ever told him. To-day it can harm nobody but myself and I may as well tell it here.

I was asked by Professor Bruzelius, the leading physician of Sweden in those days, to go to San Remo and accompany home a patient of his, a boy of eighteen who had spent the winter there in an advanced stage of consumption. He had had several haemorrhages of late. His condition was so serious that I only consented to take him home if he were accompanied by a member of the family or at least a competent Swedish nurse, the possibility of his dying on the way having to be considered. Four days later his mother arrived at San Remo. We were to break our journey in Basel and Heidelberg and to take the Swedish steamer from Lübeck to Stockholm. We arrived at Basel in the evening after a very anxious journey. In the night the mother had a heart attack which nearly killed her. The specialist I called in in the morning agreed with me, that she would in no case be able to travel for a couple of weeks. The choice lay between letting the boy die in Basel or continuing the journey with him alone. Like all those who are about to die he was longing to get home. Rightly or wrongly I decided to go on to Sweden with him. The day after our arrival at the Hôtel Victoria in Heidelberg he had another severe haemorrhage from the lungs and all hope of continuing the journey had to be abandoned. I told him we were to wait where we were a couple of days for his mother. He was very reluctant to postpone our journey a single day. He was eagerly studying the trains in the evening. He was sleeping peacefully when I went to have a look at him after midnight. In the morning I found him dead in his bed, no doubt from an internal haemorrhage. I wired my colleague in Basel to communicate the news to the mother of the boy and let me have her instructions The professor wired back that her condition was so serious that he dared not tell her. Convinced as I was that she wanted her son to be buried in

Sweden, I put myself in communication with an undertaker for all the necessary arrangements. I was informed by the undertaker that according to the law the body must be embalmed, price two thousand marks. I knew the family was not rich. I decided to embalm the body myself. There was no time to lose, it was the end of July, the heat was extreme. With the aid of a man from the Anatomical Institution I made a summary embalmment in the night at the cost of about two hundred marks. It was the first embalmment I had ever done, I am bound to say it was not a success, very far from it. The lead coffin was soldered in my presence, the outer oak coffin was enclosed in an ordinary deal packing-case according to the railway regulations. The rest was to be done by the undertaker in charge of the transport of the body by rail to Lübeck and from there by ship to Stockholm. The sum of money I had received from the mother for the journey home was hardly sufficient to pay the bill of the hotel. I protested in vain against the exorbitant charge for the bedding and the carpet in the room the boy had died in. When all was settled I had barely enough money left to pay my own journey to Paris. I had never been out of the house since my arrival, all I had seen of Heidelberg had been the garden of the Hôtel de l'Europe under my windows. I thought I might at least have a look at the famous old ruined castle before leaving Heidelberg where I hoped never to return. As I was standing by the parapet of the castle terrace looking down upon the Neckar valley at my feet, a dachshund puppy came rushing up to me as fast as his crooked little legs could carry his long, slender body, and started licking me all over the face. His cunning eyes had discovered my secret at the first glance. My secret was that I had always been longing to possess just such a little Waldmann as these fascinating dogs are called in their own native country. Hard up though I was I bought Waldmann at once for fifty marks and we returned in triumph to the Hôtel Victoria, Waldmann trotting close to my heels without a leash, quite certain that his master was I and nobody else. There was an extra charge in the morning for something about the carpet in my room. My patience was at an end, I had already spent eight hundred marks on carpets in the Hôtel Victoria. Two hours later I presented the carpet in the boy's room to an old cobbler I had seen sitting mending a pair of boots outside his poor home full of ragged children. The director of the hotel was speechless with rage, but the cobbler got his carpet. My mission in Heidelberg was ended, I decided to take the morning train for Paris. In the night I changed my mind and decided to go to Sweden anyhow. My arrangements

143

for being away from Paris for a fortnight were already made, Norstrom was to look after my patients during my absence, I had already wired to my brother that I was coming to stay with him in the old home for a couple of days, surely such an opportunity for a holiday in Sweden would never return. My one thought was to clear out from the Hôtel Victoria. It was too late to catch the passenger train for Berlin, I decided to take the goods train in the evening, the same that was conveying the body of the boy to Lübeck and to go on with the same Swedish steamer to Stockholm. As I was sitting down to my supper in the buffet of the station I was informed by the waiter that dogs were 'verboten' in the restaurant. I put a five-mark piece in his hand and Waldmann under the table, and was just beginning to eat my supper when a stentorian voice from the door called out:

'Der Leichenbegleiter!'

All the occupants of the tables looked up from their plates scanning each other, but nobody moved.

'Der Leichenbegleiter!'

The man banged the door to return a moment later with another man whom I recognized as the undertaker's clerk. The owner of the stentorian voice came up to me and roared in my face:

'Der Leichenbegleiter!'

Everybody looked at me with interest. I told the man to leave me alone, I wanted to have my supper. No, I must come at once, the stationmaster wanted to speak to me on most urgent business. A giant with bristling porcupine moustaches and gold-rimmed spectacles handed me a pile of documents and shrieked in my ear something about the van having to be sealed and that I must take my place in it at once. I told him in my best German that I had already reserved my place in a second-class compartment. He said it was 'verboten,' I must be locked up with the coffin in the van at once.

'What the devil do you mean?'

'Aren't you der Leichenbegleiter? Don't you know that it is "verboten" in Germany for a corpse to travel without his Leichenbegleiter and that they must be locked up together?'

I showed him my second-class ticket for Lübeck, I told him I was an independent traveller going for a holiday to Sweden. I had nothing whatsoever to do with the coffin.

'Are you or are you not the Leichenbegleiter?' he roared angrily.

'I am certainly not. I am willing to try my hand at any job but I refuse to be a Leichenbegleiter, I do not like the word.'

The stationmaster looked bewildered at his bundle of papers, and announced that unless the Leichenbegleiter turned up in less than five minutes the van containing the coffin for Lübeck would be shunted off on the side-track and remain in Heidelberg. As he spoke, a little hunchback with restless eyes and a face ravaged with small-pox rushed up to the stationmaster's desk with a pile of documents in his hands.

'Ich bin der Leichenbegleiter,' he announced with unmistakable dignity.

I nearly embraced him, I have always had a sneaking liking for hunchbacks. I said I was delighted to make his acquaintance, I was going on to Lübeck with the same train as he and to take the same steamer to Stockholm. I had to hold on to the stationmaster's desk when he said he was not going to Stockholm, but to St. Petersburg with the Russian general and from there to Nijni-Novgorod.

The stationmaster looked up from his bundle of documents, his porcupine moustaches bristling with bewilderment.

'Potzdonnerwetter!' he roared, 'there are two corpses going on to Lübeck by this train! I have only one coffin in the van, you cannot put two corpses in one coffin, it is "verboten." Where is the other coffin?'

The hunchback explained that the coffin of the Russian general was just being unloaded from the cart to be put in the van, it was all the fault of the carpenter who had only finished the second packing-case in the nick of time. Who could have dreamt that he was to provide two such huge packing-cases on the same day!

The Russian general! I suddenly remembered having been told that an old Russian general had died of an apoplectic stroke in the hotel opposite ours the same day as the boy. I even remembered having seen from my window a fierce-looking old gentleman with a long grey beard in a bath chair in the hotel gardens. The porter had told me that he was a famous Russian general, a hero of the Crimean war. I had never seen a more wild-looking man.

While the stationmaster returned to the perusal of his entangled documents, I took the hunchback aside, patted him cordially on the back and offered him fifty marks cash and another fifty marks I meant to borrow from the Swedish Consul in Lübeck if he would undertake to be the Leichenbegleiter of the coffin of the boy as well as of that of the Russian general. He accepted my offer at once. The stationmaster said it was an unprecedented case, it raised a delicate point of law, he felt sure it was 'verboten' for two corpses to travel with one Leichenbegleiter between them. He must consult the Kaiserliche Oberliche Eisenbahn Amt Direktion Bureau, it would take at least a week to get an answer. It was Waldmann who saved the situation. Several times during our discussions I had noticed a friendly glance from the stationmaster's gold-rimmed spectacles in the direction of the puppy and several times he had stretched his enormous hand for a gentle stroke on Waldmann's long, silky ears. I decided on a last desperate attempt to move his heart. Without saying a word I deposited Waldmann on his lap. As the puppy licked him all over the face and started pulling at his porcupine moustaches his harsh features softened gradually into a broad, honest smile at our helplessness. Five minutes later the hunchback had signed a dozen documents as the Leichenbegleiter of the two coffins, and I with Waldmann and my Gladstone bag was flung into a crowded second-class compartment as the train was starting. Waldmann offered to play with the fat lady next to us, she looked sternly at me and said that it was 'verboten' to take a dog in a second-class compartment, was he at least 'stubenrein'? Of course he was 'stubenrein,' he had never been anything else. Waldmann now turned his attention to the basket on the fat lady's lap, sniffed eagerly and started barking furiously. He was barking still when the train stopped at the next station. The fat lady called the guard and pointed to the floor. The guard said it was 'verboten' to travel with a dog without a muzzle. In vain did I open Waldmann's mouth to show to the guard that he had hardly any teeth, in vain did I put my last five-mark piece in the guard's hand, Waldmann must be taken at once to the dog-box. Bent on revenge I pointed to the basket on the fat lady's lap and asked the guard if it was not 'verboten' to travel with a cat without a ticket? Yes, it was 'verboten.' The fat lady and the guard were still quarrelling when I climbed down on the platform. The travelling accommodation for dogs was in those days shamefully inadequate, a dark cell just over the wheels, saturated with fumes from the locomotive, how could I put Waldmann there? I rushed to the luggage van and implored the guard to take charge of the puppy, he said it was 'verboten.' The sliding doors of the next van were cautiously drawn aside, just enough to let the head of the Leichenbegleiter pop out, a long pipe in his mouth. With the agility of a cat I climbed into the van with Waldmann and the Gladstone bag.

Fifty marks payable on arrival if he would hide Waldmann in his van till Lübeck! Before he had time to answer the doors were bolted from outside, a sharp whistle from the locomotive and the train began to move. The big van was quite empty but for the two packing-cases containing the two coffins. The heat was tremendous but there was ample room to stretch out one's legs. The puppy fell asleep immediately on my coat, the Leichenbegleiter produced a bottle of hot beer from his provision basket, we lit our pipes and sat down on the floor to discuss the situation. We were quite safe, nobody had seen me jump in with the dog, I was assured that no guard ever came near the van. When an hour later the train slowed down for the next stop I told the Leichenbegleiter that nothing but sheer force could make me part company with him, I meant to remain where I was till we reached Lübeck. The hours passed in agreeable conversation chiefly kept going by the Leichenbegleiter, I speak German very badly though I understand it quite well. My friend said he had made this same journey many times, he even knew the name of each station we stopped at although we never saw anything of the outside world from our prison van. He had been a Leichenbegleiter for more than ten years, it was a pleasant and comfortable job, he liked travelling and seeing new countries. He had been in Russia six times before, he liked the Russians, they always wanted to be buried in their own country. A large number of Russians were coming to Heidelberg to consult its many famous Professors. They were their best clients. His wife was by profession a Leichenwäscherin. Hardly any embalmment of importance was made without their assistance. Pointing to the other packing-case he said he felt rather vexed that neither he nor his wife had been called in for the Swedish gentleman. He suspected that he was the victim of some intrigue, there was much professional jealousy between him and his two other colleagues. There was a certain mystery about the whole affair, he had not even been able to find out what doctor had made the embalmment. They were not all equally good about it. Embalmment was a very delicate and complicated business, one never knew what might happen during a long journey in hot weather like this. Had I assisted at many embalmments?

Only at one, said I with a shudder.

'I wish you could see the Russian general,' said the Leichenbegleiter enthusiastically, pointing with his pipe to the other packing-case. 'He is perfectly wonderful, you would never believe it was a corpse, even his eyes are wide-open. I wonder why the stationmaster was so particular about you,' he went on. 'It is true you are rather young to be a Leichenbegleiter but so far as I can see you are respectable enough. All you need is a shave and a brush-up, your clothes are all covered with dog's hair and surely you cannot present yourself to-morrow at the Swedish Consulate with such a chin,

I am sure you have not shaved for a week, you look more like a brigand than a respectable Leichenbegleiter. What a pity I have not got my razors with me or I would shave you myself at the next stop.'

I opened my Gladstone bag and said I would be much obliged if he would spare me the ordeal, I never shaved myself if I could help it. He examined my razors with the eyes of a connoisseur, said the Swedish razors were the best in the world, he never used any others himself. He had a very light hand, he had shaved hundreds of people and never heard a word of complaint.

I have never been better shaved in my life and I told him so with my compliments when the train began to move again.

'There is nothing like travelling in foreign countries,' said I as I washed the soap off my face, 'every day one learns something new and interesting. The more I see of this country the more I realize the fundamental differences between the Germans and other people. The Latin and the Anglo-Saxon races invariably adopt the sitting-up position for being shaved, in Germany you are made to lie flat on your back. It is all a matter of taste, *chacun tue ses puces à sa façon*, as they say in Paris.'

'It is a matter of habit,' explained the Leichenbegleiter, 'you cannot make a corpse sit up, you are the first living man I have ever shaved.'

My companion spread a clean napkin over his packing-case and opened his provision basket. An amalgamated scent of sausage, cheese and sauerkraut tickled my nostrils, Waldmann woke up instantaneously, we watched him with hungry eyes. My joy was great when he invited me to partake of his supper, even the sauerkraut had lost its horror to my palate. He won my heart when he presented a large slice of Blutwurst to Waldmann. The effect was fulmineous and lasted till Lübeck. When we had finished our second bottle of Moselle my new friend and I had few secrets left to reveal to one another. Yes, one secret I jealously kept to myself – that I was a doctor. Experience in many lands had warned me that any hint of a class distinction between my host and myself would deprive me of my unique opportunity of seeing life from the visual angle of a Leichenbegleiter. What little I know of psychology I owe to a certain inborn facility for adapting myself to the social level of my interlocutor. When I am having supper with a duke I feel quite at home with him and that I am his equal. When I am having supper with a Leichenbegleiter I become as far as in my power a Leichenbegleiter myself.

Indeed when we started our third bottle of Moselle it only rested with me to become a Leichenbegleiter in earnest.

'Cheer up, Fritz,' said my host with a merry twinkle in his eye, 'don't look so dejected! I know you are out of cash and that something must have gone wrong with you. Never mind, have another glass of wine and let us talk business. I have not been a Leichenbegleiter for more than ten years without learning what sort of people I am dealing with! Intelligence is not everything. I am sure you were born under a lucky star or you would not be here sitting by my side. Here is your chance, the chance of your life! Deliver your coffin in Sweden while I am delivering mine in Russia and come back to Heidelberg by the first train. I will make you my partner. As long as Professor Friedreich is alive there will be work for two Leichenbegleiters or my name is not Zaccharias Schweinfuss! Sweden is no good for you, there are no famous doctors there, Heidelberg is full of them, Heidelberg is the place for you.'

I thanked my new friend cordially and said I would give him my definite answer in the morning when our heads had cleared a little. A few minutes later we were both fast asleep on the floor of the Leichenwagen. I had an excellent night, Waldmann less so. When the train rolled into the Lübeck station it was broad daylight. A clerk from the Swedish Consulate was waiting on the platform to superintend the transporting of the coffin on board the Swedish steamer for Stockholm. After a cordial 'Aufwiedersehen' to the Leichenbegleiter I drove to the Swedish Consulate. As soon as the Consul saw the puppy he informed me that the importation of dogs was forbidden, there having of late been several cases of hydrophobia in Northern Germany. I might try with the captain but he felt sure that Waldmann would not be admitted on board. I found the captain in a very bad temper, all sailors are when they have a coffin among their cargo. All my pleading was in vain. Encouraged by my success with the stationmaster in Heidelberg I decided to try him with the puppy. Waldmann licked him in vain all over the face. I then decided to try him with my brother. Yes, of course he knew Commandor Munthe quite well, they had sailed together on the 'Vanadis' as midshipmen, they were great friends.

Could he be so cruel as to leave my brother's beloved puppy stranded in Lübeck among total strangers?

No, he could not be so cruel. Five minutes later Waldmann was locked up in my cabin to be smuggled in on my own responsibility on our arrival in Stockholm. I love the sea, the ship was comfortable, I dined at the captain's table, everybody on board was most

149

polite to me. The stewardess looked somewhat sulky when she came to make up my cabin in the morning, but she became our ally as soon as the offender began to lick her all over the face, she had never seen a more fascinating puppy. When Waldmann appeared surreptitiously on the foredeck all the sailors began to play with him and the captain looked on the other side in order not to see him. It was late at night when we laid alongside the quay in Stockholm and I jumped on shore from the bow of the ship with Waldmann in my arms. I called in the morning on Professor Bruzelius who showed me a telegram from Basel that the mother was out of danger and that the funeral of the boy was postponed till her arrival in about a fortnight's time. He hoped I would still be in Sweden, the mother would be sure to wish to hear from me of her son's last moments and of course I must assist at the funeral. I told him I was going on a visit to my brother before returning to Paris, I was in a great hurry to be back to my patients.

I had never forgiven my brother for having dumped on me our terrible heirloom of Mamsell Agata, I had written him an angry letter on the subject. Luckily he seemed to have forgotten all about it. He said he was delighted to see me and both he and his wife hoped I would remain in the old home for at least a fortnight. Two days after my arrival he expressed his surprise that a busy doctor like me could be away from his patients so long, what day was I leaving? My sister-in-law had become glacial. There is nothing to do with people who dislike dogs but to pity them and start with your puppy on a walking-tour, knapsack on back. There is nothing better for a puppy than camping out in the open and sleeping under friendly firs on a carpet of soft moss instead of a carpet from Smyrna. My sister-in-law had a headache and did not come down to breakfast the morning I was starting, I wanted to go to her room to wish her good-bye. My brother advised me not to do it. I did not insist after he had told me that the housemaid had just found under my bed his wife's new Sunday hat, her embroidered slippers, her feather boa, two volumes of the 'Encyclopædia Britannica' torn to pieces, the remains of a rabbit, and her missing kitten, his head almost bitten off. As to the Smyrna carpet in the drawing-room, the flower-beds in the garden and the six ducklings in the pond. . . . I looked at my watch and told my brother I always liked to be in good time at the station.

'Olle,' shouted my brother to my father's old coachman as we drove away, 'for Heaven's sake see that the Doctor does not miss his train.'

A fortnight later I was back in Stockholm. Professor Bruzelius told me that the mother had arrived from the continent that same morning, the funeral was to take place next day, of course I must attend. To my horror he went on to say that the poor mother insisted on seeing her son before he was buried, the coffin was to be opened in her presence in the early morning. Of course I would never have embalmed the body myself had such a possibility ever entered my head. I knew I had meant well, but done badly, that in all probability the opening of the coffin would reveal a terrible sight. My first thought was to bolt and take the night train for Paris. My second thought was to stay where I was and play the game. There was no time to lose. With the powerful help of Professor Bruzelius I succeeded with great difficulty in obtaining the permission to open the coffin in order to proceed to a summary disinfection of the remains if it should prove necessary, which I was convinced was the case. Shortly after midnight I descended to the vault under the church accompanied by the custodian of the cemetery and a workman who was to open the two coffins. When the lid of the inner lead coffin was unsoldered the two men stood back in silent reverence before the awe of death. I took the lantern from the custodian and uncovered the face. The lantern fell on the floor, I reeled back as if struck by an invisible hand.

I have often wondered at my presence of mind that night, I must have had nerves of steel in those days.

'It is all right,' said I, rapidly covering the face again, 'screw on the lid, there is no need for any disinfection, the body is in perfect state of preservation.'

I called on Professor Bruzelius in the early morning. I told him that the sight I had seen in the night would haunt the poor mother for life, that he must at all costs prevent the opening of the coffin.

I assisted at the funeral. I have never assisted at another since that day. The coffin was carried to the grave on the shoulders of six of the boy's school-fellows. The clergyman in a moving allocution said that God in His inscrutable wisdom had willed it, that this young life so full of promise and joy should be cut short by cruel death. It was at least a comfort to those who stood mourning around his premature grave that he had come back to rest among his own people in the land of his birth. They would at least know where to lay their flowers of loving memory, where to pray. A choir of undergraduates from Upsala sang the traditional:

151

'Integer vitae scelerisque purus.'

I have hated this beautiful Ode of Horace ever since that day.

Supported by her aged father the mother of the boy advanced to the open grave and lowered a wreath of lilies of the valley on the coffin.

'It was his favourite flower,' she sobbed.

One by one the other mourners came forth with their bunches of flowers and looked down into the grave with tear-filled eyes for the last farewell. The choir sang the customary old hymn:

'Rest in peace, the strife is ended.'

The grave-diggers began to shovel the earth over the coffin, the ceremony was over.

When they had all gone I looked down in the half-filled grave in my turn.

'Yes, rest in peace, grim old fighter, the strife is ended! Rest in peace! Do not haunt me any longer with those wide-open eyes of yours or I shall go crazy! Why did you stare so angrily at me when I uncovered your face last night in the vault under the chapel? Do you think I was more pleased to see you than you were to see me? Did you take me for a grave-plunderer who had broken open your coffin to rob you of the golden ikon on your breast? Did you think it was I who brought you here? No, it was not I. For all I know it was the Archfiend himself in the shape of a drunken hunchback who caused you to come here! For who but Mephisto, the eternal jester, could have staged the ghastly farce just enacted here? I thought I heard his mocking laughter ringing through their sacred chant, God forgive me, I was not far from laughing myself when your coffin was lowered into this grave. But what matters it to you whose grave it is? You cannot read the name on the marble cross, what matters it to you what name it is? You cannot hear the voices of the living overhead, what matters it to you what tongue they speak? You are not lying here amongst strangers, you are lying side by side with your own kinsmen. So is the Swedish boy who was laid to rest in the heart of Russia while the buglers of your old regiment were sounding the Last Post by your grave. The kingdom of death has no borders, the grave has no nationality. You are all one and the same people now, you will soon even look exactly the same. The same fate awaits you all wherever you are laid to rest, to be forgotten and to moulder into dust, for such is the law of life. Rest in peace, the strife is ended.'

XI

Madame Réquin

Not far from Avenue de Villiers there lived a foreign doctor, a specialist, I understood, in midwifery and gynecology.

He was a coarse and cynical fellow who had called me in consultation a couple of times, not so much to be enlightened by my superior knowledge as to shift some of his responsibility onto my shoulders. The last time he had called me in had been to assist at the agony of a young girl dying of peritonitis under very suspicious circumstances, so much so that it was with hesitation I consented to put my name next to his on the death certificate. On coming home late one night I found a cab waiting for me at the door with an urgent request from this man to come at once to his private clinic in Rue Granet. I had decided to have nothing more to do with him but the message was so urgent that I thought I had better go with the cab anyhow. I was let in by a stout, unpleasant-looking woman who announced herself as Madame Réquin, sage-femme de 1-ère classe, and took me to a room on the top floor, the same room in which the girl had died. Blood-soaked towels, sheets and blankets were lying all over the place, blood dripping from under the bed with a sinister sound. The doctor, who thanked me warmly for having come to his rescue, was in a great state of agitation. He said there was no time to lose and he was right there, for the woman lying unconscious on her 'lit de travail' looked more dead than alive. After a rapid examination I asked him angrily why he had not sent for a surgeon or an accoucheur instead of me, since he knew that neither of us two was fit to deal with such a case. The woman rallied a little after a couple of syringes of camphor and ether. I decided with some hesitation to make him give her a little chloroform while I set to work. With my usual luck all went tolerably well and after vigorous artificial respiration even the half-suffocated child returned to life to our great surprise. But it was a narrow escape for both mother and child. There was no more cotton-wool, linen or dressing material of any sort to stem the haemorrhage, but luckily we came upon a half-open Gladstone bag full of fine linen and ladies' underwear which we tore rapidly to pieces for tampons.

'I never saw such beautiful linen,' said my colleague holding up a linen chemise, 'and look,' he exclaimed, pointing to a coronet embroidered in red over the letter M, 'ma foi, mon cher confrère, we are moving in good society! I assure you she is a very fine girl though there is not much left of her now, an exceptionally beautiful girl, I would not mind renewing her acquaintance if ever she pulls through.

'Ah, la jolie broche,' he exclaimed, picking up a diamond brooch which had evidently fallen on the floor when we were ransacking the bag. 'Ma foi! it looks to me as if it might make up for my bill if it comes to the worst. One never knows with these foreign ladies, she might choose to clear out as mysteriously as she came, God knows from where.'

'We are not there yet,' said I, snatching the brooch from his red fingers and putting it in my pocket, 'according to French law the bill of the undertaker passes before the bill of the doctor, we don't yet know which of the two bills will be presented for payment first. As to the child . . .'

'Never mind the child,' he giggled, 'we have plenty of babies here and to spare to substitute for it if it comes to the worst. Madame Réquin is dispatching every week half-a-dozen babies with the 'train des nourrices' from the Gare d'Orléans. But I cannot afford to let the mother slip through my fingers, I have to be careful about my statistics, I have already signed two death certificates from this place in two weeks.'

The woman was still half-unconscious when I left at daybreak, but the pulse had steadied itself and I told the doctor I thought she would live. I must have been in a pretty bad state myself or I would never have accepted the cup of black coffee Madame Réquin offered me in her sinister little parlour as I staggered downstairs.

'Ah, la jolie broche,' said Madame Réquin as I handed her the brooch for custody. 'Do you think the stones are real?' she wondered, holding the brooch close to the gaslight. It was a very fine diamond brooch with a letter M, surmounted with a coronet in rubies. The flash from the stones was all right, but the glare in her greedy eyes was suspect.

'No,' said I to make up for my stupidity for having handed her the brooch, 'I am sure it is all imitation.'

Madame Réquin hoped I was mistaken, the lady had not had time to pay in advance as was the rule of the establishment, she had arrived in the nick of time in a half-fainting condition, there was no name on her luggage, it was labelled London.

'That's enough, don't worry, you will be paid all right.'

Madame Réquin expressed a hope soon to see me again and I left the house with a shudder.

A couple of weeks later I received a letter from my colleague that all had gone well, the lady had left for an unknown destination as soon as she could stand on her feet, all bills having been paid and a large sum left in the hands of Madame Réquin for the adoption of the child by some respectable foster-parents. I returned his bank-note in a short letter begging him not to send for me next time he was about to kill somebody. I hoped never to set eyes again either upon him or Madame Réquin.

My hope was realized as to the Doctor. As to Madame Réquin I shall have to tell you more about her in due time.

XII

The Giant

As time went on, I realized more and more how rapidly Norstrom's practice was dwindling away, and that the day might come when he would have to put up the shutters altogether. Soon even the numerous Scandinavian colony, rich and poor, was drifting away from Rue Pigalle to Avenue de Villiers. I tried in vain to stay the tide, luckily Norstrom never doubted my loyalty, we remained friends to the last. God knows it was not a lucrative practice, this Scandinavian clientèle. During my whole life as a doctor in Paris it was like a stone round my neck that might have drowned me had it not been for my firm footing in the English and American colony and among the French themselves. As it was, it took away a great deal of my time and brought me into all sorts of troubles, it ended even by bringing me to prison. It is a funny story, I often tell it to my friends who write books, as a striking application of the law of coincidence, the hard-worked cheval de bataille of novelists.

Apart from the Scandinavian workmen in Pantin and La Villette, over one thousand in all, always in need of a doctor, there was the artist colony in Montmartre and Montparnasse always in need of money. Hundreds of painters, sculptors, authors of unwritten chef-d'oeuvres in prose and verse, exotic survivals of Henri Murger's 'Vie de Bohême.' A few of them were already on the eve of success like Edelfeld, Carl Larson, Zorn and Strindberg, but the majority had to subsist on hope alone. Biggest in size but shortest in cash was my sculptor friend, the Giant, with the flowing blond beard of a Viking and the guileless blue eyes of a child. He seldom appeared in the Café de l'Hermitage where most of his comrades spent their evenings. How he got his fill for his six-feet-eight body was a mystery to all. He lived in an enormous, ice-cold hangar in Montparnasse adapted as a sculptor's studio, where he worked, cooked his food, washed his shirt and dreamt his dreams of future fame. Size was what he needed for himself and for his statues, all of superhuman proportions, never finished for want of clay. One day he appeared at Avenue de Villiers with a request to me to act as his best man for his marriage next Sunday in the Swedish church, to be followed by a reception in his new apartment to 'pendre la crémaillère.' The choice of his heart turned out to be a frail Swedish miniature painter less than half his size. Of course I was delighted to accept. The ceremony over, the Swedish chaplain made a nice little speech to the newly married couple seated side by side in front of the altar. They reminded me of the colossal statue of Ramses II seated in the temple of Luxor beside his little wife barely reaching his hip. An hour later we knocked at the door of the studio, full of expectations. We were ushered in by the Giant himself with great precaution through a lilliputian paper vestibule into his salon where we were cordially invited to partake of the refreshments and sit in turn on his chair. His friend Skornberg – you may have seen his full-size portrait in the Salon that year, easy to remember for he was the tiniest hunchback I have ever seen – proposed the health of our host. Raising his glass with an enthusiastic wave of his hand he happened to knock down the partition wall, revealing to our marvelling eyes the bridal chamber with the nuptial couch, adapted with skilful hands out of the packing case of a Bechstein Concert grand. While Skornberg was finishing his speech without further accidents the Giant rebuilt rapidly the partition wall with a couple of 'Figaros.' Then he lifted a curtain and showed us, with a cunning glance at his blushing bride, still another room, built of 'Le Petit Journal' – it was the nursery.

We left the paper house an hour later to meet for supper in the Brasserie Montmartre. I had to see some patients first, it was nearly midnight when I joined the party. In the centre of the big room sat my friends all red in their faces singing at the tops of their voices the Swedish Anthem in a deafening chorus, interpolated with solos of thunder from the Giant's broad breast and the shrill piping of the little hunchback. As I was making my way through the crowded room a voice called out: 'A la porte les Prussiens! A la porte les Prussiens!' A beer glass flew over my head and struck the Giant straight in the face. Streaming with blood he sprang from his seat, seized the wrong Frenchman by the collar and tossed him like a tennis ball across the counter into the lap of the proprietor, who screamed at the top of his voice: 'La police! La police!' A second bock struck me on the nose, smashing my eyeglasses, and another bock hurled Skornberg under the table. 'Throw them out! Throw them out!' roared the whole brasserie closing on us. The Giant with a chair in each hand mowed down his assailants like ripe corn, the little hunchback flew out from under the table screaming and biting like an infuriated monkey till another bock knocked him senseless on the floor. The Giant picked him up, patted his best friend on the back and holding him tight under one arm he covered as best as he could our inevitable retreat towards the door where we were seized by half-a-dozen policemen and escorted to the Commissariat in Rue Douai. After having given our names and addresses we were locked up in a room with bars before the windows, we were *au violon*. After two hours of meditation we were brought before the Brigadier who, addressing me in a rough voice, asked if I was Doctor Munthe of Avenue de Villiers. I said I was. Looking at my nose swollen to twice its size and my torn bloodstained clothes he said I did not look like it. He asked me if I had anything to say since I seemed to be the least drunk of this band of German savages and besides the only one who seemed to speak French. I told him we were a peaceful Swedish wedding party who had been brutally assailed in the brasserie, no doubt being mistaken for Germans. As the interrogation went on his voice became less stern and he glanced now and then with something like admiration at the Giant with the half-unconscious little Skornberg like a child in his lap. At last he said with true French gallantry that it would indeed be a pity to keep a bride waiting the whole night for such a magnificent specimen of a bridegroom, and that he would let us off for the present pending the inquiry. We thanked him profusely and stood up to go. To my horror he said to me:

'Please remain, I have to talk to you.' He looked again at his papers, consulted a register on the table and said sternly:

'You have given a false name, I warn you it is a very serious offence. To show you my good will I give you another chance to retract your statement to the police. Who are you?'

I said I was Doctor Munthe.

'I can prove you are not,' he answered severely. 'Look at this,' he said, pointing to the register. 'Doctor Munthe of Avenue de Villiers is Chevalier de la Légion d'Honneur, I can see plenty of red spots on your coat but I can see no red ribbon.'

I said I did not often wear it. Looking at his empty buttonhole he said with a hearty laugh that he had yet to live to learn that there existed a man in France who had the red ribbon and did not wear it. I suggested sending for my concierge to identify me, he answered me it was unnecessary, it was a case to be dealt with by the Commissaire de Police himself in the morning. He rang the bell.

'Search him,' he said to the two policemen.

I protested indignantly and said he had no right to have me

searched. He said it was not only his right, it was, according to the police regulations, his duty for my own protection. The depôt was crowded with all sorts of ruffians, he could not guarantee that any valuables in my possession might not be stolen from me. I said I had no valuables in my pockets except a small sum of money which I handed him.

'Search him,' he repeated.

There was plenty of strength in me in those days, two policemen had to hold me while a third was searching me. Two gold repeaters, two old Breguet watches, and an English hunting watch were found in my pockets.

Not a word was said to me, I was immediately locked up in an evil-smelling cell. I sank down on the mattress wondering what would happen next. The right thing was of course to insist on communicating with the Swedish Legation, but I decided to wait till next morning. The door opened to let in a sinister-looking individual half Apache, half souteneur, who made me understand at a glance the wisdom of the prison regulations to have me searched.

'Cheer up, Charlie,' said the new-comer, 'on t'a pincé, eh? Don't look so dejected, never mind, you will be restored to society in twelve months if you are lucky, and surely you must be lucky or you would never have grabbed five watches in one single day. Five watches! Fichtre! I take my hat off to you, there is nothing like you English!'

I said that I was not English and that I was a collector of watches. He said so was he. He threw himself on the other mattress, wished me good night and pleasant dreams and was snoring in a minute. From the other side of the partition wall a drunken woman started singing in a hoarse voice. He growled angrily:

'Shut up, Fifine, ou je te casserai la gueule!' The singer stopped immediately and whispered:

'Alphonse, I have something important to tell you. Are you alone?' He answered he was with a charming young friend who was anxious to know what o'clock it was as he had unfortunately forgotten to wind up the five watches he was always carrying in his pockets. He soon fell asleep again, the babel of the ladies' voices gradually died away and all was still except for the coming of the guard every hour to look at us through the guichet. As the clock struck seven in St. Augustin, I was taken out of the cell and brought before the Commissaire de Police himself. He listened attentively to my adventure fixing me with his intelligent penetrating eyes the whole time. When I came to telling him of my mania for clocks and watches, that I had been on my way to Le Roy the whole day to have these five watches overhauled and had forgotten all about them when I was searched, he burst into laughter and said it was the best story he had ever heard, it was pure Balzac. He opened a drawer of the writing-table and handed me my five watches.

'I have not been sitting at this table for twenty years without learning something about classifying my visitors, you are all right.' He rang the bell for the Brigadier who had locked me up for the night.

'You are suspended for a week for having disobeyed the regulations to communicate with the Swedish Consul. Vous êtes un imbécile!'

XIII

Mamsell Agata

The old grandfather clock in the hall struck half-past seven as I entered Avenue de Villiers silently as a ghost. It was the hour when punctually to the minute Mamsell Agata started to rub the patina off my old refectory table in the dining-room, there was a fair chance to reach in safety my bedroom, my only harbour of refuge. The rest of the house was all in the hands of Mamsell Agata. Silent and restless as a mongoose she used to move about from room to room the whole day, a dust towel in her hand, in search of something to scrub or a torn letter to pick up from the floor. I stopped annihilated as I opened the door of my consulting-room. Mamsell Agata stood bending over the writing-table examining my morning mail. She lifted her head, her white eyes stared in grim silence at my torn, bloodstained clothes, for once her lipless mouth did not find immediately the right unpleasant word.

'Good heavens, where has he been?' she hissed at last. She always used to call me 'he' when she was angry, alas! she seldom called me anything else.

'I have had a street accident,' said I. I had long ago taken to lying to Mamsell Agata in legitimate self-defence. She examined my rags with the scrutinizing eye of the connoisseur, always on the look-out for anything to patch, to darn or to mend. I thought her voice sounded a little kinder as she ordered me to hand her my whole outfit at once. I slunk into my bedroom, had a bath, Rosalie brought me my coffee, nobody could make a cup of coffee like Mamsell Agata.

'Pauvre Monsieur,' said Rosalie as I handed her my clothes to be taken to Mamsell Agata, 'I hope you are not hurt?'

'No,' said I, 'I am only afraid.'

Rosalie and I had no secrets from one another in what concerned Mamsell Agata, we both lived in deadly fear of her, we were comrades in arms in our daily defenceless battle for life. Rosalie, whose real profession was that of a charwoman, had come to my rescue the day the cook had bolted, and now since the housemaid had also cleared out she had remained with me as a sort of bonne à tout faire. The cook I was very sorry to lose but I soon had to admit that I had never eaten a better dinner than since Mamsell Agata had taken possession of the kitchen. The departed housemaid, a sturdy Bretonne, had also been much to my liking, she had always scrupulously observed our agreement that she should never go near my writing-table and never touch the antique furniture. A week after Mamsell Agata's arrival she had shown signs of declining health, her hands had begun to tremble, she had dropped my finest old Faenza vase, and soon after she had fled in such a hurry that she had even forgotten to take her aprons with her. The very day of her departure Mamsell Agata had set to work rubbing and scrubbing my dainty Louis XVI chairs, beating mercilessly my priceless Persian rugs with a hard stick, washing the pale marble face of my Florentine Madonna with soap and water, she had even succeeded in getting off the wonderful lustre of the Gubbio vase on the writing-table. If Mamsell Agata had been born four hundred years ago no trace of mediaeval art would have remained to-day. But how long ago was she born? She looked exactly the same as when I had seen her as a boy in my old home in Sweden. My elder brother had inherited her when the old home broke up. A man of exceptional courage as he is, he had succeeded in getting rid of her and handing her over to me. Mamsell Agata was the very thing for me, he had written, there never was a housekeeper like her. He was right there. Ever since, I in my turn had tried to get rid of her. I used to invite my bachelor friends and stray acquaintances for luncheon, they all said I was lucky indeed to have such a wonderful cook. I told them I was going to get married, that Mamsell Agata only liked bachelors and was looking out for another place. They were all very interested and wanted to see her. That settled it, they never wanted to see her again if they could help it. To describe what she looked like is beyond me. She had thin golden locks arranged in a sort of early Victorian fashion – Rosalie said it was a wig but I do not know. An exceptionally high and narrow forehead, no eyebrows, small white eyes and hardly any face at all, only a long hook nose overhanging a narrow slit which seldom opened to show a row of long pointed teeth like those of a ferret. The colour of her face and her fingers was a cadaverous blue, the touch of her hand was slimy and cold like that of a corpse. Her smile – no, I think I won't tell you what her smile was like, it was what Rosalie and I feared most. Mamsell Agata only spoke Swedish but quarrelled fluently in French and English. I believe she must have ended by understanding a little French or she would not have picked up all she seemed to know about my patients. I often found her listening behind the door of my consulting-room especially when I received ladies. She had a great liking for dead people, she always seemed more cheerful when one of my patients was on the point of dying, she seldom failed to appear on the balcony when a funeral passed down Avenue de Villiers. She hated children, she never forgave Rosalie for having given a piece of the Christmas cake to the children of the concierge. She hated my dog, she always went about blowing Keating's flea-powder on the carpets and started scratching herself as soon as she saw me, in sign of protestation. My dog hated her from the very first, perhaps because of the most peculiar smell which radiated from her whole person. It reminded me of the odeur de souris of Balzac's Coúsin Pons but with a special blend of her own I have only noticed once in my life. That was when many years later I entered an abandoned tomb in the Valley of the Kings at Thebes full of hundreds of large bats hanging in black clusters from its walls.

Mamsell Agata never left the house except on Sundays when she sat all by herself in a pew in the Swedish church Boulevard Ornano, praying to the God of Wrath. The pew was always empty, nobody dared to sit near her, my friend the Swedish chaplain told me that the first time he put the bread in her mouth during the Holy Communion she glared at him so savagely that he was afraid she might bite off his finger.

Rosalie had lost all her former cheerfulness, she looked thin and wretched, spoke of going to live with her married sister in Touraine. Of course it was easier for me, who was away the whole day. As soon as I returned home all the strength seemed to go out of my body, and a deadly grey weariness to fall over my thoughts like dust. Since I had discovered that Mamsell Agata was a sleep-walker, my nights had become still more agitated and restless, I often thought I smelt her even in my bedroom. At last I opened my heart to Flygare, the Swedish chaplain, who was a frequent visitor to my house and had, I think, a vague suspicion of the terrible truth.

'Why don't you send her away,' said the chaplain one day, 'you cannot go on like this, really I am beginning to believe that you are afraid of her. If you haven't the courage to send her away, I will do it for you.'

I offered him a thousand francs for his church fund if he could send her away.

'I shall give notice to Mamsell Agata to-night, don't worry, come to the sacristy to-morrow after service and you will have good news.'

There was no service in the Swedish church the next day, the chaplain had been taken suddenly ill the evening before, too late for finding a substitute. I went at once to his house Place des Ternes, his wife said she was just going to send for me. The chaplain had returned home the evening before in an almost fainting condition, he looked as if he had seen a ghost, said his wife.

Perhaps he has seen one, thought I, as I went to his room. He said he had just begun to tell Mamsell Agata his errand, he had expected her to be very angry but instead of that she had only smiled at him. Suddenly he noticed a most peculiar smell in the room, he felt as if he was going to faint, he was sure it was the smell.

'No,' said I, 'it was the smile.'

I ordered him to remain in bed till I called again, he asked what on earth was the matter with him, I said I did not know – this was not true, I knew quite well, I recognized the symptoms.

'By the bye,' said I, as I stood up to go, 'I wish you would tell me something about Lazarus, you who are a chaplain surely know more about him than I do. Isn't there an old legend. . ∴.'

'Lazarus,' said the chaplain in a feeble voice, 'was the man who returned alive to his dwelling house from his grave where for three days and nights he had lain under the sway of death. There is no doubt about the miracle, he was seen by Mary and Martha and many of his former friends.'

'I wonder what he looked like?'

'The legend says that the destruction wrought by death on his body, arrested by miraculous power, was still apparent in the cadaverous blueness of his face and his long fingers, cold with the cold of death; his dark finger nails had grown immeasurably long, the rank odour of the grave still hung to his clothes. As Lazarus advanced among the crowd that had gathered to welcome him back to life, their joyous words of greeting died on their lips, a terrible shadow descended like dust over their thoughts. One by one they fled away, their souls benumbed by fear.'

As the chaplain recited the old legend his voice grew weaker and weaker, he tossed uneasily in his bed, his face grew white as the pillow under his head.

'Are you sure that Lazarus is the only one who has risen from the grave,' said I, 'are you sure that he had not a sister?'

The chaplain put his hands over his face with a shriek of terror.

On the stairs I met Colonel Staaff the Swedish military attaché who just came to inquire about the chaplain. The Colonel invited me to drive home with him, he wanted to speak to me on urgent business. The Colonel had served with great distinction in the French army during the war of '70 and had been wounded at Gravelotte. He had married a French lady and was a great favourite in Paris society.

'You know,' said the Colonel, as we sat down to tea, 'you know I am your friend and more than twice your age, you must not take amiss what I am going to tell you in your own interest. Both my wife and I have often heard of late complaints about you for the tyrannical sort of way you treat your patients. Nobody likes to have the words discipline and obedience constantly thrown into their faces. Ladies, specially French ladies, are not accustomed to such rough handling by a young fellow like you, they already call you Tiberius as a nickname. The worst of it is that I fear it seems as natural to you to command as you imagine it is natural to others to obey. You are mistaken, my young friend, nobody likes to obey, everybody likes to command.'

'I disagree, most people, and almost all women, like to obey.'

'Wait till you get married,' said my gallant friend with a furtive glance towards the door of the sitting-room.

'Now to a far more serious matter,' the Colonel went on. 'There is a rumour going about, that you are very careless as to appearances in regard to your private life, that there is a mysterious woman living with you in the assumed position of your housekeeper. Even the wife of the English Consul hinted something of the sort to my wife who defended you most energetically. What would the Swedish Minister and his wife, who treat you as if you were their own son, say if they got hold of this rumour, which they are sure to do sooner or later? I tell you, my friend, this won't do for a doctor in your position with lots of ladies, English and French, coming to consult you. I repeat this won't do! If you must indulge in a mistress, go ahead! It is your affair, but for Heaven's sake get her out of your house, not even the French can stand such a scandal!'

I thanked the Colonel, I said he was quite right, that I had often tried to get her out of my house but had not had the strength.

'I know it is not easy,' admitted the Colonel, 'I have been young myself. If you haven't got the courage to get her out of the house, I will help you! I am your man, I have never been afraid of anybody, man or woman, I have charged the Prussians at Gravelotte, I have faced death in six big battles. . . .'

'Wait till you face Mamsell Agata Svenson,' said I.

'You don't mean to say she is Swedish? So much the better, if it comes to the worst I shall have her turned out of France by the legation. I shall be at Avenue de Villiers to-morrow morning at ten, be sure to be there.'

'No thank you, not I, I never go near her when I can help it.'

'Et pourtant tu couches avec elle,' ejaculated the Colonel, looking stupefied at me.

I was just on the point of going to be sick on his carpet when he handed me a stiff brandy and soda in time and I reeled out of the house after having accepted his invitation for dinner next day to celebrate the victory.

I dined alone with Madame Staaff the next day. The Colonel was not very well, I was to go and see him after dinner, the old wound from Gravelotte was troubling him again, thought his wife. The gallant Colonel was lying on his bed with a cold compress on the top of his head, he looked very old and feeble, there was a vacant expression in his eyes I had never seen before.

'Did she smile?' I asked him.

He shuddered as he stretched his hand towards his brandy and soda.

'Did you notice the long black hook on her thumb nail, like the hook of a bat?'

He grew pale and wiped the perspiration from his forehead

'What shall I do?' I said dejectedly, my head between my two hands.

'There is only one possible escape for you,' answered the Colonel in a weak voice, 'get married or you will take to drink.'

XIV

Vicomte Maurice

I did not get married and I did not take to drink. I took to something else; I abandoned Avenue de Villiers altogether. Rosalie brought my tea and my 'Figaro' to my bedroom at seven o'clock, half-an-hour later I was off not to return till two o'clock for my consultation. I was off again with my last patient to come back late at night to creep to my bedroom stealthily as a thief. Rosalie's wages had been doubled. She stuck bravely to her post, she only complained of having nothing to do but to open the door. Everything else, the beating of the carpets, the mending of my clothes, the cleaning of my boots, the washing of my linen, the cooking of my food was done by Mamsell Agata. Realizing the necessity of a liaison between herself and the outer world and the need of somebody at hand to quarrel with, Mamsell Agata now tolerated Rosalie's presence with grim resignation. She had even smiled at her once, said Rosalie with a slight trembling in her voice. Soon Tom also took to abandoning Avenue de Villiers for fear of Mamsell Agata. He spent his days driving about with me visiting patients, he seldom had a meal at home, he never went into the kitchen as all dogs love to do. As soon as he returned from his day's work, he slunk to his basket in my bedroom where he knew he was in relative safety. As my practice increased it became more and more difficult to snatch time for our usual Sunday afternoon romp in the Bois de Boulogne. Dogs as well as men must have an occasional sniff at Mother Earth to keep up their spirits. There is nothing like a brisk walk among friendly trees be it even the half-tamed trees of the Bois de Boulogne, and an occasional game of hide and seek among the thickets with a stray acquaintance. One day, as we were strolling down a side alley enjoying each other's company, we suddenly heard far behind us a desperate panting and wheezing accompanied by fits of coughing and choking. I thought it was a case of asthma but Tom diagnosed it at once as a case of a half-suffocated small bulldog or pug approaching at full speed and imploring us with his last breath to wait for him. A minute later Loulou sank down half-dead at my feet, too fat to breathe, too exhausted to speak, his black tongue almost fallen out from his mouth, his blood-shot eyes protruding from their sockets with joy and emotion.

'Loulou! Loulou!' a despairing voice screamed from a coupé driving past on the high road.

'Loulou! Loulou!' called out a footman running towards us behind the thickets. The footman said he was escorting the Marquise and Loulou on their usual five minute constitutional by the side of the carriage when Loulou suddenly began to sniff furiously in all directions and cantered off with such a speed through the bushes that he was lost sight of at once. The Marquise had been put back in the carriage by her maid in a fainting condition, he himself had been hunting for Loulou for half-an-hour while the coachman was driving up and down the high road asking every passer-by for news of Loulou. The Marquise burst into a flood of tears of joy when I deposited Loulou on her lap, still speechless for want of breath. He was going to have an apoplectic stroke, she sobbed. I roared into the ear trumpet that it was only emotion. The truth was that he was as near having a stroke as a fat old pug can be. Being the involuntary cause of it all, I accepted the invitation of his mistress to have tea with her. When Tom jumped on my lap, Loulou had a fit of rage that nearly suffocated him. The rest of the drive he lay motionless on his mistress' lap in a state of complete collapse, glaring savagely at Tom with one eye and blinking affectionately at me with the other.

'I have smelt many things in my life,' said the eye, 'but I have never forgotten your own most particular smell, I like it much better than the smell of anybody else. What a joy to have found you at last! Do take me on your lap instead of that black mongrel. No fear, I shall settle his account as soon as I get a breath of air!'

'Never mind what you say, snub-nosed little monster,' said Tom loftily. 'I never saw such a sight, it almost makes one ashamed of being a dog! A champion poodle like me does not growl at a sausage, but you had better hold your black tongue lest it should drop out of your ugly mouth altogether.'

After our second cup of tea Monsieur l'Abbé entered the drawing-room for his usual afternoon call. The kind Abbé reproached me for not having let him know of my return to Paris. The Count had often inquired about me and would be delighted to see me. The Countess had gone to Monte Carlo for a change of air. The Countess was now in excellent health and spirits. Unfortunately he could not say the same in regard to the Count, who had returned to his sedentary life, spending the whole day in his arm-chair smoking his cigars. The Abbé thought he had better warn me that the Vicomte Maurice was furious with me for having played such a joke upon him at Château Rameaux. I had hypnotized both him and the little village doctor into the belief that he had colitis in order to prevent him from gaining the Gold Medal at the shooting competition of the Société du Tir de France. The Abbé implored me to keep out of his way, he was known for his violent, uncontrollable temper, he was always quarrelling with people, not later than a month ago he had fought another duel, God knows what might happen if we met.

'Nothing would happen,' said I. 'I have nothing to fear from this brute, for he is afraid of me. I proved last autumn in the smoking-room of the Château Rameaux that I was the stronger of the two and I am glad to hear from you that he has not forgotten his lesson. His one superiority over me is that he can drop a swallow or a sky-lark with his revolver at fifty yards while I should probably miss an elephant at the same distance. But he is not likely ever to take advantage of this superiority of his, he would never challenge me for he considers me his social inferior. You mentioned the word hypnotism, well I am getting sick of the very word, it is constantly thrown in my face because I have been a pupil of Charcot's. Understand once for all that all this nonsense about hypnotic power is an exploded theory denied by modern science. It is not a case of hyp-notism, it is a case of imagination. This fool imagines that I have hypnotized him, it is not I who have put this silly idea in his head, he has done it all by himself, we call it auto-suggestion. So much the better for me. It makes him powerless to harm me at least face to face.'

'But could you hypnotize him if you wanted to do so?'

'Yes, easily, he is an excellent subject, Charcot would be delighted to demonstrate him at his Tuesday lectures at the Salpêtrière.'

'Since you say that there is no such thing as hypnotic power, do you mean to say that I for instance could make him obey my orders as he obeyed yours?'

'Yes, granted he believed that you possessed this power, which he certainly does not believe.'

'Why not?'

'The real difficulty begins here, a satisfactory answer to your question cannot be given to-day. This is a relatively new science, still in its infancy.'

'Could you make him commit a crime?'

'Not unless he was capable of committing such a crime of his own initiative. Since I am convinced that this man has criminal instincts, the answer is in this particular case in the affirmative.'

'Could you make him give up the Countess?'

'Not unless he wished it himself and submitted to a methodic treatment by hypnotic suggestion. Even so it would take considerable time, the sexual instinct being the strongest force in human nature.'

'Promise me to keep out of his way, he says he is going to horsewhip you the first time he meets you.'

'He is welcome to try, I know how to deal with such an emergency, don't worry. I am quite capable of taking care of myself.'

'Luckily he is with his regiment at Tours and not likely to return to Paris for a long time.'

'My dear Abbé, you are far more naïve than I thought, he is actually in Monte Carlo with the Countess and will be back in Paris when she returns from her change of air.'

The very next day I was asked to see the Count professionally. The Abbé was right, I found the Count in a very unsatisfactory condition both physically and mentally. You cannot do much for an elderly gentleman who sits in his arm-chair the whole day smoking endless cigars, thinking of nothing but his beautiful young wife who has gone to Monte Carlo for a change of air. Neither can you do much for him when she returns to resume her position as one of the most admired and coveted ladies of the Paris society, spending her days at Worth's trying on new gowns and her evenings at theatres and balls, after a frosty kiss of good night on her husband's cheek. The more I saw of the Count the more I liked him, he was the most perfect type of a French aristocrat of the old régime I had ever seen. The real reason why I liked him was no doubt because I felt sorry for him. It had not dawned upon me in those days that the only people I really liked were those I felt sorry for. I suppose that was why I did not like the Countess the first time I saw her again after our last meeting under the lime-tree in the park of the Château Rameaux when the moon was full and the owl saved me from liking her too much. No, I did not like her at all as I sat watching her by the side of the Abbé, across the dining-room table, laughing merrily at the silly jokes of Vicomte Maurice, some of them about myself, I gathered from his insolent side-glances. Neither of them said a single word to me. The only sign of recognition I had received from the Countess was an absent-minded handshake before dinner. The Vicomte had ignored my presence altogether. The Countess was as beautiful as ever but she was not the same woman. She looked in splendid health and spirits, the yearning expression in her large eyes was no more there. I saw at the first glance that there had been full moon in the park of Monte Carlo and no warning owls in the lime-trees. The Vicomte Maurice looked exceedingly pleased with himself, there was an unmistakable air of the conquering hero in his whole bearing which was particularly irritating.

'Ça y est,' said I to the Abbé as we sat down in the smoking-room after dinner. 'Surely love is blind, if this is to be called love. She deserved a better fate than to fall into the arms of this degenerate fool.'

'Do you know that it is not a month ago since the Count paid his gambling debts in order to save him from being cashiered from the army, there is also a rumour about a dishonoured cheque. They say he is spending fabulous sums on a famous cocotte. To think that this is the man who is going to take the Countess to the Bal Masqué of the Opera to-night.'

'I wish I could shoot.'

'For Heaven's sake do not speak like that, I wish you would go away, he is sure to come here for his brandy and soda.'

'He had better be careful with his brandies and sodas, did you not notice how his hand was trembling when he dropped his patent medicine into his wine-glass. At any rate it is a good omen for the swallows and the skylarks. Don't look so uneasily at the door, he is having a good time making love to the Countess in the drawing-room. I am besides going away, my carriage is at the door.'

I went upstairs to see the Count a moment before leaving, he was already going to bed, he said he was very sleepy, lucky man! As I was wishing him good night I heard the desperate howling of a dog from below. I knew that Tom was waiting for me in the hall in his usual corner by a standing invitation from the Count who was a great lover of dogs and had even provided him with a special little carpet for his comfort. I sprang downstairs as fast as I could. Tom was lying huddling against the front door groaning feebly, blood was flowing from his mouth. Bent over him stood Vicomte Maurice kicking him furiously. I fell on the brute so unexpectedly that he lost his balance and rolled on the floor. A second well-aimed blow knocked him down again as he was springing to his feet. Snatching my hat and my coat I sprang with the dog in my arms to my carriage and drove full speed to Avenue de Villiers. It was evident from the

171

first that the poor dog was suffering from severe internal injuries. I sat up with him the whole night, his breathing became more and more difficult, the haemorrhage never ceased. In the morning I shot my faithful friend with my own hands to spare him further sufferings.

It was a relief to me when I received in the afternoon a letter from two of Vicomte Maurice's fellow officers with a request to be put in communication with my seconds, the Vicomte having decided after some hesitation to do me the honour etc, etc.

I succeeded with difficulty in persuading Colonel Staaff, the Swedish military attaché, to see me through this business. My friend Edelfeld, the well-known Finnish painter, was to be my other second. Norstrom was to assist me as surgeon.

'Never in my life have I had such luck as these last twenty-four hours,' said I to Norstrom as we were sitting at dinner at our usual table in Café de la Régence. 'To tell you the truth I was terribly afraid that I was going to be afraid. Instead of that my curiosity to know how I was going to face the music has occupied my thoughts so constantly, that I have had no time to think of anything else. You know how interested I am in psychology.'

Norstrom was evidently not in the least interested in psychology that evening, besides he never was. He was unusually silent and solemn, I noticed a certain tender expression in his dull eyes which made me feel almost ashamed of myself.

'Listen, Axel,' he said in a somewhat husky voice, 'listen. . . .'

'Don't look at me like that, and above all don't be sentimental, it doesn't suit your style of beauty. Scratch your silly old head and try to understand the situation. How can you imagine for a moment that I should be such a fool as to face this savage to-morrow morning in the Bois de St. Cloud if I did not know that he cannot kill me. The idea is too absurd to be considered for a moment. These French duels are besides a mere farce, you know it as well as I do. We have both of us assisted as doctors at more than one of these performances where the actors now and then hit a tree but never each other. Do let us have a bottle of Chambertin and go straight to bed, Burgundy makes me sleepy, I have hardly had any sleep since my poor dog died, I must sleep to-night at any cost.'

The morning was cold and misty. My pulse was steady at eighty but I noticed a curious twitching in the calves of my legs and a considerable difficulty in speaking, and try as I might I did not succeed in swallowing the drop of brandy Norstrom handed me from his pocket-flask as we stepped out from the. carriage. The endless preliminary formalities seemed particularly irritating to me since I did not understand a word of what they were talking about. How silly all this is and what a waste of time, thought I, how much simpler would it not be to give him a sound thrashing *à l'anglaise* and be done with it! Somebody said that the mist had now lifted sufficiently to allow a clear sight. I was surprised to hear it, for it seemed to me that the fog was thicker than ever. Still I could see quite well Vicomte Maurice standing in front of me with his usual air of insolent nonchalance, a cigarette between his lips, very much at his ease, thought I. At that very moment a redbreast started singing from the thicket behind me, I was just wondering what on earth the little fellow had to do so late in the year in the Bois de St. Cloud, when Colonel Staaff put a long pistol in my hand.

'Aim low!' he whispered.

'Fire!' a sharp voice called out.

I heard a shot. I saw the Vicomte letting fall his cigarette from his lips and Professor Labbé rushing up to him. A moment later I found myself sitting in Colonel Staaff's carriage with Norstrom on the opposite seat, a broad grin on his face. The Colonel patted me on the shoulder but nobody spoke.

'What has happened, why didn't he shoot? I am not going to accept any mercy from this brute, I am going to challenge him in my turn, I am going to. . . .'

'You are going to do nothing of the sort, you are going to thank God for your miraculous escape,' interrupted the Colonel. 'Indeed he tried his best to kill you and no doubt he would have done so had you given him time for a second shot. Luckily you fired simultaneously. Had you waited the fraction of a second you would not be sitting by my side now. Didn't you hear the bullet whizzing over your head? Look!'

Suddenly as I looked at my hat the curtain went down over my performance as a hero. Stripped of his ill-fitting make-up as a brave man, the real man appeared, the man who was afraid of death. Shaking with fear I sank back in my corner of the carriage.

'I am proud of you, my young friend,' the Colonel went on. 'It did my old soldier's heart good to watch you, I could not have done it better myself! When we charged the Prussians at Gravelotte. . . .'

The chattering of my teeth prevented me from catching the end of the sentence. I felt sick and faint, I wanted to tell Norstrom to let down the window for a breath of air but I could not articulate a word. I wanted to fling open the door and bolt like a rabbit but I could move neither arms nor legs.

'He was losing lots of blood,' chuckled Norstrom, 'Professor Labbé said the bullet had passed clean through the base of the right lung, he will be a lucky man if he escapes with two months in bed.'

The chattering of my teeth ceased instantly, I listened attentively.

'I did not know you were such a fine shot,' said the gallant Colonel. 'Why did you tell me you had never handled a pistol before?'

Suddenly I burst into a roar of laughter, I did not in the least know why.

'There is no cause for laughter,' said the Colonel sternly, 'the man is dangerously wounded, Professor Labbé looked very grave, it may end in a tragedy.'

'So much the worse for him,' said I, miraculously regaining my power of speech, 'he kicked my defenceless old dog to death, he spends his leisure hours killing swallows and skylarks, he deserves all he gets. Do you know that the Areopagus of Athens pronounced a death sentence on a boy for having stung out the eyes of a bird?'

'But you are not the Areopagus of Athens.'

'No, but neither am I the cause of this man's death if it comes to the worst. I had not even time to take aim at him, the pistol went off all by itself. It was not I who sent this bullet through his lung, it was somebody else. Besides, since you are so sorry for this brute, may I ask if it was in order to miss him that you whispered in my ear to aim low when you handed me the pistol?'

'I am glad to hear you have got your tongue back in its right place, you old swaggerer,' smiled the Colonel. 'I could hardly understand a word you said when I dragged you into my carriage nor did you yourself, I am sure, you went on muttering the whole time something about a redbreast.'

When we entered Porte Maillot I had already resumed full command over my silly nerves and was feeling very pleased with myself. As we approached Avenue de Villiers, Mamsell Agata's Medusa face loomed out of the morning mist, staring menacingly at me with her white eyes. I looked at my watch, it was half-past seven, my courage rose.

'She is just now rubbing the patina off the refectory table in the dining-room,' thought I. 'Another bit of luck and I shall manage to slink unnoticed into my bedroom and signal to Rosalie to bring me my cup of tea.'

Rosalie came on tiptoe with my breakfast and my 'Figaro.'

'Rosalie, you are a brick! For Heaven's sake keep her out of the hall, I mean to slip out in half-an-hour. Good Rosalie, just give me a brush-up before you go, I need it badly.'

'But really Monsieur cannot go about visiting his patients in this old hat, look! there is a round hole in front and here is another behind, how funny! It cannot be made by a moth, the whole house is stinking with naphthaline ever since Mamsell Agata came. Can it be a rat? Mamsell Agata's room is full of rats, Mamsell Agata likes rats.'

'No, Rosalie, it is the death-watch beetle, it has got teeth as hard as steel and can make just such a hole in a man's skull as well as in his hat, if luck is not on his side.'

'Why does not Monsieur give the hat to old Don Gaetano, the organ grinder, it is his day for coming and playing under the balcony to-day.'

'You are welcome to give him any hat you like but not this one, I mean to keep it, it does me good to look at those two holes, it means luck.'

'Why does not Monsieur go about in a top-hat like the other doctors, it is much more chic.'

'It is not the hat that makes the man but the head. My head is all right as long as you keep Mamsell Agata out of my sight.'

XV

John

I sat down to my breakfast and my 'Figaro.' Nothing very interesting. Suddenly my eyes fell on the following notice under the big headlines: AN UGLY BUSINESS.

'Madame Réquin, sage-femme de première classe, Rue Granet, has been arrested in connection with the death of a young girl under suspicious circumstances. There is also an order of arrest against a foreign doctor who has it is feared already left the country. Madame Réquin is also accused for having caused the disappearance of a number of new-born children confided to her care.'

The paper fell from my hand. Madame Réquin, sage-femme de première classe, Rue Granet! I had been surrounded with so much suffering, so many tragedies had been enacted before my eyes during these last years that I had forgotten the whole affair. As I sat there staring at the notice in the 'Figaro' it all came back to me as vividly as had it happened yesterday instead of three years ago, the dreadful night when I had made the acquaintance of Madame Réquin. As I sat sipping my tea and reading the notice in the 'Figaro' over and over again, I felt greatly pleased to know that this horrible woman had been caught at last. I felt equally pleased at the recollection that in that unforgettable night it had been granted to me to save two lives, the life of a mother and the life of a child from being murdered by her and her ignoble accomplice. Suddenly another thought flashed through my head. What had I done for these two lives I had caused to live? What had I done for this mother already abandoned by another man in the hour she needed him most?

'John! John!' she had called out under the chloroform with a ring of despair. 'John! John!'

Had I done better than he? Had not I also abandoned her in the hour she needed me most? What agonies must she not have gone through before she fell in the hands of this terrible woman and this brutal colleague of mine, who would have murdered her had it not been for me? What agonies had she not gone through when her awakening consciousness brought her back to the ghastly reality of her surroundings. And the half-asphyxiated child who had looked at me with his blue eyes as he drew his first breath with the life-giving air I had breathed into his lungs, my lips to his lips! What had I done for him? I had snatched him from the arms of merciful death to throw him in the arms of Madame Réquin! How many new-born babies had not already sucked death from her enormous bosom? What had she done with the blue-eyed little boy? Was he among the eighty per cent of the helpless little travellers in the 'train des nourrices' who according to official statistics succumbed during the first year of their life, or among the remaining twenty per cent who survived to perhaps an even worse fate?

An hour later I had applied and obtained from the prison authorities the permission to visit Madame Réquin. She recognized me at once and gave me such a warm welcome that I felt very uncomfortable indeed before the prison official who had accompanied me to her cell.

The boy was in Normandy and very happy, she had just received excellent news about him from his foster parents who loved him tenderly. Unfortunately she could not lay her hands on their address, there had been some confusion in her register. It was just possible, though not likely, that her husband might remember their address.

I felt sure the boy was dead but to leave nothing undone I said sternly that unless I received the address of the foster parents in forty-eight hours I would denounce her to the authorities for child murder and also for the theft of a valuable diamond brooch left in her custody by me. She managed to squeeze a few tears from her cold glittering eyes and swore that she had not stolen the brooch, she had kept it as a souvenir from this lovely young lady whom she had nursed as tenderly as if she had been her own daughter.

'You have forty-eight hours,' said I, leaving Madame Réquin to her meditations.

The morning of the second day I received the visit of Madame Réquin's worthy husband with the pawn ticket of the brooch and the names of three villages in Normandy where Madame used to dispatch her babies that year. I wrote at once to the three maires of the respective villages with a request to find out if a blue-eyed boy about three years old were among the adoptive children in their villages. After a long delay I received negative answers from two of the maires, no answer from the third. I then wrote to the three curés of these villages and after months of waiting the curé of Villeroy informed me that he had discovered with a shoemaker's wife a little boy who might answer to my description. He had arrived from Paris three years ago and certainly he had blue eyes.

I had never been in Normandy, it was Christmas time and I thought I deserved a little holiday. It was actually on Christmas Day I knocked at the door of the shoemaker. No answer. I entered a dusky room with the shoemaker's low table by the window, muddy and worn-out boots and shoes of all sizes strewn over the floor, some newly washed shirts and petticoats were hanging to dry on a rope across the ceiling. The bed had not been made up, the sheets and the blankets looked indescribably dirty. On the stone floor of the evil-smelling kitchen sat a half-naked little child eating a raw potato. He gave me a terrified look from his blue eyes, dropped his potato, lifted instinctively his emaciated arm as if to avoid a blow and crawled as fast as he could into the other room. I caught him up just as he was creeping under the bed and sat down at the shoemaker's table by the window to examine his teeth. Yes, the boy was about three years and a half I should say, a little skeleton with emaciated arms and legs, a narrow chest and a stomach blown up to twice its proper size. He sat absolutely still on my lap, he did not utter a sound even when I opened his mouth to examine his teeth. There was no doubt about the colour of his tired joyless eyes, they were as blue as my own. The door was flung open and with a terrific curse the shoemaker reeled into the room blind drunk. Behind him in the open door stood a woman with a baby at her breast and two small children hanging on to her skirt, staring stupefied at me. The shoemaker said he was damned glad to get rid of the boy, but he must have the overdue money paid down first. He had written several times to Madame Réquin but had had no answer. Did she think he was going to feed that wretched marmot with his own hard earnings? His wife said that now since she had a child of her own and two other children en pension she was only too glad to get rid of the boy. She muttered something to the shoemaker and their eyes wandered attentively from my face to that of the boy. The same terrified look had come back in the boy's eyes as soon as they had entered the room, his little hand I was holding in mine was trembling slightly. Luckily I had remembered in time it was Christmas and I produced a wooden horse from my pocket. He took it in silence, in an uninterested sort of way quite unlike that of a child, he did not seem to care much for it.

'Look,' said the shoemaker's wife, 'what a beautiful horse your

178

papa has brought you from Paris, look, Jules!'

'His name is John,' said I.

'C'est un triste enfant,' said the shoemaker's wife, 'he never says anything, not even "mama," he never smiles.'

I wrapped him up in my travelling rug and went to see Monsieur le Curé who was kind enough to send his housekeeper to buy a woollen shirt and a warm shawl for our journey.

The curé looked at me attentively and said:

'It is my duty as a priest to condemn and chastise immorality and vice, but I cannot refrain from telling you, my young friend, that I respect you for trying at least to atone for your sin, a sin so much the more heinous as the punishment falls on the heads of innocent little children. It was high time to take him away, I have buried dozens of these poor abandoned little babies and I would have buried your boy as well ere long. You have done well, I thank you for it,' said the old curé, tapping me on the shoulder.

We were just on the point of missing the night express for Paris, there was no time for explanations. John slept peacefully the whole night well wrapped in his warm shawl while I sat by his side wondering what on earth I was going to do with him. I really believe that had it not been for Mamsell Agata I would have taken him straight from the station to Avenue de Villiers. I drove instead to the Crèche St. Joseph in Rue de Seine, I knew the nuns well. They promised to keep the boy for twenty-four hours till a suitable home had been found for him. The nuns knew of a respectable family, the husband was working in the Norwegian margarine factory in Pantin, they had just lost their only child. The idea suited me, I drove there at once and the next day the boy was installed in his new home. The woman seemed clever and capable, somewhat quick-tempered I should have thought from the look of her eyes, but the nuns had told me she had been a devoted mother to her own child. She was given the money needed for his outfit and paid three months in advance, less than I spend on my cigarettes. I preferred not to give her my address, God knows what would have happened if Mamsell Agata had got to know of his existence. Joséphine was to report to the nuns if anything went wrong or if the child got ill. It did not take long before she had to report. The boy caught scarlet fever and nearly died. All the Scandinavian children in the Pantin quarter were down with scarlet fever, I had to go there constantly. Children with scarlet fever need no medicine, only careful nursing and a toy for their long convalescence. John got both, for his new foster mother was evidently very kind to him and I had long ago

179

learned to include dolls and wooden horses in my pharmacopoeia.

'He is a strange child,' said Joséphine, 'he never says even "mama," he never smiles, not even when he got the Father Christmas you sent him.'

For it was Christmas once more, the boy had been with his new foster mother a whole year, of toil and worries for me but relative happiness for him. Joséphine was certainly hot-tempered, often impertinent to me when I had to scold her for not keeping the boy tidy or for never opening the window. But I never heard her say a rough word to him, and although I do not think he cared for her I could see by his eyes that he was not afraid of her. He seemed strangely indifferent to everybody and everything. Gradually I became more and more uneasy about him and more dissatisfied with his foster mother. The boy had got back that frightened look in his eyes, and it was evident that Joséphine was neglecting him more and more. I had several rows with her, it generally ended by her saying angrily that if I was not satisfied I had better take him away, she had had more than enough of him. I well understood the reason, she was to become a mother herself. It got much worse after the birth of her own child, I told her at last that I was determined to take the boy away as soon as I had found the right place for him. Warned by experience I was determined there should be no more mistakes about him.

A couple of days later in coming home for my consultation I heard as I opened the front door the angry voice of a woman resounding from my waiting-room. The room was full of people waiting with their usual patience to see me. John sat huddled up in the corner of the sofa next to the wife of the English parson. In the middle of the room stood Joséphine talking at the top of her voice and gesticulating wildly. As soon as she saw me in the doorway she rushed to the sofa, took hold of John and literally threw him at me, I had barely time to catch him in my arms.

'Of course I'm not good enough to look after a young gentleman like you, Master John!' shouted Joséphine, 'you'd better stay with the doctor, I've had enough of his scoldings and all his lies about your being an orphan. One has only to look at your eyes to see who is your father!' She lifted the portière to rush out of the room and nearly fell over Mamsell Agata who shot me a glance from her white eyes that riveted me to the spot. The parson's wife rose from the sofa and walked out of the room lifting her skirts as she passed before me.

'Kindly take this boy to the dining-room and remain there with him till I come,' said I to Mamsell Agata. She stretched out her arms in horror in front of her as if to protect herself against something unclean, the slit under her hook nose parted in a terrible smile and she vanished in the wake of the parson's wife.

I sat down at my luncheon, gave John an apple and rang for Rosalie.

'Rosalie,' said I, 'take this money, go and get yourself a cotton dress, a couple of white aprons and whatever else you need to look respectable. From to-day you are promoted to be a nurse to this child. He will sleep in my room to-night, from to-morrow you are to sleep with him in Mamsell Agata's room.'

'But Mamsell Agata?' asked Rosalie, terror-struck.

'Mamsell Agata will be dismissed by me when I have finished my luncheon.'

I sent away my patients and went to knock at her room. Twice I raised my hand to knock, twice I let it fall. I did not knock. I decided it was wiser to postpone the interview till after dinner when my nerves had cooled down a little. Mamsell Agata was invisible. Rosalie produced an excellent pot-au-feu for dinner and a milk pudding which I shared with John – all Frenchwomen of her class are good cooks. After a couple of extra glasses of wine to cool my nerves I went to knock at Mamsell Agata's room still trembling with rage. I did not knock. It suddenly dawned upon me that it would cost me my night's sleep if I had a row with her now, and sleep was what I needed more than ever. Much better postpone the interview till to-morrow morning

While I was having my breakfast I came to the conclusion that the proper thing would be to give her notice in writing. I sat down to write her a thundering letter but hardly had I begun when Rosalie brought me a note in the small sharp handwriting of Mamsell Agata saying that no decent person could remain a day longer in my house, that she was leaving for good this same afternoon and that she never wanted to see me again – the very words I had hoped to say to her in my letter.

The invisible presence of Mamsell Agata still haunting the house, I went down to Le Printemps to get a cot for John and a rocking-horse as a reward for what I owed him. The cook came back the next day happy and content. Rosalie was beaming with joy, even John seemed pleased with his new surroundings when I went to have a look at him in the evening in his snug little bed. I myself felt happy as a schoolboy on his holidays.

But as to holidays, there wasn't much of them. I was hard at work from morning till night with my patients and not seldom also with the patients of some of my colleagues who were beginning to call me in consultation to share their responsibility – greatly to my surprise, for even then I seemed never to be afraid of responsibility. I discovered later in my life that this was one of the secrets of my success. Another secret of my success was of course my constant luck, more striking than ever before, so much so that I was beginning to think that I had got a mascot in the house. I even began to sleep better since I had taken to have a look at the little boy asleep in his cot before I went to bed.

I had been chucked by the wife of the English parson, but plenty of her compatriots were taking her place on the sofa in my waiting-room. Such was the lustre that surrounded the name of Professor Charcot that some of its light reflected itself even upon the smallest satellites around him. English people seemed to believe that their own doctors knew less about nervous diseases than their French colleagues. They may have been right or wrong in this, but it was good luck for me in any case. I was even called to London for a consultation just then. I did not know the patient but I had been exceptionally lucky with another member of her family which, no doubt, was the cause of my being summoned to her. It was a bad case, a desperate case according to my two English colleagues, who stood by the bed-side watching me with gloomy faces while I examined their patient. Their pessimism had infected the whole house, the patient's will to recover was paralysed by despondency and fear of death. It is very probable that my two colleagues knew their pathology far better than I. But I knew something they evidently did not know: that there is no drug as powerful as hope, that the slightest sign of pessimism in the face or words of a doctor can cost his patient his life. Without entering into medical details it is enough to say that as a result of my examination I was convinced that her gravest symptoms derived from nervous disorders and mental apathy. My two colleagues watched me with a shrug of their broad shoulders while I laid my hand on her forehead and said in a calm voice that she needed no morphia for the night. She would sleep well anyhow, she would feel much better in the morning; she would be out of danger before I left London the following day. A few minutes later she was fast asleep, during the night the temperature dropped almost too rapidly to my taste, the pulse steadied itself, in the morning she smiled at me and said she felt much better.

Her mother implored me to remain a day longer in London, to see her sister-in-law, they were all very worried about her. The colonel, her husband, wanted her to consult a nerve specialist, she herself had tried in vain to make her see Doctor Phillips, she felt sure she would be all right if she only had a child. Unfortunately she had an inexplicable dislike of doctors, and would certainly refuse to consult me, but it might be arranged that I should sit next her at dinner so as at least to form an opinion of her case. Maybe Charcot could do something for her? Her husband adored her, she had everything life could give, a beautiful house in Grosvenor Square, one of the finest old country seats in Kent. They had just returned from a long cruise to India in their yacht. She never had any rest, was always wandering about from place to place as if in search of something. There was a haunting expression of profound sadness in her eyes. Formerly she had been interested in art, she painted beautifully, she had even spent a winter in Julien's atelier in Paris. Now she took interest in nothing, cared for nothing, yes, she was interested in children's welfare, she was a large subscriber to their summer holidays fund and their orphanages.

I consented reluctantly to remain, I was anxious to return to Paris, I was worrying about John's cough. My hostess had forgotten to tell me that her sister-in-law, who sat by my side during dinner, was one of the most beautiful women I had ever seen. I was also much struck with the sad expression in her magnificent dark eyes. There was something lifeless in her whole face. She seemed bored with my company and took little trouble to conceal it. I told her there were some good pictures in the Salon that year, that I had heard from her sister-in-law that she had been an artist student in Julien's atelier. Had she met Marie Baschkirzeff there? No, she had not, but had heard about her.

Yes, everybody had. 'Moussia' was spending most of her time in advertising herself. I knew her very well, she was one of the cleverest young persons I had ever met but she had little heart, she was above all a poseuse, incapable of loving anybody but herself. My companion looked more bored than ever. Hoping for better luck I told her I had spent the afternoon in the children's hospital in Chelsea, it had been a revelation to me who was a frequent visitor to the Hôpital des Enfants Trouvés in Paris.

She said she thought our children's hospitals were very good.

I told her it was not so, that the mortality amongst French children inside and outside the hospitals was frightful. I told her about the thousands of abandoned babies dumped on the provinces

183

in the train des nourrices.

She looked at me for the first time with her sad eyes, the hard lifeless expression in her face gone, I said to myself she was perhaps a kind-hearted woman after all. In saying good-bye to my hostess I told her that it was not a case for me nor for Charcot himself, Doctor Phillips was the man, her sister-in-law would be all right when she had a baby.

John seemed pleased to see me but he looked pale and thin as he sat by my side at the luncheon table. Rosalie said he coughed a lot in the night. There was a slight rise in the temperature in the evening and he was kept in bed for a couple of days. Soon he resumed the daily routine of his little life, assisted in his usual grave silence at my luncheon and was taken in the afternoon to Parc Monceau by Rosalie. One day, a couple of weeks after my return from London, I was surprised to find the colonel sitting in my waiting-room. His wife had changed her mind, and wanted to come to Paris for some shopping, they were to join the yacht next week at Marseilles for a cruise in the Mediterranean. I was invited to lunch at the Hôtel du Rhin the next day, his wife would be very pleased if I would take her to visit one of the children's hospitals after luncheon. As I could not lunch, it was arranged that she should fetch me at Avenue de Villiers after my consultation. My waiting-room was still full of people when her elegant landau drove up before the door. I sent down Rosalie to ask her to go for a drive and come back in half-an-hour, unless she preferred to wait in the dining-room till I had finished with my patients. Half-an-hour later I found her sitting in the dining-room with John on her lap greatly interested in his demonstration of his various toys.

'He has got your eyes,' said she, looking from John to me, 'I did not know you were married.'

I said I was not married. She blushed a little and resumed her perusal of John's new picture book. She soon picked up her courage and with the usual tenacious curiosity of a woman she asked if his mother was Swedish, his hair was so blond, his eyes were so blue.

I knew quite well what she was driving at. I knew that Rosalie, the concierge, the milkman, the baker were sure I was John's father, I had heard my own coachman speak about him as 'le fils de Monsieur.' I knew it was quite useless to explain, I would not have convinced them, I had besides ended by almost believing it myself. But I thought this kind lady had a right to know the truth. I told her laughingly I was no more his father than she was his

184

mother, that he was an orphan with a very sad history. She had better not ask me, it would only give her pain. I drew back his sleeve and pointed to an ugly scar on his arm. He was all right now with Rosalie and me, but I should not be sure that he had forgotten the past until I had seen him smile. He never smiled.

'It is true,' she said gently. 'He has not smiled a single time as other children do when they show their toys.'

I said we knew very little of the mentality of small children, we were strangers in the world they lived in. Only the instinct of a mother could now and then find its way among their thoughts.

For all answer she bent her head over him and kissed him tenderly. John looked at her with great surprise in his blue eyes.

'It is probably the first kiss he has ever had,' said I.

Rosalie appeared to take him for his usual afternoon walk in Parc Monceau, his new friend suggested taking him for a drive in her landau instead. I was delighted to get out of the projected visit to the hospital, I accepted with pleasure.

From that day a new life began for John and I think also for somebody else. Every morning she came to his room with a new toy, every afternoon she drove him in her landau to the Bois de Boulogne with Rosalie in her best Sunday clothes on the back seat. Often he rode gravely on the top of a camel in Jardin d'Acclimatation surrounded by dozens of laughing children.

'Do not bring him so many rich toys,' said I, 'children like cheap toys just as well and there are so many who get none. I have often noticed that the humble doll à treize sous is always a great success even in the richest nurseries. When children learn to understand the money value of their toys they are driven out of their paradise, they cease to be children. John has besides already too many toys, it is time to teach him to give away some of them to those who have none. It is a somewhat difficult lesson to learn for many children. The relative facility with which they learn this lesson is a safe index to foretell what sort of men and women they will become.'

Rosalie told me that when they returned from their drive the beautiful lady always insisted on carrying John upstairs herself. Soon she remained to assist at his bath, and ere long it was she who gave him his bath, Rosalie's rôle being limited to handing her the bath towels. Rosalie told me something that touched me very much. She told me that when the lady had dried his thin little body she always kissed the ugly scar on his arm before putting on his shirt. Soon it was she who put him to bed and remained with him till he had fallen asleep. I myself saw little of her, I was out the whole day, and I feared that the poor colonel did not see much of her either, she was spending her whole day with the boy. The colonel told me that the Mediterranean cruise had been abandoned. They were to remain in Paris, he did not know for how long, nor did he care as long as his wife was happy, she had never been in a better mood than now. The colonel was right, the whole expression of her face had changed, an infinite tenderness shone in her dark eyes.

The boy slept badly, often when I went to have a look at him before going to bed I thought his face looked flushed, Rosalie said he coughed a good deal in the night. One morning I heard the ominous crepitation in the top of his right lung. I knew only too well what it meant. I had to tell his new friend, she said she already knew, she had probably known it before I did. I wanted to get a nurse to help Rosalie, but she would not hear of it. She implored me to take her as his nurse and I gave way. There was indeed nothing else to do, the boy seemed to fret even in his sleep as soon as she left the room. Rosalie went to sleep with the cook in the attics, the daughter of the duke slept on the bed of the charwoman in John's room. A couple of days later he had a slight haemorrhage, the temperature rose in the evening, it became evident that the course of the disease was going to be rapid.

'He won't live long,' said Rosalie, putting her handkerchief to her eyes, 'he has already got the face of an angel.'

He liked to sit up for a while on the lap of his tender nurse while Rosalie was making up his bed for the night. I had always thought John an intelligent and sweet-looking child but I would never have called him a beautiful child. As I looked at him now the very features of his face seemed changed, his eyes seemed much larger and of a darker hue. He had become a beautiful child, beautiful as the Genius of Love or the Genius of Death. I looked at the two faces, cheek leaning against cheek. My eyes filled with wonder. Was it possible that the infinite love that radiated from the heart of this woman towards this dying child could recast the soft outlines of his little face into a vague likeness to her own? Did I witness another undreamt-of mystery of Life? Or was it Death, the great sculptor, already at work with masterly hand, to remould and refine the features of this child before closing his eyelids? The same pure forehead, the same exquisite curve of the eyebrows, the same long eyelashes. Even the graceful moulding of the lips would be the same could I ever see him smile as I saw her smile the night when in his sleep he murmured for the first time the word all children love to say and all women love to hear, 'Mama! Mama!'

She put him back to bed, he had a restless night, she never left his side. Towards morning his breathing seemed a little easier, he dozed off to sleep. I reminded her of her promise to obey me and forced her with difficulty to lie down on her bed for an hour, Rosalie would call her as soon as he woke up. When I returned to his room as dawn was breaking, Rosalie, her finger on her lips, whispered that they were both asleep.

'Look at him!' she whispered, 'look at him! He is dreaming!'

His face was still and serene, his lips were parted in a beautiful smile. I put my hand over his heart. He was dead. I looked from the smiling face of the boy to the face of the woman asleep on Rosalie's bed. The two faces were the same.

She washed him and dressed him for the last time. Not even Rosalie was allowed to help her to lay him in his coffin. She sent her out twice in search of the right kind of pillow, she did not think his head looked comfortable.

She implored me to postpone screwing on the lid till the next day. I told her she knew the bitterness of Life, she knew little of the bitterness of Death, I was a doctor, I knew of both. I told her death had two faces, one beautiful and serene, another forbidding and terrible. The boy had parted from life with a smile on his lips, death would not leave it there for long. It was necessary to close the coffin to-night. She bent her head and said nothing. As I lifted the lid she sobbed and said she could not part with him and leave him all alone in the foreign cemetery.

'Why part with him,' said I, 'why not take him with you, he weighs so little, why don't you take him to England in your yacht and bury him near your beautiful parish church in Kent?'

She smiled through her tears, the same smile as the boy's smile. She sprang to her feet.

'Can I? May I?' she called out almost with joy.

'It can be done, it shall be done if you let me screw on the lid now, there is no time to lose or he will be taken to the cemetery in Passy to-morrow morning.'

As I lifted up the lid she laid a little bunch of violets close to his cheek.

'I have nothing else to give him,' she sobbed, 'I wish I had something to give him to take with him from me!'

'I think he would like to take this with him,' said I, taking the diamond brooch from my pocket and pinning it to his pillow. 'It belonged to his mother.'

She did not utter a sound, she stretched out her arms towards her child and fell senseless on the floor. I lifted her up and laid her on Rosalie's bed, screwed on the lid of the coffin and drove to the Bureau des Pompes Funèbres in Place de la Madeleine. I had a private interview with the undertaker, alas, we had met before. I authorized him to spend any sum he liked if the coffin could be put on board an English yacht in the harbour of Calais the next night. He said it could be done if I promised not to look at the bill. I said nobody would look at the bill. I then drove to the Hôtel du Rhin, woke up the colonel and told him his wife wished the yacht to be in Calais in twelve hours. While he wrote out the telegram to the captain I sat down to write a hurried note to his wife that the coffin would be on board their yacht in Calais harbour the next night. I added in a postscript that I had to leave Paris early in the morning, and this was to bid her good-bye.

I have seen John's grave, he lies buried in the little churchyard of one of the most beautiful parish churches in Kent. Primroses and violets were growing on his grave, and blackbirds were singing over his head. I have never seen his mother again. Better so.

XVI

A Journey to Sweden

I think I have already told you something about the illness of the Swedish Consul, it happened just about that time, here is the story. The Consul was a nice, quiet little man with an American wife and two small children. I had been there in the afternoon. One of the children had a feverish cold but insisted on getting up for the festival home-coming of their father that same evening. The house was full of flowers and the children had been allowed to sit up for dinner in honour of the occasion. Their mother was very pleased to show me two most affectionate telegrams from her husband, one from Berlin, one from Cologne, announcing his return. They seemed to me somewhat long. At midnight I received an urgent message from his wife to come at once. The door was opened by the Consul himself in his night-shirt. He said that the dinner had been postponed to await the arrival of the King of Sweden and the President of the French Republic, who had just made him a Grand Cross of the Legion of Honour. He had just bought Le Petit Trianon as a summer residence for his family. He was in a rage with his wife for not wearing the Marie Antoinette pearl necklace he had given her, called his little boy Le Dauphin and announced himself as Robespierre – folie de grandeur! The children were screaming with terror in the nursery, his wife was prostrated with grief, his faithful dog lay under the table growling with fear. My poor friend suddenly got violent, I had to lock him up in the bedroom where he smashed everything and nearly succeeded in throwing us both through the window. In the morning he was taken to Doctor Blanche's asylum in Passy. The famous alienist suspected from the first general paralysis. Two months later the diagnosis was clear, the case was incurable. La Maison Blanche being very expensive, I decided to have him removed to the government asylum in Lund, a small town in the South of Sweden. Doctor Blanche was against it. He said it would be a risky and expensive undertaking, that his temporary lucidity was not to be trusted, that he must in any case be accompanied by two capable warders. I said the little money left must be saved for the children, the journey must be undertaken in the cheapest possible way, I was going to take him to Sweden alone. When I signed the papers for his release from the asylum, Doctor Blanche renewed his warnings in writing, but of course I knew better. I drove him straight to Avenue de Villiers. He was quite calm and reasonable during dinner except that he tried to make love to Mamsell Agata, surely the only chance she had ever had. Two hours later we were locked up in a first-class compartment in the night express for Cologne, there were no corridor trains in those days. I happened to be the doctor of one of the Rothschilds, the owners of the Chemin de Fer du Nord. Orders had been given to facilitate our journey in every way, the conductors were told to leave us undisturbed, my patient being apt to become agitated at the sight of a stranger. He was very quiet and docile and we both lay down on our couches to sleep. I was awakened by the grip of a madman round my throat, twice I knocked him down, twice he sprang at me again with the agility of a panther, he nearly succeeded in strangling me. The last thing I remember was dealing him a blow on his head which seemed to stun him. On entering Cologne in the morning we were found both lying unconscious on the floor of the compartment and taken to the Hôtel du Nord, where we remained for twenty-four hours, each in his bed, in the same room. As I had to tell the doctor who came to stitch my wound – he had nearly bitten off my ear – the proprietor sent word that no lunatics were allowed in the hotel. I decided to go on to Hamburg with the morning train. He was very amiable the whole way to Hamburg, sang 'La Marseillaise' as we drove through the town to the Kiel station. We embarked all right on the steamer to Korsuer – at that time the quickest route between the continent and Sweden. A couple of miles off the Danish coast our steamer was blocked by pack ice driven down from the Cattegatt by a raging northern gale, a not very uncommon occurrence during a severe winter. We had to walk for over a mile on floating ice-flakes, my friend enjoyed it hugely, and were taken in open boats into Korsuer. As we were entering the harbour my friend jumped into the sea, I after him. We were picked up, and sat in an unheated train to Copenhagen, our clothes frozen to ice, the temperature 20 Centigrade below zero. The rest of the journey went remarkably well, the cold bath seemed to have done my friend a lot of good. One hour after the crossing to Malmö I handed over my friend in the railway station at Lund to two warders from the asylum. I drove to the hotel – there was only one hotel in Lund in those days – and ordered a room and breakfast. I was told I could have breakfast but no room, all the rooms being reserved for the theatrical company which was giving a gala performance in the Municipal Hall that same evening. While I was having my breakfast the waiter brought me with great pride the programme for the night's performance of 'Hamlet,' a tragedy in five acts by William Shakespeare. Hamlet in Lund! I glanced at the programme:

Hamlet, Prince of Denmark .... Mr. Erik Carolus Malmborg.

I stared at the programme, Erik Carolus Malmborg! Could it be possible that it was my old pal from the university days in Upsala! Erik Carolus Malmborg was to become a priest in those days. I had crammed him for his exams, had written his first proof sermon as well as his love-letters to his fiancée during a whole term. I had flogged him regularly every evening when he came home drunk to sleep in my spare room, he had been kicked out for disorderly conduct from his own lodgings. I had lost sight of him when I had left Sweden many years ago. I knew he had been sent down from the University and had gone from bad to worse. Suddenly I also remembered having heard that he had taken to the stage, of course it must be my ill-starred old friend who was the Hamlet of to-night! I sent my card to his room, he came like a shot overjoyed to see me after a lapse of so many years. My friend told me a distressing story. After a disastrous series of performances to empty houses in Malmö the company, decimated to one third of its members, had reached Lund the evening before for a last desperate battle against fate. Most of their costumes and portable belongings, the jewels of the queen mother, the crown of the king, Hamlet's own sword which he was to run through Polonius, even Yorick's skull, had been seized by the creditors in Malmö. The king had got a sharp attack of sciatica and could neither walk nor sit on his throne, Ophelia had a fearful cold, the Ghost had got drunk at the farewell supper in Malmö and missed the train. He himself was in magnificent form, Hamlet was his finest creation – it might have been expressly written for him. But how could he alone carry the immense burden of the five-act tragedy on his shoulders! All the tickets for the performance to-night were sold out, if they should have to return the money, complete collapse was inevitable. Perhaps I could lend him two hundred kronor for old friendship's sake?

I rose to the occasion. I summoned a meeting of the leading stars of the company, instilled new blood into their dejected hearts with several bottles of Swedish punch, curtailed ruthlessly the whole scene with the actors, the scene with the grave-diggers, the killing of Polonius, and announced that, ghost or no ghost, the performance was to take place.

It was a memorable evening in the theatrical annals of Lund. Punctually at eight the curtain rose over the royal palace of Elsinore, as the crow flies not an hour's distance from where we were. The crowded house chiefly composed of boisterous undergraduates from the University proved less emotional than we had expected. The entrance of the Prince of Denmark passed off almost unnoticed, even his famous 'To be or not to be' missed fire. The king limped painfully across the stage and sank down with a loud groan on his throne. Ophelia's cold had assumed terrific proportions. It was evident that Polonius could not see straight. It was the Ghost that saved the situation. The Ghost was I. As I advanced in ghost-like fashion on the moonlit ramparts of the castle of Elsinore, carefully groping my way over the huge packing-cases which formed its very backbone, the whole fabric suddenly collapsed and I was precipitated up to the armpits in one of the packing-cases. What was a ghost expected to do in similar circumstances? Should I duck my head and disappear altogether in the packing-case or should I remain as I was, awaiting further events? It was a nice question to settle! A third alternative was suggested to me by Hamlet himself in a hoarse whisper: why the devil didn't I climb out of the infernal box? This was, however, beyond my power, my legs being entangled in coils of rope and all sorts of paraphernalia of stage craft. Rightly or wrongly I decided to remain where I was, ready for all emergency. My unexpected disappearance in the packing-case had been very sympathetically received by the audience, but it was nothing compared to the success when, with only my head popping out from the packing-case, I began again in a lugubrious voice my interrupted recital to Hamlet. The applause became so frenetic that I had to acknowledge them with a friendly waving of my hand, I could not bow in the delicate position I was in. This made them completely wild with delight, the applause never ceased till the end. When the curtain fell over the last act I appeared with the leading stars of the company to bow to the audience. They kept on shouting: 'The Ghost! The Ghost!' so persistently that I had to come forth alone several times to receive their congratulations, with my hand on my heart.

We were all delighted. My friend Malmborg said he had never had a more successful evening. We had a most animated midnight supper. Ophelia was charming to me and Hamlet raised his glass to my health offering me in the name of all his comrades the leadership of the company. I said I would have to think it over. They all accompanied me to the station. Forty-eight hours later I was back to my work in Paris not in the least tired. Youth! Youth!

XVII

Doctors

A large number of foreign doctors were practising in Paris in those days. There was a great jalousie de métier amongst them, of which I got my share and no wonder. Nor were we much liked by our French colleagues for our monopoly of the wealthy foreign colony, no doubt a far more lucrative clientèle than their own. Of late an agitation had even been started in the press to protest against the steadily increasing number of foreign doctors in Paris, often, it was hinted, not even provided with regular diplomas from well-recognized universities. It resulted in an order by the Préfet de Police that all foreign doctors were to present their diplomas for verification before the end of the month. I with my diploma as M.D. of the faculty of Paris was of course all right, I nearly forgot all about it and turned up the very last day at the Commissariat of my quartier. The Commissaire, who knew me slightly, asked me if I knew a Doctor X., who lived in the same avenue as I did. I answered that all I knew about him was that he must have a very large practice, I had often heard his name mentioned, and I had often admired his elegant carriage waiting outside his house.

The Commissaire said I would not have to admire it for long, he was on their black list, he had not presented himself with his diploma because he had none to present, he was a quack, he was going to be *pincé* at last. He was said to be making two hundred thousand francs a year, more than many of the leading celebrities in Paris. I said there was no reason why a quack might not be a good doctor, a diploma meant little to his patients as long as he was able to help them. I heard the end of the story a couple of months later from the Commissaire himself. Doctor X. had presented himself at the very last moment with a request for a private interview with the Commissaire. Presenting his diploma as M.D. of a well-known German university, he implored the Commissaire to keep his secret, he said he owed his enormous practice to the circumstance that he was considered by everybody to be a quack. I told the Commissaire this man would soon become a millionaire if he knew his medicine half as well as he knew his psychology.

As I was walking home I did not envy my colleague his two hundred thousand francs of income but I envied him for knowing what sum his income amounted to. I had always been longing to know what my earnings were. That I was making lots of money seemed certain, I had always plenty of cash whenever I wanted money for something. I had a fine apartment, a smart carriage, an excellent cook; now, since Mamsell Agata had left, I often had my friends to dinner at Avenue de Villiers with the best of everything. Twice I had rushed down to Capri, once to buy Mastro Vincenzo's house, another time to offer a high sum of money to the unknown owner of the ruined little chapel at San Michele – it took me ten years to settle that business. Already then a keen lover of art, my rooms in Avenue de Villiers were full of treasures of bygone times, and over a dozen fine old clocks chimed every hour of my often sleepless nights. For some inexplicable reason these periods of wealth were not seldom interrupted by moments when I had no money at all. Rosalie knew it, the concierge knew it, even the *fournisseurs* knew it. Norstrom also knew it for I often had to borrow money from him. He said it could only be explained by some defect in my mental machinery, the remedy was to keep proper accounts and to send regular bills to my patients like everybody else. I said it was hopeless to try to keep accounts and as to writing bills I had never done it and was not going to do it. Our profession was not a trade but an art, this trafficking in suffering was a humiliation to me. I blushed scarlet when a patient put his twenty-franc piece on my table and when he put it in my hand I felt as if I wanted to hit him. Norstrom said it was nothing but sheer vanity and conceit on my part, that I should grab all the money I could lay my hands on, as all my colleagues did, even if handed me by the undertaker. I said our profession was a holy office on the same level as that of the priest, if not higher, where surplus money-making should be forbidden by law. The doctors should be paid by the State and well paid like the judges in England. Those who did not like this arrangement should leave the profession and go on the Stock Exchange or open a shop. The doctors should walk about like sages honoured and protected by all men. They should be welcome to take what they liked from their rich patients for their poor patients and for themselves, but they should not count their visits or write any bills. What was to the heart of the mother the value in cash of the life of her child you had saved? What was the proper fee for taking the fear of death out of a pair of terror-stricken eyes by a comforting word or a mere stroke of your hand? How many francs were you to charge for every second of the death-struggle your morphia syringe had snatched from the executioner? How long were we to dump on suffering mankind all these expensive patent medicines and drugs with modern labels but with roots sprung from mediaeval superstition? We well knew that our number of efficacious drugs could be counted on the ends of our fingers and were handed to us by benevolent Mother Nature at a cheap price. Why should I, who was a fashionable doctor, drive about in a smart carriage, while my colleague in the slums had to walk on foot? Why did the State spend many hundred times more money on teaching the art of killing than the art of healing? Why didn't we build more hospitals and fewer churches, you could pray to God everywhere but you could not operate in a gutter! Why did we build so many comfortable homes for professional murderers and housebreakers and so few for the homeless poor in the slums? Why shouldn't they be told that they should feed themselves? There is no man or woman who cannot even while shut up in prison earn his or her daily bread if given the choice between eating or not eating. We were constantly told that the majority of the prison population was made up from weak-minded, unintelligent, more or less irresponsible individuals. This was a mistake. Their standard of intelligence was as a rule not below but above the average. All first offenders should be condemned to a much shorter term of imprisonment on a very low diet combined with repeated and severe corporal punishments. They should make room for the fathers of abandoned and illegitimate children, and for the *souteneurs* now at large in our midst. Cruelty to helpless animals was to the eyes of God a far greater sin than housebreaking, yet it was only punished by a small fine. We all knew that excessive accumulation of wealth was, as often as not, cleverly concealed theft from the poor. I had never come across a millionaire in prison. The trick of making money out of almost anything was a special gift of very doubtful moral value. The possessors of this faculty should only be tolerated to carry on, on the understanding that, as with the bees, a large slice of their golden combs should be distributed among those who have no honey to put on their daily bread.

As to the rest of the prison population, the inveterate criminals, the cold-blooded murderers, etc., instead of spending a lifetime in relative comfort at a rate of expense exceeding the price of a permanent bed in a hospital, they should be given a painless death, not as punishment, for we had no right either to judge or to punish, but for the sake of protection. England was right as usual. Even so these evil-doers had indeed no right to complain of being treated harshly by society. They were rewarded for their crimes with the greatest privilege that can be granted to living man, a privilege as a rule denied to their fellow creatures as a reward for their virtues – that of a rapid death.

Norstrom advised me to abandon reforming society – he thought it was not in my line – and to stick to medicine. So far I had no right to complain of the result. He had however grave doubts as to the smooth working of my scheme to walk about as a sage among my patients exchanging my services for portable goods. He stuck to his belief that the old system of writing bills was safer. I said I was not so sure of that. Although it was true that some of my patients after a couple of unanswered letters asking for their bills went away without paying me anything – it never happened with the English – others as often as not sent me sums exceeding what I would have asked of them if I had sent a bill. Although the majority of my patients seemed to prefer to part with their money than with their goods, I had applied my system with success on several occasions. One of my most treasured possessions is an old Loden cape I once took from Miss C. the day she was leaving for America. As she was driving about with me in my carriage to gain time to say all she had to say about her eternal gratitude and her inability to repay all my kindness, I noticed an old Loden cape over her back. It was the very thing I wanted. So I wrapped it over my knees and said I was going to keep it. She said she had bought it ten years ago in Salzburg and was very fond of it. I said so was I. She suggested we should drive immediately to Old England, she would be delighted to present me with the most expensive Scotch cape to be had. I said I did not want any Scotch cape. I must tell you that Miss C. was a somewhat irascible lady who had given me lots of trouble for years. She got so angry that she jumped from the carriage without even saying goodbye, she sailed for America the next day. I have never seen her again.

I also remember the case of Lady Maud B. who called on me in Avenue de Villiers before leaving for London. She said she had written in vain three times for her bill, I had placed her in a very embarrassing position, she did not know what to do. She was overwhelming in her praise of my skill and my kindness, money had nothing to do with her gratitude, all her possessions could not repay me for having saved her life. I thought it very nice to be told all this by such a charming young lady. As she spoke I was admiring

197

her new dark red silk frock, and so was she with an occasional side-glance in the Venetian mirror over the mantelpiece. Looking attentively at her tall, slender figure I said I would take her frock, it was exactly what I wanted. She burst into a merry laugh which soon changed into blank consternation when I announced that I would send Rosalie to her hotel at seven o'clock to fetch the frock. She rose to her feet pale with rage and said that she had never heard of such a thing. I said it was very likely. She had told me there was nothing she would not give me. I had chosen the frock for reasons of my own. She burst into tears and rushed out of the room. A week later I met the English Ambassador's wife at the Swedish Legation. This kind lady told me that she had not forgotten the consumptive English governess I had recommended to her, she had even sent her an invitation to her garden-party for the English colony.

'No doubt she looks very ill,' said the ambassadress, 'but surely she cannot be as poor as you say, I am sure she gets her clothes from Worth.'

I much resented Norstrom's saying that my inability to write bills and to pocket my fee without blushing derived from vanity and conceit. If Norstrom was right I must admit that all my colleagues seemed singularly free from this defect. They all sent their bills just as tailors do, and grabbed with greatest ease the louis d'or their patients put in their hands. In many consulting-rooms it was even the etiquette that the patient should put his money on the table before opening his mouth to relate his woes. Before an operation it was the established rule that half of the sum should be paid in advance. I knew of a case where the patient was roused from the chloroform and the operation postponed in order to verify the validity of a cheque. When one of us smaller lights called in a celebrity for consultation, the big man put a slice of his fee in the hands of the small man as a matter of course. Nor did it stop there. I remember my stupefaction the first time I called in a specialist for an embalmment when this man offered me five hundred francs from his fee. The charge for an embalmment was scandalously high.

Many of the professors I used to consult in difficult cases were men of world-wide reputation, at the very top of the tree in their speciality, extraordinarily exact and amazingly quick in their diagnosis. Charcot for instance was almost uncanny in the way he went straight to the root of the evil, often apparently only after a rapid glance at the patient from his cold eagle eyes. During the last years of his life maybe he relied too much upon his eye, the examination of his patients was often far too rapid and superficial. He never admitted a mistake and woe to the man who ever dared to hint at his being in the wrong. On the other hand he was surprisingly reserved before pronouncing a fatal prognosis, even in clearly hopeless cases. L'imprévu est toujours possible, he used to say. Charcot was the most celebrated doctor of his time. Patients from all over the world flocked to his consulting-room in Faubourg St. Germain, often waiting for weeks before being admitted to the inner sanctuary where he sat by the window in his huge library. Short of stature, with the chest of an athlete and the neck of a bull, he was a most imposing man to look at. A white clean-shaven face, a low forehead, cold penetrating eyes, an aquiline nose, sensitive cruel lips, the mask of a Roman Emperor. When he was angry, the flash in his eyes was terrible like lightning, nobody who has ever faced those eyes is likely to forget them. His voice was imperative, hard, often sarcastic. The grip of his small, flabby hand was unpleasant. He had few friends amongst his colleagues, he was feared by his patients and his assistants for whom he seldom had a kind word of encouragement in exchange for the superhuman amount of work he imposed upon them. He was indifferent to the sufferings of his patients, he took little interest in them from the day of establishing the diagnosis until the day of the post-mortem examination. Among his assistants he had his favourites whom he often pushed forward to privileged positions far above their merits. A word of recommendation from Charcot was enough to decide the result of any examination or concours, in fact he ruled supreme over the whole faculty of medicine.

Sharing the fate of all nerve specialists he was surrounded by a bodyguard of neurotic ladies, hero-worshippers at all costs. Luckily for him he was absolutely indifferent to women. His only relaxation from his incessant toil was music. Nobody was allowed to speak a word about medicine on his Thursday evenings all devoted to music. Beethoven was his favourite. He was very fond of animals, every morning as he descended heavily from his landau in the inner court of Salpêtrière he produced from his pocket a piece of bread for his two old Rosinantes. He always cut short any conversation about sport and killing animals. His dislike of the English derived, I think, from his hatred of fox hunting.

Professor Potain shared with Charcot the position of the greatest medical celebrity in Paris in those days. There never were two people more unlike one another than these two great doctors. The famous clinicien of Hôpital Necker was a very plain, insignificant-looking man, who would have passed unnoticed in a crowd where the head of Charcot would have been singled out among thousands. Compared to his illustrious confrère, he looked almost shabby in his ill-fitting old frockcoat. His features were dull, his words few and spoken as if with great difficulty. He was beloved like a god by all his patients, rich and poor seemed exactly the same to him. He knew the name of every single patient in his enormous hospital, patted them young and old on their cheek, listened with infinite patience to their tales of woe, often paid from his own pocket for extra dainties for their tired palates. He examined his poorest hospital patients with the same extreme attention as his royalties and millionaires, he had plenty of both. No sign of disorder of lungs or heart however obscure seemed to escape his phenomenally acute ear. I do not believe there ever was a man who knew more of what goes on in the breast of another man than he did. What little I know of diseases of the heart I owe to him. Professor Potain and Guéneau de Mussy were almost the only two consulting doctors I dared to turn to when in need of advice for a penniless patient. Professor Tillaux the famous surgeon was the third. His clinic in Hôtel Dieu was run on the same lines as Potain's in Hôpital Necker, he was like a father to all his patients, the poorer they looked the more interest he seemed to take in their welfare. As a teacher he was the best I have ever seen, his book on 'Anatomie Topographique' is moreover the best book ever written on the subject. He was a wonderful operator and always did all the dressing himself. There was something almost northern about this man with his straight simple manners and his blue eyes, he was in fact a Breton. He was extraordinarily kind and patient with me and my many shortcomings, that I did not become a good surgeon is certainly not his fault. As it is, I owe him a lot, I am convinced I even owe him that I can still walk about on my two legs. I think I had better tell you this story here in parenthesis.

*   *   *

I had been working very hard during the long, hot summer without a single day of rest, harassed by insomnia and its usual companion, despondency. I was irritable with my patients, ill tempered with everybody, and when autumn came even my phlegmatic friend Norstrom began to lose his patience with me. At last he informed me one day we were dining together that unless I went

200

away at once for a three weeks' rest cure in a cool place, I should go to pieces, altogether. Capri was too hot, Switzerland was the right place for me. I had always bowed to my friend's superior common-sense. I knew he was right although his premises were wrong. It was not overwork but something else that had reduced me to such a lamentable condition; but don't let us talk about that here. Three days later I arrived in Zermatt and set to work at once to find out whether life above the snow-line was more cheerful than below it. The ice-axe became a new toy to me to play with in the old game of lose and win between life and death. I began where most other climbers end, with the Matterhorn. Roped to the ice-axe on a slanting rock twice the size of my dining-room table, I spent the night under the shoulder of the angry mountain in a raging snow-storm. I was interested to learn from my two guides that we were hanging on to the very rock from where Hadow, Hudson, Lord Francis Douglas and Michel Croz were hurled down on to the Matterhorn glacier four thousand feet below during Whymper's first ascent. At daybreak we came upon Burckhardt. I scratched the fresh snow from his face, peaceful and still as that of a man asleep. He had frozen to death. At the foot of the mountain we overtook his two guides dragging between them his half-dazed companion, Davies, whose life they had saved at the peril of their own.

Two days later the Schreckhorn, the sullen giant, hurled his usual avalanche of loose rocks against the intruders. He missed us, but it was a fine shot anyhow at such a distance, a piece of rock that would have smashed a cathedral thundered past us at a distance of less than twenty yards. A couple of days later, as dawn was breaking in the valley below, our bewitched eyes watched the Jungfrau putting on her immaculate robe of snow. We could just see the virgin's rosy cheek under her white veil. I started at once to conquer the enchantress. It looked at first as if she might say yes, but when I tried to pluck a few Edelweiss from the hem of her mantle she suddenly got shy and went to hide herself behind a cloud. Try as I might, I never succeeded in approaching the beloved. The more I advanced the further she seemed to draw away from me. Soon a shroud of vapour and mist all aglow with sunrays hid her entirely from our view like the screen of fire and smoke that descends round her virgin sister Brünnhilde in the last act of the Walkyrie. An old witch whose business it was to watch over the fair maiden like a jealous old nurse, allured us further and further away from our goal among desolated crags and yawning precipices ready to engulf us at any moment. Soon the guides declared they had lost their way and that nothing remained but to return from where we came and the sooner the better. Defeated and lovesick, I was dragged down to the valley again by the stout rope of my two guides. No wonder I was downhearted, it was the second time in that year I had been thrown over by a young lady. But youth is a great healer of heart wounds. With a little sleep and a cool head one soon gets over them. Sleep I got but little, but luckily I did not lose my head. The following Sunday – I remember even the date for it was my birthday – I smoked my pipe on the top of Mont Blanc, where according to my two guides most people hang out their tongues gasping for breath. What happened that day I have related elsewhere, but since the little book is out of print I must tell it you here to make you understand what I owe to Professor Tillaux.

The ascent of Mont Blanc, winter and summer, is, comparatively speaking, easy. Nobody but a fool attempts the ascent in the autumn before the sun of the day and the frost of the night has had time to fix the fresh snow to the vast slopes of the mountain. The king of the Alps relies for his defence against intruders on his avalanches of fresh snow just as the Schreckhorn relies on his projectiles of loose rocks.

It was luncheon time when I lit my pipe on the top. All the foreigners in the hotels of Chamonix were looking in turn through their telescopes at the three flies crawling about on the white *calotte* that covered the head of the old mountain king. While they were having their luncheon, we were groping our way through the snow in the couloir under Mont Maudit, soon to appear again in their telescopes on the Grand Plateau. Nobody spoke, we all knew that the very sound of the voice might start an avalanche. Suddenly Boisson looked back, and pointed with his ice-axe to a black line drawn as by the hand of a giant across the white slope.

'Wir sind alle verloren,' he murmured as the immense snowfield split in two and started the avalanche with a roar of thunder, hurling us down the slope with vertiginous speed. I felt nothing, I knew nothing. Suddenly the same reflex impulse which in Spallanzani's famous experiment made his decapitated frog move its paw to the spot he was pricking with a pin – this same reflex impulse compelled the big unconscious animal to raise his hand to react against the sharp pain in his skull. The blunt peripheric sensation roused in my brain the instinct of self-preservation – the last to die. With a desperate effort I set to work to free myself from the layer of snow under which I lay buried. I saw the glistening walls of blue ice around me, I saw the light of the day above my head through the aperture of the crevasse into which I had been hurled by the avalanche. Strange to remember I felt no fear, nor was I conscious of any thought either of the past, the present or the future. Gradually I became aware of an indistinct sensation slowly groping its way through my benumbed brain till at last it reached my understanding. I recognized it at once, it was my old hobby, my incurable curiosity to know all there was to know about Death. My chance had come at last, could I only keep my head clear and look him straight in the face without flinching. I knew he was there, I fancied I could almost see him advancing towards me in his icy shroud. What would he say to me, would he be harsh and unforgiving, or would he have pity on me and just leave me where I was lying in the snow and let me freeze to everlasting sleep? Incomprehensible as it may seem I do believe that it was this last survival of my normal mentality, my curiosity about Death, that saved my life. All at once I felt the grip of my fingers round the ice-axe, I felt the rope round my waist. The rope! Where were my two companions? I pulled the rope towards me as fast as I could, there was a sudden jerk, the black-bearded head of Boisson popped out of the snow. He drew a deep gasp, pulled instantly the rope round his waist and dragged his half-dazed companion out of his grave.

'How long does it take to freeze to death?' I asked.

Boisson's quick eyes wandered round the walls of our prison and stopped riveted to a thin bridge of ice spanning the slanting walls of the crevasse like the flying buttress of a Gothic cathedral.

'If I had an ice-axe and if I could reach that bridge,' he said, 'I believe I could cut my way out.'

I handed him the ice-axe my fingers were clasping with an almost cataleptic grip.

'Steady, for God's sake steady,' he repeated as, standing on my shoulders like an acrobat, he swung himself on to the ice bridge above our heads. Hanging on to the slanting walls with his hands he cut his way step by step out of the crevasse and dragged me up with the rope. With great difficulty we hoisted up the other guide still half stunned. The avalanche had swept away the usual traces of the landmarks, we had only one ice-axe between us to warn us against falling into some crevasse hidden under the fresh snow. That we reached the hut after midnight was according to Boisson even a greater miracle than that we got out of the crevasse. The hut was almost buried under the snow, we had to break a hole through the roof to enter it. We fell headlong on the floor. I drank to the last drop the rancid oil of the little oil lamp while Boisson rubbed my frozen feet with snow, after having cut open my heavy mountain shoes with his knife. The rescue party from Chamonix having spent the whole morning in a fruitless search for our bodies on the track of the avalanche, found us all fast asleep on the floor of the hut. The next day I was taken in a hay cart to Geneva and put in the night express to Paris.

Professor Tillaux stood washing his hands between two operations as I staggered into the amphitheatre of Hôtel Dieu the next morning. As they unwrapped the cotton wool round my legs he stared at my feet, and so did I, they were black as those of a negro.

'Sacré Suédois, where the devil have you come from?' thundered the Professor.

He gave me an anxious look from his kind blue eyes which made me feel quite ashamed of myself. I said I had been having a rest cure in Switzerland, I had had a misadventure on a mountain, such as might happen to any tourist, I was very sorry.

'Mais c'est lui,' shouted an interne, 'pour sûr c'est lui!' Taking a 'Figaro' from the pocket of his blouse he began to read aloud a telegram from Chamonix about the miraculous escape of a foreigner who with his two guides had been carried away by an avalanche on descending Mont Blanc.

'Nom de tonnerre, nom de nom de nom! Fiche moi la paix sacré Suédois, qu'est-ce que tu viens faire ici, va-t-en à l'Asile St. Anne chez les fous!

'Allow me to demonstrate to you the skull of a Lapland bear,' he went on while he was dressing the ugly cut on the top of my skull. 'A knock-down blow that would have stunned an elephant, but not a fracture, not even a commotion cérébrale! Why take the long journey to Chamonix, why don't you climb up to the top of the tower of Notre-Dame and throw yourself down in the square under our windows, there is no danger as long as you fall on your head!'

I was always delighted when the Professor chaffed me as it was a sure sign I was in his good graces. I wanted to drive straight to Avenue de Villiers but Tillaux thought I would be more comfortable for a couple of days in a separate room in the hospital. I was surely his worst pupil, still he had taught me enough of surgery to make me realize that he meant to amputate me. For five days he came to look at my legs, three times a day, on the sixth day I was on my sofa in Avenue de Villiers all danger over. The punishment was severe in any case, I was laid up for six weeks, I got so nervous that I had to write a book – don't be afraid, it is out of print. I hobbled about on two sticks for another month, then I was all right again.

I tremble at the thought of what would have happened to me had I fallen into the hands of one of the other leading surgeons in Paris in those days. Old Papa Richet in the other wing of Hôtel Dieu would surely have made me die of gangrene or blood poisoning, it was his speciality, it was rampant all over his mediaeval clinic. The famous Professor Péan, the terrible butcher of Hôpital St. Louis, would have chopped off both my legs on the spot and thrown them on the top of some stumps of arms and legs, half-a-dozen ovaries and uteruses and various tumours, all in a heap on the floor of his amphitheatre besmeared with blood like a slaughterhouse. Then, his enormous hands still red with my blood, he would have plunged his knife with the dexterity of a conjurer into his next victim, half conscious under insufficient anaesthesia, while half-a-dozen others, screaming with terror on their brancards, were awaiting their turn of torture. The massacre en masse at an end, Péan would wipe the sweat from his forehead, rub a few spots of blood and pus from his white waistcoat and dresscoat – he always operated in evening dress – and with a: Voilà pour aujourd'hui, Messieurs! he would rush out of the amphitheatre to his pompous landau and drive full speed to his private clinic in Rue de la Santé to cut open the abdomens of half-a-dozen women driven there by a gigantic réclame like helpless sheep to the slaughterhouse of La Villette.

XVIII

La Salpêtrière

I seldom failed to attend Professor Charcot's famous *Leçons du Mardi* in the Salpêtrière, just then chiefly devoted to his *grand hystérie* and to hypnotism. The huge amphitheatre was filled to the last place with a multicoloured audience drawn from tout Paris, authors, journalists, leading actors and actresses, fashionable demi-mondaines, all full of morbid curiosity to witness the startling phenomena of hypnotism almost forgotten since the days of Mesmer and Braid. It was during one of these lectures that I became acquainted with Guy de Maupassant, then already famous for his *Boule de Suif* and his unforgettable *Maison Tellier*. We used to have endless talks on hypnotism and all sorts of mental troubles, he never tired of trying to draw from me what little I knew on these subjects. He also wanted to know everything about insanity, he was collecting just then material for his terrible book 'Le Horla,' a faithful picture of his own tragic future. He even accompanied me once on a visit to Professor Bernheim's clinic in Nancy which opened my eyes to the fallacies of the Salpêtrière school in regard to hypnotism. I also stayed as his guest for a couple of days on board his yacht. I well remember our sitting up the whole night talking about death in the little saloon of his *Bel Ami* riding at her anchor off Antibes harbour. He was afraid of death. He said the thought of death was seldom out of his mind. He wanted to know all about the various poisons, their rapidity of action and their relative painlessness. He was particularly insistent in questioning me about death at sea. I told him my belief that death at sea without a lifebelt was a relatively easy death, with the lifebelt perhaps the most terrible of all. I can see him now fixing his sombre eyes on the lifebelts hung by the cabin door and saying he would throw them overboard next morning. I asked him if he meant to send us to the bottom of the sea during our projected cruise to Corsica. He sat silent for a while.

'No,' he said at last, he thought after all he wanted to die in the arms of a woman. I told him at the rate he was going he had a fair chance to see his wish fulfilled. As I spoke Yvonne woke up, asked half dazed for another glass of champagne and fell asleep again, her head on his lap. She was a ballet dancer, barely eighteen, reared by the vicious caresses of some vieux marcheur in the coulisses of the Grand Opera, now helplessly drifting to total destruction on board the *Bel Ami* in the lap of her terrible lover. I knew that no lifebelt could save her, I knew she would have refused it if I had offered it to her. I knew she had given her heart as well as her body to this insatiable male who had no use for anything but her body. I knew what her fate would be, it was not the first girl I had seen asleep, her head on his lap. How far he was responsible for his doings is another question. The fear that haunted his restless brain day and night was already visible in his eyes, I for one considered him already then as a doomed man. I knew that the subtle poison of his own *Boule de Suif* had already begun its work of destruction in this magnificent brain. Did he know it himself? I often thought he did. The MS. of his 'Sur l'Eau' was lying on the table between us, he had just read me a few chapters, the best thing he had ever written I thought. He was still producing with feverish haste one masterpiece after another, slashing his excited brain with champagne, ether and drugs of all sorts. Women after women in endless succession hastened the destruction, women recruited from all quarters, from Faubourg St. Germain to the Boulevards, actresses, ballet-dancers, midinettes, grisettes, common prostitutes – 'le taureau triste' his friends used to call him. He was exceedingly proud of his successes, always hinting about mysterious ladies of the highest society admitted to his flat in Rue Clauzel by his faithful valet François – the first symptom of his approaching folie de grandeur. He often used to rush up the steps of Avenue de Villiers to sit down in a corner of my room looking at me in silence with that morbid fixity of his eyes I knew so well. Often he used to stand for minutes staring at himself in the mirror over the mantelpiece as if he was looking at a stranger. One day he told me that while he was sitting at his writing-table hard at work on his new novel he had been greatly surprised to see a stranger enter his study notwithstanding the severe vigilance of his valet. The stranger had sat down opposite him at the writing-table and began to dictate to him what he was about to write. He was just going to ring for François to have him turned out when he saw to his horror that the stranger was himself.

A couple of days later I was standing by his side in the coulisses of the Grand Opera watching Mademoiselle Yvonne dancing a pas de quatre, smiling on the sly at her lover whose flaming eyes never left her. We had late supper in the elegant little flat Maupassant had just taken for her. She had washed off the rouge from her face, I was shocked to see how pale and worn she looked compared with when I had first seen her in the yacht. She told me she always took ether when she was dancing, there was nothing like ether for a pick-me-up, all her comrades took ether, even Monsieur le Directeur du Corps de Ballet himself – as a matter of fact I saw him die of it many years later in his villa in Capri. Maupassant complained that she was getting too thin and that she was keeping him awake at night by her incessant coughing. At his request I examined her the next morning, there was serious trouble at the top of one of her lungs. I told Maupassant she must have complete rest, I advised him to send her for the winter to Menton. Maupassant said he was quite willing to do all that could be done for her, besides he did not fancy thin women. She refused point blank to go, she said she would rather die than leave him. She gave me lots of trouble during the winter and also lots of new patients. One after another her comrades began to turn up at Avenue de Villiers, to consult me on the sly, afraid as they were to be put on half pay by the regular doctor of the Opera. The coulisses of the Corps de Ballet were a new world to me, not exempt from danger to the inexperienced explorer for, alas, it was not only to the altar of the Goddess Terpsichore that these young vestals brought the garlands of their youth. Luckily for me their Terpsichore had been turned out of my Olympus with the last forgotten strains of Gluck's *Chaconne* and Mozart's *Menuet*, what remained to-day was to my eyes acrobatics pure and simple. Not so with the other onlookers in the coulisses. I never ceased to wonder at the facility with which these decrepit Don Giovannis lost their balance while watching all these half-naked girls keeping theirs on the tips of their toes.

Yvonne had her first haemorrhage and the trouble began in earnest. Maupassant like all authors who write about illness and death hated to watch it at close quarters. Yvonne drank bottles of cod-liver oil by the dozen in order to get fat, she knew her lover did not like thin women. It was all in vain, soon nothing remained of her fair youth but her wonderful eyes, lustrous with fever and ether. Maupassant's purse remained open to her, but his arms soon closed round the body of one of her comrades. Yvonne threw a bottle of vitriol at the face of her rival, luckily she nearly missed her. She escaped with two months' imprisonment, thanks to Maupassant's powerful influence and to a certificate from me that she had only a couple of months to live. Once out of prison she refused to return to her flat notwithstanding Maupassant's entreaties. She vanished into the vast unknown of the immense city like the doomed animal hiding to die. I found her by a mere accident a month later in a bed at St. Lazare – the last stage in the Via Crucis of all the fallen and forlorn women of Paris. I told her I would let Maupassant know, I felt sure he would come to see her at once. I called at Maupassant's house the same afternoon, there was no time to lose, it was evident that she had not many days to live. The faithful François was at his usual post as a Cerberus, watching over his master against any intruders. I tried in vain to be admitted, the orders were severe, no visitor was to be admitted under any circumstances, it was the usual story about the mysterious lady. All I could do was to scribble a note about Yvonne to his master which François promised to deliver at once. Whether he got it or not I never knew, I hope he did not, it is quite probable, for François was always trying to keep his beloved master away from his entanglements with women. When I came to St. Lazare the next day, Yvonne was dead. The nun told me she had spent the whole morning putting rouge on her face and arranging her hair, she had even borrowed from an old prostitute in the next bed a little red silk shawl, last vestige of past splendour, to cover her emaciated shoulders. She told the nun she was expecting her Monsieur, she waited eagerly the whole day but he never came. In the morning they found her dead in her bed, she had swallowed to the last drop her portion of chloral.

Two months later I saw Guy de Maupassant in the garden of Maison Blanche in Passy, the well-known asylum. He was walking about on the arm of his faithful François, throwing small pebbles on the flower beds with the geste of Millet's Semeur. 'Look, look,' he said, 'they will all come up as little Maupassants in the spring if only it will rain.'

* * *

To me who for years had been devoting my spare time to study hypnotism these stage performances of the Salpêtrière before the public of tout Paris were nothing but an absurd farce, a hopeless muddle of truth and cheating. Some of these subjects were no doubt real somnambulists faithfully carrying out in a waking state the various suggestions made to them during sleep – post-hypnotic suggestions. Many of them were mere frauds, knowing quite well what they were expected to do, delighted to perform their various tricks in public, cheating both doctors and audience with the amazing cunning of the hystériques. They were always ready to 'piquer une attaque' of Charcot's classical grande hystérie, arc-en-ciel and all, or to exhibit his famous three stages of hypnotism: lethargy, catalepsy, somnambulism, all invented by the Master and hardly ever observed outside the Salpêtrière. Some of them smelt with delight a bottle of ammonia when told it was rose water, others would eat a piece of charcoal when presented to them as chocolate. Another would crawl on all fours on the floor, barking furiously when told she was a dog, flap her arms as if trying to fly when turned into a pigeon, lift her skirts with a shriek of terror when a glove was thrown at her feet with a suggestion of its being a snake. Another would walk with a top-hat in her arms rocking it to and fro and kissing it tenderly when she was told it was her baby. Hypnotized right and left, dozens of times a day, by doctors and students, many of these unfortunate girls spent their days in a state of semi-trance, their brains bewildered by all sorts of absurd suggestions, half conscious and certainly not responsible for their doings, sooner or later doomed to end their days in the salles des agités if not in a lunatic asylum. While condemning these Tuesday gala performances in the amphitheatre as unscientific and unworthy of the Salpêtrière, it would be unfair not to admit that serious work was done in the wards to investigate many of the still obscure phenomena of hypnotism. I myself was just then by the permission of the chef de clinique carrying out some interesting experiments in post-hypnotic suggestion and telepathy with one of these girls, one of the best somnambulists I have ever met.

I had already then grave doubts as to the correctness of Charcot's theories, accepted without opposition by his blindfolded pupils and the public by means of what can only be explained as a sort of suggestion en masse. I had returned from my last visit to Professor Bernheim's clinic in Nancy as an obscure but resolute supporter of the so-called Nancy school in opposition to the teachings of Charcot. To speak of the Nancy school at the Salpêtrière was in those days considered almost as an act of lèse-majesté. Charcot himself flew into a rage at the very mention of Professor Bernheim's name. An article of mine in the 'Gazette des Hôpitaux' inspired by my last visit to Nancy was shown to the Master by one of his assistants who disliked me cordially. For several days Charcot seemed to ignore my presence altogether. Some time later appeared in the 'Figaro' a violent article under the nom de plume of 'Ignotus,' one of the leading journalists of Paris, denouncing these public demonstrations of hypnotism as a dangerous and ridiculous spectacle of no scientific value, unworthy of the great Master of the Salpêtrière. I was present when this article was shown to Charcot during the morning round, I was amazed at his furious resentment against a mere newspaper article, it seemed to me he could have well afforded to ignore it. There was plenty of jealousy among his pupils, I had a large share of it. Who started the lie I do not know, but to my horror I soon became aware of a rumour that 'Ignotus' had got his most damaging facts from me. Charcot never said a word to me about it, but from that day his usual cordial attitude to me had changed. Then came the blow, one of the bitterest I ever received in my life. Fate had set the trap, with my usual impulsive foolhardiness I walked straight into it.

One Sunday as I was leaving the hospital I came upon a pair of old peasants sitting on a bench under the plane-trees in the inner court. They smelt of the country, of the orchard, the fields and the cow-house, it did my heart good to look at them. I asked them where they came from and what they were doing there. The old man in his long blue blouse lifted his hand to his béret, the old woman in her neat white coiffe curtseyed to me with a friendly smile. They said they had arrived there the same morning from their village in Normandy on a visit to their daughter who had been kitchen maid in the Salpêtrière for over two years. It was a very good job, she had been taken there by one of the nuns in their village who was now undercook in the hospital kitchen. But there was lots to do on the farm, they had now three cows and six pigs and they had come to take their daughter home, she was a very strong and healthy girl and they were getting too old to work the farm alone. They were so tired from the long night journey in the train that they had had to sit down on the bench to rest for a while. Would I be so kind as to show them where the kitchen was? I said they had to cross three courts and pass through endless corridors, I had better take them to the kitchen myself and help them to find their daughter. God knows how many kitchen maids there were in the immense kitchen which prepared food for nearly three thousand mouths! We trotted off to the kitchen pavilion, the old woman never ceasing to tell me about their apple-orchard, their crop of potatoes, the pigs, the cows, the excellent cheese she was making. She produced from her basket a little fromage de crème she had just made for Geneviève, but she would be very pleased if I would accept it. I looked at her face as she handed me the cheese.

How old was Geneviève?

She was just twenty.

Was she fair and very good-looking?

'Her father says she looks exactly like me,' answered the old mother simply.

The old man nodded approvingly.

'Are you sure she is working in the kitchen?' I asked with an involuntary shudder, looking again attentively at the wrinkled face of the old mother.

For all answer the old man fumbled about in the immense pocket of his blouse and produced Geneviève's last letter. I had been a keen student of calligraphy for years, I recognized at a glance the curiously twisted and naïve, but remarkably neat handwriting, gradually improved during hundreds of experiences in automatic handwriting, even under my own supervision.

'This way,' I said taking them straight up to the Salle St. Agnes, the ward of the grandes hystériques.

Geneviève was sitting dangling her silk-stockinged legs from the long table in the middle of the ward with a copy of 'Le Rire' in her lap with her own portrait on the title-page. At her side sat Lisette, another of the leading stars of the company. Geneviève's coquettishly arranged hair was adorned with a blue silk ribbon, a row of false pearls hung round her neck, her pale face was made up with rouge, her lips painted. To all appearance she looked more like an enterprising midinette off for a stroll on the Boulevards than the inmate of a hospital. Geneviève was the prima donna of the Tuesday stage performances, spoiled and petted by everybody, very pleased with herself and her surroundings. The two old peasants stared bewildered at their daughter. Geneviève looked back at them with an indifferent, silly air, she did not seem to recognize them at first. Suddenly her face began to twitch and with a piercing scream she fell headlong on the floor in violent convulsions, to be followed immediately by Lisette in the classic arc-en-ciel. Obeying the law of imitation a couple of other hystériques started to 'piquer' their attacks from their beds, one in convulsive laughter, one in a flood of tears. The two old folk speechless with terror were rapidly pushed out of the ward by the nuns. I joined them on the stairs and took them down to the bench under the plane-trees. They were still too frightened even to cry. It was not easy to explain the situation to these poor peasants. How their daughter had landed in the salle des hystériques from the kitchen I did not know myself. I spoke to them as gently as I could, I said their daughter would soon be all right again. The old mother began to cry, the small twinkling eyes of the father began to shine with an evil light. I urged them to return to their village, I promised them that their daughter should be sent home as soon as possible. The father wanted to take her away at once but the mother backed me up by saying that it was wiser to leave her where she was till she got better, she was sure her daughter was in good hands. After repeating my promise to arrange as soon as possible with the professor and the director of the hospital the necessary formalities for sending Geneviève home in charge of a nurse I succeeded with great difficulty in putting them in a cab to drive to Gare d'Orléans to catch the next train. The thought of the two old peasants kept me awake the whole night. How was I to keep my promise? I knew only too well that I was just then the most unsuitable of all men to speak to Charcot about their daughter, I knew equally well that she would never consent to leave the Salpêtrière and return to her humble old home of her own free will. I could see only one solution, to conquer that will of hers and replace it by my own will. I knew Geneviève well as an excellent somnambulist. She had been trained by others and by myself to carry out post-hypnotic suggestions to be transformed into act with the fatality of a falling stone, with an almost astronomic punctuality and amnesia, i.e. complete ignorance in her waking state of what she had been told to do. I applied to the chef de clinique to continue my experiments with Geneviève in telepathy, just then the order of the day. He was himself keenly interested in the subject, offered me to work undisturbed in his own cabinet for an hour every afternoon and wished me good luck. I had told him a lie. The very first day I suggested to Geneviève under deep hypnosis to stay in bed the following Tuesday instead of going to the amphitheatre, to dislike her life in the Salpêtrière and to wish to return to her parents. For a week I repeated daily these suggestions to her with no apparent result. The following week she was absent and much missed during the Tuesday performance in the amphitheatre. I was told she had a cold and was in bed. A couple of days later I found her with a railway guide in her hands, she put it rapidly in her pocket as soon as she saw me, an excellent sign that I could rely on her amnesia. Soon afterwards it was suggested to her to go to the Bon Marché the following Thursday – the day out – to buy herself a new hat. I saw her show it with great pride to Lisette the next morning. Two days later she was ordered to leave the Salle St. Agnes at twelve o'clock the next day while the nuns were busy distributing the midday meal, to slip out of the porter's lodge while he was having his luncheon, jump into a cab and drive straight to Avenue de Villiers. On returning home to my consultation I found her sitting in my waiting-room. I asked her what was the matter, she looked very embarrassed and muttered something about wanting to see my dogs and the monkey I had told her about. She was entertained by Rosalie in the dining-room with a cup of coffee and put into a cab to drive back to the hospital.

'C'est une belle fille,' said Rosalie, putting her finger to her forehead, 'mais je crois qu'elle a une araignée dans le plafond. Elle m'a dit qu'elle ne savait pas du tout pourquoi elle était venue ici.'

The success of this preliminary experiment made me decide with my usual impulsiveness to carry out my plan at once. Geneviève was ordered to come to Avenue de Villiers with the same precaution and at the same hour two days later. It was on a Monday, I had invited Norstrom for luncheon, I wanted him there as a witness in case of unforeseen complications. When I told him of my plan, he warned me of the serious consequences it might have to myself whether in case of failure or success, he was besides certain she would not turn up.

'Suppose she has told somebody,' said Norstrom.

'She cannot tell what she does not know herself, she will not know she is coming to Avenue de Villiers till the clock strikes twelve.'

'But could it not be got out of her under hypnotic sleep?' he insisted.

'There is only one man who could wrench it out of her – Charcot himself. But since he takes little notice of her except during his Tuesday lectures, I have eliminated this possibility.'

I said it was besides too late for discussions, I was sure she had already left the hospital and would turn up in less than half-an-hour.

The grandfather clock in the hall chimed a quarter to one, I thought it was going too fast, for the first time its deep voice irritated my ears.

'I wish you would chuck all this nonsense about hypnotism,' said Norstrom lighting his big cigar. 'You have got it on the brain, you will end by getting crazy yourself if you are not already. I do not believe in hypnotism, I have tried to hypnotize several people, but I have never succeeded.'

'I would not believe in hypnotism myself if you had,' I retorted angrily

The front bell rang. I sprang to open the door myself. It was Miss

Anderssen, the nurse I had ordered to be there at one o'clock to take Geneviève home. She was to start with her by the night express to Normandy with a letter from me to the curé of the village explaining the situation and begging him to prevent at all costs Geneviève's return to Paris.

I sat down at the dining-table again smoking furiously cigarette after cigarette.

'What has the nurse to say to all this?' asked Norstrom.

'She says nothing, she is English. She knows me well, she trusts my judgment absolutely.'

'I wish I did,' growled Norstrom puffing at his cigar.

The Cromwell clock on the mantelpiece struck half-past one, confirmed with uncanny precision by the voice of half-a-dozen old clocks from every room.

'Failure,' said Norstrom phlegmatically, 'and so much the better for both of us, I am d——d glad not to be mixed up in this business.'

I did not close my eyes that night, this time it was Geneviève and not the two peasants that kept me awake. I had long since been so spoiled by luck that my nerves were ill adapted for failure. What had happened?

I felt sick and slightly faint as I entered the amphitheatre of the Salpêtrière the next morning. Charcot had already begun his Tuesday lecture on hypnotism, Geneviève was not there in her usual place on the platform. I slipped out of the room and went up to the Salle de Gardes. One of the internes told me he had been summoned from his luncheon yesterday to Salle St. Agnes where he found Geneviève in a state of cataleptic coma interrupted by the most violent convulsions he had ever seen. One of the nuns had met her outside the hospital half-an-hour before as she was jumping into a cab. She had looked so agitated that the nun had brought her back to the porter's lodge with the greatest difficulty and she had had to be carried upstairs to the Salle St. Agnes. The whole night she had fought desperately like a wild animal trying to escape from its cage, they had had to put her into a strait-jacket. She was now shut up in a separate room with a heavy dose of bromide and a bonnet d'irrigation on her head. Nobody understood the cause of this sudden change. Charcot himself had visited her and succeeded with great difficulty in putting her to sleep. We were interrupted by the entering of the chef de clinique who told me he had been hunting for me all over the hospital, Charcot wished to speak to me, he was to take me to his cabinet as soon as the lesson in the amphitheatre was finished. He did not say a single word to me as we passed through the adjoining laboratories. He knocked at the door and I entered the well-known little sanctuary of the Master for the last time in my life. Charcot sat in his usual chair by the table, bent over the microscope. He raised his head and flashed his terrible eyes on me. Speaking very slowly, his deep voice trembling with rage, he said I had tried to allure to my house an inmate of his hospital, a young girl, a deséquilibrée, half unconscious of her acts. According to her own confession she had already been once to my house, my diabolical plan to take advantage of her a second time had only miscarried by a mere accident. It was a criminal offence, he ought to hand me over to the police but for the honour of the profession and the red ribbon in my buttonhole he would let me off by turning me out of the hospital, he wished never to set his eyes on me again.

I felt as if struck by lightning, my tongue stuck to my palate, I could not utter a word. Suddenly as I realized the real meaning of his abominable accusation my fear left me. I answered angrily that it was he and his followers and not I who had brought ruin to this girl who had entered the hospital as a strong and healthy peasant girl and would leave it as a lunatic if she remained there much longer. I had adopted the only course open to me to return her to her old parents. I had failed to rescue her and I was sorry I had failed.

'Assez, Monsieur!' he shouted.

He turned to the chef de clinique and told him to accompany me to the porter's lodge with orders from himself to refuse to let me enter the hospital again, adding that if his own authority was not sufficient to exclude me from his clinic he would report the matter to the Assistance Publique. He rose from his chair and walked out of the room with his slow, heavy step.

XIX

Hypnotism

The famous platform performances in the amphitheatre of the
Salpêtrière which brought on my disgrace, have long since been
condemned by every serious student of hypnotic phenomena.
Charcot's theories on hypnotism imposed by the sheer weight of
his authority on a whole generation of doctors have fallen into
discredit after having retarded our knowledge of the true nature of
these phenomena for over twenty years. Almost every single one of
Charcot's theories on hypnotism has proved wrong. Hypnotism is
not, as he said, an artificially induced neurosis only to be encountered in hysteria, in hypersensitive, weak-minded and ill-
balanced people. The contrary is the truth. Hysterical subjects are
as a rule less easily hypnotizable than well-balanced and mentally
sound people. Intelligent, strong-willed and domineering people
are more easy to hypnotize than dull, stupid, superficial, weak-
minded people. Idiots and lunatics are in the majority of cases
refractory to hypnotic influence. People who say they don't believe
in hypnotism, laugh at you and say they are sure they cannot be
hypnotized, are as a rule most easy to put to sleep. All children are
easily hypnotizable. Hypnotic sleep cannot be produced by mech-
anical means alone. The shining glass balls, the revolving mirrors
borrowed from the bird-catcher, the magnets, the fixed staring in
the eyes of the subject, the classical mesmeric passes used at the
Salpêtrière and the Charité are sheer nonsense.

The therapeutic value of hypnotism in medicine and surgery is
not negligible as Charcot said. On the contrary it is immense if in
the hands of competent doctors with clear heads and clean hands,
and thoroughly acquainted with the technique. The statistics of
thousands of well-investigated cases prove this beyond dispute.
Speaking of myself who have never been what is called a hypnotis-
eur but a nerve doctor compelled to make use of this weapon when
other remedies had proved useless, I have often obtained marvellous results by this still misunderstood method of healing. Mental
disorders of various kinds with or without loss of will power,
alcoholism, morphinomania, cocainomania, nymphomania can

as a rule be cured by this method. Sexual inversion is more difficult to tackle. In many if not most cases it cannot be considered as a disease but as a deviation of the sexual instinct natural to certain individuals where an energetic interference often does more harm than good. Whether and how far our social laws should interfere, is a very complicated question I do not mean to discuss here. What is certain is that the actual formulation of the law is founded upon a misunderstanding of the uncomfortable position in our midst of this numerous class of people. They are no criminals, but mere victims of a momentary absent-mindedness of Mother Nature, perhaps at their birth, perhaps at their conception. What is the explanation of the enormous increase of sexual inversion? Does nature revenge herself on the masculinized girl of to-day by rearing an effeminate son from her straightened hips and flattened breasts? Or are we the bewildered spectators of a new phase of evolution with a gradual amalgamation of two distinct animals into a new, hitherto unknown specimen, last survival of a doomed race on a worn-out planet, missing link between the Homo sapiens of to-day and the mysterious Super-Homo of to-morrow?

The great benefit derived from hypnotic anaesthesia in surgical operations and childbirth is now admitted by everybody. Even more striking is the beneficial effect of this method in the most painful of all operations, as a rule still to be endured without anaesthesia – Death. What it was granted to me to do for many of our dying soldiers during the last war is enough to make me thank God for having had this powerful weapon in my hands. In the autumn of 1915 I spent two unforgettable days and nights among a couple of hundred dying soldiers, huddled together under their blood-stained great-coats on the floor of a village church in France. We had no morphia, no chloroform, no anaesthetics whatsoever to alleviate their tortures and shorten their agony. Many of them died before my eyes, insensible and unaware, often even a smile on their lips, with my hand on their forehead, my slowly repeated words of hope and comfort resounding in their ears, the terror of death gradually vanishing from their closing eyes.

What was this mysterious force which almost seemed to emanate from my hand? Where did it come from? Did it come from the stream of consciousness within me below the level of my waking life, or was it after all the mysterious 'odylic force,' the magnetic fluid of the old mesmerists? Of course modern science has done away with the magnetic fluid and replaced it with a dozen new, more or less ingenious theories. I know them all, none of them satisfies me so far. Suggestion alone, the very keystone of the now universally accepted theory on hypnotism, cannot explain all its startling phenomena. The word suggestion as used by its chief promoters, the Nancy school, differs besides only in name from this now ridiculed odylic force of Mesmer. Let us admit, as we must do, that the miracle is not done by the operator but by the subconscious mind of the subject. But how are we to explain the success of the one operator and the failure of another? Why does the suggestion of one operator re-echo as a word of command in the subterranean workshop of the subject's mind to bring its hidden forces into action while this same suggestion made by another operator is intercepted by the subject's consciousness and remains ineffective? I, of all people, am anxious to know it, because ever since I was a boy, I have been aware that I myself possessed this power, whatever name is given to it, in an exceptional degree. Most of my patients, young and old, men and women, seemed to find it out sooner or later and often spoke to me about it. My comrades in the hospital wards all knew about it, Charcot himself knew about it and often utilized it. Professor Voisin, the famous alienist of Asile St. Anne, often made me assist him in his desperate endeavours to hypnotize some of his lunatics. We used to work for hours with these poor lunatics screaming and raving with rage in their strait-jackets, unable to do anything but to spit in our faces, as they often did. The result of our efforts was in most cases negative, but on several occasions I succeeded in calming down some of them when the Professor himself had failed, notwithstanding his marvellous patience. All the keepers in the Jardin Zoologique and Ménagerie Pezon knew about it. It was a familiar trick of mine to put their snakes, lizards, tortoises, parrots, owls, bears and big cats into a state of lethargy, quite similar to Charcot's first stage of hypnosis, often I even succeeded in inducing profound sleep. I think I have already mentioned how I opened an abscess and extracted a splinter from the paw of Léonie the magnificent lioness in the Ménagerie Pezon. It could not be explained but as a case of local anaesthesia under slight hypnosis. Monkeys, notwithstanding their restlessness, are easily put to sleep thanks to their high intelligence and impressionable nervous system. Snake charming is of course a hypnotic phenomenon. I have myself put a cobra into a state of catalepsy in the temple of Karnak. The training of wild elephants has, I suspect, also something to do with hypnotic influence. The way I once heard a mahout talking for hours to one of the elephants of the Zoo who had become restive, sounded exactly like hypnotic suggestion. Most birds are easily hypnotizable, everybody knows how easily it is done with chickens. In all dealings with animals, wild and tame, the soothing influence of the monotonous sound of slowly repeated words can easily be verified by every observer, so much so that it almost seems as if they understood the very meaning of what one said to them – what would I not give if I could understand what they said to me! Still it is obviously impossible to speak of mental suggestion here. There must be some other power at work, I ask again and in vain, what is this power?

Among my patients I had handed over to Norstrom during my absence in Sweden was a bad case of morphinomania nearly cured by hypnotic suggestion. As I was anxious that the treatment should not be interrupted I made Norstrom assist at the last séance. He said it was quite easy and the patient seemed to like him. On my return to Paris she had fallen back into her old habits, my colleague had been unable to hypnotize her. I tried to make her explain the reason of his failure, she said she could not understand it herself, she was very sorry, she had tried her best and so had Norstrom whom she said she liked very much.

Charcot once sent me a young foreign diplomat, a bad case of sexual inversion. Both Professor Kraft-Ebing, the famous specialist of Vienna, and Charcot himself had been unable to hypnotize this man. He himself was most anxious to be cured, he was living in constant fear of blackmail and was most distressed over their failure. He said he was convinced it was his only chance, that he felt sure he would be all right if he could be put to sleep.

'But you *are* asleep,' said I, barely touching his forehead with the top of my fingers, no passes, no staring in his eyes, no suggestion. The words were hardly out of my mouth before his eyelids closed with a slight tremor, he was in deep hypnotic sleep in less than a minute. It looked hopeful at first, a month later he returned to his country full of confidence for the future, far more so than I was. He said he was going to propose to a young lady he had become fond of of late, he was most anxious to marry and have children. I lost sight of him. A year later I heard by a mere accident that he had killed himself. Had this unhappy man consulted me a few years later when I had acquired more knowledge of sexual inversion I would never have attempted the hopeless task of curing him.

Outside the Salpêtrière I have hardly ever come across Charcot's famous three stages of hypnosis so strikingly exhibited during his Tuesday lectures. They were all invented by himself, grafted on his hysterical subjects and accepted by his pupils by the powerful suggestion of the Master. The same affirmation holds good in regard to his special hobby, his grande hystérie then rampant all over the Salpêtrière, ward after ward full of it, now almost extinct.

The fact that all these experiments in hypnotism were done on hysterical subjects, is the only possible explanation of his inability to understand the true nature of these phenomena. If the statement of the Salpêtrière school that only hysterical subjects are hypnotizable was correct it would mean that at least eighty-five per cent of mankind was suffering from hysteria.

But on one point Charcot was surely right, whatever the Nancy school, Forel, Moll and many others may say. Experiments in hypnotism are not without their danger, to the subjects as well as to the spectators. Personally I think public demonstrations of hypnotic phenomena should be forbidden by law. Specialists in nervous and mental disorders can no more do without hypnotism than can surgeons without chloroform and ether. One need only remember the thousands and thousands of helpless cases of shell-shock and traumatic neuroses during the last war cured as by enchantment by this method. Hypnotic treatment in the great majority of cases does not necessitate hypnotic sleep with abolition of waking consciousness. An operator well acquainted with its complicated technique and who knows something about psychology – both these qualifications are necessary for success – will as a rule obtain remarkable, often amazing results, by the mere use of what is called suggestion à l'état de veille. The Nancy school maintains that hypnotic sleep and natural sleep are identical. It is not so. As yet we do not know what hypnotic sleep is and until we know more about it we had better refrain from inducing it in our patients except in cases of absolute necessity. This being said, let me add that most of the accusations against hypnotism are grossly exaggerated. So far I know of no well-authenticated proof of a criminal act committed by a subject under post-hypnotic suggestion. I have never seen a suggestion made under hypnosis carried out by the subject which he or she would refuse to carry out if made during normal waking state. I affirm that if a blackguard should suggest to a woman under profound hypnosis that she should surrender herself to him and she should carry out this

221

suggestion, it would mean that she would as readily have done so had the suggestion been made to her in a normal condition of waking life. There is no such thing as blind obedience. The subject knows quite well what is going on the whole time and what he is willing or unwilling to do. Camille, Professor Liéjoie's famous somnambulist in Nancy, who would remain impassive and indifferent when a pin was stuck full length through her arm or a piece of burning charcoal put in her hand, would blush scarlet when the Professor pretended to make a gesture as if to disarrange her clothes, and wake up instantaneously. This is only one of the many baffling contradictions familar to students of hypnotic phenomena and most difficult for outsiders to understand. The fact that the person cannot be hypnotized without his or her will, must not be overlooked by the alarmists. Of course all talk about an unwilling and unaware person being hypnotized at a distance is sheer nonsense. So also is Psycho-Analysis.

XX

Insomnia

Norstrom with his usual kind thoughtfulness had invited me to dinner the evening of the fatal day. It was a gloomy dinner, I was still smarting under the humiliation of my defeat, and Norstrom sat scratching his head in silent meditation how he was to raise the three thousand francs due to his landlord the next day. Norstrom refused point-blank to accept my explanation of my disaster – bad luck and the most unexpected interference of the unforeseen with my carefully prepared plans. Norstrom's diagnosis of my case was Don Quixottish foolhardiness and immeasurable conceit. I said that unless I received that very day some sign from Fortuna, my beloved goddess, that she felt sorry for having forsaken me and would take me back in her favour, I would accept his diagnosis. As I spoke the words, my eyes were miraculously transferred from the bottle of Médoc between us to Norstrom's gigantic hands.

'Have you ever gone in for massage?' I asked abruptly.

For all answer Norstrom opened his broad, honest hands and showed me with great pride a pair of thumb balls the size of an orange. There was no doubt of his speaking the truth when he said he had done a lot of massage in Sweden in former days.

I told the waiter to bring a bottle of Veuve Clicquot, the best he could lay his hands on, and raised my glass to drink to my defeat of to-day and to his victory of to-morrow.

'I thought you told me a moment ago you were out of cash,' said Norstrom, looking at the bottle of champagne.

'Never mind,' I laughed, 'a brilliant idea, worth a hundred bottles of Veuve Clicquot, has just shot through my brain, have another glass while I am working it out.'

Norstrom always used to say that I had two different brains working alternatively in my head, the well-developed brain of a fool and the undeveloped brain of a sort of genius. He stared bewildered at me when I told him I would come to Rue Pigalle the next day at his consultation hour between two and three to explain it all. He said it was the best hour for a quiet talk. I was sure to find him alone. We left the Café de la Régence arm in arm, Norstrom still pondering over which of my two brains my brilliant idea had sprung from, I in tearing spirits, having almost forgotten having been turned out of the Salpêtrière in the morning.

At two o'clock sharp the following day I entered the sumptuous consulting-room of Professor Guéneau de Mussy in Rue du Cirque, the famous physician of the Orléans family whose exile he had shared – now one of the leading medical celebrities in Paris. The Professor, who had always been very kind to me, asked me what he could do for me. I told him that when I had called on him a week ago he had done me the honour of introducing me to Monseigneur le Duc d'Aumale, as he was leaving the room supported by his valet and leaning heavily on his stick. He had told me that the Duke was suffering from sciatica, that his knees were giving way, that he was almost unable to walk, that he had consulted in vain all the leading surgeons of Paris. I said I had ventured to come to-day to tell the Professor that unless I was greatly mistaken the Duke could be cured by massage. A compatriot of mine, a great authority on sciatica and massage, was actually in Paris, I took the liberty of suggesting that he should be called in to examine the Duke. Guéneau de Mussy, who like most French doctors of his time knew next to nothing about massage, accepted at once. As the Duke was leaving for his Château de Chantilly the next day it was arranged that I should come at once with my illustrious compatriot to his hôtel in the Faubourg St. Germain. Later in the afternoon Norstrom and I arrived at the hôtel where we were met by Professor Guéneau de Mussy. Norstrom had been instructed by me to try his best to look like a famous specialist on sciatica but for God's sake to avoid lecturing on the subject. A rapid examination made it clear to us both that it was indeed an excellent case for massage and passive movements. The Duke left for the Château de Chantilly the next day accompanied by Norstrom. A fortnight later I read in the 'Figaro' that the famous Swedish specialist Doctor Norstrom of world-wide reputation had been called to Chantilly to attend the Duc d'Aumale. Monseigneur had been seen walking unaided in the park of his château, it was a marvellous recovery. Doctor Norstrom was also attending the Duc de Montpensier crippled with gout for years and now rapidly improving.

Then came the turn of Princess Mathilde, soon to be followed by Don Pedro of Brazil, a couple of Russian Grand Dukes, an Austrian Arch-Duchess and the Infanta Eulalia of Spain.

My friend Norstrom, who after his return from Chantilly obeyed me blindly, had been forbidden by me to accept any other patients but royalties until further orders. I assured him this was sound tactics, founded on solid psychological facts. Two months later Norstrom was back in his smart apartment at the Boulevard Haussmann, his consulting-room crammed with patients from all countries, Americans heading the list. In the autumn appeared his 'Manuel de Massage Suédois' by Doctor Gustave Norstrom, Paris, Librairie Hachette, concocted by us with feverish haste from different Swedish sources, an American edition appearing simultaneously in New York. In the early winter Norstrom was summoned to Newport to attend old Mr. Vanderbilt, the fee to be fixed by himself. To his dismay I forbade him to go, a month later the old multimillionaire was shipped to Europe to take his place among Norstrom's other patients – a living réclame in gigantic letters, visible all over the United States. Norstrom was hard at work from morning till night rubbing his patients with his enormous thumbs, his thumb balls gradually assuming the proportions of a small melon. Soon he even had to give up his Saturday evenings in the Scandinavian club where, streaming with perspiration, he used to gallop round the room with all the ladies in turn for the sake of his liver. He said there was nothing like dancing and perspiring to keep your liver going.

Norstrom's success made me so happy that for some time I almost forgot my own disgrace. Alas, it all came back to me soon in all its horror, first in my dreams, then in my waking thoughts. Often just as I was falling to sleep I saw under my closing eyelids the ignominious last scene of the tragedy before the curtain went down over my future. I saw Charcot's terrible eyes flashing through the darkness, I saw myself escorted by two of his assistants like a criminal between two policemen, walking out of the Salpêtrière for the last time. I saw my own folly, I understood that Norstrom's diagnosis – 'Don Quixottish foolhardiness and immeasurable conceit' – was right after all. Don Quixote again!

Soon I ceased to sleep altogether, an acute attack of insomnia set in, so terrible that it nearly made me go off my head. Insomnia does not kill its man unless he kills himself – sleeplessness is the most common cause of suicide. But it kills his joie de vivre, it saps his strength, it sucks the blood from his brain and from his heart like a vampire. It makes him remember during the night what he was meant to forget in blissful sleep. It makes him forget during the day what he was meant to remember. Memory is the first to go overboard, soon friendship, love, sense of duty, even pity itself are one after another washed away. Despondency alone sticks to the doomed ship to sheer it on the rocks to total destruction. Voltaire was right when he placed sleep on the same level as hope.

I did not go off my head, I did not kill myself. I staggered on with my work as best I could, careless, indifferent what happened to myself, and what happened to my patients. Beware of a doctor who suffers from insomnia! My patients began to complain that I was rough and impatient with them, many of them left me, many stuck to me still and so much the worse for them. Only when they were about to die did I seem to wake up from my torpor, for I continued to take a keen interest in Death long after I had lost all interest in Life. I could still watch the approach of my grim colleague with the same keenness I used to watch him with when I was a student at the Salle Ste. Claire, hoping against hope to wrench his terrible secret from him. I could still sit the whole night by the bed-side of a dying patient after having neglected him when I might have been able to save him. They used to say I was very kind to sit up like that the whole night when the other doctors went away. But what did it matter to me whether I sat on a chair by the bed-side of somebody else or lay awake in my own bed? Luckily for me my increasing diffidence of drugs and narcotics saved me from total destruction, hardly ever did I myself take any of the numerous sleeping-draughts I had to write out the whole day for others. Rosalie was my medical adviser. I swallowed obediently tisanes after tisanes concocted by her, French fashion, from her inexhaustible pharmacopoeia of miraculous herbs. Rosalie was very worried about me. I even found out that often on her own initiative she used to send away my patients when she thought I looked too tired. I tried to get angry but I had no strength left to scold her.

Norstrom was also very worried about me. Our mutual position had now changed, he was ascending the slippery ladder of success, I was descending. It made him kinder than ever, I constantly marvelled at his patience with me. He often used to come to share my solitary dinner in Avenue de Villiers. I never dined out, never asked anybody to dinner, never went out in society where I used to go a lot before. I now thought it a waste of time, all I longed for was to be left alone and to sleep.

Norstrom wanted me to go to Capri for a couple of months, for a thorough rest, he felt sure I would return to my work all right again. I said I would never return to Paris if I went there now, I hated this artificial life of a big city more and more. I did not want to waste my time any longer in this atmosphere of sickness and decay. I wanted to go away for good. I did not want to be a fashionable doctor any longer, the more patients I got the heavier did I feel my chains. I had plenty of other interests in life than to look after rich Americans and silly neurotic females. What was the good of his talking about throwing away 'my splendid opportunities'? He knew quite well I had not the stuff in me to become a first-rate doctor. He knew equally well that I could neither make money nor keep it. Besides I did not want any money, I should not know what to do with it, I was afraid of money, I hated it. I wanted to lead a simple life amongst simple, unsophisticated people. If they could neither read nor write, so much the better. All I needed was a white-washed room with a hard bed, a deal table, a couple of chairs and a piano. The twitter of birds outside my open window and the sound of the sea from afar. All the things I really cared for could be got for very little money, I should be quite happy in the humblest surroundings as long as I had nothing ugly around me.

Norstrom's eyes wandered slowly round the room from the primitive pictures on gold ground on the walls to the Florentine Cinquecento Madonna on the prie-Dieu, from the Flemish tapestry over the door to the lustrous Cafaiolo vases and the frail Venetian glasses on the sideboard to the Persian rugs on the floor.

'I suppose you got this at the Bon Marché,' said Norstrom, staring maliciously at the priceless old Bukhara rug under the table.

'I will give it to you with pleasure in exchange for a single night's natural sleep. You are welcome to this unique Urbino vase signed by Maestro Giorgio himself if you can make me laugh. I do not want all this stuff any more, it says nothing to me, I am sick of it. Stop that irritating smile of yours, I know what I am saying, I am going to prove it to you.

'Do you know what I did when I was in London last week for that consultation about the lady with angina pectoris? Well, I had another consultation there that same day about another far worse case, a man this time. This man was me or rather my double, my Doppelgänger, as Heine called him.

' "Look here, my friend," I said to my Doppelgänger as we were leaving St. James's Club arm in arm, "I want to make a careful examination of your inside. Pull yourself together and let us stroll slowly up New Bond Street from Piccadilly to Oxford Street. Now listen carefully to what I say: put on your strongest glasses and look attentively in every shop-window, examine carefully every object you see. It is a fine opportunity for you who are fond of beautiful things, the richest shops of London are here. Everything money can buy will be displayed before your eyes, within the reach of your hand. Anything you would like to possess shall be handed over to you, all that you have to say is that you would like to have it. But only on one condition; what you select must remain with you for your own use or enjoyment, you cannot give it away."'

'We turned the corner of Piccadilly, the experiment began. I watched my Doppelgänger carefully from the corner of my eye as we strolled up Bond Street looking at every shop-window. He stopped a moment in front of Agnew, the art dealer's, looked carefully at an old Madonna on gold ground, said it was a very fine picture, early Sienna school, it might be Simone di Martino himself. He made a gesture towards the window-pane as if he wanted to grab the old picture, then he shook his head dejectedly, put his hand in his pocket and moved on. He greatly admired a fine old Cromwell clock at Hunt and Roskell's but with a shrug of his shoulders he said he did not care what time it was, he could besides guess it by looking at the sun. In front of Asprey's display of all imaginable bibelots and trinkets of silver and gold and precious stones he said he felt sick and declared he would smash the window-pane and all that was behind it if he had to look at all this confounded rubbish any longer. As we passed before the tailor to His Royal Highness the Prince of Wales, he said he thought old clothes were more comfortable to wear than new ones. As we moved on up the street he became more and more indifferent and seemed to be more interested in stopping to pat the numerous dogs trotting behind their owners on the trottoir than to explore the shop-windows. When we reached Oxford Street at last he had an apple in one hand and a bunch of lilies of the valley in the other. He said he wanted nothing else of all that he had seen in Bond Street, except perhaps the little Aberdeen terrier who had been sitting waiting patiently for his master outside Asprey's. He began to eat his apple, and said it was a very good apple, and looked tenderly at his bunch of lilies of the valley saying they reminded him of his old home in Sweden. He said he hoped I had finished my experiment and asked me if I had found out what was the matter with him – was it the head?

'I said No, it was the heart.

'He said I was a very clever doctor, he had always suspected it was the heart. He begged me to keep my professional secret and not to tell it to his friends, he did not want them to know what did not concern them.

'We returned to Paris the next morning. He seemed to enjoy the crossing between Dover and Calais, he said he loved the sea. Since then he has hardly ever left Avenue de Villiers, wandering restlessly from room to room as if he could not sit down for a minute. He is always hanging about in my waiting-room, pushing his way among the rich Americans to ask me for a pick-me-up, he says he is so tired. The rest of the day he drives about with me from place to place waiting patiently in the carriage with the dog while I am visiting my patients. During dinner he sits opposite me in the chair you are sitting in now, staring at me with his tired eyes, says he has no appetite, all he wants is a stiff sleeping-draught. In the night he comes and bends his head over my pillow, imploring me for God's sake to take him away, he says he cannot stand it much longer or ...'

'Neither can I,' Norstrom interrupted angrily, 'for Heaven's sake stop this confounded nonsense about your Doppelgänger, mental vivisection is a dangerous game for a man who cannot sleep. If you go on like this a little longer, both you and your Doppelgänger will end in Asile St. Anne. I give you up. If you wish to chuck your career, if you do not want either reputation or money, if you prefer your white-washed room in Capri to your luxurious apartment in Avenue de Villiers, by all means be off, the sooner the better, to your beloved island, and be happy there instead of becoming a lunatic here! As to your Doppelgänger you are welcome to tell him from me with all my respects that he is a humbug. I bet you anything you like that he will soon pick up another Bukhara rug to spread under your deal table, a Siennese Madonna and a Flemish gobelin to hang on the walls of your white-washed room, a Cinquecento Gubbio plate for eating your macaroni, and an old Venetian glass for drinking your Capri Bianco!'

XXI

The Miracle of Sant'Antonio

Sant'Antonio had done another miracle. I was living in a little contadino house in Anacapri, whitewashed and clean with a sunny pergola outside the open windows and friendly, simple people all around me. Old Maria Porta-Lettere, La Bella Margherita, Annarella and Gioconda were all delighted to see me back amongst them. Don Dionisio's Capri Bianco was better than ever and it dawned upon me more and more that the parroco's Capri Rosso was equally good. From sunrise till sunset I was hard at work in what had been Mastro Vincenzo's garden, digging the foundations of the huge arches of the loggia outside my future home. Mastro Nicola and his three sons were digging by my side and half-a-dozen girls with laughing eyes and swinging hips were carrying away the earth in huge baskets on their heads. A yard below the surface we had come upon the Roman walls, opus reticulatum as hard as granite with nymphs and bacchantes dancing on the intonaco of Pompeian red. Below appeared the mosaic floor framed with vineleaves of nero antico and a broken pavement of beautiful palombino now in the centre of the big loggia. A fluted column of cipollino, now supporting the little loggia in the inner courtyard, lay across the pavement where it had fallen two thousand years ago, crushing in its fall a big vase of Parian marble, the lion-headed handle of which is now lying on my table Roba di Timberio, said Mastro Nicola picking up a mutilated head of Augustus split in two – you can see it in the loggia to-day.

When the macaroni in the parroco Don Antonio's kitchen were ready the bells in the church rang mezzogiorno, we all sat down for a hearty meal round an enormous plate of insalata di pomidoro, minestrone or macaroni, soon to be at work again till sunset. When the bells below in Capri rang Ave Maria my fellow-workers all made the sign of the cross and went away with a Buon riposo, Eccellenza, buona notte signorino. Their wish was overheard by Sant'Antonio, he worked another miracle, I slept soundly the whole night, as I had not slept for years. I rose with the sun, sprang down to the lighthouse for my morning bath and was back in the garden as the others returned to work from the five o'clock morning mass.

None of my fellow-workers could read or write, none had ever worked at the building of any other houses than those of contadini, all more or less alike. But Mastro Nicola knew how to build an arch as did his father and his grandfather from untold generations, the Romans had been their masters. That this was going to be a different house from any they had ever seen before, had already dawned upon them, they were all tremendously interested, nobody knew so far what it was going to look like, nor did I. All we had to go by was a rough sort of sketch drawn by myself with a piece of charcoal on the white garden-wall, I cannot draw anything, it looked as if drawn by the hand of a child.

'This is my house,' I explained to them, 'with huge Roman columns supporting its vaulted rooms and of course small Gothic columns in all the windows. This is the loggia with its strong arches, we will decide by and by how many arches there will be. Here comes a pergola, over a hundred columns, leading up to the chapel, never mind the public road running straight across my pergola now, it will have to go. Here looking out on Castello Barbarossa comes another loggia, I do not quite see what it looks like for the present, I am sure it will spring out of my head at the right moment. This is a small inner court, all white marble, a sort of atrium with a cool fountain in its midst and heads of Roman Emperors in niches round the walls. Here behind the house we are going to knock down the garden-wall and build a cloister something like the Lateran cloister in Rome. Here comes a large terrace where all you girls will dance the tarantella on summer evenings. On the top of the garden we shall blast away the rock and build a Greek theatre open on all sides to sun and wind. This is an avenue of cypresses leading up to the chapel which we will of course rebuild as a chapel with cloister stalls and stained-glass windows, I intend to make it my library. This is a colonnade with twisted Gothic columns surrounding the chapel and here looking out over the bay of Naples we are going to hoist an enormous Egyptian sphinx of red granite, older than Tiberius himself. It is the very place for a sphinx. I do not see for the present where I shall get it from but I am sure it will turn up in time.'

They were all delighted and eager to finish the house at once. Mastro Nicola wanted to know where the water for the fountains was to come from.

Of course from Heaven where all the water on the island came from. I intended besides to buy the whole mountain of Barbarossa and build an enormous cistern there for collecting the rain water, and supply the whole village with water, now so badly needed, it was the least I could do for them to repay all their kindness to me. When I drew the outlines of the little cloister with my stick in the sand I saw it at once just as it stands now, encircling with its graceful arcades its little court of cypresses with the dancing fawn in its midst. When we found the earthenware vase full of Roman coins, they became tremendously excited, every contadino on the island has been on the look-out for il tesoro di Timberio for two thousand years. It was only later on when cleaning these coins that I found amongst them the gold coin fresh as if it had been coined to-day, 'fleur de coin' indeed, the finest likeness of the old Emperor I had ever seen. Close by we found the two bronze hoofs of an equestrian statue, one still in my possession, the other stolen ten years later by a tourist.

The whole garden was full of thousands and thousands of polished slabs of coloured marble, africano, pavonazetto, giallo antico, verde antico, cipollino, alabastro, all now forming the pavement of the big loggia, the chapel and some of the terraces. A broken cup of agate of exquisite shape, several broken and unbroken Greek vases, innumerable fragments of early Roman sculpture, including, according to Mastro Nicola, la gamba di Timberio, dozens of Greek and Roman inscriptions came to light as we were digging. While we were planting the cypresses bordering the little lane to the chapel, we came upon a tomb with a skeleton of a man, he had a Greek coin in his mouth, the bones are still there where we found them, the skull is lying on my writing-table.

The huge arcades of the big loggia rose rapidly out of the earth, one by one the hundred white columns of the pergola stood out against the sky. What had once been Mastro Vincenzo's house and his carpenter workshop was gradually transformed and enlarged into what was to become my future home. How it was done I have never been able to understand, nor has anybody else who knows the history of the San Michele of to-day. I knew absolutely nothing about architecture, nor did any of my fellow-workers, nobody who could read or write ever had anything to do with the work, no architect was ever consulted, no proper drawing or plan was ever made, no exact measurements were ever taken. It was all done *all' occhio* as Mastro Nicola called it.

Often of an evening when the others had gone away I used to sit alone on the broken parapet outside the little chapel where my sphinx was to stand, watching with my mind's eye the castle of my dreams rise out of the twilight. Often as I sat there I thought I saw a tall figure in a long mantle wandering about under the half-finished vaults of the loggia below, carefully examining the day's work, testing the strength of the new structures, bending over the rudimentary outlines drawn by me on the sand. Who was the mysterious overseer? Was it the venerable Sant'Antonio himself who had climbed down on the sly from his shrine in the church to work another miracle here? Or was it the tempter of my youth who twelve years ago had stood by my side on this very spot offering me his help in exchange for my future? It had become so dark that I could no longer see his face but I thought I saw the blade of a sword glistening under a red mantle. When we returned to work next morning just on the point where we had stopped short the evening before in great perplexity as to what to do and how to do it, all my difficulties seemed to have been removed during the night. All hesitation had left me. I saw it all in my mind's eye clearly as if it had been drawn by an architect in its minutest details.

Maria Porta-Lettere had brought me a couple of days before a letter from Rome. I had flung it unopened in the drawer of my deal table to join a dozen of other unread letters. I had no time for the world outside Capri, there is no post in Heaven. Then an unheard-of thing happened, there came a telegram to Anacapri. Painfully signalled two days before from the semaphore at Massa Lubrense it had in the course of time reached the Capri semaphore by the Arco Naturale. Don Ciccio, the semaphorist, after a vague guess at its meaning, had offered it in turn to various people in Capri. Nobody could understand a word of it, nobody wanted to have anything to do with it. It had then been decided to try it on Anacapri and it had been put on the top of Maria Porta-Lettere's fish basket. Maria Porta-Lettere, who had never seen a telegram before, handed it with great precaution to the parroco. Il Reverendo Don Antonio, unfamiliar with reading anything he did not know by heart, told Maria Porta-Lettere to take it to the schoolmaster, Il Reverendo Don Natale, the most learned man in the village. Don Natale was certain it was written in Hebrew but was unable to translate it on account of the bad spelling. He told Maria Porta-Lettere to take it to the Reverendo Don Dionisio, who had been in Rome to kiss the hand of the Pope and was the right man to read the mysterious message. Don Dionisio, the greatest authority in the village on roba antica, recognized it at once as being written in the secret telegraphic code of Timberio himself, little wonder nobody could understand it. His opinion was confirmed by the farmacista but strenuously opposed by the barber who swore it was written in English. He shrewdly suggested that it should be taken to La Bella Margherita whose aunt had married un lord inglese. La Bella Margherita burst into tears as soon she saw the telegram, she had dreamt in the night that her aunt was ill, she felt sure the telegram was for her and was sent by the lord inglese to announce the death of her aunt. While Maria Porta-Lettere was wandering from house to house with the telegram the excitement in the village increased more and more, and soon all work ceased. A rumour that war had broken out between Italy and the Turks was contradicted at noon by another rumour brought on naked boy's feet from Capri that the king had been assassinated in Rome. The Municipal Council was urgently summoned but Don Diego, the sindaco, decided to postpone unfolding the flag at half-mast until another telegram confirmed the sad news. Shortly before sunset Maria Porta-Lettere, escorted by a crowd of notables of both sexes, arrived with the telegram at San Michele. I looked at the telegram and said it was not for me. Who was it for? I said I did not know, I had never heard of any living or dead person afflicted with a similar name, it was not a name, it seemed an alphabet in an unknown tongue. Wouldn't I try to read the telegram and tell what was in it? No, I would not, I hated telegrams. I did not want to have anything to do with it? Was it true there was war between Italy and the Turks? yelled the crowd under the garden wall.

I did not know, I did not care in the least if there was a war as long as I was left in peace to dig in my garden.

Old Maria Porta-Lettere sank down dejectedly on the column of cipollino, she said she had been on her legs with the telegram since daybreak with nothing to eat, she could do no more. She had besides to go and feed the cow. Would I take care of the telegram till tomorrow morning? It would not be safe to leave it in her, keeping, with all the grand-children playing about the room, not to speak of the chickens and the pig. Old Maria Porta-Lettere was a great friend of mine, I felt sorry for her and for the cow. I put the telegram in my pocket, she was to resume her wanderings with it the next morning.

The sun sank into the sea, the bells rang Ave Maria, we all went home to our supper. As I was sitting under my pergola with a bottle of Don Dionisio's best wine before me, a terrible thought suddenly flashed through my brain – fancy if the telegram was for me after all! Having fortified myself with another glass of wine, I put the telegram on the table before me and set to work to try to translate its mysterious meaning into human language. It took me the whole bottle of wine to satisfy myself that it was not for me, I fell asleep, my head on the table, the telegram in my hand.

I slept late the next morning. There was no need for hurry, nobody was working in my garden to-day, surely they were all in church since morning mass, it was Good Friday. As I strolled up to San Michele a couple of hours later, I was greatly surprised to find Mastro Nicola with his three sons and all the girls, hard at work in the garden as usual. Of course they knew how anxious I was to go on with the work full speed, but I would never have dreamt to ask them to work on Good Friday. Indeed it was kind of them, I told them I was very grateful. Mastro Nicola looked at me with evident surprise and said it was no festa to-day.

'No holiday to-day!' Did he not know it was Good Friday, the day of the crucifixion of our Lord Jesus Christ?

'Va bene,' said Mastro Nicola, 'but Jesus Christ was not a Saint.'

'Of course He was a Saint, the greatest Saint of all.'

'But not as great as Sant'Antonio who has done more than one hundred miracles. How many miracles has Gesù Cristo done?' he asked with a malicious look at me.

Nobody knew better than I that Sant'Antonio was not easy to beat on miracles, what greater miracle could have been made than bringing me back to his village? Avoiding Mastro Nicola's question I said that with all honour due to Sant'Antonio he was but a man, while Jesus Christ was the Son of our Lord in Heaven who in order to save us all from Hell had suffered death on the Cross this very day.

'Non è vero,' said Mastro Nicola, resuming his digging with great vigour. 'L'hanno fatto morire ieri per abbreviare le funzioni nella chiesa. It is not true. They put him to death yesterday to shorten the functions in the church.'

I had barely time to recover from this announcement when a well-known voice called me by name from outside the garden wall. It was my friend the newly appointed Swedish Minister in Rome. He was furious for not having had an answer to his letter, announcing his intention to come and spend the Easter with me and still more offended that I had not had the decency to meet him at the Marina with a donkey on the arrival of the post boat as he had begged me to do in his telegram. He would never have come to

Anacapri had he known he would have to climb all by himself those seven hundred and seventy-seven Phoenician steps leading up to my wretched village. Would I have the cheek to say I had not got his telegram?

Of course I got it, we all got it, I nearly got drunk over it. He softened a little when I handed him the telegram, he said he wanted to take it to Rome to show it to the Ministero delle Poste e Telegrafi. I snatched it from him, warning him that any attempt to improve the telegraphic communications between Capri and the mainland would be strenuously opposed by me.

I was delighted to show my friend over the place and to explain to him all the future wonders of San Michele with an occasional reference to my sketch on the wall in order to make him understand it more clearly, which he said was much needed. He was full of admiration, and when he looked down from the chapel on the fair island at his feet he said he believed it was the most beautiful view in the world. When I pointed out to him the place for the huge Egyptian sphinx of red granite he gave me an uneasy side-glance, and when I showed him where the mountain was going to be blasted away for the erection of my Greek theatre he said he felt somewhat giddy and asked me to take him to my villa and give him a glass of wine, he wanted to have a quiet talk with me.

His eyes wandered round my whitewashed room, he asked me if this was my villa, I answered I had never been so comfortable in my life. I put a flask of Don Dionisio's wine on the deal table, invited him to sit down on my chair and threw myself on the bed ready to listen to what he had to say. My friend asked me if I had not been spending much of my time these last years at the Salpêtrière among more or less queer and unhinged people, somewhat shaky in their upper storey?

I said he was not far from the truth, but that I had given up the Salpêtrière altogether.

He said he was very glad to hear it, he thought it was high time, I had better take up some other speciality. He was very fond of me, in fact he had come down to try to persuade me to return at once to my splendid position in Paris instead of wasting my time among these peasants in Anacapri. Now since he had seen me he had changed his mind, he had come to the conclusion I was in need of a thorough rest.

I said I was very glad he approved of my decision, I really could not stand the strain any longer, I was tired out.

'In the head?' he asked sympathetically.

I told him it was useless to ask me to return to Paris, I was going to spend the rest of my days in Anacapri.

'You mean to say that you are going to spend your life in this wretched little village all alone among these peasants who can neither read nor write! You who are a man of culture, who are you going to associate with?'

'With myself, my dogs and perhaps a monkey.'

'You always say you cannot live without music, who is going to sing to you, who is going to play to you?'

'The birds in the garden, the sea all around me. Listen! Do you hear that wonderful mezzo-soprano, it is the golden oriole, isn't his voice more beautiful than the voice of our celebrated compatriot Christine Nilson or Patti herself? Do you hear that solemn andante of the waves, isn't that more beautiful than the slow movement of Beethoven's Ninth Symphony?'

Changing abruptly the conversation, my friend asked me who was my architect and in what style was the house going to be built?

I told him I had no architect and that so far I did not know in what style the house was going to be built, all that would settle itself as the work went on.

He gave me another uneasy side-glance and said he was at least glad to know I had left Paris a rich man, surely it needed a large fortune to build such a magnificent villa as I had described to him.

I opened the drawer of my deal table and showed him a bundle of banknotes tucked in a stocking. I said it was all I possessed in this world after twelve years' hard work in Paris, I believe it amounted to something like fifteen thousand francs, maybe a little more, maybe a little less, probably a little less.

'Listen, incorrigible dreamer, to the voice of a friend,' said the Swedish Minister. Tapping his forehead with his finger he went on, 'You do not see straighter than your ex-patients in the Salpêtrière, the trouble is evidently catching. Make an effort to see things as they are in reality and not in your dreams. At the rate you are going your stocking will be empty in a month's time, and so far I saw no trace of a single room to live in, I saw nothing but half-finished loggias, terraces, cloisters and pergolas. With what are you going to build your house?'

'With my hands.'

'Once established in your house, what are you going to live on?'

'Macaroni.'

'It will cost at least half a million to build your San Michele as you see it in your imagination, where are you going to get the money from?'

I was dumbfounded. I had never thought of it, it was altogether a new point of view.

'What on earth am I going to do?' I said at last, staring at my friend.

'I will tell you what you are to do,' said my friend with his resolute voice. 'You are to stop work at once on your crazy San Michele, clear out of your whitewashed room and since you decline to return to Paris, you are to go to Rome to take up your work as a doctor. Rome is the very place for you. You need only spend the winters there, you will have the long summers to go on with your building. You have got San Michele on the brain but you are not a fool, or at least most people have not found it out so far. You have besides luck in everything you lay your hands on. I am told there are forty-four foreign doctors practising in Rome, if you pull yourself together and set to work in earnest you can beat them all with your left hand. If you work hard and hand over your earnings to me I will bet you anything you like, that in less than five years you will have made enough money to finish your San Michele and live happily the rest of your life in the company of your dogs and your monkeys.'

After my friend had left I spent a terrible night wandering up and down in my little contadino room like an animal in a cage. I dared not even go up to the chapel to say good night to the sphinx of my dreams as was my wont. I was afraid that the tempter in the red mantle might once more stand by my side in the twilight. When the sun rose I rushed down to the lighthouse and sprang into the sea. When I swam ashore my head was clear and cool like the waters of the gulf.

Two weeks later I was established as a doctor in Keats' house in Rome.

XXII

Piazza di Spagna

My very first patient was Mrs. P, the wife of the well-known English banker in Rome. She had been laid upon her back for nearly three years after a fall from her horse while riding to hounds in the Campagna. All the foreign doctors in Rome had been attending her in turn, a month ago she had even consulted Charcot, who had given her my name, I did not know he was aware of my having settled in Rome. As soon as I had examined her, I understood that the prophecy of the Swedish Minister was going to be fulfilled. I knew that once more Fortuna stood by my side, invisible to all but myself. It was indeed a lucky case to start my Roman practice, the patient was the most popular lady in the foreign colony. I realized that it was the shock and no permanent injury to her spine that had paralysed her limbs and that faith and massage would put her on her legs in a couple of months. I told her what nobody else had ever dared to tell her and I kept my word. She began to improve before I had begun the massage. In less than three months she was seen by half the fashionable Roman society stepping out of her carriage in Villa Borghese and walking about under the trees leaning on her stick. It was looked upon as a miraculous achievement, it was in reality a very simple and easy case, granted the patient had faith and the doctor patience. It opened the doors of every house in the numerous British colony in Rome and of many Italian houses as well. Next year I became doctor to the British Embassy and had more English patients than all the eleven English-born doctors put together – I leave it to you to imagine what were their feelings towards me. An old friend of mine from the École des Beaux Arts, now a pensionnaire in Villa Medici, brought me into contact with the French colony. My lifelong friend Count Giuseppe Primoli sang my praise in the Roman society, a faint echo from my luck in Avenue de Villiers did the rest to fill my consulting-room with patients. Professor Weir-Mitchell, the leading nerve specialist of America, with whom I had already had some dealings in my Paris days, continued to send me his surplus of dilapidated millionaires and their unstrung wives. Their exuberant daughters who had invested their vanity in the first available Roman prince, also began to send for me in their sombre old palaces to consult me about their various symptoms of disillusion. The rest of the vast crowd of Americans followed like a flock of sheep. The twelve American doctors soon shared the fate of their English colleagues. The hundreds of models on the steps of the Trinità dei Monti under my windows in their picturesque costumes from the mountains round Montecassino were all patients of mine. All the flower-sellers of Piazza di Spagna threw a little bunch of violets into my carriage as I drove past in exchange for a cough mixture for some of their innumerable babies. My ambulatorio in Trastevere spread my fame all over the poor quarters in Rome. I was on my legs from morning till night, I slept like a king from night till morning unless I was called out, which happened as often as not, it mattered nothing to me, I never knew what fatigue meant in those days. Soon, to gain time and to satisfy my love of horses, I drove about Rome full speed in a smart red-wheeled victoria drawn by a pair of splendid Hungarian horses, my faithful Tappio, the Lapland dog, seated by my side. I can now see that it was maybe a little showy and might have been mistaken for réclame had I not already then passed the need of any. Anyhow, it hit my forty-four colleagues badly in the eye, there is no doubt about it. Some of them drove about in gloomy-looking old coaches from the time of Pio Nono, to all appearances as if intended to be adapted at a moment's notice as hearses for their dead patients. Others walked about on foot on their lugubrious errands in long frock-coats, their top-hats pushed down over their foreheads as if in deep meditation on whom they were to embalm next. They all glared savagely at me as I drove past, they all knew me by sight. Soon they had to know me in person as well, as, whether they wanted it or not, I began to be called in consultation by their dying patients. I tried my best to observe rigorously the etiquette of our profession and to tell their patients they were lucky indeed to be in such good hands, but it was not always easy. We were indeed a sad crew, shipwrecks from various lands and seas, landed in Rome with our scanty kit of knowledge. We had to live somewhere, there was surely no reason why we shouldn't live in Rome as long as we didn't interfere with the living of our patients.

Soon it became very difficult for any foreigner in Rome to die without my being called in to see him through. I became to the dying foreigners what the Illustrissimo Professore Baccelli was to the dying Romans – the last hope, alas, so seldom fulfilled. Another person who never failed to turn up on these occasions was Signor Cornacchia, undertaker to the foreign colony and director of the Protestant Cemetery by Porta San Paolo. He never seemed to have to be sent for, he always turned up in good time, his big hook nose seemed to smell the dead at a distance like the carrion-vulture. Correctly dressed in a long frock-coat and top-hat, in the fashion of a colleague, he was always hanging about in the corridor waiting for his turn to be called in. He seemed to have taken a great liking to me, saluting me most cordially with a waving of his top-hat whenever he met me in the street. He always expressed his regrets when I was the first to leave Rome in the spring, he always greeted me with outstretched hands and a friendly: Ben tornato, Signor Dottore, when I returned in the autumn. There had been a slight misunderstanding between us the previous Christmas when he had sent me twelve bottles of wine with his hopes for a fruitful co-operation during the coming season. He seemed deeply hurt by my inability to accept his gift, he said none of my colleagues had ever refused his little token of sympathy. The same unfortunate mis-understanding had besides cooled down for some time the cordial relations between myself and the two foreign chemists.

One day I was greatly surprised to receive a visit from old Doctor Pilkington who had very particular reasons for hating me. He said that he and his colleagues had so far waited in vain for my calling on them according to the unwritten rules of etiquette. Since the mountain had not come to Mahomet, Mahomet had come to the mountain. He had nothing in common with Mahomet except his long, white, venerable beard, he looked more like a false prophet than a real one. He said he had come in his quality of the doyen of the resident foreign doctors in Rome to invite me to become a member of their recently formed Society for Mutual Protection with the object of putting an end to the war which had been raging amongst them for so long. All his colleagues had become members except that old ruffian Doctor Campbell with whom none of them were on speaking terms. The thorny question of their professional fees had already been settled to everybody's satisfaction by a mutual agreement fixing the minimum fee at twenty francs, maxi-mum fee at the discretion of each member according to circum-stances. No embalmment of man, woman or child was to be made for less than five thousand francs. He was sorry to have to tell me that the Society had of late received several complaints of gross carelessness on my part in collecting my fees and even for not having collected any fees at all. Not later than yesterday Signor Cornacchia, the undertaker, had confided to him almost with tears in his eyes that I had embalmed the wife of the Swedish parson for a hundred lire, a most deplorable breach of loyalty to all my colleagues. He felt sure I would realize the advantages to myself of my becoming a member of their Society for Mutual Protection and would be glad to welcome me amongst them at their next meeting to-morrow.

I answered I was sorry I could not see the advantage either for me or for them of my becoming a member, that anyhow I was willing to discuss with them the fixing of a maximum fee but not of a minimum fee. As to the injections of sublimate they called embalmment, its cost did not exceed fifty francs. Adding another fifty for the loss of time, the sum I had charged for embalming the parson's wife was correct. I intended to earn from the living, not from the dead. I was a doctor, not a hyaena.

He rose from his seat at the word hyaena with a request not to disturb myself in case I ever wished to call him in consultation, he was not available.

I said it was a blow both to myself and to my patients, but that we would have to try to do without him.

I was sorry I had lost my temper, and I told him so at our next meeting, this time in his own house in Via Quattro Fontane. Poor Doctor Pilkington had had a slight stroke the very day after our interview and had sent for me to attend him. He told me the Society for Mutual Protection had broken down, they were all at daggers drawn again, he felt safer in my hands than in theirs. Luckily there was no cause for alarm, in fact I thought he looked livelier after his stroke than before. I tried to cheer him up as well as I could, said there was nothing to worry about and that I had always believed he had already had several slight strokes before. He was soon on his legs again, more active than ever, he was still flourishing when I left Rome.

Soon afterwards I made the acquaintance of his deadly enemy Doctor Campbell, whom he had called an old ruffian. Judging from my first impression he seemed to have hit upon the right diagnosis this time. A more savage-looking old gentleman I never saw, wild blood-shot eyes and cruel lips, the flushed face of a drunkard, all covered with hair like a monkey, and a long, unkempt beard. He was said to be over eighty, the retired old English chemist told me he looked exactly the same thirty years ago when he first arrived in Rome. Nobody knew from where he came, it was rumoured he had been a surgeon in the Southern army in the American war. Surgery was his speciality, he was in fact the only surgeon among the foreign doctors, he was on speaking terms with none of them. One day I found him standing by my carriage patting Tappio.

'I envy you that dog,' he said abruptly in a rough voice. 'Do you like monkeys?'

I said I loved monkeys.

He said I was his man, he begged me to come and have a look at his monkey who had been scalded almost to death by upsetting a kettle of boiling water.

We climbed up to his flat at the top of the corner house of Piazza Mignanelli. He begged me to wait in his salon and appeared a minute later with a monkey in his arms, a huge baboon all wrapped up in bandages.

'I am afraid he is very bad,' said the old doctor in quite a different voice, tenderly caressing the emaciated face of his monkey. 'I do not know what I shall do if he dies, he is my only friend. I have brought him up on the bottle since he was a baby, his dear mother died when she gave birth to him. She was almost as big as a gorilla, you never saw such a darling, she was quite human. I do not mind in the least cutting my fellow creatures to pieces, I rather like it, but I have no more courage left in me to dress his scalded little body, he suffers so horribly when I try to disinfect his wounds that I cannot stand it any longer. I am sure you like animals, will you take him in hand?'

We unwrapped the bandages soaked with blood and pus, it was a pitiful sight, his whole body was one terrible wound.

'He knows you are a friend or he would not sit as still as he does, he never allows anybody but me to touch him. He knows everything, he has more brains than all the foreign doctors in Rome put together. He has eaten nothing for four days,' he went on, with a tender expression in his blood-shot eyes. 'Billy, my son, won't you oblige your papa by trying this fig?'

I said I wished we had a banana, there was nothing monkeys liked better.

He said he would telegraph at once to London for a bunch of bananas, never mind the cost.

I said it was a question of keeping up his strength. We poured a little warm milk into his mouth, but he spat it out at once.

'He cannot swallow any more,' groaned his master, 'I know what

243

it means, he is dying.'

We improvised with a sort of feeding tube and this time he kept the milk to the delight of the old doctor.

Billy got slowly better. I saw him every day for a fortnight, and I ended by becoming quite fond both of him and his master. Soon I found him sitting in his specially constructed rocking-chair on their sunny terrace by the side of his master, a bottle of whisky on the table between them. The old doctor was a great believer in whisky to steady one's hand before an operation. To judge from the number of empty whisky bottles in the corner of the terrace, his surgical practice must have been considerable. Alas! they were both addicted to drink. I had often caught Billy helping himself to a little whisky and soda out of his master's glass. The doctor had told me whisky was the best possible tonic for monkeys, it had saved the life of Billy's beloved mother after her pneumonia. One evening I came upon them on their terrace, both blind drunk. Billy was executing a sort of negro dance on the table round the whisky bottle, the old doctor sat leaning back in his chair clapping his hands to mark the time, singing in a hoarse voice:

'Billy, my son, Billy, my sonny, soooooooonny!' They neither heard nor saw me coming. I stared in consternation at the happy family. The face of the intoxicated monkey had become quite human, the face of the old drunkard looked exactly like the face of a gigantic gorilla. The family likeness was unmistakable.

'Billy, my son, Billy, my son, soooooooony!'

Was it possible? No, of course it was not possible but it made me feel quite creepy. . . .

A couple of months later I found the old doctor standing again by my carriage talking to Tappio. No, thank God, Billy was all right, it was his wife who was ill this time, would I oblige him by having a look at her?

We climbed once more up to his flat, I had so far had no idea that he shared it with anybody but Billy. On the bed lay a young girl, almost a child, with closed eyes, evidently unconscious.

'I thought you said it was your wife who was ill, is this your daughter?'

No, it was his fourth wife, his first wife had committed suicide, the second and the third had died of pneumonia, he felt sure this one was going the same way.

My first impression was that he was quite right. She had double pneumonia, but an enormous effusion in the left pleura had evidently escaped his notice. I gave her a couple of hypodermic injections of camphor and ether with his dirty syringe, and we started rubbing her limbs vigorously with apparently little effect.

'Try to rouse her, speak to her!' I said.

He bent over her livid face and roared in her ear:

'Sally, my dear, pull yourself together, do get well or I shall marry again!'

She drew a deep breath and opened her eyes with a shudder.

The next day we tapped her pleura, youth did the rest, she recovered slowly, as if unwillingly. My suspicion of some chronic mischief in her lungs soon proved well founded. She was in an advanced state of consumption. I saw her every day for a couple of weeks, I could not help feeling very sorry for her. She was evidently in terror of the old man and no wonder, for he was horribly rough with her, though perhaps he did not mean it. He had told me she came from Florida. As autumn came I advised him to take her back there the sooner the better, she would never survive a Roman winter. He seemed to agree, I soon found out that the chief difficulty was what to do with Billy. It ended by my offering to keep the monkey during his absence in my little courtyard under the Trinità dei Monti steps, already occupied by various animals. He was to be back in three months. He never came back, I never knew what became of him nor did anybody else. I heard a rumour that he had been shot during a brawl in a public house but I do not know if it was true. I have often wondered who this man was and whether he was a doctor at all. I once saw him amputate an arm with amazing rapidity, he must have known something about anatomy but evidently very little about dressing and disinfecting a wound, and his instruments were incredibly primitive. The English chemist had told me he always wrote out the same prescriptions often with wrong spelling and wrong dosage. My own belief is that he was no doctor at all but a former butcher or perhaps an orderly in an ambulance who had had some good reason for leaving his own country.

Billy stayed with me in Piazza di Spagna till the spring when I took him down to San Michele where he gave me a hell of a time for the rest of his happy life. I cured him of dipsomania, he became in many ways a quite respectable monkey. You will hear more about him later on.

XXIII

More Doctors

One day there appeared in my consulting-room a lady in deep mourning with a letter of introduction from the English chaplain. She was of decidedly mature age, of very voluminous dimensions, arrayed in loose flying garments of a very unusual cut. Seating herself with great precaution on the sofa she said she was a stranger in Rome. The death of the Reverend Jonathan, her lamented husband, had left her alone and unprotected in the world. The Reverend Jonathan had been everything to her, husband, father, lover, friend. . . .

I looked sympathetically at her round, blank face and silly eyes and said I was very sorry for her.

The Reverend Jonathan had . . .

I said I was unfortunately in a great hurry, the waiting-room was full of people, what could I do for her? She said she had come to put herself in my hands, she was going to have a baby. She knew that the Reverend Jonathan was watching over her from his heaven, but she could not help feeling very anxious, it was her first child. She had heard a lot about me, now, since she had seen me, she felt sure she would be as safe in my hands as in the hands of the Reverend Jonathan. She had always had a great liking for Swedes, she had even once been engaged to a Swedish parson, love at first sight which however had not lasted. She was surprised to find me so young-looking, just the same age as the Swedish parson, she even thought there was a certain likeness between us. She had a strange feeling as if we had met before, as if we could understand each other without words. As she spoke she looked at me with a twinkle in her eye which would have made the Reverend Jonathan feel very uncomfortable had he been watching over her just at that moment.

I hurried to tell her that I was no accoucheur but that I felt sure she would be safe in the hands of any of my colleagues who, I understood, were all specialists in this branch of our profession. There was for instance my eminent colleague Doctor Pilkington. . . .

No, she wanted me and nobody else. Surely I could not have the heart to leave her alone and unprotected amongst strangers, alone with a fatherless child! There was besides no time to lose, the baby was expected any day, any moment. I rose rapidly from my seat and offered to send for a cab to take her at once to Hôtel de Russie where she was staying.

What would not the Reverend Jonathan have given, had it been granted to him to see their child, he who had loved its mother so passionately! Theirs had been a love-match if ever there was one, a melting into one of two ardent lives, of two harmonious souls. She burst into a paroxysm of tears ending in a fit of convulsion which shook her whole body in a most alarming way. Suddenly she turned pale and sat quite still clasping her hands protectively over her abdomen. My fears turned into terror. Giovannina and Rosina were in Villa Borghese with the dogs, Anna was also away, there was no woman in the house, the waiting-room was full of people. I sprang from my chair and looked attentively at her. All of a sudden I recognized that face, I knew it well, it was not in vain I had spent fifteen years of my life among hysterical women from all lands and of all ages. I told her sternly to wipe off her tears, pull herself together and listen to me without interruption. I put a few professional questions to her, her evasive answers roused my interest in the Reverend Jonathan and his untimely death. Untimely indeed for the demise of her lamented husband proved to have taken place at a very awkward time of the previous year from my point of view as a doctor. I told her at last as gently as I could that she was not going to have any baby at all. She bounded from the sofa, her face scarlet with rage, and rushed out of the room shrieking at the top of her voice that I had insulted the memory of the Reverend Jonathan!

A couple of days later I met the English chaplain in the Piazza and thanked him for having recommended me to Mrs. Jonathan, expressing my regret for not having been able to take charge of her. I was struck by the chaplain's reserved manner. I asked him what had become of Mrs. Jonathan. He left me abruptly saying she was in the hands of Doctor Jones, she was expecting her baby at any moment.

It all came out in less than twenty-four hours. Everybody knew it, all the foreign doctors knew it and loved it, all their patients knew it, the two English chemists knew it, the English baker in Via Babuino knew it, Cook's knew it, all the *pensions* in Via Sistina knew it, in all the English tea-rooms people talked of nothing else. Soon every member of the British colony in Rome knew that I had committed a colossal blunder and that I had insulted the Reverend Jonathan's memory. Everybody knew that Doctor Jones had not left the Hôtel de Russie and that the midwife had been sent for at midnight. The next day the English colony in Rome split into two hostile camps. Was there going to be a baby or was there not going to be a baby? All the English doctors and their patients, the clergy and the faithful congregation, the English chemist in Via Condotti, were all certain there was going to be a baby. All my patients, the rival chemist in Piazza Mignanelli, all the flower-sellers in Piazza di Spagna, all the models on the Trinità dei Monti steps under my windows, all the dealers in roba antica, all the scalpellini in Via Margutta, denied emphatically that there was going to be a baby. The English baker was wavering. My friend the English Consul was, though reluctantly, forced to take up his position against me for reasons of patriotism. The position of Signor Cornacchia, the undertaker, was a particularly delicate one, requiring careful handling. There was on one hand his un-shaken faith in my efficiency as his principal collaborator. There was on the other hand the undeniable fact that his prospects as an undertaker were much brighter if I proved to be wrong than if I proved to be right. Soon the rumour spread that old Doctor Pilkington had been called to the Hôtel de Russie in consultation and had discovered that there were to be two babies instead of one. Signor Cornacchia realized that the only right policy was to wait and see. When it became known that the English chaplain had been warned to hold himself in readiness at any hour of the day or the night for a christening in articulo mortis in view of the prolonged strain, there was no more room for hesitation. Signor Cornacchia went over to the enemy's camp, bag and baggage, abandoning me to my fate. From Signor Cornacchia's professional point of view as an undertaker a baby was as good as a full-grown person. But why not two babies! And why not also . . . ?

Already when a wet nurse in her picturesque costume from the Sabine mountains had been seen entering the Hôtel de Russie unmistakable signs of discouragement had become apparent among my allies. When a perambulator arrived from England and was placed in the hall of the hotel, my position became almost critical. All the tourist ladies in the hotel gave a friendly glance at the perambulator as they crossed the hall, all the waiters were offering bets of two to one on twins, all the betting on no baby at all having ceased. I was cut by several people at the garden party at the English Embassy, where Doctor Pilkington and Doctor Jones, once more on speaking terms, formed the centre of an animated group of listeners to the last news from the Hôtel de Russie. The Swedish Minister took me aside and told me in an angry voice he did not want to have anything more to do with me, he had had more than enough of my eccentricities, to use a mild word. Last week he had been told I had called a most respectable old English doctor a hyaena. Yesterday the wife of the English chaplain had told his own wife that I had insulted the memory of a Scotch parson. If I meant to go on in this way, I had better return to Anacapri before the whole foreign colony turned its back upon me.

After another week of intense suspense signs of reaction began to set in. The betting among the waiters now stood at evens, with a few timid offers of five lire on no baby at all. When the news spread that the two doctors had quarrelled and that Doctor Pilkington had retired with the second baby under his long frock-coat, all the betting on twins came to an end. As time went on the numbers of deserters increased day by day, the English chaplain and his congregation still rallying bravely round the perambulator. Doctor Jones, the midwife and the nurse were still sleeping in the hotel but Signor Cornacchia warned by his keen scent had already abandoned the sinking ship.

Then came the crash in the shape of a shrewd-looking old Scotsman who walked one day into my consulting-room and sat down on the sofa where his sister had sat. He told me he had the misfortune to be Mrs. Jonathan's brother. He said he had arrived straight from Dundee the evening before. He did not seem to have wasted his time. He had settled his accounts with Doctor Pilkington by paying him one third of his bill, he had kicked out Doctor Jones, he now asked me for the address of a cheap lunatic asylum. The doctor, he thought, ought to be locked up in another place.

I told him that, unfortunately for him, his sister's case was not a case for a lunatic asylum. He said that if she was not a case for a lunatic asylum he did not know who was. The Reverend Jonathan had died of old age and softening of the brain over a year ago, she was not likely to have been exposed to any further temptations, the crazy old thing. She had already made herself the laughing-stock of the whole of Dundee in the same way she had now made herself the laughing-stock of the whole of Rome. He said he had had enough of her, he did not want to have anything more to do with her. I said neither did I, I had been surrounded by hysterical

249

females for fifteen years, I wanted a rest. The only thing was to take her back to Dundee.

As to her doctor, I am sure he had acted to the best of his ability. I understood he was a retired Indian army doctor with limited experience in hysteria. I believe what we called 'phantom tumour' was rarely met with in the English army. It was not very rare with hysterical women.

Did I know she had had the cheek to order the perambulator from the stores in his name, he had had to pay five pounds for it, she could have got an excellent second-hand one in Dundee for two pounds. Could I help him to find a purchaser for the perambulator? He did not want to make any profits on it, but he would like to get his money back.

I told him that if he left his sister in Rome she would be quite capable of ordering another perambulator from the stores. He seemed much impressed by this argument. I lent him my carriage to take his sister to the station. I have never seen them again.

* * *

So far the prophecy of the Swedish Minister had been fulfilled, I had been an easy winner. Soon however I had to deal with a far more serious rival who had just then taken up his practice in Rome. I was told and I believe it was true that it was my rapid success which had made him give up his lucrative practice in —— and settle in the capital. He enjoyed an excellent reputation among his countrymen as an able doctor and a charming man. He soon became a conspicuous figure in the Roman society from which I was vanishing more and more, having learned what I wanted to know. He drove about in a carriage as smart as my own, he entertained a lot in his sumptuous apartment in the Corso, his rise was as rapid as my own had been. He had called on me, we had agreed there was room in Rome for both of us, he was always very courteous to me whenever we met. He had evidently a very large practice, chiefly drawn from wealthy Americans, many of them flocking to Rome, I was told, in order to be under his care. He had his own staff of nurses, his own private nursing home outside Porta Pia. I understood at first he was a ladies' doctor, but heard later that he was a specialist in diseases of the heart. He evidently possessed the inestimable gift of inspiring confidence in his patients, I never heard his name mentioned except with praise and gratitude. It did not surprise me for, compared with the rest of us, he was in fact a rather striking personality, a fine forehead, extraordinarily penetrating and intelligent eyes, a remarkable facility for speaking, very winning manners. He ignored completely his other colleagues, but he had called me in consultation a couple of times, chiefly for nervous cases. He seemed to know his Charcot pretty well, he had also visited several German clinics. We nearly always agreed as to diagnosis and treatment, I soon came to the conclusion that he knew his business at least as well as I did.

One day he sent me a rapidly scribbled note asking me to come at once to the Hôtel Constanzi for a consultation. He seemed more excited than usual. He told me in a few rapid words that the patient had been under his care for some weeks, had at first much benefited by his treatment. These last days there had been a change for the worse, the action of the heart was unsatisfactory, he would like to have my opinion. Above all I was not to alarm the patient nor his family. Judge of my surprise when I recognized in his patient a man I had loved and admired for years as did everybody else who had ever met him, the author of 'Human Personality and its Survival of Bodily Death.' His breathing was superficial and very difficult, his face was cyanotic and worn, only his wonderful eyes were the same. He gave me his hand and said he was glad I had come at last, he had been longing for my return. He reminded me of our last meeting in London, when I dined with him at the Society for Psychical Research, how we had been sitting up the whole night talking about death and thereafter. Before I had time to answer, my colleague told him he was not to speak for fear of another attack and handed me his stethoscope. There was no need for a prolonged examination, what I had seen was enough. Taking my colleague aside I asked him if he had told the family. To my intense surprise he did not seem to realize the situation, spoke of repeating the injections of strychnine at shorter intervals, of trying his serum next morning, of sending to the Grand Hôtel for a bottle of burgundy of a special vintage. I said I was against stimulants of any kind, their only possible effect might be to rouse once more his capacity for suffering, already subdued by merciful nature. There was nothing else for us to do but help him not to suffer too much. As we were speaking, Professor William James, the famous philosopher, one of his nearest friends, entered the room. I repeated to him that the family must be told at once, it was a question of hours. As they all seemed to believe more in my colleague than in myself, I insisted that another doctor should be called at once in consultation. Two hours later arrived Professor Baccelli, the leading consulting doctor in Rome. His examination was even more summary than my own, his verdict still shorter.

'Il va mourir aujourd'hui,' he said in his deep voice.

William James told me of the solemn pact between him and his friend that whichever of them was to die first should send a message to the other as he passed over into the unknown – they both believed in the possibility of such a communication. He was so overcome with grief that he could not enter the room, he sank down on a chair by the open door, his note-book on his knees, pen in hand, ready to take down the message with his usual methodical exactitude. In the afternoon set in the Cheyne-Stokes respiration, that heartrending sign of approaching death. The dying man asked to speak to me. His eyes were calm and serene.

'I know I am going to die,' he said, 'I know you are going to help me. Is it to-day, is it to-morrow?'

'To-day.'

'I am glad, I am ready, I have no fear. I am going to know at last. Tell William James, tell him . . .'

His heaving chest stood still in a terrible minute of suspense of life.

'Do you hear me?' I asked bending over the dying man, 'do you suffer?'

'No,' he murmured, 'I am very tired and very happy.'

These were his last words.

When I went away William James was still sitting leaning back in his chair, his hands over his face, his open note-book still on his knees. The page was blank.

I saw a good deal of my colleague and also of several of his patients during that winter. He was always talking about the marvellous results of his serum, and of another new remedy for angina pectoris he had been using of late in his nursing home with wonderful success. Upon my telling him how interested I had always been in angina pectoris he consented to take me to his nursing home and show me some of his patients cured by the new remedy. I was greatly surprised to recognize in one of them a former patient of mine, a wealthy American lady with all the classical stigmas of hysteria, classified by me as a malade imaginaire, looking remarkably well as she had always done. She had been in bed for over a month, attended night and day by two nurses, temperature taken every four hours, hypodermic injections of unknown drugs several times a day, the minutest details of her diet regulated with utmost scrupulosity, sleeping-draughts at night, in fact, everything she wanted. She no more had angina pectoris than I had. Luckily for her she was as strong as a horse and quite capable of resisting any treatment. She told me my colleague had saved her life. Soon it dawned upon me that the majority of the patients in the nursing home consisted of more or less similar cases under the same severe hospital régime with nothing the matter with them except an idle life, too much money and a craving for being ill and being visited by the doctor. What I saw seemed to me at least as interesting as angina pectoris. How was it done, what was his method? As far as I could make it out the method consisted in putting these women to bed at first sight with a stunning diagnosis of some grave ailment and to allow them to recover slowly by gradually lifting the load of the suggestion from their confused brains. To classify my colleague as the most dangerous doctor I had ever met was easy. To classify him as a mere charlatan I was not prepared. That I considered him as an able doctor was of course quite compatible with his being a charlatan – the two go well together, the chief danger of charlatans lies there. But the charlatan operates single-handed like the pick-pocket and this man had taken me to his nursing home to demonstrate his most damaging cases with great pride. Of course he was a charlatan, but surely a charlatan of an unusual type, well worth a closer study. The more I saw of him the more was I struck with the morbid acceleration of his whole mental machinery, his restless eyes, the extraordinary rapidity of his speech. But it was the way he handled digitalis, our most powerful but most dangerous weapon in combating heart diseases, that sounded the first note of alarm in my ears. One night I received a note from the daughter of one of his patients begging me to come at once at the urgent request of the nurse. The nurse took me aside and said she had sent for me as she feared something was wrong, she was feeling very uneasy about what was going on. She was right there. The heart had been kept too long under digitalis, the patient was in immediate danger of his life from the effect of the drug. My colleague was just going to give him another injection when I snatched the syringe from him and read the terrible truth in his wild eye. He was not a charlatan, he was a madman.

What was I to do? Denounce him as a charlatan? It would only increase the number of his patients and maybe of his victims. Denounce him as a lunatic? It would mean the irreparable ruin of his whole career. What proofs could I produce? The dead could not speak, the living would not speak. His patients, his nurses, his friends, would all side against me, I who of all men would profit most by his downfall. Do nothing, and leave him in his place, a maniac arbiter of life and death?

After long hesitation I decided to speak to his ambassador who was, I knew, on very friendly terms with him. The ambassador refused to believe me. He had known my colleague for years, he had always looked upon him as an able and reliable doctor, he had himself greatly benefited by his treatment and so had his family. He had always considered him a very excitable and somewhat eccentric man, but as to the lucidity of his mind he was sure he was as sound in his head as we were. Suddenly the ambassador burst into one of his usual roars of laughter. He said he could not help it, it was too funny, he felt sure I would not take it amiss, he knew I was not devoid of a certain sense of humour. He then told me that my colleague had called upon him that same morning to ask him for a letter of introduction to the Swedish Minister, to whom he had to speak on a very grave matter. He thought it his duty to warn the Swedish Minister to keep an eye on me, he was convinced there was something wrong with my head. I pointed out to the ambassador that it was a valuable piece of evidence, it was exactly what a lunatic might do under the circumstances, the cunning of a madman could never be overrated.

On coming home I was handed an almost illegible note from my colleague which I made out as an invitation to luncheon the next day – the change of his handwriting had already attracted my attention. I found him in his consulting-room, standing before the mirror, staring with his protruding eyes at the slight swelling of his throat, the enlargement of his thyroid gland I had already noticed. The extraordinary rapidity of his pulse made the diagnosis easy. I told him he had Graves' disease. He said he had suspected it himself and asked me to take him in hand. I told him he was overworked and must give up his practice for some time, the best thing for him to do was to return to his country for a long rest. I succeeded in keeping him in bed till the arrival of his brother. He left Rome a week later, never to return again. He died the following year, I understand, in an asylum.

XXIV

Grand Hôtel

When Doctor Pilkington introduced himself to me as the doyen of the foreign doctors he usurped the title which belonged to another man, far superior to the rest of us foreign doctors in Rome. Let me write here his real name in full letters as it is written in my memory in letters of gold -- old Doctor Erhardt, one of the best doctors and one of the most kind-hearted men I have ever met. A survivor from the vanished Rome of Pio Nono, his reputation had stood the wear and tear of over forty years of practice in the Eternal City. Although over seventy he was still in full possession of his mental and physical vigour, day and night on the go, always ready to help, rich and poor all the same to him. He was the most perfect type I have ever seen of the family doctor of bygone times, now almost extinct -- so much the worse for suffering humanity. It was impossible not to love him, impossible not to trust him. I am sure he had never had an enemy during his long life except Professor Baccelli. He was a German by birth, and had there been many like him in the Fatherland in 1914 there would never have been a war.

That so many people even among his former patients would flock to Keats' house to ask advice from me when a man like old Erhardt was living in the same Piazza will always remain a mystery to me. He was the only one of my colleagues I used to consult when in doubt, he always turned out to be right and I not seldom wrong, but he never gave me away, he stood up for me whenever he had a chance and he had it often enough. Maybe he was somewhat unfamiliar with the latest conjuring tricks of our profession and kept aloof from many of our newest miraculous patent drugs from all lands and creeds. But he handled his well-tested old pharmacopoeia with masterly skill, his penetrating eyes detected the mischief wherever it lay lurking, there were no secrets left in lung or heart once he had put his stethoscope to his old ear. No modern discovery of any importance escaped his notice. He was keenly interested in bacteriology and serotherapeutics, then almost a new science, he knew his Pasteur at least as well as I did. He was the first doctor in Italy to experiment with Behring's anti-diphtheric serum, then not out of the experimental stage, and not available for the public, now saving the lives of hundreds of thousands of children every year.

I am not likely ever to forget this experiment of his. Late one evening I was summoned to the Grand Hôtel by an urgent message from an American gentleman with a letter of introduction from Professor Weir-Mitchell. I was met in the hall by a furious-looking little man who told me in great agitation he had just arrived by the train de luxe from Paris. Instead of the best suite of rooms he had reserved, he and his family had been crammed into two small bedrooms with no sitting-room and not even a bath-room. The director's wire that the hotel was full had been sent too late and never reached him. He had just telegraphed to Ritz to protest against this sort of treatment. To make matters worse his little boy was ill with a feverish cold, his wife had been sitting up with him the whole night in the train, would I be kind enough to come and see him at once? Two little children were lying asleep in one bed, face to face, almost lips to lips. The mother looked anxiously at me and said the boy had been unable to swallow his milk, she feared he had a sore throat. The little boy was breathing laboriously with wide-open mouth, his face was almost blue. I put the little girl still asleep on the mother's bed and told her the boy had diphtheria and that I must send for a nurse at once. She said she wanted to nurse the boy herself. I spent the night scraping off the diphtheric membranes from the boy's throat, he was almost choking. Towards daybreak I sent for Doctor Erhardt to help me with the tracheotomy, the boy was on the point of suffocation. The action of the heart was already so bad that he dared not give him chloroform, we both hesitated to operate, we feared the boy might die under the knife. I sent for the father, at the mention of the word diphtheria he rushed out of the room, the rest of the conversation took place through the half-opened door. He would not hear of an operation, spoke of sending for all the leading doctors of Rome to have their opinion. I said it was unnecessary and besides too late, the decision of operation or no operation remained with Erhardt and me. I wrapped a blanket round the little girl and told him to take her to his room. He said he would give a million dollars to save the life of his son, I told him it was not a question of dollars and banged the door in his face. The mother remained by the side of the bed, watching us with terror in her eyes, I told her that the operation might have to be done at any moment, it would take at least an hour to get a nurse, she would have to help us. She nodded her assent without saying a word, her face twitching under the effort to keep back her tears, she was a brave and a fine woman. While I was putting a clean towel on the table under the lamp and preparing the instruments, Erhardt told me that by a strange coincidence he had received that very morning through the German Embassy a sample of Behring's new anti-diphtheric serum sent to him at his request from the laboratory in Marburg. It had, as I knew, already been tried with remarkable success in several German clinics. Should we try the serum? There was no time for discussion, the boy was sinking rapidly, we both thought his chances very small. With the consent of the mother we decided to inject the serum. The reaction was terrific and almost instantaneous. His whole body turned black, his temperature sprang up to a hundred and six, suddenly to drop under normal in a violent shivering fit. He was bleeding from his nose and from his bowels, the action of the heart became very irregular, symptoms of immediate collapse set in. None of us left the room during the whole day, we expected him to die any moment. To our surprise his breathing became easier towards evening, the local conditions of the throat seemed somewhat better, the pulse less irregular. I begged old Erhardt to go home for a couple of hours' sleep, he said he was too interested in watching the case to feel any fatigue. With the arrival of Sœur Philippine, the English Blue Sister, one of the best nurses I have ever had, the rumour that diphtheria had broken out on the top floor had spread like wildfire all over the crowded hotel. The director sent me word that the boy must be removed at once to a hospital or nursing home. I answered that neither Erhardt nor I would take the responsibility, he would certainly die on the way. Besides we knew of no place to take him to, the arrangements for dealing with such an emergency case were in those days hopelessly inadequate. A moment later the Pittsburgh millionaire told me through the half-open door that he had ordered the director to clear out the whole top floor at his expense, he would rather buy the whole Grand Hôtel than have his son removed at the peril of his life. Towards the evening it became evident that the mother had caught the infection. Next morning the whole wing of the top floor had been evacuated. Even the waiters and the chambermaids had fled. Only Signor Cornacchia, the undertaker, was slowly patrolling up and down the deserted corridor, top-hat in hand. Now and then the father looked in through the half-open door almost crazy with terror. The mother grew worse and worse, she was removed to the adjoining room in charge of Erhardt and

257

another nurse, I and Sister Philippine remaining with the boy. Towards noon he collapsed and died of paralysis of the heart. The condition of the mother was then so critical that we dared not tell her, we decided to wait till next morning. When I told the father that the body of the boy was to be taken to the mortuary of the Protestant Cemetery the same evening and must be buried in twenty-four hours, he staggered and nearly fell into the arms of Signor Cornacchia who stood bowing respectfully by his side. He said his wife would never forgive him for leaving the boy in a strange land, he must be buried in the family vault in Pittsburgh. I answered it was impossible, it was forbidden by the law in such a case as this to send the body away. A moment later the Pittsburgh millionaire handed me through the half-open door a cheque for a thousand pounds to be used at my discretion, he was willing to write out another cheque for whatever sum I liked but the body must be sent to America. I locked myself up in another room with Signor Cornacchia and asked him what would be the approximate price for a first-class funeral and a grave in perpetuo in the Protestant Cemetery. He said times were hard, there had of late been a rise in the price of coffins, aggravated by an unforeseen falling off in the number of clients. It was a point of honour to him to make the funeral a success, ten thousand lire excluding tips would cover everything. There was also the gravedigger who, I knew, had eight children, the flowers of course would be extra. Signor Cornacchia's oblong, feline pupils widened visibly as I told him that I was authorized to hand him the double of that sum if he could arrange to have the body sent to Naples and put on board the next steamer for America. I wanted his answer in two hours, I knew it was against the law, he had to consult his conscience. I had already consulted my own. I was going to embalm the body myself that same night and have the lead coffin soldered in my presence. Having thus satisfied myself that all possible danger of infection was excluded I was going to sign a death certificate that the cause of death was septic pneumonia followed by paralysis of the heart, omitting the word diphtheria. Signor Cornacchia's consultation with his conscience took less time than anticipated, he returned an hour later, accepting the bargain on condition that half of the sum should be paid in advance and without a receipt. I handed him the money. An hour later Erhardt and I performed tracheotomy on the mother, there is no doubt that the operation saved her life.

The memory of that night haunts me still whenever I visit the beautiful little cemetery by Porta San Paolo. Giovanni, the grave-digger, stood waiting for me at the gate with a dim lantern. I suspected by the way he greeted me that he had had an extra glass of wine to steady himself for the night's work. He was to be my only assistant, I had good reasons for wanting nobody else. The night was stormy and very dark with pelting rain. A sudden gust of wind blew out the lantern, we had to grope our way as best we could in pitch darkness. Half-way across the cemetery my foot stumbled against a heap of upturned earth, and I fell headlong into a half-finished grave. Giovanni said he had been digging it the same afternoon by order of Signor Cornacchia, luckily it was not very deep, it was the grave of a small child.

The embalmment proved to be a difficult and even dangerous undertaking. The body was already in an advanced state of decom-position. The light was insufficient, and to my horror I cut myself slightly in the finger. A big owl kept on hooting the whole time behind the Cestius Pyramid, I remember it well because it was the first time the sound seemed to disagree with me, me who have always been a great lover of owls.

I was back in the Grand Hôtel early in the morning. The mother had had a good night, her temperature had dropped to normal, Erhardt considered her out of danger. It was impossible to post-pone any longer telling her that her son was dead. As neither the father nor Erhardt wanted to tell her it fell to me to do it. The nurse said she thought she already knew. As she had been sitting by her side, the mother had suddenly woken up from her sleep and tried to spring out of bed with a cry of distress, but fallen back in a swoon. The nurse thought she was dead and was just rushing to call me when I came in and said the boy had died that moment. The nurse was right in her belief. Before I had time to speak the mother looked me straight in the eyes and said she knew her son was dead. Erhardt seemed quite broken down by the death of the boy, he reproached himself for having recommended the serum. Such was the integrity and the straightforwardness of this fine old man that he wanted to write a letter to the father almost accusing himself of having caused the death of his son. I told him the res-ponsibility was mine, I being in charge of the case, and that such a letter might make the father, already half-crazy with grief, go off his head altogether. The next morning the mother was carried down and put into my carriage and taken to the nursing home of the Blue Sisters where I had also succeeded in getting a room for her little girl and her husband. Such was his fear of diphtheria that

259

he presented me with his whole wardrobe, two big trunks full of clothes, not to speak of his ulster and his top-hat. I was delighted, second-hand clothes are often more useful than drugs. I persuaded him with difficulty to keep his gold repeater, his pocket aneroid is still in my possession. Before leaving the hotel the Pittsburgh millionaire settled quite unconcerned the gigantic bill, which made me stagger. I superintended myself the disinfection of the rooms and, remembering my trick in the Hôtel Victoria in Heidelberg, I spent an hour crawling about on my knees in the room the boy had died in, detaching the Brussels carpet nailed to the floor. That there could be any spare room left in my head for thinking of the Little Sisters of the Poor at that moment passes my understanding. I can still see the faces of the hotel officials when I had the carpet brought down to my carriage and taken to the Municipal Disinfection Establishment on the Aventine. I told the director that the Pittsburgh millionaire after having paid for the carpet over three times its value, had presented it to me as a souvenir.

At last I drove home to Piazza di Spagna. I posted on the front door a notice in French and English that the Doctor was ill, please address yourself to Dr. Erhardt, Piazza di Spagna 28. I made myself a hypodermic injection of a triple dose of morphia and sank down on the couch in my consulting-room with a swollen throat and a temperature of a hundred and five. Anna was quite frightened and was most anxious to send for Doctor Erhardt. I told her I was all right, all I wanted was twenty-four hours' sleep, she was not to disturb me unless the house was on fire.

The blessed drug began to spread forgetfulness and peace in my exhausted brain, even the haunting terror of the cut in my finger dropped out of my benumbed thoughts. I was falling asleep. Suddenly the front bell rang repeatedly, furiously. I heard from the hall the loud voice of a woman of unmistakable nationality arguing with Anna in broken Italian.

'The doctor is ill, please address yourself to Doctor Erhardt next door.'

No, she must speak at once to Doctor Munthe on very urgent business.

'The doctor is in bed, please go away.'

No, she must see him at once, 'take in my card.'

'The doctor is asleep, please. . . .'

Asleep, with that terrible voice screaming in the hall, not I!

'What do you want?'

Anna had not time to hold her back, she lifted the curtain to my room, a picture of health, strong as a horse, Mrs. Charles W. Washington Longfellow Perkins, Junior.

'What do you want?'

She wanted to know if there was any danger of her catching diphtheria in the Grand Hôtel, she had been given a room on the top floor, was it true the boy had died on the first floor, she must not run any risk.

'What is the number of your room?'

'Three hundred and thirty-five.'

'By all means stay where you are. It is the cleanest room in the whole hotel, I have disinfected it myself. It is the room the boy died in.'

I sank back on the bed, through the bed it seemed to me, the morphia set to work once more.

The front bell rang again. Again I heard the same pitiless voice in the hall telling Anna she had just remembered the other question she had come to ask me, most important.

'The doctor is asleep.'

'Throw her downstairs,' I roared to Anna, half her size.

No, she would not go, she must ask me that question.

'What do you want?'

'I have broken a tooth, I fear it must be pulled out, what is the name of the best dentist in Rome?'

'Mrs. Washington Perkins, Junior, can you hear me?'

Yes, she could hear me quite well.

'Mrs. Perkins, Junior, for the first time in my life I am sorry I am not a dentist, I would just love to pull out all your teeth.'

XXV

The Little Sisters of the Poor

The Little Sisters of the Poor in San Pietro in Vincoli, about fifty in number and most of them French, were all friends of mine, and so were many of the three hundred old men and women sheltered in the huge building. The Italian doctor who was supposed to look after all these people never showed me any sign of professional jealousy, not even when the Pittsburgh millionaire's carpet from the Grand Hôtel, duly disinfected, was spread over the ice-cold stone floor of the chapel to the greatest delight of the Little Sisters. How these Sisters managed to provide food and clothing for all their inmates was a mystery to me. Their rickety old cart crawling about from hotel to hotel to collect whatsoever scraps of food could be got, was a familiar sight to all visitors to Rome in those days. Twenty Little Sisters, two by two, were on their feet from morning till night with their huge hamper and their moneybox. Two of them were generally to be found standing in the corner of my hall at the hour of my consultation, many of my former patients will no doubt remember them. Like all nuns they were very jolly and full of fun, and they thoroughly enjoyed a little chat whenever there was a chance. They were both young and rather pretty – the Mother Superior had long ago confided to me that old and plain nuns were no good for collecting money. In return for her confidence I had told her that a young and attractive-looking nurse had a far greater chance of being obeyed by my patients than a plain one, and that a sulky nurse was never a good nurse. These nuns who knew so little of the world at large, knew a lot about human nature. They knew at first sight who was likely to put something in their moneybox and who was not. Young people, these nuns told me, gave generally more than old people, children alas! seldom gave anything except when told by their English nurses. Men gave more than women, people on foot more than people sitting in their carriages. The English were their best customers, then came the Russians. French tourists there were so few about. The Americans and the Germans were more reluctant to part with their money, the upper-class Italians were still worse but the Italian poor were very generous.

Royalties and clergy of all nationalities were as a rule not very good clients. The hundred and fifty old men in their care were on the whole easy to handle, not so the hundred and fifty old women, who were always quarrelling and fighting with one another. Terrible drames passionels were not seldom enacted between the two wings of the home, when the Little Sisters had to try to extinguish the fires smouldering under the cinders to the best of their limited understanding.

The pet of the house was Monsieur Alphonse, the tiniest little Frenchman you ever saw, who lived behind a pair of blue curtains in the corner of the big ward, sixty beds in all. None of the other beds were provided with curtains, this was a privilege granted to Monsieur Alphonse alone as being the senior of the whole house. He himself said he was seventy-five, the Sisters believed he was over eighty, judging from the state of his arteries I put him down as not far from ninety. He had come there several years ago with a small handbag, a threadbare frock-coat and a top-hat, nobody knew from where. He spent his days behind his curtains in strictest seclusion from all the other inmates, only to appear on Sundays when he strutted off to the chapel, top-hat in hand. What he did behind his curtains the whole day nobody knew. The Sisters said that when they brought him his plate of soup or his cup of coffee, another privilege, he was always sitting on his bed fumbling among his bundle of papers in the old bag or brushing his top-hat. Monsieur Alphonse was very particular about receiving visitors. You were supposed to knock first at the little table by the side of the bed. He would then carefully lock up all his papers in his bag, call out in his piping voice: 'Entrez, Monsieur!' and invite you with an apologetic waving of his hand to sit down by his side on the bed. He seemed to enjoy my visits and we soon became great friends. All my efforts to know something of his past life proved in vain, all I knew was that he was a Frenchman but nct I should say a Parisian. He did not speak a word of Italian and seemed to know nothing of Rome. He had not even been in St. Peter's, but he meant to go there un de ces quatre matins, as soon as he had time. The Sisters said he would never go there, he would never go anywhere, though he was quite capable of trotting about if he wanted to. The real reason why he stayed at home on Thursdays, the day out for men, was the irremediable collapse of his top-hat and of his old frock-coat from constant brushing.

The memorable day when he was made to try on the Pittsburgh millionaire's top-hat and brand new frock-coat, latest American fashion, opened the last chapter in Monsieur Alphonse's life, and perhaps the happiest. All the Sisters of the wards, even the Mother Superior, were down at the entrance door the following Tuesday to see him off as he stepped into my smart victoria, solemnly raising his new top-hat to his admirers.

'Est-il chic!' they laughed as we drove off. 'On dirait un milord anglais!' We drove down the Corso and made a short appearance on the Pincio before we stopped at the Piazza di Spagna where Monsieur Alphonse had been invited to luncheon by me.

I should like to see the face of the man who could have resisted the temptation to make this invitation a standing one for every Thursday to follow. Sharp at one o'clock on every Thursday of that winter my victoria deposited Monsieur Alphonse at 26 Piazza di Spagna. An hour later when my consultation began he was escorted by Anna to the waiting carriage for his accustomed drive round the Pincio. Then half-an-hour's stop at Café Aragno where Monsieur Alphonse sat down in his reserved corner for his cup of coffee and his 'Figaro' with the air of an old ambassador. Another half-hour of glorious life driving down the Corso, eagerly looking out for some of his acquaintances from Piazza di Spagna to whom to raise his new top-hat. Then to vanish again behind his blue curtains till the following Thursday when he began brushing his top-hat at daybreak, according to the Little Sisters. As often as not a friend or two dropped in to share the luncheon party to the huge delight of Monsieur Alphonse. More than one of them will surely still remember him. None of them ever had the slightest suspicion of where he came from. He looked besides very neat and dapper in his long, smart frock-coat and in his new top-hat which he was most reluctant to part with even while at table. Not knowing myself what to make out of Monsieur Alphonse, I had ended by turning him into a retired diplomat. All my friends addressed him as 'Monsieur le Ministre,' and Anna invariably called him 'Vostra Eccellenza,' you should have seen his face! Luckily he was extremely deaf, and the conversation was generally limited to a few polite remarks about the Pope or about the scirocco. Anyhow I had to keep a vigilant eye and ear upon the proceedings, ready to interfere at any moment to put aside the decanter or to come to his rescue at some embarrassing question or some even more embarrassing answer after his second glass of Frascati. Monsieur Alphonse was an ardent royalist, ready to overthrow the French Republic at any cost. He was expecting news any day from a very confidential source to return to Paris at any moment. So far we were on safe ground, I had heard many Frenchmen abolish the republic. But when he began to talk family matters I had to be very careful lest he should let the jealously kept secret of his past out of the bag. Luckily I was always warned in time by his brother-in-law: mon beau-frère le sous-préfet. It was a tacit understanding between my friends and me that at the very mentioning of this mysterious personage the decanter was to be put away and not another drop of wine poured in Monsieur Alphonse's glass.

I remember it quite well, Waldo Storey, the well-known American sculptor and a particular friend of Monsieur Alphonse, was lunching with us that Thursday. Monsieur Alphonse was in tearing spirits and unusually talkative. Already before he had finished his first glass of Frascati he was consulting Waldo about raising an army of ex-Garibaldians to invade France and march on Paris to overthrow the Republic. After all it was only a question of money, five million francs would be ample, he was willing to raise one million himself if it came to the worst.

I thought he looked somewhat flushed, I felt sure his brother-in-law was not far away. I gave Waldo the usual signal not to give him another drop of wine.

'Mon beau-frère le sous-préfet. . . .' he chuckled.

He stopped short as I pushed the decanter out of his reach and looked down on his plate as he used to do when he was somewhat vexed.

'Never mind,' said I, 'here's another glass of wine to your health, sorry to have vexed you, and a bas la République! since you want it so.'

To my surprise he did not stretch out his hand towards his glass. He sat quite still staring at his plate. He was dead.

Nobody knew better than I what it would mean to Monsieur Alphonse and me, had I followed the usual course and sent for the police according to the law. Inspection of the body by the Medico-Legal Officer, perhaps a post-mortem, intervention of the French Consulate, last not least the stealing from the dead of his only possession, the secret of his past. Anna was sent down to tell the coachman to put up the hood, Monsieur Alphonse had had a fainting fit, I was going to take him home myself. Five minutes later Monsieur Alphonse was sitting by my side in the carriage in his usual corner, the collar of the Pittsburgh millionaire's ulster well pulled over his ears, his top-hat deep down on his forehead as was his custom. He looked exactly as he used to do, only that he looked much smaller than in life, all dead people do.

'By the Corso?' asked the coachman.

'Yes, of course by the Corso, it is Monsieur Alphonse's favourite drive.'

The Mother Superior was somewhat uneasy at first, but my certificate of 'death from heart failure' dated from the home made it all right with the police regulations. In the evening Monsieur Alphonse was put in his coffin with his bag as a pillow for his old head, its key still on its ribbon round his neck. The Little Sisters do not ask any questions either of the living or of the dead. All they want to know of those who come to them for shelter is that they are old and hungry. The rest concerns God and not them nor anybody else. They know quite well that many of their inmates live and die among them under assumed names. I wanted to let him take his beloved top-hat with him in the coffin, but the Sisters said it would not do. I said I was sorry, I felt sure he would have liked it.

*   *   *

One night I was awakened by an urgent message from the Little Sisters of the Poor to come at once. All the wards of the huge building were dark and silent but I heard the Sisters praying in the chapel. I was let into a small room in the Sisters' quarters where I had never been before. On the bed lay a nun, still young, her face white as the pillow under her head, her eyes closed, her pulse hardly perceptible. It was La Mère Générale des Petites Soeurs des Pauvres who had arrived the same evening from Naples on her way back to Paris from a journey of inspection round the world. She was in immediate danger of death from a severe disease of the heart. I have stood by the bedside of kings and queens and of famous men at an hour when their lives were at stake, maybe even in my hands. But I never felt the responsibility of my profession more heavily than I did that night when this woman slowly opened her wonderful eyes and looked at me:

'Faites ce que vous pouvez, Monsieur le Docteur,' she murmured, 'car quarante mille pauvres dépendent de moi.'

*   *   *

The Little Sisters of the Poor are toiling from morning till night at their work, the most useful and the most unappreciated form of charity I know of. You need not come to Rome to find them, poverty and old age are all over the world and so are the Little Sisters of the Poor with their empty hamper and their empty moneybox. Do put your suit of old clothes in their hamper, never

266

mind your size, all sizes will do for the Little Sisters of the Poor. Top-hats are getting out of fashion, you had better give them your top-hat as well. There will always be in their wards an old Monsieur Alphonse, hidden behind a pair of blue curtains, busy brushing his broken-down top-hat, the last vestige of bygone prosperity. Do send him on his day out for a joy-ride down the Corso in your smart victoria. It is much better for your liver to go for a long walk in the Campagna with your dog. Do invite him to luncheon next Thursday, there is no better stimulant for lost appetite than to watch a hungry man having his fill. Give him his glass of Frascati wine to help him to forget, but put the decanter away when he begins to remember.

Do put some of your savings in the Little Sisters' moneybox, even a penny will do, believe me you never made a safer investment. Remember what I have written on another page of this book – what you keep to yourself you lose, what you give away you keep for ever. Besides you have no right to keep this money to yourself, it does not belong to you, money belongs to nobody up here. All money belongs to the Devil who sits at his counter night and day behind his sacks of gold trading with human souls. Do not hold on too long to the dirty coin he puts in your hand, get rid of it as soon as you can or the cursed metal will soon burn your fingers, penetrate your blood, blind your eyes, infect your thoughts and harden your heart. Put it into the moneybox of the Little Sisters, or throw the damned stuff into the nearest gutter, it is the very place for it! What is the good of hoarding your money, it will soon be taken from you in any case. Death has another key to your safe.

The gods sell all things at a fair price, said an old poet. He might have added that they sell their best goods at the cheapest rate. All that is really useful to us can be bought for little money, it is only the superfluous that is put up for sale at a high price. All that is really beautiful is not put up for sale at all but is offered us as a gift by the immortal gods. We are allowed to watch the sun rise and set, the clouds sailing along in the sky, the forests and the fields, the glorious sea, all without spending a penny. The birds sing to us for nothing, the wild flowers we may pick as we are walking along by the roadside. There is no entrance fee to the starlit hall of the Night. The poor man sleeps better than the rich man. Simple food tastes in the long run better than food from Ritz. Contentment and peace of mind thrive better in a small country cottage than in the stately palace in a town. A few friends, a few books, indeed a very few, and a dog is all you need to have about you as long as you have

267

yourself. But you should live in the country. The first town was planned by the Devil, that is why God wanted to destroy the tower of Babel.

Have you ever seen the Devil? I have. He was standing leaning his arms against the parapet of the tower of Notre Dame. His wings were folded, his head was resting in the palms of his hands. His cheeks were hollow, his tongue was protruding between his foul lips. Pensive and grave he looked down on Paris at his feet. Motionless and rigid as if he were of stone, he has been standing there for nearly a thousand years gloating over the city of his choice as if he could not tear his eyes away from what he saw. Was this the arch-fiend whose very name had filled me with awe since I was a child, the formidable champion of evil in the struggle between right and wrong?

I looked at him with surprise. I thought he looked far less wicked than I had imagined, I had seen worse faces than his. There was no glimmer of triumph in those stony eyes, he looked old and weary, weary of his easy victories, weary of his Hell.

Poor old Beelzebub! Maybe when all is said it is not altogether your fault when things go wrong up here in our world. After all it was not you who gave life to this world of ours, it was not you who let loose sorrow and death amongst men. You were born with wings and not with claws, it was God who turned you into a devil and hurled you to His hell to be the keeper of His damned. Surely you would not have stood here in storm and rain on the top of the tower of Notre Dame for a thousand years had you liked your job. I am sure it is not easy to be a devil for one who was born with wings. Prince of Darkness, why don't you extinguish the fire in your subterranean kingdom and come up to settle amongst us in a big town – believe me the country is no place for you – as a private gentleman of means with nothing to do the whole day but eat and drink and hoard your money. Or if you must increase your capital and try your hand at some new congenial job, why don't you open another gambling hell in Monte Carlo or start a brothel or become a usurer to the poor or the proprietor of a travelling menagerie with defenceless wild animals starving behind their iron bars! Or if you want a change of air why don't you go to Germany and start another factory for your latest poison gas! Who but you could have directed their blind air raid over Naples and dropped their incendiary bomb on the home of the Little Sisters of the Poor among their three hundred old men and women!

But will you allow me in return for the advice I have given you to ask you a question ? Why do you put out your tongue like that ? I do not know how it is looked upon in hell, but, with all respect to you, amongst us it is looked upon as a sign of defiance and disrespect. Pardon me, sire, at whom are you putting out your tongue the whole time ?

Miss Hall

Many of my patients of those days will surely remember Miss Hall, indeed once seen she was not easily forgotten. Great Britain alone, Great Britain at its very best, could have produced this unique type of the early Victorian spinster, six feet three inches, dry and stiff like a stick, *arida nutrix* of at least two unborn generations of Scotchmen. During the fifteen years I knew Miss Hall I never saw any change in her appearance, always the same glorious face enshrined by the same curls of faded gold, always the same gaily coloured dress, always the same bower of roses in her hat. How many years of uneventful life Miss Hall had spent in various second-class Roman pensions in search of adventure, I do not know. But I know that the day she met Tappio and me in the Villa Borghese her real mission in life began, she had found herself at last. She spent her mornings brushing and combing the dogs in my ice-cold back sitting-room under the Trinità dei Monti steps only to return to her pension for luncheon. At three o'clock she sailed forth from Keats' house across the Piazza with Giovannina and Rosina, half her size, on each side of her in their wooden shoes with their red handkerchiefs round their heads and surrounded by all my dogs barking joyously in anticipation of their walk in Villa Borghese – a familiar sight to the whole Piazza di Spagna in those days. Giovannina and Rosina belonged to the San Michele household, better servants I have never had, light of hand and foot, singing the whole day at their work. Of course nobody but I could ever have dreamt of taking these two half-tamed Anacapri girls to Rome. It would besides never have worked had not Miss Hall turned up in time to become a sort of foster-mother to them, to watch over them with the solicitude of an old hen over her chickens. Miss Hall said she could never understand why I did not allow the girls to walk about alone in the Villa Borghese, she had been walking all over Rome by herself for many years without anybody ever having taken any notice of her or said a word to her. True to her type Miss Hall had never succeeded in saying a single word of comprehensible Italian, but the girls understood her quite well and were very fond of her, although I fear they did not take her more seriously than I did. Of me Miss Hall saw very little, and I saw even less of her, I never looked at her when I could help it. On the rare occasions when Miss Hall was invited to be present at my luncheon, a huge flower-vase was always placed on the table between us. Although Miss Hall was strictly forbidden to look at me, she nevertheless managed now and then to pop her head over the flower-vase and have a shot at me from the corner of her old eye. Miss Hall never seemed to understand how beastly selfish and ungrateful I was in return for all she did for me. Considering her limited means of communication – Miss Hall was not allowed to ask me any questions – she succeeded somehow in finding out a good deal of what was going on in the house and what people I saw. She kept a vigilant eye on all my lady patients, she used to patrol the Piazza for hours to see them coming in and out during my consultations. With the opening of the Grand Hôtel, Ritz had dealt a final blow to the vanishing simplicity of Roman life. The last invasion of the barbarians had begun, the Eternal City had become fashionable. The huge hotel was crammed with the smart set from London and Paris, American millionaires and leading rastaqouères from the Riviera. Miss Hall knew all these people by name, she had watched them for years through the society columns of the 'Morning Post.' As to the English nobility Miss Hall was a perfect encyclopaedia. She knew by heart the birth and the coming of age of their sons and heirs, the betrothal and the marriage of their daughters, the dresses they had worn when presented at Court, their dances, their dinner-parties, their journeys abroad. Many of these smart people ended by becoming my patients whether they wanted it or not, to the huge delight of Miss Hall. Others, unable to be alone a single moment, invited me to lunch or dinner. Others called at Piazza di Spagna to see the room Keats had died in. Others stopped their carriages in the Villa Borghese to pat my dogs with some complimentary words to Miss Hall on how well they were groomed. Gradually Miss Hall and I emerged hand in hand from our natural obscurity into the higher spheres of society. I went out a good deal that winter. I had still a lot to learn from these easy-going idlers, their capacity for doing nothing, their good spirits, their good sleep puzzled me. Miss Hall now kept a special diary of the social events of my daily life. Beaming with pride she trotted about in her best frock leaving my cards right and left. The lustre of our ascending star grew brighter and brighter, higher and higher went our way, nothing could stop us any more. One day as Miss Hall was walking with the dogs in the

Villa Borghese a lady with a black poodle on her lap signalled to her to come up to her carriage. The lady patted the Lapland dog and said it was she who had given Tappio as a tiny puppy to the doctor. Miss Hall felt her old knees shaking under her, it was H.R.H. the Crown Princess of Sweden! A beautiful gentleman, seated by her illustrious side, stretched out his hand with a charming smile and actually said:

'Hullo, Miss Hall, I have heard a lot about you from the doctor.'

It was H.R.H. Prince Max of Baden, the husband of nobody less than the niece of her beloved Queen Alexandra! From that memorable day Miss Hall abandoned the smart set of the Grand Hôtel to devote all her spare time to royalties, there were at least half-a-dozen of them that winter in Rome. She stood for hours outside their hotels waiting for a chance to see them coming in or out, she watched them with bent head driving on the Pincio or in the Villa Borghese, she followed them like a detective in the churches and the museums. On Sundays she sat in the English church in Via Babuino as near to the Ambassador's pew as she dared, with one eye on her prayer-book and the other on a Royal Highness, straining her old ear to catch the particular sound of the royal voice in the singing of the congregation, praying for the Royal Family and their relations in every land with the fervour of an early Christian.

Soon Miss Hall started another diary, entirely devoted to our associations with Royalty. The previous Monday she had had the honour to carry a letter from the doctor to H.R.H. the Grand Duchess of Weimar at the Hôtel Quirinale. The porter had given her an answer adorned with the Grand-ducal crown of Saxe and Weimar. The envelope had been graciously presented to her by the doctor as a precious souvenir. On Wednesday she had been entrusted with a letter for H.R.H. the Infanta Eulalia of Spain in the Grand Hôtel. Unfortunately there was no answer. One afternoon, as she was with the dogs in the Villa Borghese, Miss Hall had noticed a tall lady in black walking rapidly up and down a side alley. She recognized her at once as the same lady she had seen in the garden of San Michele, standing motionless by the Sphinx and looking out over the sea with her beautiful, sad eyes. As the lady passed before her now, she said something to her companion and stretched out her hand to pat Gialla, the borzoi. Judge of Miss Hall's consternation when a detective came up to her and told her to move on at once with the dogs – it was H.I.H. the Empress of Austria and her sister Countess Trani! How could the doctor have been so cruel not to have told her in the summer? Only by a mere accident did she know much later that a week after the lady's visit to San Michele the doctor had received a letter from the Austrian Embassy in Rome with an offer to buy San Michele and that the would-be purchaser was no less a person than the Empress of Austria. Luckily the doctor had declined the offer, it would indeed be a pity if he should sell a place like San Michele with such unique opportunities for seeing Royalties! Had she not last summer for weeks been watching at a respectful distance a granddaughter of her own beloved Queen Victoria, painting in the pergola! Had not a cousin of the Tsar himself been living there for a whole month! Had she not had the honour to stand behind the kitchen door to see the Empress Eugénie pass before her at an arm's length the first time she came to San Michele. Had she not heard with her own ears H.I.H. say to the doctor that she had never seen a more striking likeness to the great Napoleon than the head of Augustus the doctor had dug up in his garden! Had she not several years later heard the commanding voice of the Kaiser himself lecturing to his suite on the various antiquities and works of art as they passed along accompanied by the doctor who hardly opened his mouth! Close to where she stood hidden behind the cypresses, H.I.H. had pointed to a female torso half covered by the ivy and told his suite that what they saw was worthy of a place of honour in his Museum in Berlin, for all he knew it might be an unknown masterpiece by Phidias himself. Horror-struck Miss Hall had heard the doctor say it was the only fragment in San Michele that was not good. It had been dumped upon him by a well-meaning patient who had bought it in Naples, it was Canova at his worst. To Miss Hall's great regret the party had left almost immediately for the Marina to embark on their dispatch boat Sleipner for Naples.

A propos of the Empress of Austria, I must tell you that Miss Hall was a K.C. of the Imperial Order of St. Stefan. This high distinction had been bestowed upon Miss Hall one day by me when my conscience must have been particularly bad, as a reward for her faithful services to me and my dogs. Why it had been bestowed upon myself I had never succeeded in understanding. Miss Hall received this decoration from my hands with bent head and tear-filled eyes. She said she would take it with her to her grave. I said I saw no objection, she was sure to go to Heaven anyhow. But that she would take it with her to the British Embassy I had not antici-pated. I had succeeded in obtaining from kind Lord Dufferin an invitation for Miss Hall to the reception at the Embassy in honour of the Queen's birthday, all the English colony in Rome having been invited except poor Miss Hall. Overwhelmed with joyful anticipation Miss Hall had been invisible for several days, hard at work with her toilette. Judge of my consternation when on presenting Miss Hall to her ambassador I saw Lord Dufferin screw in his monocle and stare speechless at Miss Hall's sternum. Luckily Lord Dufferin was not an Irishman for nothing. All he did was to take me aside with a roar of laughter and make me promise to keep Miss Hall out of the sight of his Austrian colleague. Miss Hall told me as we drove home that it had been the proudest day of her life. Lord Dufferin had been most gracious to her, everybody had smiled at her, she felt sure her toilette had been a great success.

Yes, it is all very well to make fun of Miss Hall! But I should like to know what will become of Royalty when Miss Hall is no more there to keep a diary of their doings, to watch them with shaking knees and bent head driving on the Pincio and in the Villa Borghese, to pray for them in the English church of Via Babuino? What will become of their stars and ribbons when mankind will have outgrown playing with toys? Why not give them all to Miss Hall and be done with them! There will always remain the V.C., we all uncover our heads to courage face to face with death. Do you know why the V.C. is so rare in the British Army? Because bravery in its highest form, Napoleon's courage de la nuit, seldom gets the V.C. and because courage unassisted by luck bleeds to death unrewarded.

Next after the V.C. the most coveted English decoration is the Garter – it would be an evil day for England if the order should ever be reversed.

'I like the Garter,' said Lord Melbourne, 'there is no damned merit about it.'

My friend the Swedish Minister in Rome showed me only the other day the copy of a letter of mine written nearly twenty years ago. The original he said he had forwarded to the Swedish Foreign Office for perusal and meditation. It was a belated answer to a repeated official request from the Swedish Legation that I should at least have the decency to acknowledge with thanks the receipt of the Messina medal bestowed on me by the Italian Government for something I was supposed to have done during the earthquake. The letter ran as follows:

Your Excellency,
My guiding principle in the matter of decorations has so far been only to accept a decoration if I had done nothing whatso-

274

ever to deserve it. A glance at the Red Book will make you realize the remarkable results of my strict adherence to this principle during a number of years. The new method suggested by your Excellency's letter, i.e. to seek public recognition for what little useful work I may have tried to do, seems to me a risky undertaking of doubtful practical value. It would only bring confusion into my philosophy, and it might irritate the immortal gods. I slipped unnoticed out of the cholera slums of Naples, I mean to do the same from the ruins of Messina. I need no commemorative medal to remember what I saw.

*   *   *

As it happens, I must admit that this letter is all humbug. The Swedish Minister never returned my Messina medal to the Italian Government, I have got it somewhere in a drawer, with a clear conscience and no greater confusion in my philosophy than before. There was in fact no reason why I should not accept this medal, for what I did in Messina was very little compared with what I saw hundreds of unnamed and unrecorded people do at the peril of their lives. I myself was in no peril except that of dying from hunger and from my own stupidity. It is true that I brought a number of half-suffocated people back to life by means of artificial respiration, but there are few doctors, nurses or coastguards who have not done the same for nothing. I know that I dragged single-handed an old woman from what had been her kitchen but I also know that I abandoned her in the street screaming for help, with her two legs broken. There was indeed nothing else for me to do, until the arrival of the first hospital ship, no dressing material and no medicine whatsoever was obtainable. There was also the naked baby I found late one evening in a courtyard, I took it to my cellar where it slept peacefully the whole night, tucked under my coat, now and then sucking my thumb in its sleep. In the morning I took it to the nuns of S. Teresa in what remained of their chapel where already over a dozen babies were lying on the floor screaming with hunger, as for a whole week not a drop of milk could be found in Messina. I always marvelled at the number of unhurt babies picked out of the ruins or found in the streets, it almost looked as if Almighty God had shown a little more pity on them than on the grown-up people. The aqueduct having been broken, there was no water either except from a few stinking wells, polluted by the thousands of putrefied bodies strewn all over the town. No bread, no meat, hardly any macaroni, no vegetables, no fish, most of the fishing-boats having

275

been swamped or smashed to pieces by the tidal wave which swept over the beach, carrying away over a thousand people, huddled there for safety. Hundreds of them were hurled back on the sand, where they lay for days rotting in the sun. The biggest shark I have ever seen – the strait of Messina is full of sharks – was also thrown up on the sand, still alive. I watched with hungry eyes when he was being cut open, hoping to snatch a slice for myself. I had always been told that the flesh of the shark is very good. In his belly was the whole leg of a woman in a woollen red stocking and a thick boot, amputated as by a surgeon's knife. It is quite possible that there were other than sharks that tasted human flesh during those days, the less said about it the better. Of course the thousands of homeless dogs and cats, sneaking about the ruins during night, lived on nothing else, until they were caught and devoured by the living whenever there was a chance. I myself have roasted a cat over my spirit lamp. Luckily there were plenty of oranges, lemons and mandarins to steal in the gardens. Wine was plentiful, the looting of the thousands of wine cellars and wine shops began the very first day, most people were more or less drunk in the evening, myself included, it was a real blessing, it took away the fainting sensation of hunger, and few people would have dared to fall asleep had they been sober. Shocks occurred almost every night, followed by the roar of falling houses and renewed screams of terror from the people in the streets. On the whole I slept rather well in Messina notwithstanding the inconvenience of having constantly to change my sleeping quarters. The cellars were of course the safest place to sleep in if one could overcome the haunting fear of being entrapped like a rat by a falling wall. Better still was to sleep under a tree in an orange grove but after two days of torrential rain the nights became too cold for a man whose whole outfit was in the haversack on his back. I tried to console myself as best I could for the loss of my beloved Scotch cape by the thought that it was probably wrapped round some even more dilapidated garments than my own. I would however not have exchanged them for anything better even had I had a chance. Only a very brave man would have felt comfortable in a decent suit of clothes among all these people saved in their nightshirts, maddened by terror, hunger and cold – he would besides not have kept it for long. That robbery from the living and the dead, assaults, even murders, occurred frequently before the arrival of the troops and the declaration of martial law is not to be wondered at. I know of no country where they would not have occurred under similar indescribable circumstances. To make

276

matters worse, the law of irony had willed it that while of the eight hundred carabinieri in the Collegio Militare only fourteen escaped alive, the first shock opened the cells for over four hundred unhurt professional murderers and thieves on life sentences in the prison by the Capuccini. That these gaol-birds, after having looted the shops for clothes and the armourers for revolvers, had a real good time in what remained of the rich city is certain. They even broke open the safe of the Banco di Napoli, killing two night watchmen. Such was however the terror that prevailed in all minds that many of these bandits preferred to give themselves up and be locked up in the hull of a steamer in the harbour, rather than remain in the doomed city, notwithstanding their unique opportunities. As far as I am concerned I was never molested by anybody, on the contrary they were all touchingly kind and helpful to me as they were to each other. Those who had got hold of any clothing or food were always glad to share it with those who had not. I was even presented by an unknown shoplifter with a smart quilted ladies' dressing-gown, one of the most welcome presents I have ever received. One evening, in passing by the ruins of a palazzo, I noticed a well-dressed man throwing down some pieces of bread and a bundle of carrots to two horses and a little donkey imprisoned in their underground stable, I could just see the doomed animals through a narrow chink in the wall. He told me he came there twice a day with whatever scraps of food he could get hold of, the sight of these poor animals dying of hunger and thirst was so painful to him that he would rather shoot them with his revolver if only he had the courage, but he had never had the courage to shoot any animal, not even a quail.[1] I looked in surprise at his handsome, intelligent and rather sympathetic face and asked him if he was a Sicilian, he said he was not but that he had lived in Sicily for several years. It began to rain heavily and we walked away. He asked me where I was living and when I answered nowhere in particular, he looked at my drenched clothes and offered to put me up for the night, he was living with two friends close by. We groped our way among huge blocks of masonry and piles of smashed furniture of all descriptions, descended a flight of steps and stood in a large underground kitchen dimly lit by an oil-lamp under a colour print of the Madonna stuck up on the wall. There were three mattresses on the floor, Signor Amedeo said I was welcome to sleep on his, he and his two friends were to be away the

[1] It might interest animal lovers to know that these two horses and the little donkey were got out alive on the seventeenth day after the earthquake and that they recovered.

whole night to search for some of their belongings under the ruins of their houses. I had an excellent supper, the second decent meal I had had since my arrival at Messina. The first had been a couple of days before when I had unexpectedly come upon a joyous luncheon party in the garden of the American Consulate, presided over by my old friend Winthrop Chanler, who had arrived the same morning in his yacht loaded with provisions for the starving city. I slept soundly the whole night on Signor Amedeo's mattress, only to be awakened in the morning by the safe return of my host and his two friends from their perilous night expedition – perilous indeed, as I knew that troops were ordered to shoot at sight any person attempting to carry anything away, were it even from the ruins of his own house. They flung their bundles under the table and themselves on their mattresses and were all fast asleep when I left. Dead tired though he looked, my kind host had not forgotten to tell me that I was welcome to stay with him as long as I liked, and of course I asked for nothing better. The next evening I had supper again with Signor Amedeo, his two friends were already fast asleep on their mattresses, they were all three to be off again for their night's work after midnight. A kinder man than my host I never saw. When he heard I was out of cash, he offered at once to lend me five hundred lire, I regret to say I owe him them still. I could not help expressing my surprise that he was willing to lend his money to a stranger of whom he knew nothing. He answered me with a smile that I would not be sitting by his side if he did not trust me.

Late the following afternoon as I was crawling among the ruins of the Hôtel Trinacria in search of the corpse of the Swedish Consul, I was suddenly confronted with a soldier pointing his rifle at me. I was arrested and taken to the nearest post. Having overcome the preliminary difficulty of locating my obscure country and having scrutinized my permit signed by the prefect, the officer in charge let me off, my only *corpus delicti* consisting in a half-carbonized Swedish Consular Register. I left the post rather uneasy, for I had noticed the somewhat puzzled look in the officer's eye when I had told him I was unable to give my exact address, I did not even know the name of the street my kind host was living in. It was already quite dark, soon I started running, for I imagined I heard stealthy footsteps behind me as if somebody was following me, but I reached my sleeping quarters without further adventures. Signor Amedeo and his two friends were already asleep on their mattresses. Hungry as usual I sat down to the supper my kind host had left for me on the table. I meant to keep awake till they were about to start and offer Signor Amedeo to help him that night in his search for his belongings. I was just saying to myself that it was the least I could do in return for his kindness to me when I suddenly heard a sharp whistle and the sound of footsteps. Somebody was coming down the stairs. In an instant the three men asleep on the mattresses sprang to their feet. I heard a shot, a carabiniere fell headlong down the stairs on the floor at my feet. As I bent rapidly over him to see if he was dead I distinctly saw Signor Amedeo pointing his revolver at me. The same instant the room was full of soldiers, I heard another shot, after a desperate struggle the three men were overpowered. As my host passed before me, handcuffed, with a stout rope tied round his arms and legs, he raised his head and looked at me with a wild flash of hatred and reproach that made the blood freeze in my veins. Half an hour later I was back again at the same post, where I was locked up for the night. In the morning I was interrogated again by the same officer to whose intelligence and kindness I probably owe my life. He told me the three men were escaped prisoners on life sentence in the prison by the Capuccini, all 'pericolosissimi.' Amedeo was a famous bandit who had terrorized the country round Girgenti for years with a record of eight homicides. It was also he and his gang who had broken into the Banco di Napoli and killed the watchmen the previous night while I was sound asleep on his mattress. The three men had been shot at daybreak. They had asked for a priest, had confessed their sins and had died fearlessly. The police officer said he wished to compliment me for the important rôle I had played in their capture. I looked him in the eye and said I was not proud of my achievement. I had realized long ago that I was not fit to play the rôle of an accuser and still less the rôle of an executioner. It was not my business, maybe it was his, maybe it was not. God knew how to strike when He wished to strike, He knew how to take a life as well as how to give it.

Unfortunately for me my adventure reached the ears of some newspaper correspondents hanging about outside the Military Zone – no newspaper correspondents could enter the town in those days for good reason – in search of sensational news, the more incredible the better; and surely this story would seem incredible enough to those who were not in Messina during the first week after the earthquake. Only a lucky mutilation of my name saved me from becoming famous. But when I was informed by those who knew the long arm of the *Mafia* that it would not save me from being murdered if I remained in Messina, I sailed the next day with some coastguards across the straits to Reggio.

Reggio itself, where twenty thousand people had been killed outright by the first shock, was indescribable and unforgettable. Still more terrifying was the sight of the small coast towns strewn among the orange groves, Scilla, Canitello, Villa S. Giovanni, Gallico, Archi, San Gregorio, formerly perhaps the most beautiful land in Italy, now a vast cemetery for more than thirty thousand dead and several thousand wounded lying among the ruins during two nights of torrential rain followed by an ice-cold tramontana, without any assistance whatsoever, and many thousands of half-naked people running about in the streets like lunatics, screaming for food. Further south the intensity of the seismic convulsion seemed to have reached its climax. In Pellaro, for instance, where only a couple of hundred of its five thousand inhabitants escaped alive, I was unable to distinguish even where the streets had been. The church, crammed with terrified people, collapsed at the second shock, killing them all. The churchyard was strewn with split-open coffins, literally shot out of the graves – I had already seen the same ghastly sight in the cemetery of Messina. On the heap of ruins where the church had stood sat a dozen women shivering in their rags. They did not cry, they did not speak, they sat there quite still with bent heads and half-closed eyes. Now and then one of them lifted her head and stared with vacant eyes towards a shabby old priest gesticulating wildly among a group of men close by. Now and then he raised his clenched fist with a terrific curse in the direction of Messina across the waters, Messina, the city of Satan, the Sodom and Gomorrah in one, the cause of all their misery. Had he not always prophesied that the city of the sinners would end with ——? A series of undulatory gesticulations with both his hands in the air left no doubt what the prophecy had been. Castigo di Dio! Castigo di Dio!

I gave the woman next to me with a baby in her lap a little loaf of stale bread from my haversack. She grabbed it without saying a word, handed me instantly an orange from her pocket, bit off a piece of the bread to put it in the mouth of the woman behind her who was on the point of becoming a mother, and started devouring the rest ravenously like a starving animal. She told me in a low, monotonous voice how she, with the baby at her breast, had escaped, she did not know how, when the house tumbled down at the first 'staccata,' how she had worked till the following day to try to drag out her other two children and their father from the wreckage, she could hear their moans till it was broad daylight. Then came another staccata and all was silent. She had an ugly cut across the forehead, but her 'creatura' – the touching word the mothers call their babies here – was quite unhurt, grazie a Dio. As she spoke, she put the baby to the breast, a magnificent little boy, entirely naked, strong as the infant Hercules, evidently not in the least the worse for what had happened. In a basket by her side slept another baby under some wisps of rotten straw; she had picked it up in the street, nobody knew to whom it belonged. As I stood up to go, the motherless baby began to fret, she snatched it from the basket and put it to her other breast. I looked at the humble Calabrian peasant woman, strong limbed and broad bosomed with the two splendid babies sucking vigorously at her breasts, and suddenly I remembered her name. She was the Demeter of the Magna Graecia where she was born, the Magna Mater of the Romans. She was Mother Nature, from her broad bosom flowed the river of life as before over the graves of the hundred thousand dead. O Death, where is Thy sting? O Grave, where is Thy victory?

* * *

To return to Miss Hall: With all these royalties on her hands it became increasingly difficult for her to control the coming and going of my lady patients. My hope to have done with neurotic women when I left Paris had not been fulfilled, my consulting-room in the Piazza di Spagna was full of them. Some of them were old and dreaded acquaintances from Avenue de Villiers, others had been dumped upon me in ever-increasing numbers by various worn-out nerve specialists in legitimate self-defence. The dozens of undisciplined and unhinged ladies of all ages that Professor Weir-Mitchell alone used to hand over to me would be enough to test the solidity of any man's brain and patience. Professor Kraft-Ebing of Vienna, the famous author of 'Psychopathia Sexualis,' was also constantly sending me patients of both sexes and of no sex, all more or less difficult to handle, specially the women. To my great surprise and satisfaction I had also been attending of late a good many patients with various nervous disorders, undoubtedly addressed to me by the master of the Salpêtrière, though never with a word in writing. Many of these patients were ill-defined border-cases more or less irresponsible for their acts. Some were nothing less than disguised lunatics, up to anything. It is easy to be patient with lunatics, I confess to a sneaking liking for them. With a little kindness one comes to terms with most of them as often as not. But it is not easy to be patient with hysterical women, and as to being kind to them, one had better think it over twice before being too kind to them, they ask for nothing better. As a rule you can do but little for these patients, at least outside the hospital. You can stun their nerve centres with sedatives but you cannot cure them. They remain what they are, a bewildering complex of mental and physical disorders, a plague to themselves and to their families, a curse to their doctors. Hypnotic treatment, so beneficial in many hitherto incurable mental troubles, is as a rule contraindicated in the treatment of hysterical women of all ages, hysteria has no age limit. It should in any case be limited to Charcot's suggestion à l'état de veille. It is besides unnecessary, for these helpless women are in any case already too willing to be influenced by their doctor, to depend upon him too much, to imagine he is the only one who can understand them, to hero-worship him. Sooner or later the photographs begin to turn up, there is nothing to be done, 'il faut passer par la,' as Charcot used to say with his grim smile. My dislike of photographs is of old date, personally I have never submitted to be photographed since I was sixteen years old except for the unavoidable snapshots for my passport when I served in the Red Cross during the war. I have never taken any interest even in the photographs of my friends, I can at will reproduce their unretouched features on my retina with far more exactitude than can the best of photographers. For the student of psychology an ordinary photograph of a human face is besides of scant value. But old Anna was tremendously interested in photographs. From the memorable day of her promotion from the humblest of all the flower-sellers in Piazza di Spagna to open the door in Keats' house, Anna had become a keen collector of photographs. Often, after having blown her up too harshly for some of her many shortcomings, I used to despatch the dove of peace with a photograph in her beak to Anna's little dugout under the Trinità dei Monti steps. When at last worn out by insomnia, I left Keats' house for good, Anna grabbed a whole drawer in my writing-table full of photographs of all sizes and descriptions. For the sake of truth I am bound to admit I was glad to get rid of them. Anna is quite innocent, I alone am the culprit. On a short visit to London and Paris the following spring, I was struck by the aloofness, not to say coolness of several of my former patients and their relatives. In passing through Rome on my return journey to Capri I had just time to dine at the Swedish Legation. I thought the Minister seemed rather sulky, even my charming hostess was unusually silent. As I was leaving for the station to catch the night train to Naples, my old friend told me it was high time I returned to San Michele to remain there for the rest of my days among my dogs and monkeys. I was not fit for any other society, I had broken my own record with my last performance when leaving Keats' house. In a furious voice he went on to tell me that on Christmas Eve on passing through Piazza di Spagna, thronged with tourists as usual that day, he had come upon Anna in the doorway of Keats' house before a table full of photographs, yelling to the passers-by in a shrill voice:

'Venite a vedere questa bellissima signorina coi cappelli ricci, ultimo prezzo due lire.'

'Guardate la Signora Americana, guardate che collana di perle, guardate che orecchini con brillanti, ve la do per due cinquanta, una vera combinazione!'

'Non vi fate scappare questa nobile marchesa, tutta in pelliccia!'

'Guardate questa duchessa, tutta scollata, in veste di ballo e con la corona in testa, quattro lire, un vero regalo!'

'Ecco la Signora Bocca Aperta, prezzo ridotto una lira e mezzo.'

'Ecco la Signora Mezza Pazza, rideva sempre, ultima prezzo una lira!'

'Ecco la Signora Capa Rossa che puzzava sempre di liquore, una lira e mezzo.'

'Ecco la Signorina dell'Albergo di Europa che era impazzita per il Signor Dottore due lire e mezzo.'

'Vedete la Signora Francese che portava via il porta sigarette sotto il mantello, povera signora, non era colpa sua, non aveva la testa apposto, prezzo ristretto una lira.'

'Ecco la Signora Russa che voleva ammazzare la civetta, due lire, ne anche un soldo di meno.'

'Ecco la Baronessa Mezzo Uomo Mezza Donna, mamma mia, non si capisce niente, il Signore Dottore diceva che era nata cosi, due lire venti cinque, una vera occasione.'

'Ecco la Contessina Bionda che il Signore Dottore voleva tanto bene, guardate com'e carina, non meno di tre lire!'

'Ecco la . . .'

In the midst of all the ladies was throned his own cabinet photo, in full dress uniform, decorations and cocked hat and in the corner: 'To A.M. from his old friend C.B.' Anna said she was willing to part with it at the reduced price of one lira as she was dealing chiefly in ladies' photographs. The Legation had received heaps of letters from several of my former patients, their fathers, husbands and sweethearts, protesting indignantly against this scandal. An infuriated Frenchman who on his honeymoon in Rome had discovered a large photo of his bride for sale in the shop-window of a barber in Via Croce, had appealed for my address, he was going to challenge me to a duel with pistols at the frontier. The Minister hoped that the Frenchman was a good shot, he had besides always predicted that I should not die a natural death.

Old Anna is still selling flowers in Piazza di Spagna, you had better buy a bunch of violets from her unless you prefer to give her your photograph. Times are hard, old Anna has cataracts in both eyes.

So far as I know there is no way of getting rid of these patients, any suggestion in that direction would be welcomed by me. To write to their families to come and take them home is useless. All their relations have got tired of them long ago and will stop at no sacrifice to make them remain with you. I well remember a dejected-looking little man who entered my consulting-room one day after my other patients had gone. He sank down on a chair and handed me his card. His very name was hateful to me, Mr. Charles W. Washington Longfellow Perkins, Junior. He apologized for not having answered my two letters and my cable, he had preferred to come himself to make a last appeal to me. I repeated my request, I said it was not fair to throw the whole burden of Mrs. Perkins, Junior, on me. I could do no more. He said neither could he. He said he was a business man, he wanted to treat the question on business lines, he was willing to part with half of his annual income payable in advance. I said it was not a question of money, I was in need of rest. Did he know that for more than three months she had been bombarding me with letters at an average rate of three letters a day, and that I had had to stop my telephone in the evening? Did he know that she had bought the fastest horses in Rome and was following me all over the town, that I had had to give up my evening walks on the Pincio? Did he know that she had taken a flat in the opposite corner house of Via Condotti to watch through a powerful telescope the people who were coming and going in and out of my house?

Yes, it was a very good telescope. Dr. Jenkins of St. Louis had had to move to another house because of that telescope.

Did he know that I had been summoned three times in the night to the Grand Hôtel to pump her stomach for an overdose of laudanum?

He said she always used veronal with Dr. Lippincott, he suggested I should wait till the morning next time she sent for me, she was always very careful about the dose. Any river about this town?

Yes, we called it the Tiber. She had thrown herself from Ponte

284

Sant'Angelo last month, a policeman had jumped after her and picked her up.

He said it had been unnecessary, she was an excellent swimmer, she had kept afloat off Newport for over half-an-hour. He was surprised to hear that his wife was still in the Grand Hôtel, as a rule she never remained in any place more than a week.

I said it was her last chance, she had already been in all the other hotels of Rome. The director had just told me it was impossible to keep her any longer, she was quarrelling with all the waiters and chambermaids the whole day and was moving the furniture in her sitting-room the whole night. Could he not stop her allowance, her only chance would be if she should have to earn her living by hard work.

She had ten thousand dollars a year in her own right and another ten thousand from her first husband, who had got out of it cheap.

Couldn't he have her locked up in America?

He had tried in vain, she was not supposed to be mad enough, he would like to know what more was wanted of her. Couldn't I have her locked up in Italy?

I feared not.

We looked at each other with growing sympathy.

He told me that according to Dr. Jenkins's statistics she had never been in love with the same doctor for more than a month, the average was a fortnight, my time would soon be up in any case, wouldn't I have pity on him and hold out until the spring?

Alas, Dr. Jenkins's statistics proved wrong, she remained my chief tormentor during my whole stay in Rome. She invaded Capri in the summer. She wanted to drown herself in the Blue Grotto. She climbed the garden-wall of San Michele; in my exasperation I nearly threw her over the precipice. I almost think I would have done it had not her husband warned me before we parted that a drop of a thousand feet would mean nothing to her.

I had good reason for believing him, only a couple of months before a half-crazy German girl had jumped over the famous wall of the Pincio and escaped with a broken ankle. After she had worn out all the resident German doctors in turn I had become her prey. It was a particularly trying case, for Fraulein Frida had an uncanny facility for writing poetry, her lyrical output averaging ten pages a day, all dumped on me. I stood it for a whole winter. When spring came – these cases always get worse at springtime – I told her silly mother that unless she returned with Miss Frida from whence

285

they came, I would stop at nothing to have her locked up. They were to leave for Germany in the morning. I was awakened in the night by the arrival of the fire brigade to the Piazza di Spagna, the first floor of the Hôtel de l'Europe next door was on fire. Miss Frida in her night-gown spent the remainder of the night in my sitting-room writing poetry in tearing spirits. She had got what she wanted, they had to remain a whole week in Rome for the police investigations and the settlement of the damage, the fire having broken out in their sitting-room. Miss Frida had soaked a towel with petroleum, thrown it in the piano and set it on fire.

One day as I was leaving my house I was stopped at the door by a spanking-looking American girl, the very picture of health, nothing wrong with the nerves, this time, thank God. I said she looked as if we might postpone the consultation till to-morrow, I was in a hurry. She said so was she, she said she had come to Rome to see the Pope and Doctor Munthe who had kept Aunt Sally out of mischief for a whole year, a thing which no other doctor had succeeded in doing. I offered her a very handsome colour-print of Botticelli's Primavera if she would take her aunt back with her to America, she said she would not hear of it if I offered her the original. The aunt was not to be depended upon. I do not know if the Keats Society who bought the house when I left it has put in new doors in the room Keats had died in and where I might have died myself had my number been up. If the old door is still there, there is also a small bullet-hole in the left corner at about the height of my head, filled with stucco and painted over by myself.

Another constant visitor to my consulting-room was a timid-looking, otherwise quite well-behaved lady who one day with a pleasant smile stuck a long hat-pin in the leg of an Englishman next to her on the sofa. The company also included a couple of klepto-maniacs who used to carry away under their cloaks any object they could lay their hands on, to the consternation of my servants. Some of my patients were not fit at all to be admitted to the waiting-room but had to be established in the library or in the back sitting-room under the vigilant eye of Anna who was wonderfully patient with them, much more so than I. To gain time some of them were admitted to the dining-room to tell me their tales of woe while I was having my luncheon. The dining-room opened on a little courtyard under the Trinità dei Monti steps, transformed by me into a sort of infirmary and convalescent home for my various animals. Among them was a darling little owl, a direct descendant from the owl of Minerva. I had found it in the Campagna with a broken wing half dead of hunger. Its wing healed, I had twice taken it back where I had found it and set it free, twice it had flown back to my carriage to perch on my shoulder, it would not hear of our parting. Since then the little owl was sitting on her perch in the corner of the dining-room, looking lovingly at me with her golden eyes. She had even given up sleeping in the day in order not to lose sight of me. When I used to stroke her soft little person she would half close her eyes with delight and nibble gently at my lips with her tiny, sharp beak, as near to a kiss as an owl can get. Among the patients admitted to the dining-room was a very excitable young Russian lady, who was giving me lots of trouble. Would you believe it, this lady got so jealous of the owl, she used to glare at the little bird so savagely that I had to give strict orders to Anna never to leave these two alone in the room. One day on coming in for luncheon Anna told me that the Russian lady had just called with a dead mouse wrapped in paper. She had caught it in her room, she felt sure the owl would like it for breakfast. The owl knew better, after having bitten off its head, owl fashion, she refused to eat it. I took it to the English chemist, it contained enough arsenic to kill a cat.

* * *

To give Giovannina and Rosina a treat I had invited their old father to come to Rome to spend Easter with us. Old Pacciale had been a particular friend of mine for many years. In his early days he had been a coral-fisher like most of the male population of Capri in those days. After various vicissitudes he had ended by becoming the official gravedigger of Anacapri, a bad job in a place where nobody dies as long as he keeps clear of the doctor. Even after I had established him and his children in San Michele he would not hear of giving up his job as a gravedigger. He had a peculiar liking for handling dead people, he positively enjoyed burying them. Old Pacciale arrived on Easter Thursday in a state of complete bewilderment. He had never travelled on the railway before, he had never been in a town, he had never sat in a carriage. He had to get up at three o'clock every morning when he went down on the Piazza to wash his hands and face in Bernini's fountain under my window. After having been taken by Miss Hall and the children to kiss the bronze toe of St. Peter and to crawl up the Scala Santa and by his colleague Giovanni of the Protestant Cemetery to inspect the various cemeteries of Rome, he said he would not see anything more. He spent the rest of his time seated by the window overlooking the Piazza, in his long fisherman's cap of Phrygian cut which he never took off his head. He said it was the finest view in Rome, nothing could beat Piazza di Spagna. So thought I for the matter of that. I asked him why he liked Piazza di Spagna best.

'Because there are always funerals passing,' explained old Pacciale.

XXVII

Summer

Spring had come and gone, it was getting on towards Roman
summer. The last foreigners were vanishing from the stuffy streets.
The marble goddesses in the empty museums were enjoying their
holidays, cool and comfortable in their fig-leaves. St. Peter was
taking his siesta in the shade of the Vatican gardens. The Forum
and the Coliseum were sinking back into their haunted dreams.
Giovannina and Rosina were looking pale and tired, the roses in
Miss Hall's hat were drooping. The dogs were panting, the monkeys under the Trinità dei Monti steps were yelling for a change of
air and scenery. My beautiful little cutter was riding at her anchor
off Porto d'Anzio, waiting for the signal to hoist sail for my island
home, where Mastro Nicola and his three sons were scanning the
horizon from the parapet of the chapel for my return. My last visit
before leaving Rome was to the Protestant Cemetery by Porta San
Paolo. The nightingales were still singing to the dead, who did not
seem to mind being forgotten in so sweet a place, so fragrant with
lilies, roses and myrtle in full bloom. Giovanni's eight children
were all down with malaria, there was plenty of malaria in the
outskirts of Rome in those days, Baedeker might say what he liked.
The eldest girl, Maria, was so emaciated by repeated attacks of
fever that I told her father that she would not survive the summer
if she was left in Rome. I offered him to let her spend the summer in
San Michele with my household. He hesitated at first, the poor class
Italians are most reluctant to be separated from their sick children,
they prefer to let them die at home rather than to have them taken
to a hospital. He ended by accepting when he was told to take his
daughter to Capri himself to see with his own eyes how well she
would be looked after by my people. Miss Hall with Giovannina
and Rosina and all the dogs went by rail to Naples as usual. I with
Billy the baboon, the mongoose and the little owl had a glorious sail
in the yacht. We rounded Monte Circeo as the sun was rising,
caught the morning breeze from the Bay of Gaeta, darted at racing
speed under the Castle of Ischia and dropped anchor at the Marina
of Capri as the bells were ringing *mezzogiorno*. Two hours

later I was at work in the garden of San Michele with hardly any clothes on.

After five long summers' incessant toil from sunrise till sunset San Michele was more or less finished, but there was still a lot to be done in the garden. A new terrace was to be laid out behind the house, another loggia to be built over the two small Roman rooms which we had discovered in the autumn. As to the little cloister court I told Mastro Nicola we had better knock it down, I did not like it any more. Mastro Nicola implored me to leave it as it was, we had already knocked it down twice, if we kept on knocking down everything as soon as it was built, San Michele would never be finished. I told Mastro Nicola that the proper way to build one's house was to knock everything down never mind how many times and begin again until your eye told you that everything was right. The eye knew much more about architecture than did the books. The eye was infallible, as long as you relied on your own eye and not on the eye of other people. As I saw it again I thought San Michele looked more beautiful than ever. The house was small, the rooms were few but there were loggias, terraces and pergolas all around it to watch the sun, the sea and the clouds – the soul needs more space than the body. Not much furniture in the rooms but what there was could not be bought with money alone. Nothing superfluous, nothing unbeautiful, no bric-a-brac, no trinkets. A few primitive pictures, an etching of Dürer and a Greek bas-relief on the whitewashed walls. A couple of old rugs on the mosaic floor, a few books on the tables, flowers everywhere in lustrous jars from Faenza and Urbino. The cypresses from Villa d'Este leading the way up to the chapel had already grown into an avenue of stately trees, the noblest trees in the world. The chapel itself which had given its name to my home had at last become mine. It was to become my library. Fine old cloister stalls surrounded the white walls, in its midst stood a large refectory table laden with books and terra-cotta fragments. On a fluted column of giallo antico stood a huge Horus of basalt, the largest I have ever seen, brought from the land of the Pharaohs by some Roman collector, maybe by Tiberius himself. Over the writing-table the marble head of Medusa looked down upon me, fourth century B.C., found by me at the bottom of the sea. On the huge Cinquecento Florentine mantel-piece stood the Winged Victory. On a column of africano by the window the mutilated head of Nero looked out over the gulf where he had caused his mother to be beaten to death by his oarsmen. Over the entrance door shone the beautiful Cinquecento stained-glass window presented to Eleonora Duse by the town of Florence and given by her to me in remembrance of her last stay in San Michele. In a small crypt five feet below the Roman floor of coloured marble slept in peace the two monks I had come upon quite unaware when we were digging for the foundations of the mantelpiece. They lay there with folded arms just as they had been buried under their chapel nearly five hundred years ago. Their cassocks had mouldered almost to dust, their dried-up bodies were light as parchment, but their features were still well preserved, their hands were still clasping their crucifixes, one of them wore dainty silver buckles on his shoes. I was sorry to have disturbed them in their sleep, with infinite precautions I laid them back in their little crypt. The lofty archway with Gothic columns outside the chapel looked just right, I thought. Where are such columns to be found to-day? Looking down from the parapet on the island at my feet, I told Mastro Nicola that we were to begin at once the emplacement for the sphinx, there was no time to lose. Mastro Nicola was delighted, why didn't we fetch the sphinx at once, where was it now? I said it was lying under the ruins of the forgotten villa of a Roman Emperor somewhere on the mainland. It had been lying waiting for me there for two thousand years. A man in a red mantle had told me all about it the first time I looked out over the sea from the very spot where we now stood. So far I had only seen it in my dreams. I looked down on the little white yacht on the Marina under my feet and said I was quite sure I would find the sphinx at the right time. The difficulty would be to bring it across the sea, it was in fact far too heavy a cargo for my boat, it was all of granite and weighed I did not know how many tons. Mastro Nicola scratched his head and wondered who was going to drag it up to San Michele? He and I of course.

The two small Roman rooms under the chapel were still full of débris from the fallen ceiling but the walls were intact to a man's height, the garland of flowers and the dancing nymphs on the red intonaco looked as though they had been painted yesterday.

'Roba di Timberio?' asked Mastro Nicola.

'No,' said I, looking attentively at the delicate pattern of the mosaic floor with its dainty border of vine leaves of nero antico, 'this floor was made before his time, it dates from Augustus. The old Emperor was also a great lover of Capri, he started building a villa here, God knows where, but he died at Nola on his return to Rome before it was finished. He was a great man and a great Emperor but, mark my word, Tiberius was the greatest of them all.'

The pergola was already covered with young vines; roses, honeysuckle and Epomea were clustering round the long row of white columns. Among the cypresses in the little cloister court stood the Dancing Faun and his column of cipollino, in the centre of the big loggia sat the bronze Hermes from Herculaneum. In the little marble court outside the dining-room all ablaze with sun, sat Billy the baboon, hard at work catching Tappio's fleas, surrounded by all the other dogs drowsily awaiting their turn for the customary completion of their morning toilette. Billy had a wonderful hand for catching fleas, no jumping or crawling thing escaped his vigilant eye, the dogs knew it quite well and enjoyed the sport as much as he did. It was the only sport tolerated by the law of San Michele. Death was fulmineous and probably painless, Billy had swallowed his prey before there was time to realize the danger. Billy had given up drinking and become a respectable monkey in the full bloom of manhood, alarmingly like a human being, on the whole well behaved though somewhat boisterous when I was out of sight, making fun of everybody. I often wondered what the dogs really thought of him at the back of their heads. I am not sure they were not afraid of him, they generally turned their heads away when he looked at them. Billy was afraid of nobody but me. I could always see by his face when he had a bad conscience which was generally the case. Yes, I think he was afraid of the mongoose who was always sneaking about the garden on restless feet, silent and inquisitive. There was something very manly about Billy, he could not help it, his Maker had made him so. Billy was not at all insensible to the attractions of the other sex. Billy had taken a great liking at first sight to Elisa, the wife of my gardener, who stood for hours staring at him with fascinated eyes, where he sat in his private fig-tree smacking his lips at her. Elisa was expecting a baby as usual, I had never known her otherwise. Somehow I did not quite like this sudden friendship with Billy, I had even told her she had better look at somebody else.

Old Pacciale had gone down to the Marina to receive his colleague, the gravedigger of Rome, who was to arrive at noon with his daughter by the Sorrento sailing boat. As he had to be back at his job at the Protestant Cemetery the eve of the following day, he was to be taken in the afternoon to inspect the two cemeteries of the island. In the evening my household was to offer a dinner with vino a volontà on the garden terrace to their distinguished visitor from Rome.

The bells in the chapel rang Ave Maria. I had been on my legs since five o'clock in the morning hard at work in the blazing sun. Tired and hungry I sat down to my frugal supper on the upper loggia, grateful for another happy day. On the garden terrace below sat my guests in their Sunday clothes, round a gigantic plate of macaroni and a huge piretto of San Michele's best wine. In the place of honour at the head of the table sat the gravedigger of Rome with the two gravediggers of Capri, one on each side of him. Next sat Baldassare my gardener and Gaetano my sailor, and Mastro Nicola with his three sons, all talking at the top of their voices. Round the table stood their womenfolk in admiration, according to Neapolitan custom. The sun was slowly sinking over the sea. For the first time in my life it seemed a relief to me when it disappeared at last behind Ischia. Why was I longing for the twilight and the stars, I the sun-worshipper, who had been afraid of darkness and night ever since I was a child? Why had my eyes been burning so when I looked up to the glorious sun god? Was he angry with me, was he going to turn his face away from me and leave me in the dark, I who was working on my knees to build him another sanctuary? Was it true what the tempter in the red mantle had told me twenty years ago when I looked down upon the fair island for the first time from the chapel of San Michele? Was it true that too much light was not good for mortal eyes?

'Beware of the light! Beware of the light!' His sinister warning echoed in my ears.

I had accepted his bargain, I had paid his price, I had sacrificed my future to gain San Michele, what else did he want of me? What was the other heavy price he had said I would have to pay before I died?

A dark cloud suddenly descended over the sea and over the garden at my feet. My burning eyelids closed with terror . . .

'Listen, compagni!' shouted the gravedigger of Rome from the terrace below, 'listen to what I tell you! You peasant folk who only see him going about in this wretched little village, barefooted and with no more clothes on than you have, do you know that he is driving about the streets of Rome with a carriage and pair, they say he even went to see the Pope when he had influenza? I tell you, compagni, there is nobody like him, he is the greatest doctor in Rome, come with me to my cemetery and you will see for yourself! Sempre lui! Sempre lui! As to me and my family I do not know what we should do without him, he is our benefactor. To whom do you think my wife is selling all her wreaths and flowers, if not to his customers! And all these foreigners who ring the bell at the gate and give their penny to my children for being let in, why do you think they have come there, what do you think they want? Of course my children don't understand what they are talking about, and often had to wander all over the cemetery with them before they found what they wanted. Now as soon as some foreigners ring the bell my children know at once what they want and take them straight to his row of graves, and they are always very pleased and give the children an extra penny. Sempre lui! Sempre lui! There is hardly a month he does not cut open some of his patients in the mortuary chapel to try to find out what was the matter with them, he gives me fifty lire apiece for putting them back in their coffins. I tell you, compagni! there is nobody like him. Sempre lui! Sempre lui!'

The cloud had already drifted away, the sea was once more radiant with golden light, my fear was gone. The devil himself can do nothing to a man as long as he can laugh.

The dinner party broke up. Glad to be alive, and with plenty of wine in our heads, we all went to bed to sleep the sleep of the just.

*　　*　　*

Hardly had I fallen asleep, than I found myself standing on a lonely plain strewn with débris of broken masonry, huge blocks of travertine and fragments of marbles half hidden by ivy, rosemary and wild honeysuckle, cistus and thyme. On a crumbling wall of *opus reticulatum* sat an old shepherd playing on the flute of Pan to his flock of goats. His wild, long-bearded face was scorched by sun and wind, his eyes were burning like fire under his bushy eyebrows, his lean emaciated body was shivering under his long blue cloak of a Calabrian shepherd. I offered him a little tobacco, he handed me a slice of fresh goat-cheese and an onion. I understood him with difficulty.

What was the name of this strange place?

It had no name.

Where did he come from?

From nowhere, he had always been here, this was his home.

Where did he sleep?

He pointed with his long staff to a flight of steps under a tumble-down archway. I climbed down the steps hewn in the rock and stood in a dim, vaulted room. In the corner a straw mattress with a couple of sheep-skins as bedcover. Suspended round the walls and from the ceiling bunches of dried onions and tomatoes, an earthen-ware jug of water on the rough table. This was his home, these were his belongings. Here he had lived his whole life, here he would lie down one day to die. In front of me opened a dark subterranean passage half filled with débris from the fallen roof. Where did it lead to?

He did not know, he had never been there. He had been told as a boy that it led to a cave haunted by an evil spirit who had lived there for thousands of years, in the shape of a huge werewolf who would devour any man who should approach his cave.

I lit a torch and groped my way down a flight of marble steps. The passage widened more and more, an ice-cold blast of air blew in my face. I heard an uncanny moan which made the blood freeze in my veins. Suddenly I stood in a large hall. Two huge columns of African marble still supported a part of the vaulted roof, two others lay across the mosaic floor wrenched from their pedestals by the grip of the earthquake. Hundreds of huge bats were hanging in black clusters round the walls, others were fluttering in wild flight round my head, blinded by the sudden light of the torch. In the midst of the hall crouched a huge granite sphinx, staring at me with stony, wide-open eyes . . .

I started in my sleep. The dream vanished. I opened my eyes, the day was breaking.

Suddenly I heard the call of the sea, imperious, irresistible like a command. I sprang to my feet, flung myself into my clothes and rushed up to the parapet of the chapel to hoist the signal to the yacht to make ready for the start. A couple of hours later I boarded my boat with provisions for a week, coils of stout rope, pick-axes and spades, a revolver, all my available money, a bundle of torches of resinous wood, such as fishermen use for night fishing. A moment later we hoisted sail for the most stirring adventure of my life. The following night we dropped anchor in a lonely cove, unknown to all but a few fishermen and smugglers. Gaetano was to wait for me there with the yacht for a week and to run for shelter to the nearest port in case bad weather set in. We knew this dangerous coast well, with no safe anchorage for a hundred miles. I also knew its wonderful inland, once the Magna Graecia of the Golden Ages of Hellenic art and culture, now the most desolate province of Italy abandoned by man to malaria and earthquake.

Three days later I stood on the same lonely plain strewn with broken masonry and huge blocks of travertine and fragments of marbles half hidden under ivy-rosemary and wild honeysuckle, cistus and thyme. On the crumbling wall of *opus reticulatum* sat the old shepherd playing on his pipe to his flock of goats. I offered him a little tobacco, he handed me a slice of fresh goat-cheese and an onion. The sun had already gone down behind the mountains, the deadly mist of malaria was slowly creeping over the desolate plain. I told him I had lost my way, I dared not wander about alone in this wilderness, might I stay with him for the night?

He led the way to his underground sleeping-quarters I knew so well from my dream. I lay down on his sheep-skins and fell asleep.

It is all too weird and fantastic to be translated into written words, you would besides not believe me if I tried to do so. I hardly know myself where the dream ended and where reality began. Who steered the yacht into this hidden, lonely cove? Who led my way across this trackless wilderness to the unknown ruins of Nero's villa? Was the shepherd of flesh and blood or was he not Pan himself who had come back to his favourite haunts of old to play the flute to his flock of goats?

Do not ask me any questions, I cannot tell you, I dare not tell you. You may ask the huge granite sphinx who lies crouching on the parapet of the chapel in San Michele. But you will ask in vain. The sphinx has kept her own secret for five thousand years. The sphinx will keep mine.

*   *   *

I returned from the great adventure, emaciated from hunger and hardships of all sorts, and shivering with malaria. Once I had been kidnapped by brigands, there were plenty of them in Calabria in those days. It was my rags that saved me. Twice I had been arrested by the coastguards as a smuggler. Several times I had been stung by scorpions, my left hand was still in a bandage from the bite of a viper. Off Punta Licosa, where Leucosia, the Siren sister of Parthenope, lies buried, we were caught in a south-westerly gale and would have gone to the bottom of the sea with our heavy cargo had not Sant'Antonio taken the helm in the nick of time. Votive candles were still burning before his shrine in the church of Anacapri when I entered San Michele. The rumour that we had been wrecked in the heavy gale had spread all over the island. All my household was overjoyed to welcome me home.

Yes, all was well at San Michele, grazie a Dio. Nothing had happened in Anacapri, as usual nobody had died. The parroco had sprained his ankle, some people said he had slipped when descending the pulpit last Sunday, others said it was the parroco of Capri who had made him mal'occhio, everybody knew the parroco of Capri had the evil eye. Yesterday morning the Canonico Don

Giacinto had been found dead in his bed down in Capri. The Canonico had been quite well when he went to bed, he had died in his sleep. He had been lying in state during the night before the High Altar, he was to be buried with great pomp this morning, the bells had been ringing since daybreak.

In the garden the work had been going on as usual. Mastro Nicola had found another testa di cristiano when knocking down the cloister wall, and Baldassare had come upon another earthenware jar full of Roman coins while taking up the new potatoes. Old Pacciale who had been digging in my vineyard at Damecuta took me aside with an air of great mystery and importance. Having ascertained that nobody overheard us, he produced from his pocket a broken clay pipe black with smoke, it might have belonged to some soldier of the Maltese regiment who camped at Damecuta in 1808.

'La pipa di Timberio!' said old Pacciale.

The dogs had had their baths every midday and their bones twice a week according to the regulations. The little owl was in good spirits. The mongoose was on his legs day and night always on the look-out for something or somebody. The tortoises seemed very happy in their own quiet way.

Had Billy been good?

Yes, Elisa hurried to answer, Billy had been very good, un vero angelo.

I thought he did not look like one as I watched him grinning at me from the top of his private fig-tree. Contrary to his habit he did not come down to greet me. I felt sure he had been up to some mischief, I did not like the look of his face. Was it really true that Billy had been good?

Gradually the truth came out. The very day I had sailed Billy had thrown a carrot at the head of a forestiere who was passing under the garden-wall and smashed his eye-glass. The forestiere was very angry and was going to lodge a complaint at Capri. Elisa protested vigorously, it was all the fault of the forestiere who had no business to stand and laugh at Billy like that, everybody knew he got angry when people laughed at him. The next day there had been a terrible fight between Billy and the fox-terrier, all the dogs had thrown themselves into the fray, Billy had fought like Il Demonio and even wanted to bite Baldassare when he tried to separate the belligerents. The battle had suddenly ceased with the arrival of the mongoose, Billy had leaped to his tree and all the dogs had slunk away as they always did when the little mongoose turned up. Billy and the dogs

297

had been at daggers drawn ever since, he had even refused to continue to catch their fleas. Billy had chased the Siamese kitten all over the garden and ended up by carrying it up to the top of his fig-tree and proceeded to pull off all its hair. Billy had been constantly teasing the tortoises. Amanda the biggest tortoise had laid seven eggs as big as pigeon-eggs to be hatched by the sun, tortoise-fashion, Billy had gulped them down in an instant. Had they at least been careful not to leave any wine-bottles about? There was an ominous silence. Pacciale, the most trustworthy of the household, admitted at last that on two occasions Billy had been seen sneaking out of the wine-cellar with a bottle in each hand. Three days ago two more wine-bottles had been discovered in the corner of the monkey-house, carefully buried under the sand. According to the instructions Billy had been immediately locked up in the monkey-house on water and bread pending my return. The next morning the monkey-house had been found empty, Billy had broken out in the night in some inexplicable way, the bars were intact, the key to the padlock was in Baldassare's pocket. The whole household had been hunting for Billy in vain all over the village. Baldassare had caught him at last this very morning high up on the mountain of Barbarossa, fast asleep, with a dead bird in his hand. While the investigation was going on, Billy was sitting at the top of his tree looking defiantly at me, there could be no doubt that he understood every word we said. Stern disciplinary measures were necessary. Monkeys like children must learn to obey until they can learn to command. Billy was beginning to look uneasy. He knew I was the master, he knew I could catch him with the lasso as I had done before, he knew that the whip in my hand was for him. The dogs knew it equally well where they sat in a circle round Billy's tree wagging their tails with clear consciences, thoroughly enjoying the situation – dogs rather like to assist at the whipping of somebody else. Suddenly Elisa put her hands over her abdomen with a piercing scream and was dragged on to her bed in the cottage in the nick of time by Pacciale and me while Baldassare rushed to fetch the midwife. When I returned to his tree Billy had vanished, so much the better for him and for me, I hate to punish animals.

I had besides other things to think about. I had always taken a keen interest in Don Giacinto. I was most anxious to know something more about his death, about his life I knew quite enough. Don Giacinto had the reputation of being the richest man on the island, he was said to possess an income amounting to twenty-five lire every hour of his life, 'anche quando dorme,' even when he was asleep. I had watched him for many years squeezing the last penny out of his poor tenants, evicting them from their homes when the olives had failed and they could not pay their rent, leaving them to starve when they were getting old and had no more strength to toil for him. I had never heard of his giving away a penny, nor had anybody else. I knew I should cease to believe in any divine justice on this side of the grave if Almighty God had bestowed upon this old bloodsucker the greatest blessing He can bestow upon any living man – to die in his sleep. I decided to go and see my old friend the parroco, Don Antonio, he would be sure to be able to tell me what I wanted to know, Don Giacinto had been his deadly enemy for half a century. The parroco was sitting up in his bed, his foot wrapped up in an enormous bundle of blankets, his face beaming. The room was full of priests, in their midst stood Maria Porta-Lettere, her tongue almost dropping out of her mouth with excitement: Fire had broken out in the church of San Costanzo during the night, while Don Giacinto was lying in state on the catafalque, the coffin had been consumed by the flames! Some people said it was il Demonio who had knocked down the wax candelabra by the catafalque to set Don Giacinto on fire. Others said that it had been done by a band of brigands who had come to steal the silver statue of San Costanzo. The parroco was sure that it was il Demonio who had knocked down the wax candelabra, he had always believed that Don Giacinto would end in flames.

Maria Porta-Lettere's account of Don Giacinto's death seemed plausible enough. Il Demonio had appeared in the window while il Canonico was reading his evening prayers. Don Giacinto had called out for help and been carried to his bed in a fainting condition and had died of fright shortly afterwards.

I was greatly interested, I thought I had better go down to Capri myself to investigate the matter. The Piazza was packed with people all screaming at the tops of their voices. In their midst stood the Sindaco and the municipal councillors eagerly awaiting the arrival of the carabinieri from Sorrento. On the steps leading to the church stood a dozen priests gesticulating wildly. The church was closed pending the arrival of the authorities. Yes, said the Sindaco coming up to me with a grave face, it was all true! The sacristan in coming to open the church in the morning had found it full of smoke. The catafalque was half consumed by the fire, the coffin itself was badly scorched, of the precious pall of embroidered velvet and a dozen wreaths from the Canonico's relatives and children nothing remained but a heap of smouldering ashes. Three of the huge wax candelabra round the catafalque were still burning, the fourth had evidently been knocked down by a sacrilegious hand to set fire to the pall. So far it was impossible to ascertain whether it was the work of il Demonio or of some criminals, but the Sindaco shrewdly remarked that the fact that none of the precious jewels round the neck of San Costanzo were missing made him, parlando con rispetto, incline to the former supposition. The mystery deepened more and more as I continued my investigations. In the Caffé Zum Hiddigeigei, the headquarters of the German colony, the floor was strewn with broken glasses, bottles and crockery of all sorts, on a table stood a half-empty bottle of whisky. In the Farmacia dozens of Faenza jars with precious drugs and secret compounds had been hurled from their shelves, castor-oil everywhere. Il Professore Raffaele Parmigiano showed me himself the devastation of his new Sala di Esposizione, the pride of the Piazza. His 'Eruption of Vesuvius,' his 'Procession of San Costanzo,' his 'Salto di Tiberio,' his 'Bella Carmela' lay all in a heap on the floor, their frames broken, their canvases split. His 'Tiberio swimming in the Blue Grotto' stood still on the easel all splashed over with patches of ultramarine in mad confusion. The Sindaco informed me that so far the investigations carried out by the local authorities had led to no result. The theory of brigands had been abandoned by the Liberal party since it had been ascertained that nothing of real value had been carried away. Even the two dangerous Neapolitan camorrists, in villeggiatura in the gaol of Capri for over a year, had been able to establish their alibi. It had been proved that owing to the heavy rain they had remained the whole night in the prison instead of taking their usual stroll in the village after midnight as was their custom. They were besides good Catholics and very popular and not likely to disturb themselves with such trifles.

The theory of il Demonio had been dismissed by the Clerical party out of respect for the memory of Don Giacinto. Who then were the perpetrators of these dastardly outrages? There remained one hypothesis. There remained the secular enemy, almost at their very door, Anacapri! Of course it was all the work of the Anacapresi! It explained everything! Il Canonico was the deadly enemy of the Anacapresi who had never forgiven him for having scoffed at the last miracle of Sant'Antonio in his famous sermon on the day of San Costanzo. The fierce hatred between Zum Hiddigeigei and the newly opened caffé in Anacapri was a notorious fact. In the time of Caesar Borgia Don Petruccio, the apothecary of Capri, would have thought twice before accepting any invitation from his colleague in Anacapri to partake of his macaroni. The competition between Professore Raffaele Parmigiano of Capri and Professore Michelangelo of Anacapri for the monopoly of the 'Tiberio swimming in the Blue Grotto' had of late developed into a furious war. The opening of the Sala di Esposizione had hit Professore Michelangelo badly in the eye, the sale of his 'Procession of Sant'Antonio' had almost come to a standstill.

Of course Anacapri was at the bottom of it all.

Abbasso Anacapri! Abbasso Anacapri!

I thought I had better return from where I had come, I was beginning to feel very uneasy. I did not know myself what to believe. The bitter war between Capri and Anacapri which had been raging ever since the times of the Spanish viceroys in Naples was still going on in those days with unabated fury. The two Sindacos were not on speaking terms. The peasants hated each other, the notables hated each other, the priests hated each other, the two patron saints, Sant'Antonio and San Costanzo, hated each other. A couple of years before I had seen with my own eyes a crowd of Capresi dancing round our little chapel of Sant'Antonio when a huge rock from Monte Barbarossa had smashed the altar and the statue of Sant'Antonio.

At San Michele work had already been suspended, all my people were in their Sunday clothes on their way to the Piazza where the band was to play to celebrate the event, over a hundred lire having already been collected for the fireworks. The Sindaco had sent word hoping I would assist in my quality of cittadino onorario – this unique distinction had in fact been bestowed upon me the year before.

In the midst of the pergola sat Billy by the side of the biggest tortoise, too absorbed in his favourite game to notice my coming. The game consisted in a series of rapid knocks at the back door of the tortoise-house where the tail comes out. At each knock the tortoise would pop out its sleepy head from the front door to see what was the matter, only to receive a stunning blow on the nose from Billy's fist with the rapidity of lightning. This game was forbidden by the law of San Michele. Billy knew it quite well and screamed like a child when, for once quicker than he, I got hold of the strap round his stomach.

'Billy,' said I sternly, 'I am going to have a private conversation with you under your fig-tree, there are several accounts to be settled between us. It is no good smacking your lips at me like that, you know that you deserve a good spanking and that you are going to get it. Billy, you have been drinking again! Twc empty wine-bottles have been found in a corner of the monkey-house, one bottle of Buchanan's "Black and White" is missing. Your general conduct during my absence in Calabria has been disgraceful. You have smashed the eye-glass of a forestiere with a carrot. You have been disobedient to my servants. You have quarrelled and fought with the dogs, you have even refused to catch their fleas. You have insulted the mongoose. You have been disrespectful to the little owl. You have repeatedly boxed the ears of the tortoise. You have nearly strangled the Siamese kitten. Last not least you have broken away from the premises in a state of intoxication. Cruelty to animals belongs to your nature or you would not be a candidate for humanity, but the Lords of Creation alone have the right to get drunk. I tell you I have had enough of you, I am going to send you back to America to your drunken old master Doctor Campbell, you are not fit for decent society. You are a disgrace to your father and mother! Billy, you are a disreputable man-cub, an inveterate drunkard, a . . .'

There was an awful silence.

Putting on my spectacles better to look at Billy's ultramarine finger-nails and scorched tail, I said at last:

'Billy, I rather liked your retouches to "Tiberio swimming in the Blue Grotto," I thought it an improvement on the original. It reminded me of a picture I saw last year in the Salon of the Futurists in Paris. Your former master often told me of your lamented mother. A most remarkable monkey, I understand. I suppose you have inherited your artistic talents from her. Your good looks and your sense of humour I guess you got from your father, whose identity has been fully established by recent events and who can be no other than the Devil himself. Tell me, Billy, just to satisfy my curiosity, was it you or your father who knocked down the wax candelabra and set the coffin on fire?'

XXVIII

The Bird Sanctuary

The Rev. Canonico Don Giacinto's sudden departure to another world in fire and smoke had had a most invigorating effect upon our parroco Don Antonio's general condition of health and spirits. His sprained ankle improved rapidly and soon he was able to resume his customary morning walks to San Michele to assist at my breakfast. I always invited him, according to Neapolitan custom, to 'mangiare con me' but he invariably declined my cup of tea with a polite: No, grazie, sto bene. The sole scope of his visit was to sit opposite me by the breakfast table and look at me while I was eating. Don Antonio had never seen a forestiere before at close quarters and nearly everything I said or did was a constant source of curiosity to him. He knew I was a Protestant but after some vague attempts to discuss the matter we had agreed to drop theology from the conversation and leave the Protestants alone. It was a great concession on his part, for once a week he used to send all living and dead Protestants to hell from his pulpit with the most fearful invectives. The Protestants were Don Antonio's speciality, his sheet-anchor in all his oratorical difficulties, I do not know what he would have done without the Protestants. The old parroco's memory was somewhat shaky, the feeble thread of his argumentation used to break at the most awkward moments, in the midst of his sermons there was a blank silence. His faithful congregation knew it well and did not mind it in the least, everybody continuing peacefully their meditations upon their own affairs, their olives and their vineyards, their cows and their pigs. They also knew what was to follow. Don Antonio blew his nose with a series of thunder-blasts as from the trumpets of the Last Judgment, he was on safe ground again.

'Ma questi maledetti protestani, ma questo camorrista Lutero! May il Demonio tear their cursed tongues from their mouths, may he break their bones and roast them alive. In aeternitatem!'

Once on an Easter Sunday I happened to look in at the church door with a friend of mine at the very moment when the parroco was losing his bearings, there was the usual blank silence. I whispered in my friend's ear that we were in for it now.

'Ma questo camorrista Lutero, questi maledetti protestanti! Che il Demonio . . .'

Suddenly Don Antonio caught sight of me in the doorway. The clenched fist he had just raised to smite down the cursed infidels loosened into a friendly waving of the hand and an apology in my direction: But of course not il Signor Dottore! Of course not il Signor Dottore!

I seldom failed to go to church on Easter Sunday to take up my place at the door by the side of blind old Cecatiello, the official beggar of Anacapri. We both stretched out our hands to the church-goers, he for his soldo and I for the bird in the pocket of the men, in the folds of the black mantiglia of the women, in the palms of the hands of the children. It speaks a good deal for the exceptional position I enjoyed in those days among the villagers that they accepted without resentment my interfering with their way of celebrating the resurrection of Our Lord, consecrated by the tradition of nearly two thousand years and still encouraged by their priests. From the first day of the Holy Week the traps had been set in every vineyard, under every olive-tree. For days hundreds of small birds, a string tied round their wing, had been dragged about the streets by all the boys of the village. Now, mutilated symbols of the Holy Dove, they were to be set free in the church to play their rôle in the jubilant commemoration of Christ's return to Heaven. They never returned to their sky, they fluttered about for a while helpless and bewildered, breaking their wings against the windows, before they fell down to die on the church floor. At daybreak I had been up on the church roof with Mastro Nicola holding the ladder as my unwilling assistant, in order to smash some of the window-panes, but only a very few of the doomed birds found their way to freedom.

The birds! The birds! How much happier would not my life on the beautiful island have been had I not loved them as I do! I loved to see them come every spring in thousands and thousands, it was a joy to my ear to hear them sing in the garden of San Michele. But there came a time when I almost wished that they had not come, when I wished I could have signalled to them far out on the sea to fly on, fly on with the flock of wild geese high overhead, straight to my own country far in the North where they would be safe from man. For I knew that the fair island that was a paradise to me was a hell to them, like that other hell that awaited them further on on their Via Crucis, Heligoland. They came just before sunrise. All they asked for was to rest for a while after their long flight across the Mediterranean, the goal of the journey was so far away, the land where they were born and where they were to raise their young. They came in thousands: woodpigeons, thrushes, turtle-doves, waders, quails, golden orioles, skylarks, nightingales, wagtails, chaffinches, swallows, warblers, redbreasts and many other tiny artists on their way to give spring concerts to the silent forests and fields in the North. A couple of hours later they fluttered helplessly in the nets the cunning of man had stretched all over the island from the cliffs by the sea high up to the slopes of Monte Solaro and Monte Barbarossa. In the evening they were packed by hundreds in small wooden boxes without food and water and despatched by steamers to Marseilles to be eaten with delight in the smart restaurants of Paris. It was a lucrative trade, Capri was for centuries the seat of a bishop entirely financed by the sale of the netted birds. 'Il vescovo delle quaglie,' he was called in Rome. Do you know how they are caught in the nets? Hidden under the thickets, between the poles, are caged decoy birds who repeat incessantly, automatically their monotonous call. They cannot stop, they go on calling out night and day till they die. Long before science knew anything about the localization of the various nerve-centres in the human brain, the devil had revealed to his disciple man his ghastly discovery that by stinging out the eyes of a bird with a red-hot needle the bird would sing automatically. It is an old story, it was already known to the Greeks and the Romans, it is still done to-day all along the southern shores of Spain, Italy[1] and Greece. Only a few birds in a hundred survive the operation, still it is good business, a blinded quail is worth twenty-five lire in Capri to-day. During six weeks of the spring and six weeks of the autumn, the whole slope of Monte Barbarossa was covered with nets from the ruined castle on the top down to the garden-wall of San Michele at the foot of the mountain. It was considered the best *caccia* on the whole island, as often as not over a thousand birds were netted there in a single day. The mountain was owned by a man from the mainland, an ex-butcher, a famous specialist in the blinding of birds, my only enemy in Anacapri except the doctor. Ever since I had begun building San Michele the war between him and me had been going on incessantly. I had appealed to the Prefect of Naples, I had appealed to the Government in Rome, I had been told there was nothing to be done, the mountain was his, the law was on his side. I had obtained an audience from the highest Lady in the land, she had smiled at

[1] Now forbidden by law.

me with her enchanting smile that had won her the heart of the whole of Italy, she had honoured me with an invitation to remain for luncheon, the first word I had read on the menu had been 'Paté d'alouettes farcies.' I had appealed to the Pope and had been told by a fat cardinal that the Holy Father had been carried down in his portantina that very morning at daybreak to the Vatican gardens to watch the netting of the birds, the caccia had been good, over two hundred birds had been caught. I had scraped off the rust from the little two-pounder the English had abandoned in the garden in 1808 and started firing off a shot every five minutes from midnight till sunrise in the hope of frightening away the birds from the fatal mountain. The ex-butcher had sued me for interfering with the lawful exercise of his trade, I had been fined two hundred lire damages. I had trained all the dogs to bark the whole night at the cost of what little sleep remained for me. A few days later my big Maremma dog died suddenly, I found traces of arsenic in his stomach. I caught sight of the murderer the next light lurking behind the garden-wall and knocked him down. He sued me again, I was fined five hundred lire for assault. I had sold my beautiful Greek vase and my beloved Madonna by Desiderio di Settignano in order to raise the enormous sum he had asked for the mountain, several hundred times its value. When I came with the money he renewed his old tactics and grinned at me that the price had been doubled. He knew his man. My exasperation had reached a point when I might have parted with everything I possessed to become the owner of the mountain. The bird slaughter went on as before. I had lost my sleep, I could think of nothing else. In my despair I fled from San Michele and sailed for Monte Cristo to return when the last birds had passed over the island.

The first thing I heard when I came back was that the ex-butcher was lying on the point of death. Masses were read for his salvation twice a day in the church at thirty lire apiece, he was one of the richest men in the village. Towards evening arrived the parroco asking me in the name of Christ to visit the dying man. The village doctor suspected pneumonia, the chemist was sure it was a stroke, the barber thought it was un colpo di sangue, the midwife thought it was una paura. The parroco himself, always on the look-out for the evil eye, inclined towards the mal'occhio. I refused to go. I said I had never been a doctor in Capri except for the poor and that the resident physicians on the island were quite capable of coping with any of these ailments. Only on one condition would I come, that the man would swear on the crucifix that if he pulled through he would never again sting out the eyes of a bird and that he would sell me the mountain at his exorbitant price of a month ago. The man refused. In the night he was given the Last Sacraments. At daybreak the parroco appeared again. My offer had been accepted, he had sworn on the crucifix. Two hours later I tapped a pint of pus from his left pleura to the consternation of the village doctor and to the glory of the village saint, for, contrary to my expectations, the man recovered. – Miracolo! Miracolo!

The mountain of Barbarossa is now a bird sanctuary. Thousands of tired birds of passage are resting on its slopes every spring and autumn, safe from man and beast. The dogs of San Michele are forbidden to bark while the birds are resting on the mountain. The cats are never let out of the kitchen except with a little alarm-bell tied round their necks. Billy the vagabond is shut up in the monkey-house, one never knows what a monkey or a school-boy is up to.

So far I have never said a word to belittle the last miracle of Sant'Antonio which at a low estimate saved for many years the lives of at least fifteen thousand birds a year. But when all is over for me, I mean just to whisper to the nearest angel that with all due respect to Sant'Antonio, it was I and not he who tapped the pus out of the butcher's left pleura and to implore the angel to put in a kind word for me if nobody else will. I am sure Almighty God loves the birds or He would not have given them the same pair of wings as He has given to His own angels.

XXIX

The Bambino

Sant'anna shook her head and wanted to know whether it was wise to send out such a small baby on such a windy day, and if it was at least a respectable house the grandchild was to be taken to? The Madonna said there was nothing to worry about, the child would be well wrapped up, she felt sure he would be all right, she had always heard children were welcome in San Michele. Better let the boy go since he wanted to go, didn't she know that small as he was he had already a will of his own? St. Joseph was not even consulted, it is true he never had much to say in the Family. Don Salvatore, the youngest priest of Anacapri, lifted the cradle from the shrine, the sacristan lit the wax candles and off they went.[1] First came a small choirboy ringing a bell, then came two *Figlie di Maria* in their white frocks and blue veils, then came the sacristan swinging the censer, then came Don Salvatore carrying the cradle. As they passed along through the village, the men bared their heads, the women held up their own babies that they might see the Royal Infant, a golden crown on his head, a silver rattle in the shape of a siren round his neck, and the street boys called out to one another: 'Il Bambino! Il Bambino!' At the door of San Michele stood the whole household with roses in their hands to welcome our guest. The best room in the house had been turned into a nursery, full of flowers and hung with garlands of rosemary and ivy. On a table spread with our best linen cloth burned two wax candles, for small children do not like to be left in the dark. In a corner of the nursery stood my Florentine Madonna, hugging her own baby and from the walls two putti of Luca della Robbia and a Holy Virgin of Mino da Fiesole looked down upon the cradle. From the ceiling burned the holy lamp, woe to the house if it ever flickered and went out, it meant the death of its owner before the year was over.

[1] You may not have heard of this quaint old custom. During my stay in San Michele I used to receive a visit from the Bambino every year, the greatest honour that could possibly be bestowed upon us. He generally remained at San Michele for a week.

By the cradle lay a few humble toys, such as our village could produce, to keep company with the Bambino; a bald-headed doll, sole survivor from Giovannina and Rosina's childhood, a wooden donkey lent by Elisa's eldest girl, a rattle in the shape of a horn against the evil eye. In a basket under the table lay asleep Elisa's cat with her six new-born kittens, specially brought there for the occasion. In a huge earthenware jar on the floor stood a whole bush of rosemary in flower. Do you know why rosemary? Because when the Madonna washed the linen of the Infant Jesus Christ, she hung his little shirt to dry on a bush of rosemary.

Don Salvatore deposited the cradle in its shrine and left the Bambino in the charge of my womenfolk after most detailed recommendations to watch over him and see that he had all he wanted. Elisa's children played about on the floor the whole day to keep him company and at Ave Maria the whole household kneeled before the cradle reciting their prayers. Giovannina poured a little more oil in the lamp for the night, they waited for a while till the Bambino had fallen asleep and then they went away as silently as they could. When all was still in the house I went up to the nursery to have a look at the Bambino before I went to bed. The light from the holy lamp fell on the cradle, I could just see him lying there smiling in his sleep.

Poor little smiling child, little did he know that the day should come when all of us who were kneeling by his cradle should abandon him, when those who said they loved him should betray him, when cruel hands should tear the golden crown from his brow and replace it by a crown of thorns and nail him to a cross, forsaken even by God.

The night he died a sombre old man was wandering up and down the same marble floor where I was standing now. He had risen from his couch roused in his sleep by a haunting dream. His face was dark as the sky overhead, fear shone in his eye. He summoned his astronomers and his wise men from the East and bid them to tell him the meaning of his dream, but before they could read the golden writing on the sky, one by one the stars flickered and went out. Whom had he to fear, he the ruler of the world! What mattered the life of one single man to him, the arbiter of the lives of millions of men! Who could bring him to account for the putting to death that night of an innocent man by one of his procurators in the name of the Emperor of Rome? And his procurator whose execrated name is still on our lips, was he more responsible than his Imperial Master for signing the death-warrant of an innocent man? To him, the stern upholder of Roman law and tradition in an unruly province, was it even an innocent man he was putting to death? And the cursed Jew who still wanders round the world in search of forgiveness, did he know what he was doing? Or he, the greatest evildoer of all time, when he betrayed his Master with his kiss of love? Could he have done otherwise? Did he do it of his own free will? It had to be done, he had to do it, obeying a will stronger than his. Was there not in that night on Golgotha more than one man who was made to suffer for a sin which was not his?

I bent over the sleeping child for a while and went away on tiptoe.

The Festa di Sant'Antonio

The Festa di Sant'Antonio was the greatest day in the year for Anacapri. For weeks the little village had been all astir for the solemn commemoration of our Patron Saint. The streets had been cleaned, the houses where the procession had to pass had been whitewashed, the church decorated with red silk hangings and tapestries, the fireworks ordered from Naples, the band, most important of all, hired from Torre Annunziata. The series of festivals opened with the arrival of the band on the eve of the great day. Half across the bay the band had already begun to blow all they were worth, far too far away to be heard by us in Anacapri but near enough with favourable wind to irritate the ears of the Capresi in the hated village below. On landing at the Marina the band and their gigantic instruments were packed in two big carts and taken as far as the carriage road was finished. The rest of the way they had to climb in loose formation up the steep Phoenician steps, blowing incessantly. Under the wall of San Michele they were received by a deputation from the Municipio. The magnificent bandmaster in his gorgeous uniform all covered with gold lace à la Murat raised his baton and, preceded by the boys of the village, the band made their solemn entrance into Anacapri a tempo di marcia blowing their horns, clarinets and oboes, banging their drums and cymbals and rattling their triangles as hard as they could. Inauguration concert on the Piazza all decorated with flags and crammed with people, lasting without any interval till midnight. A few hours' dreamless sleep in the old barracks where the English soldiers slept in 1806, interrupted by the bursting of the first rockets to announce that the great day was dawning. At 4 a.m. reveille through the village blowing lustily in the fresh morning breeze. At 5 the usual morning mass in church read as always by the parroco assisted, in honour of the occasion, by the band on empty stomachs. At 7 merenda, a cup of black coffee, half a kilo of bread and fresh goatcheese. At 8 the church was already filled to the last place, the men on one side, the women on the other, their babies asleep on their laps. In the centre of the church the band on their specially erected tribune. The twelve priests of Anacapri in their choir stalls behind the High Altar embarked courageously on the Missa Solennis of Pergolesi, trusting to Providence and the accompanying band to see them through. Musical intermezzo, a furious galop played by the band with great bravura, much appreciated by the congregation. At ten o'clock Messa Cantata from the High Altar with painful solos by poor old Don Antonio and tremolos of protestation and sudden cries of distress from the inside of the little organ, worn out by the wear and tear of three centuries. At 11 sermon from the pulpit in commemoration of Sant'Antonio and his miracles, each miracle illustrated and made visible by a special gesture appropriate to the occasion. Now the orator would raise his hands in ecstasy to the Saints in Heaven, now he would point his index to the floor to locate the underground dwellings of the damned. Now he would fall on his knees in silent prayers to Sant'Antonio suddenly to spring to his feet on the point of precipitating himself from the pulpit, to smite down an invisible scoffer with a blow from his fist. Now he would bend his head in rapturous silence to listen to the happy chants of the angels, now, pale with terror, he would put his hands to his ears not to hear the grinding of the teeth of il Demonio and the cries of the sinners in their cauldrons. At last, streaming with perspiration and prostrated by two hours of tears and sobs and maledictions at a temperature of 105 Fahrenheit, he would sink down on the floor of the pulpit with a terrific curse on the Protestants. 12 o'clock. Great excitement on the Piazza. Esce la processione! Esce la processione! The procession is coming out. First came a dozen small children, almost babies, hand in hand. Some wore short white tunics and angel wings like Raphael's putti. Some, entirely naked and adorned with garlands of vine-leaves and wreaths of roses round their brows, looked as if detached from a Greek bas-relief. Then came the Figlie di Maria, tall slender girls in white robes and long blue veils with the silver medal of the Madonna round their necks on a blue ribbon. Then came the *bizzocche*, in black dresses and black veils, dried-up old spinsters who had remained faithful to their first love, Jesus Christ. Then came the 'Congrega di Carità' preceded by their banner, old, grave-looking men in their quaint black and white cassocks of the time of Savonarola.

La musica! La musica!

Then came the band in their gold-laced uniforms from the time of the Bourbon kings of Naples, preceded by their magnificent bandmaster blowing for all they were worth a wild polka, a special favourite piece of the saint, I understood. Then, surrounded by all the priests in their gala robes and saluted by hundreds of crackers, appeared Sant'Antonio erect on his throne, his hand stretched out in the act of blessing. His robe was covered with precious lace and strewn with jewels and ex-votos, his mantle of magnificent old brocatello was fastened on his breast with a fibula of sapphires and rubies. From a string of multi-coloured glass beads round his neck hung a huge coral in the shape of a horn to protect him against the evil eye.

Close on the heels of Sant'Antonio came I, bareheaded, wax taper in hand, walking by the side of the Sindaco – an honour bestowed upon me by special permission from the Archbishop of Sorrento. Then came the municipal councillors relieved for the day from their grave responsibility. Then came the notables of Anacapri: the doctor, the notary, the apothecary, the barber, the tobacconist, the tailor. Then came il popolo: sailors, fishermen, contadini, followed at a respectful distance by their womenfolk and their children. In the rear of the procession walked humbly half-a-dozen dogs, a couple of goats with their kids trotting by their side, and a pig or two, on the look-out for their owners. Specially selected masters of ceremony, gilt sticks in their hands, Gold Sticks in Waiting to the Saint, rushed incessantly to and fro along the flank of the procession to keep order in the ranks and to regulate the speed. As the procession wound its way through the lanes, basketfuls of sweet-scented ginestra, the favourite flower of the saint, were thrown from every window. The broom is in fact called the fiore di Sant'Antonio. Here and there a cord had been stretched across the street from one window to another and just as the saint passed by, a gaily-coloured cardboard angel was seen performing a precipitate flight with flapping wings across the rope to the huge delight of the crowd. In front of San Michele the procession halted and the saint was reverently deposited on a specially erected stand to rest for a while. The clergy wiped the perspiration from their foreheads, the band kept on blowing their fortissimo as they had done ever since they issued from the church two hours before, Sant'Antonio looked on benevolently from his stand while my women folk threw handfuls of roses from the windows, old Pacciale rang the bells from the chapel and Baldassare lowered the flag from the roof of the house. It was a grand day for us all, everybody was proud of the honour paid to us. The dogs watched the proceedings from the pergola, well behaved and polite as usual though somewhat restless. In the garden the tortoises continued

313

impassive to ponder upon their own problems, the mongoose was too busy to give way to his curiosity. The little owl sat blinking with half-closed eyes on his perch, thinking of something else. Billy, being an unbeliever, was shut up in the monkey-house, from where he kept up an infernal din, shouting at the top of his voice, banging his water-bottle against his tin bowl, rattling his chain, shaking his bars and using the most horrible language.

Back to the Piazza where Sant'Antonio saluted by a tremendous detonation of crackers was reinstalled in his shrine in the church and the procession went home to their macaroni. The band sat down to a banquet offered by the authorities under the pergola of the Hotel Paradiso, half a kilo of macaroni per head, vino a volontà: At four the doors of San Michele were flung open, half-an-hour later the whole village was in the garden, rich and poor, men, women and children and new-born babies, cripples, idiots, blind and lame, those who could not come by themselves were carried on the shoulders of the others. Only the priests were absentees, though not by any fault of theirs. Prostrated by their long wanderings they leaned back in their choir stalls behind the High Altar in fervent prayers to Sant'Antonio, audible maybe to the saint himself in his shrine but seldom to anybody else who happened to look into the empty church. A long row of tables with huge piretti of San Michele's best wine stretched from one end of the pergola to the other. Old Pacciale, Baldassare and Mastro Nicola were hard at work re-filling the wine-glasses and Giovannina, Rosina and Elisa went round offering cigars to the men, coffee to the women, and cakes and sweets to the children. The band, by special arrangement with the authorities lent to me for the afternoon, was blowing incessantly from the upper loggia. The whole house was thrown open, nothing was locked up, all my precious belongings were lying about as usual in their apparent disorder on tables, chairs and on the floor. Over a thousand people wandered freely from room to room, nothing was ever touched, nothing was ever missing. When the bells rang Ave Maria the reception was over and they all went away after much hand-shaking, happier than ever, but that is what wine is made for. The band in better form than ever led the way to the Piazza. The twelve priests relieved and refreshed by their vigil over Sant'Antonio stood already in compact formàtion outside the church doors. The Sindaco, the municipal councillors and the notables took their seats on the terrace of the municipio. The band gasping for breath hoisted themselves and their instruments on the specially erected tribune.

The popolo stood in the Piazza packed like herrings. The majestic bandmaster raised his baton, the Gran Concerto began. Rigoletto, Il Trovatore, Gli Ughenotti, I Puritani, Il Ballo in Maschera, a choice selection of Neapolitan folk-songs, polkas, mazurkas, minuets and tarantellas in uninterrupted succession and ever increasing tempo until eleven o'clock when two thousand lire worth of rockets, Roman candles, catherine wheels and crackers exploded in the air to the glory of Sant'Antonio. At midnight the official programme for the festivity was exhausted but not so the Anacapresi and the band. Nobody went to bed, the village resounded with singing, laughter and music the whole night long. Evviva la gioia! Evviva il Santo! Evviva la musica!

The band was to depart by the six o'clock morning boat. On their way to the Marina they halted at daybreak under the windows of San Michele for their customary 'Serenata d'Addio' in my honour. I can still see Henry James looking down from his bedroom window, shaking with laughter, in his pyjamas. The band had been sadly reduced in numbers and efficiency during the night. The bandmaster had become delirious, two of the leading oboists had spat blood, the bassoon had had a rupture, the big drummer had dislocated his right shoulder-blade, the cymbalist had split his ear-drums. Two more members of the band incapacitated by emotion had had to be taken down to the Marina on donkeys. The survivors lay on their backs in the middle of the road blowing with their last breath their plaintive Serenata d'Addio to San Michele. Revived by a cup of black coffee they staggered speechless to their feet and with a friendly waving of their hands they reeled down the Phoenician steps to the Marina. The Festa di Sant'Antonio was over.

XXXI

The Regatta

It was the height of summer, a long glorious day of unbroken sunshine. The British Embassy had moved down from Rome and established its headquarters at Sorrento. On the balcony of the Hôtel Vittoria sat the ambassador in his sailor cap, scanning the horizon through his monocle for the maestrale to begin to fan the glossy waters of the gulf. In the little harbour at his feet his beloved 'Lady Hermione' lay riding at her anchor, as impatient as himself for the start. He had designed and rigged her himself with marvellous ingenuity and technical skill as a single-handed fast cruiser. He often used to say he would not mind sailing her across the Atlantic, he was prouder of her than of any of his brilliant diplomatic achievements. He used to spend the whole day in his boat, his face was as bronzed as that of a Sorrento fisherman. He knew the coast from Civita Vecchia to Punta Licosa almost as well as I did. Once he had challenged me to a race down to Messina and had beaten me badly with a following wind and a heavy sea, to his great delight.

'Wait till I get my new jackyard topsail and my silk spinnaker, ' said I.

He loved Capri and thought San Michele the most beautiful place he had ever seen, and he had seen much. He knew little of the long history of the island but was as eager as a schoolboy to know more.

I was just then exploring the Blue Grotto. Twice Mastro Nicola had dragged me half unconscious out of the famous subterranean passage leading, according to tradition, through the bowels of the earth up to the Tiberian villa six hundred feet overhead on the plain of Damecuta, maybe a corruption of Domus Augusta. I spent whole days in the Grotto and Lord Dufferin often used to come in his little dinghy to pay me a visit while I was at work. After a delicious swim in the blue waters we used to sit for hours outside the mysterious tunnel, talking about Tiberius and the Capri orgies. I told the ambassador that like all the rest of Suetonius' filthy gossip it was nonsense about the subterranean passage through which Tiberius was supposed to have come down to the Grotto to play about with his boys and girls before strangling them. The tunnel was not made by the hand of man but by the slow infiltration of sea-water through the rock. I had crawled in it for over eighty yards and convinced myself at the peril of my life that it led nowhere. That the Grotto was known to the Romans was proved by the numerous traces of Roman masonry. The island having sunk about sixteen feet since then, the Grotto was in those days entered through the huge submerged vault visible through the clear water. The small aperture through which he had entered in his dinghy was originally a window for the ventilation of the Grotto, which was of course not blue then but just like the dozens of other grottos on the island. Baedeker's information that the Blue Grotto had been discovered in 1826 by the German painter Kopisch was incorrect. The Grotto was known in the seventeenth century as Grotto Gradula and was rediscovered in 1822 by the Capri fisherman Angelo Ferraro who was even granted a life pension for his discovery. As to the sinister tradition of Tiberius handed down to posterity in the Annals of Tacitus, I told Lord Dufferin that history had never committed a worse blunder than when condemning this great Emperor to infamy on the testimony of his principal accuser, 'a detractor of humanity,' as Napoleon had called him. Tacitus was a brilliant writer but his Annals were historical novels, not history. He had to insert at random his twenty lines about the Capri orgies in order to complete his picture of the typical tyrant of the rhetorical school to which he belonged. There was no difficulty in tracing the more than suspect source from which he had got hold of these foul rumours. I was besides pointing out in my 'Psychological Study of Tiberius' that they did not even relate to the Emperor's life in Capri. That Tacitus himself did not believe in the Capri orgies is evident from his own narrative since they do not in any way weaken his general conception of Tiberius as a great emperor and a great man, 'admirable in character and in great esteem,' to use his own words. Even his far less clever follower, Suetonius, introduces his filthiest stories with the remark that they are 'scarcely allowable to be related and still less to be believed.' Before the appearance of the Annals – eighty years after the death of Tiberius – there was no public man in Roman history with a cleaner record of a noble and unblemished life than the old Emperor. None of the various writers on Tiberius, some of them his contemporaries with first-class opportunities for picking up all the gossip of the evil tongues of Rome, had a word to say about the

Capri orgies. Philo, the pious and learned Jew, distinctly speaks of the clean and simple life Caligula was forced to lead when staying with his adopted grandfather in Capri. Even the jackal Suetonius, forgetful of the wise saying of Quintilian that a liar must have a good memory, blunders into the information that Caligula, when bent on some debauchery in Capri, had to disguise himself in a wig to escape the stern eye of the old Emperor. Seneca, the castigator of vice, and Pliny – both his contemporaries – speak of the austere solitude of Tiberius in Capri. Dio Cassius, it is true, makes some casual remarks about these foul rumours but cannot help noticing himself the inexplicable contradictions into which he is falling. Even the scandal-loving Juvenal speaks of the Emperor's 'tranquil old age' in his island home, surrounded by his learned friends and astronomers. Plutarch, the severe upholder of morality, speaks of the old man's dignified solitude during the last ten years of his life. That the story of the Capri orgies is absolutely impossible from the point of view of scientific psychology was already understood by Voltaire. Tiberius was in his sixty-eighth year when he retired to Capri with an unbroken record of a life of stern morality, unchallenged even by his worst enemies. A possible diagnosis of some sinister senile dementia is excluded by the admission of all writers that the old man was in full possession of his mental health and vigour up to his death in his 79th year. The vein of insanity which runs through the Julian stock was besides absent in the Claudian. His life on the island was the life of a lonely old man, the weary ruler of an ungrateful world, a sombre idealist, heartbroken and bitter, a hypochondriac he might even be called to-day, his magnificent intellect and his rare sense of humour still surviving his belief in mankind. He distrusted and despised his contemporaries and no wonder, for almost every man or woman he had trusted had betrayed him. Tacitus has quoted his words when, the year before his retirement to Capri, he rejected the petition to erect him a temple for divine worship as had been done to Augustus. Who but the compiler of the Annals, the brilliant master of sarcasm and subtle insinuation, could have had the audacity to quote with a sneer the old Emperor's grave appeal to posterity for a fair judgment?

'As for myself, Conscript Fathers, I declare unto you that I am no more than mortal and do but discharge the duties of a man; that it suffices me if I fill worthily the principal place among you; this I would have remembered by those who live after me. Enough and more than enough will they render to my memory, if they judge me to have been worthy of my ancestors, watchful of your interests, steadfast in danger, and undaunted by the enmities encountered in the public service. These are the temples I would erect in your hearts, these are the fairest images and such as will best endure. As for those built of stone, if the judgment of posterity turn into hate, they are but dishonoured sepulchres. Hence I here invoke the Gods that to the end of my days they grant me a spirit undisturbed and discerning in my duties towards them and towards mankind; and hence I ask our citizens and allies that when I shall have departed this world, they will honour my life and my name with their approval and their kindly recollections.'

We climbed up to Damecuta. The old Emperor knew what he was doing when he built his largest villa there, next to San Michele Damecuta commands the most beautiful view on the island of Capri. I told the ambassador that many of the fragments found here had come into the hands of his colleague Sir William Hamilton, the British Ambassador to Naples in the time of Nelson, and were now in the British Museum. Many were still lying hidden under the vines, I meant to start excavations here in earnest next summer, the vineyard now belonged to me. Lord Dufferin picked up a rusty soldier's button among the débris of mosaic and coloured marble slabs. Corsican Rangers! Yes, two hundred Corsican Rangers were encamped here in 1808 but unluckily the bulk of the English garrison in Anacapri consisted of Maltese troops, who retired in disorder when the French rushed the camp. Looking down upon the cliffs at Orico I showed the ambassador where the French had landed and climbed the precipitous rock, we agreed it was indeed a marvellous performance. Yes, the English had fought with their usual gallantry but had to retire under cover of the night to what is San Michele to-day where their commander Major Hamill, an Irishman like himself, had died of his wounds. He lies buried in a corner of the cemetery of Anacapri. The two-pounder they had to abandon in their enforced retreat down the Phoenician steps to Capri the next day is still in my garden. At daybreak the French opened fire on Capri from the heights of Monte Solaro, how they got a gun up there seems almost incomprehensible. There was nothing for the English commander in the Casa Inglese in Capri to do but to sign the document of surrender. Hardly was the ink dry before the English fleet, becalmed by the Ponza islands, appeared in the offing. The document of surrender bore the name of an exceptionally unlucky man, the future gaoler of the captive eagle on another island, Sir Hudson Lowe.

As we were walking back through the village to San Michele I pointed to a small house in a little garden and told the ambassador that the owner of the house was an aunt of La Bella Margherita, the beauty of Anacapri. The aunt had married a 'milord inglese' who, unless I was mistaken, was a relation of his. Yes, he well remembered that a cousin of his had married an Italian peasant girl to the dismay of his family and had even taken her to England, but he had never seen her and did not know what had become of her after her husband's death. He was tremendously interested and wanted me to tell him all I knew about her, adding that what he knew about her husband was quite enough for him. I told him it had all happened long before my time. I had only known her long after her return from England as a widow, she was then already an old woman. All I could tell him was what I had heard from old Don Crisostomo who had been her confessor and also her tutor. Of course she could neither read nor write but with her quick Caprese mind she had soon picked up a lot of English. In order to prepare her for her life in England as the wife of a milord inglese, Don Crisostomo, who was a learned man, had been instructed to give her a few lessons in various matters to enlarge the limited range of her conversation. Grace and good manners she already possessed by birthright as all Capri girls do. As to good looks it was safe to rely on Don Crisostomo's assurance that she was the most beautiful girl in Anacapri, for I had always considered him as a great connoisseur. All efforts to rouse her interest in anything outside her own island having failed, it was decided to limit her education to the history of Capri to give her at least something to talk about to her relations. She listened gravely to the terrible tales of how Tiberio had thrown his victims from the Salto di Tiberio, how he had scratched the face of a fisherman with the claws of a crab, how he had strangled small boys and girls in the Blue Grotto. How his grandson Nero had had his own mother beaten to death by his oarsmen in view of the island, how his nephew Caligula had drowned thousands of people off Pozzuoli. At last she said in her inimitable dialect:

'They must have been very bad all these people, nothing but camorristi.'

'I should think so,' said the Professor, 'didn't you hear me say that Tiberio strangled the boys and girls in the Blue Grotto, that . . .'

'Are they all dead?'

'Yes, of course, nearly two thousand years ago.'

'But why on earth should we then trouble about them, do let us leave them alone,' she said with her enchanting smile.

Thus ended her education.

After the death of her husband she had returned to her island and gradually drifted back to the simple life of her ancestors with a lineage two thousand years older than that of her milord inglese. We found her sitting in the sun on her little pergola, a rosary in her hand and a cat in her lap, a dignified Roman matron, stately as the mother of the Gracchi. Lord Dufferin kissed her hand with the courtesy of an old courtier. She had forgotten nearly all her English and fallen back to the dialect of her childhood, and the ambassador's classical Italian was as unintelligible to her as to me.

'Tell her,' said Lord Dufferin as we rose to go, 'tell her from me that she is at least as great a lady as her milord inglese was a gentleman.'

Did the ambassador wish to see her niece, La Bella Margherita? Yes, he asked for nothing better.

La Bella Margherita received us with her charming smile and a glass of the parroco's best wine and the gallant old gentleman was quite willing to acknowledge their cousinship with a smacking kiss on her rosy cheek.

The long expected regatta was to come off the following Sunday, a triangular course: Capri, Posilipo, Sorrento, where the winner was to receive the cup from Lady Dufferin's hands. My beautiful cutter 'Lady Victoria' was as fine a boat as Scotland could build, teak and steel, ready for every emergency, safe in all weather if properly handled, and if ever I knew anything worth knowing it was how to steer a boat. The two little yachts were sister-boats, Lord Dufferin's two daughters had given them their names. Our chances were about equal. In a stiff breeze and a rough sea I should probably be a loser, but I relied on my new jackyard topsail and my new silk spinnaker to lift the cup in a light wind and a smooth sea. The new sails had arrived from England while I was still in Rome and were safely hung up in the sailroom in the sole custody of old Pacciale, the most trusted of the whole household. He well knew the importance of his position, he slept with the key under his pillow and never allowed anybody to enter the sanctuary. Although he had of late years become a passionate grave digger, his heart was still on the sea where he had lived and suffered since he was a boy as a 'pescatore di coralli.' In those days before the curse of America had fallen on Capri, almost the whole male population went coral fishing in 'Barbaria,' off Tunis and Tripoli.

321

It was a terrible job, full of hardships and privations, even dangers, for many of them never returned to their island. It took Pacciale twenty years of toil on the sea to put together the three hundred lire needed for a man to take a wife. One hundred for the boats and the fishing nets, two hundred for the bed, the couple of chairs, and a suit of Sunday clothes to get married in, the Madonna would see to the rest. The girl waited for years, spinning and weaving the house linen which it fell to her to provide. Like everybody else Pacciale had also inherited from his father a strip of land, in his case a mere strip of bare rock by the water's edge, a thousand feet below Damecuta. The earth he had carried in basketfuls on his back, year after year, till there was enough soil to plant a few vines and prickly pears. He never made a drop of wine, for the young grapes were regularly burnt by the salt spray when the S.W. was blowing. Now and then he came home with a few new potatoes, the first to ripen on the island, which he presented to me with great pride. He spent all his spare time down in his masseria, scratching the rock with his heavy mattock or sitting on a stone looking out on the sea with his clay pipe in his mouth. Now and then I used to climb down the precipitous cliffs, where a goat would hesitate where to put its foot, to pay him a visit to his huge delight. Just below our feet was a grotto, inaccessible from the sea and unknown even to-day to most people, semi-dark and hung with huge stalactites. According to Pacciale it had been habited in bygone times by a lupomanaro, the mysterious, awe-inspiring werewolf who still haunts the imagination of the islanders almost as much as Tiberio himself. I knew that the fossil tooth I had found under the sand in the cave was the tooth of a big mammal who had lain down to die here when the island was still connected with the mainland, and that the pieces of flint and obsidian were the fragments of the tools of primitive man. Maybe even a God had lived there, for the grotto faces east and Mithras, the Sun-God, was often worshipped here.

But there was no time now for exploring the Grotto, all my thoughts were settled on the coming regatta. I had sent word to Pacciale that I was coming to inspect my new sails after breakfast. The sailroom was open but to my surprise old Pacciale was not there to meet me. I thought I was going to faint as I unfolded the new sails one by one. There was a big rent in my jackyard topsail, my silk spinnaker that was to lift the cup was almost split in two, the racing jib was soiled and torn to rags. When I had recovered my speech, I roared for Pacciale. He did not come. I rushed out of the sailroom and found him at last standing against the garden wall.

Mad with rage I raised my hand to strike him, he did not move, he did not utter a sound, all he did was to bend his head and stretch out his arms horizontally against the wall. My hand fell, I knew what it meant, I had seen it before. It meant that he was going to suffer and that he was innocent, it was the crucifixion of Our Lord he reproduced with his outstretched arms and his bent head. I spoke to him as gently as I could but he did not utter a sound, he did not move from his cross of agony. I put the key of the sail-room in my pocket and summoned the whole household. Nobody had been in the sailroom, nobody had anything to say, but Giovan-nina hid her face in her apron and began to cry. I took her into my room and succeeded with the greatest difficulty in making her speak. I wish I could relate the pitiful story word by word as she told it to me between her sobs. It nearly made me cry myself when I remembered that I had been on the point of striking poor old Pacciale. It had happened two months ago on the first of May when we were still in Rome. You may remember the famous first of May many years ago when there was to be a social upheaval in all countries of Europe, an assault on the rich, a destruction of their cursed property. That was at least what the newspapers said, the smaller the paper, the bigger the impending calamity. The smallest paper of all was the 'Voce di San Gennaro' which Maria Porta-Lettere carried twice a week in her fish-basket to the parroco to be circulated among the intellectuals of the village, a faint echo from the happenings of the world resounding through the Arcadian peace of Anacapri. But it was not a faint echo that reached the ears of the intellectuals this time through the columns of the 'Voce di San Gennaro.' It was a thunderbolt from the blue sky which shook the whole village. It was the long predicted world cataclysm that was to come off on the first of May. Enlisted by il Demonio the savage hordes of Attila were to ransack the palaces of the rich and burn and destroy their belongings. It was the beginning of the end, castigo di Dio! Castigo di Dio! The news spread like wildfire all over Anacapri. The parroco hid the jewels of Sant'Antonio and the sacred vessels of the church under his bed, the notables dragged their portable belongings down to their wine-cellars. The popolo rushed to the Piazza yelling for their Patron Saint to be taken out of his shrine and carried through the streets for protection. On the eve of the fatal day Pacciale went to consult the parroco. Baldassare had already been there and had left reassured by the parroco's affirmation that the brigands would surely not care in the least for il Signor Dottore's broken stones and crockery and roba antica.

Baldassare might just as well leave all this rubbish where it was lying. As to Pacciale who was responsible for the sails, he was in a far worse plight, said the parroco. If the brigands were to invade the island they must come in boats, and sails were a most valuable booty to seafaring men. To hide them in the wine-cellar was running too great a risk, for seafaring men were also fond of good wine. Why not carry them down to his lonely masseria under the cliffs of Damecuta, it was the very place for them, the brigands would surely not risk their necks down that precipice to fetch them there.

After dark Pacciale, his brother and two trusted compagni, armed with heavy sticks, dragged my new sails down to his masseria. The night was stormy, soon it rained in torrents, the lantern went out, at the peril of their lives they groped their way down the slippery cliffs. At midnight they reached the masseria and deposited their burden in the grotto of the lupomanaro. They sat there the whole of the first of May on their bundles of drenched sails, one of them in turn standing on guard at the entrance of the cave. Towards sunset Pacciale resolved to send his unwilling brother to reconnoitre in the village without exposing himself to any undue risk. He returned three hours later to report that there was no trace of the brigands, all was going on as usual. All the people were in the Piazza, candles were lit before the altars in the church, Sant'Antonio was to come out on the Piazza to receive the thanksgivings of Anacapri for having once more saved his village from destruction. At midnight the party crept out of the grotto and climbed to the village again with my drenched sails. When Pacciale discovered the disaster he wanted to drown himself, his daughters said they did not dare to leave him out of sight for several days and nights. He had never been the same since, he hardly ever spoke. I had already noticed it myself and had several times asked him what was the matter with him. Long before Giovannina had finished her confession, all trace of anger had gone out of me, I hunted in vain for Pacciale all over the village to tell him so. I found him at last down in his masseria sitting on his usual stone looking out over the sea as was his wont. I told him I was ashamed of having raised my hand to strike him. It was all the fault of the parroco. I did not care a d——n about the new sails, the old ones were good enough for me. I meant to be off for a long cruise on the morrow, he was to come with me and we would forget all about it. He knew I had always disliked his gravedigging, better hand this job over to his brother and return to the sea. From to-day he was promoted to become my sailor in charge of the cutter. Gaetano had been blind drunk twice in Calabria and nearly made us go to the bottom, I meant to dismiss him in any case. When we came home I made him put on the new jersey just arrived from England with LADY VICTORIA R.C. Y.C. in red letters over the breast. He never took it off, he lived in it, he died in it. When I first came across Pacciale he was already an old man, how old he did not know, nor did his daughters, nor did anybody else. I had in vain tried to trace his birth in the official register of the Municipio. He had been forgotten from the very beginning. But he shall never be forgotten by me. I shall always remember him as the most honest, the most clean-minded, the most guileless man I have ever met in any land and in any station of life, gentle as a child. His own children had told me they had never heard him say a rash or unkind word to their mother or to them. He was even kind to animals, he used to take down pocketfuls of breadcrumbs to feed the birds in his vineyard, he was the only man on the island who had not trapped a bird or flogged a donkey. A devoted old servant cancels the name of master. He had become my friend, the honour was mine, he was a far better man than I. Although he belonged to another world than I, a world almost unknown to me, we understood each other quite well. During the long days and nights we were together alone on the sea he taught me many things I had not read in my books or heard from the lips of other men. He was a taciturn man, the sea had taught him its silence long ago. His thoughts were few and so much the better for him. But his sayings were full of poetry and the archaic simplicity of his similes was pure Greek. Many of his very words were Greek, he remembered them from the time he had sailed down that very coast as one of the crew in Ulysses' ship. When we were at home he continued his life as usual working in my garden or down in his beloved masseria by the sea. I did not fancy these expeditions up and down the steep cliffs, I thought his arteries were getting very hard and he often returned from his long climb rather out of breath. Otherwise he looked just the same, he never complained of anything, ate his macaroni with his usual appetite and was on his legs from daybreak till sunset. All of a sudden he refused one day to eat, we tried to coax him with all sorts of things, but he said no. He admitted that he felt 'un poco stanco,' a little tired, and seemed quite content to sit for a couple of days under the pergola looking out on the sea. Then he insisted upon going down to his masseria, it was with great difficulty I persuaded him to remain with us. I do not think he knew himself why he wanted to go there, but I knew it well. It was the instinct of primitive man that drove him there to hide from other men and lie down to die behind a rock, or under a bush or in the grotto where many thousands of years ago other primitive men had lain down to die. Towards noon he said he just wanted to lie down for a while on his bed, he who had never lain on a bed a single day of his life. I asked him several times during the afternoon how he felt, he said he felt quite well, thank you. Towards evening I had his bed moved to the window where he could see the sun going down in the sea. When I returned after Ave Maria the whole household, his brother, his compagni were sitting round the room. Nobody had told them to come, I did not even know myself it was so near. They did not speak, they did not pray, they just sat there quite still the whole night. As is the custom here, nobody was near the bed. Old Pacciale was lying there quite still and peaceful, looking out on the sea. It was all so simple and solemn, just as it was meant to be when a life is about to end. The priest came with the Last Sacrament. Old Pacciale was told to confess his sins and to ask to be forgiven. He nodded his head and kissed the crucifix. The priest gave him the absolution. Almighty God approved with a smile and said that old Pacciale was welcome to Heaven, I thought he was already there when all of a sudden he raised his hand and stroked my cheek gently, almost timidly.

'Siete buono come il mare,' he murmured.

Good as the sea!

I do not write down here these words with conceit, I write them with wonder. Where did these words come from? Surely they came from far, they came as an echo from a long-forgotten golden age when Pan was still alive, when the trees in the forest could speak and the waves of the sea could sing and man could listen and understand.

XXXII

The Beginning of the End

I have been away from San Michele a whole year, what a waste of time! I have come back with one eye less than when I went away. There is nothing more to be said about it, no doubt it was in order to prepare for such an eventuality that I was made to start life with two eyes. I have come back a different man. I seem to be looking out on the world with my one remaining eye from another angle of vision than I did before. I can no more see what is ugly and sordid, I can only see what is beautiful and sweet and clean. Even the men and women around me seem different from what they used to be. By a curious optical illusion I can see them no more as they are but as they were meant to be, as they would have liked to be if they had had a chance. I can still see with my blind eye a lot of fools strutting about, but they do not seem to get on my nerves as they used to do, I do not mind their chatter, let them have their say. Further I have not come for the present, if I am ever to love my fellow-creatures I fear I shall have to be blinded in both my eyes first. I cannot forgive them their cruelty to animals. I believe there is a sort of retrograde evolution going on in my mind which makes me drift further and further away from other people and draw closer and closer to Mother Nature and to the animals. All these men and women around me now seem to me of far less importance in the world than before. I feel as if I had been wasting too much of my time with them, as if I could do just as well without them as they can do without me. I well know they have no further use for me. Better filer à l'anglaise before one is turned out. I have plenty of other things to do and maybe there is not much time left. My wandering about the world in search of happiness is over, my life as a fashionable doctor is over, my life on the sea is over. I am going to stay where I am for good and try to make the best of it. But shall I be allowed to remain even here in San Michele? The whole bay of Naples lies shining like a mirror below my feet, the columns on the pergola, the loggias and the chapel are all ablaze with light, what will become of me if I cannot stand the glare? I have given up reading and writing and have taken up singing instead, I did not sing when all was well, I am also learning typewriting, a useful and pleasant pastime, I am told, for a single man with a single eye. Each hammer-stroke of my typewriter strikes simultaneously the MS. and my skull with a knock-out blow on the top of every thought that ventures to pop out from my brain. I have besides never been good at thinking, I seem to go on much better without it. There was a comfortable main road leading from the brain to the pen in my hand. Whatever thoughts I have had to spare have groped their way along this road ever since they began to tackle the alphabet. No wonder if they are apt to lose their bearing in this American labyrinth of cogs and wheels! In parenthesis I had better warn the reader that I can only accept responsibility for what I have written with my own hand, not for what has been concocted in collaboration with the Corona Typewriting Company. I shall be curious to see which of the two the reader will like best.

But if ever I learn to hold on to this boisterous Pegasus I mean to sing a humble song to my beloved Schubert, the greatest singer of all times, to thank him for what I owe him. I owe him everything. Even while I was lying week after week in the dark with little hope ever to get out of it, I used to hum to myself one after another of his songs, like the schoolboy who goes whistling through the dark forest to pretend that he is not afraid. Schubert was nineteen when he composed the music to Goethe's *Erlkönig* and sent it to him with a humble dedication. I shall never forgive the greatest poet of modern times for not even having acknowledged this letter with a single word of thanks to the man who had made his song immortal, the same Goethe who had ample time to write letters of thanks to Zelter for his mediocre music. Goethe's taste in music was as bad as his taste in art, he spent a year in Italy understanding nothing of Gothic art, the severe beauty of the primitives was unintelligible to him, Carlo Dolci and Guido Reni were his ideals. Even pure Greek art at its best left him cold, the Apollo Belvedere was his favourite. Schubert never saw the sea and yet no composer, no painter, no poet except Homer has ever made us understand its calm splendour, its mystery and its anger as he did. He had never seen the Nile and yet the opening bars of his wonderful *Memnon* might have sounded in the temple of Luxor. Hellenic art and literature were unknown to him, except what little his friend Mayerhofer might have told him, and yet his *Die Götter Griechenlands*, his *Prometheus*, his *Ganymede*, his *Fragment aus Aeschylus* are master-pieces from the golden age of Hellas. He had never been loved by a woman and yet no more heartrending cry of passion has ever reached our ears than his *Gretchen am Spinnrade*, no more touching resignation than his *Mignon*, no sweeter love-song has ever been sung than his *Ständchen*. He was thirty-one when he died, wretchedly poor as he had lived. He who had written *An die Musik* had not even a piano of his own! After his death all his earthly belongings, his clothes, his few books, his bed were sold at auction for sixty-three florins. In a dilapidated bag under his bed were found a score of other immortal songs worth more than all the gold of the Rothschilds in their Vienna where he lived and died.

* * *

Spring has come once more. The air is full of it. The ginestra is in bloom, the myrtle is budding, the vines are sprouting, flowers everywhere. Roses and honeysuckle are climbing the stems of the cypresses and the columns of the pergola. Anemones, crocuses, wild hyacinths, violets, orchids, cyclamens are rising out of the sweet-scented grass. Clusters of Campanula gracilis and deep-blue Lithospermum, blue as the Blue Grotto, are springing out of the very rock. The lizards are chasing each other among the ivy. The tortoises are cantering about singing lustily to themselves – perhaps you do not know that tortoises can sing? The mongoose seems more restless than ever. The little Minerva owl flaps her wings as if she meant to fly off to look up a friend in the Roman Campagna. Barbarossa, the big Maremma dog, has vanished on errands of his own, even my rickety old Tappio looks as if he would not mind a little spree in Lapland. Billy wanders up and down under his fig-tree with a twinkle in his eye and an unmistakable air of a young man about town, up to anything. Giovannina is having long talks under the garden wall with her sunburnt amoroso, it is all right, they are going to be married after Sant'Antonio. The sacred mountain above San Michele is full of birds on their way home to mate and rear their young. What a joy to me that they can rest there in peace! Yesterday I picked up a poor little skylark, so exhausted from his long journey across the sea that he didn't even attempt to fly away, he sat quite still in the palm of my hand as if he understood it was the hand of a friend, perhaps a compatriot – I asked him if he wouldn't sing me a song before he went off again, there was no bird-song I liked better than his; but he said he had no time to spare, he had to hurry home to Sweden to sing the summer in. For more than a week the flute-like notes of a golden oriole have been sounding in my garden. The other day I caught sight of his bride hiding in a laurel bush. To-day I have seen their nest, a marvel of bird-architecture. There is also much fluttering of wings and a soft murmur of bird-voices in the thicket of rosemary by the chapel. I pretend to know nothing about it, but I am pretty sure some flirtation is going on there; I wonder what bird it can be? Last night the secret came out, for just as I was going to bed a nightingale started singing Schubert's Serenade under my window:

> *Leise flehen meine Lieder*
> *Durch die Nacht zu dir*
> *In den stillen Hain hernieder*
> *Liebchen, komm zu mir.*

'What a beautiful girl Peppinella has turned out,' thought I as I was falling asleep; 'I wonder if Peppinella . . .'

IN THE OLD TOWER

I

The 'Story of San Michele' ends abruptly here just when it was about to begin, a meaningless fragment. It ends with the fluttering of wings and the twitter of birds and the air full of spring. Would that the meaningless story of my own life would end just so with the birds singing under my window and the sky bright with light! I have been thinking so much about death these last days, I do not know why. The garden is still full of flowers, the butterflies and the bees are still on the wing, the lizards are still sunning themselves among the ivy, the earth is still teeming with the life of all creeping things. Not later than yesterday I heard a belated warbler singing lustily under my window. Why should I think about death? God in His mercy has made Death invisible to the eyes of man. We know He is there, close on our heels like our shadow, never losing sight of us. Yet we never see Him, hardly ever think about Him. Strangest of all, the further we advance towards our graves, the further does Death recede from our thoughts. Indeed it needed a God to perform such a miracle!

Old people seldom talk about death, their dim eyes seem unwilling to focus anything but the past and the present. Gradually, as their memory weakens, even the past becomes more and more indistinct, and they live almost entirely in the present. That is why, granted their days are tolerably exempt from bodily suffering as nature meant them to be, old people are generally less unhappy than young people would expect them to be.

We know that we are going to die, in fact it is the only thing we know of what is in store for us. All the rest is mere guesswork, and most of the time we guess wrong. Like children in the trackless forest we grope our way through our lives in blissful ignorance of what is going to happen to us from one day to another, what hardships we may have to face, what more or less thrilling adventures we may encounter before the great adventure, the most thrilling of all, the Adventure of Death. Now and then in our perplexity we venture to put a timid question to our destiny, but we get no answer, for the stars are too far away. The sooner we realize that our fate lies in ourselves and not in the stars, so much the better for us. Happiness we can only find in ourselves, it is a waste of time to seek for it from others, few have any to spare. Sorrow we have to bear alone as best we can, it is not fair to try to shift it on others, be they men or women. We have to fight our own battles and strike as hard as we can, born fighters as we are. Peace will come one day for all of us, peace without dishonour even to the vanquished if he has tried to do his bit as long as he could.

As for me, the battle is over and lost. I have been driven out of San Michele, the labour of a lifetime. I had built it stone by stone with my own hands in the sweat of my brow, I had built it on my knees to be a sanctuary to the Sun where I was to seek knowledge and light from the glorious god I had been worshipping my whole life. I had been warned over and over again by the fire in my eyes that I was not worthy to live there, that my place was in the shade, but I had paid no heed to the warnings. Like the horses returning to their burning stables to perish in the flames, I had come back, summer after summer, to the blinding light of San Michele. Beware of the light, beware of the light!

I have accepted my fate at last, I am too old to fight a god. I have retreated to my stronghold in the old tower where I mean to make a last stand. Dante was still alive when the monks set to work to build the Tower of Materita, half monastery, half fortress, strong as the rock it stands upon. How often has not his bitter cry of: 'Nessun maggior dolore che ricordarsi del tempo felice nella miseria' echoed through its walls since I came here. But was he right after all, the Florentine seer? Is it true that there is no greater suffering than to remember our past happiness in our misery? I for one do not think so. It is with joy and not with sorrow that my thoughts go back to San Michele, where I have lived the happiest years of my life. But it is true I do not like to go there myself any more – I feel as if I were intruding upon sacred ground, sacred to a past which can never return, when the world was young and the sun was my friend.

It is good to wander about in the soft light under the olives of Materita. It is good to sit and dream in the old tower, it is about the only thing I can do now. The tower looks towards the West, where the sun sets. Soon the sun will sink into the sea, then comes the twilight, then comes the night.

It has been a beautiful day.

II

The last ray of golden light looked in through the Gothic window and wandered round the old tower from the illuminated missals and the thirteenth-century silver crucifix on the walls to the dainty Tanagras and the Venetian glasses on the refectory table, from the flower-crowned nymphs and bacchants dancing to the flute of Pan on the Greek bas-relief to the pale features on gold ground of St. Francis, the beloved Umbrian saint, with St. Claire, lilies in hand, by his side. Now a halo of gold encircled the still face of the Florentine Madonna, now the stern marble goddess, the Artemis Laphria, the swift arrow of Death in her quiver, stood out from the gloom. Now a radiant Solar Disk crowned once more the mutilated head of Akhanaten, the royal dreamer on the banks of the Nile, the Son of the Sun. Close by stood Osiris, the judge of the soul of man, and the falcon-headed Horus, the mysterious Isis and Nepthys, her sister, with Anubis, the watcher of the grave, crouching at their feet.

The light faded away, night drew near.

'God of day, Giver of light, cannot You stay with me a little longer? The night is so long for thoughts that dare not dream of sunrise, the night is so dark for eyes that cannot see the stars. Cannot you grant me a few seconds more of your radiant eternity to behold your beautiful world, the beloved sea, the wandering clouds, the glorious mountains, the rustling streams, the friendly trees, the flowers among the grass, the birds and beasts, my brothers and sisters, in the sky and in the forests and the fields? Cannot you leave me at least a few wild flowers in my hand to warm my heart, cannot you leave me a few stars in your heaven to show me the way?

'If I am no longer to see the features of men and women around me cannot you at least grant me a fugitive glance in the face of a little child or a friendly animal? I have looked into the face of man and woman for long, I know it well, it has little more to teach me. It is monotonous reading when compared to what I have read in God's own bible, in the mysterious face of Mother Nature. Dear old nurse, who has dispelled so many evil thoughts from my burning forehead by the gentle stroke of your wrinkled old hand, do not leave me alone in the dark. I am afraid of the dark! Stay with me a little longer, tell me a few more of your wonderful fairytales while you put your restless child to bed for the long night's sleep!

'Light of the world, alas! you are a God, and no prayer of mortal man has ever reached your heaven. How can I, the worm, hope for pity from you, merciless Sungod, from you who forsook even the great Pharaoh Akhanaten whose immortal Hymn to the Sun echoed over the valley of the Nile five hundred years before Homer sang:

> "*When Thou risest all the land is in joy and gladness*
> *And men say: It is Life to see Thee, it is Death not seeing Thee.*
> *West and East give praise to Thee, When Thou hast risen they*
> *live,*
> *When thou settest they die.*"'

Yet you looked on with no pity in your shining eye while the gods of old hurled the temple of your greatest worshipper in the Nile and tore the Solar Disk from his brow and the royal vulture from his breast and erased his hated name from the wrappings of sheeted gold round his frail body, condemning his nameless soul to wander in the underworld through all eternity.

Long after the gods of the Nile, the gods of Olympus and the gods of Walhalla had fallen into dust, another worshipper of yours, St. Francis of Assisi, the sweet singer of *Il Canto del Sole*, raised his arms to your heaven, immortal Sun-god, with the same prayer on his lips that I am addressing you to-day, that you should not take away your blessed light from his ailing eyes, worn out by vigil and tears. Earnestly besought by the brethren he journeyed to Rieti to consult a famous eye-doctor and submitted fearlessly to the operation advised by him. When the surgeon placed the iron in the fire to heat it, St. Francis spoke to the fire as to a friend, saying:

'Brother Fire, before all other things the Most Holy has created Thee of exceeding comeliness, powerful, beauteous and useful. Be Thou to me in this my hour merciful, be courteous. I beseech the Great Lord who has created Thee that He may temper for me Thy heat that I may be able patiently to endure Thy burning me.'

When he had finished his prayer over the iron glistening with heat, he made the sign of the cross and remained steadfastly unflinching while the hissing iron was plunged into the tender flesh, and from the ear to the eyebrow the cautery was drawn.

'Brother Medico,' said St. Francis to the physician, 'if it is not well burnt, thrust in again!'

And the physician, beholding in the weakness of the flesh such wondrous strength of spirit, marvelled and said:

'I tell you, brethren, I have seen strange things to-day!'

Alas! the saintliest of all men prayed in vain, suffered in vain, you forsook Il Poverello as you had forsaken the great Pharaoh. When on their homeward journey the faithful brethren deposited

336

the litter with its frail burden under the olive-trees by the foot of the hill, St. Francis could no longer see his beloved Assisi as he raised his hands to give it his last blessing.

How then can I, the sinner, the humblest of all your worshippers, hope for mercy from you, impassive Ruler of Life! How dare I ask for yet another favour from you, from you who has already given me so many precious gifts with lavish hands! You gave me my eyes to sparkle with joy and to fill with tears, you gave me my heart to throb with longing and to bleed with pity, you gave me sleep, you gave me hope.

I thought you gave it all to me as a gift. I was mistaken. It was only a loan, and now you want it all returned to you to be handed over to another being who will rise in his turn out of the same eternity into which I am sinking back. Lord of Light, be it so! The Lord gave and the Lord taketh away, blessed be the name of the Lord!

III

The bells in the Campanile were ringing Ave Maria. A light wind rustled through the cypresses outside the window where the birds were twittering before settling to sleep. The voice of the sea grew fainter and fainter and the blessed silence of the night fell over the old Tower.

I sat there in my Savonarola chair, weary and longing for rest. Wolf lay asleep at my feet, for days and nights he had hardly left my side. Now and then he opened his eyes and gave me a look so full of love and sorrow that it almost filled my own with tears. Now and then he sat up and laid his big head on my knees. Did he know what I knew, did he understand what I understood, that the hour for parting was drawing near? I stroked his head in silence, for the first time I did not know what to say to him, how to explain to him the great mystery I could not explain to myself

'Wolf, I am going away on a long journey, to a far-off land. This time you cannot come with me, my friend. You have to stay behind where you are, where you and I have lived together for so long, sharing good and evil. You must not mourn for me, you must forget me as everybody else will forget me, for such is the law of life. Do not worry, I shall be all right and so will you. Everything that could be done for your happiness has been done. You will live on in your own familiar surroundings where friendly people will look after you with the same loving care that I did. You will have your ample meal set before you every day as the bells ring mezzogiorno, and your succulent bones twice a week as before. The large garden where you used to romp is still yours, and even should you forget the law and start chasing a poaching cat under the olive-trees I shall continue from where I am, to turn my blind eye on the chase, closing the good one as I used to do for friendship's sake. Then when your limbs have grown stiff and your eyes dim you will rest for good under the antique marble column in the cypress grove by the old tower at the side of your comrades who have gone there before you. And when all is said, who knows if we shall not meet again? Great or small our chances are the same.'

'Do not go away, stay with me or take me with you,' pleaded the faithful eyes.

'I am going to a land I know nothing about. I do not know what will happen to me there, and still less do I know what would happen to you, if you came with me. I have read strange tales about this land, but they are only tales, nobody who went there has ever returned to tell us what he saw. One man alone might have told us, but He was the son of a God, and He went back to His Father, His lips sealed in inscrutable silence.'

I stroked the big head, but my benumbed hands no longer felt the touch of his glossy coat.

As I bent down to kiss him good-bye a sudden fear shone in his eyes, he drew back in terror and crept to his couch under the refectory table. I called him back but he did not come. I knew what it meant. I had seen it before. I had thought there might have been still another day or two left. I stood up and tried to go to the window for a deep breath of air, but my limbs refused to obey, and I sank back in my chair. I looked round the old tower. All was dark and silent, but I thought I heard Artemis, the stern goddess, taking her swift arrow from her quiver, ready to raise her bow. An invisible hand touched my shoulder. A shiver ran through my body. I thought I was going to faint, but I felt no pain and my head was clear.

'Welcome, sire! I heard the galloping of your black charger through the night, you have won the race after all, for I can still see your sombre face as you bend over me. You are no stranger to me, we have often met before ever since we stood side by side by a bed in Salle Ste. Claire. I used then to call you wicked and cruel, an executioner enjoying the slow torture of his victim. I did not know Life then as I know it now. I know now that you are by far the more merciful of the two, that what you take away with one hand you give back with the other. I know now that it was Life, not you that lit the terror in those wide-open eyes and strained the muscle in those heaving chests for yet another breath of air, yet another minute of agony.

'I for one am not going to wrestle with you to-day. Had you come to me when the blood was young it would have been another matter. There was plenty of life in me then. I would have put up a good fight and hit back as hard as I could. Now I am weary, my eyes are dim, my limbs are tired and my heart is worn out, I have only my head left to me, and my head tells me it is no use fighting. So I shall sit still in my Savonarola chair and leave you to do what you have to do. I am curious to see how you are going to set to work, I have always been interested in physiology. I had better warn you I was made of good stuff, hit as hard as you can or you might miss the mark once more as you have already missed it a couple of times unless I am mistaken. I hope, sire, that you do not bear me any grudge from bygone times. Alas! I fear I used to keep you rather busy in those days in Avenue de Villiers. Pray, sir, I am not as brave as I pretend to be, if you would just give me a few drops of your eternal sleeping-draught before you begin, I should be grateful.'

'I always do and you for one ought to know it, you who have seen me at work so often. Do you wish to send for a priest, there is still time? They always send for a priest when they see me coming.'

'It is no use sending for the priest, he can do nothing for me now. It is too late for me to repent and too early for him to condemn, and I suppose it matters little to you either way.'

'I do not care, good men or bad men are all the same to me.'

'It is no good sending for a priest who will only tell me that I was born evil, that my thoughts and my deeds were stained with sin, that I must repent it all, retract it all. I repent little I have done, I retract nothing. I have lived according to my instinct and I believe my instinct was sound. I have made a fool of myself often enough when I tried to be guided by my reason. It was because my reason was at fault, and I have already been punished for it. I wish to thank those who have been kind to me. Enemies I have had few, most of them were doctors, they did me but little harm, I went on my way just the same. I wish to ask forgiveness from those to whom I have given pain. That is all, the rest concerns God and myself, not the priest, whom I do not accept as my judge.'

'I do not like your priests. It is they who have taught men to fear my approach with their menace of eternity and their flaming hell. It is they who have torn the wings from my shoulders and disfigured my friendly face and turned me into a hideous skeleton to wander from house to house, scythe in hand, like a thief in the night and to dance their *Danse Macabre* in the frescoes on their cloister walls hand in hand with their saints and their damned. I have nothing to do either with their heaven or with their hell. I am a Natural Law.'

'I heard a golden oriole sing in the garden yesterday, and just as the sun went down a little warbler came and sang to me under the window, shall I ever hear him again?'

'Where there are angels there are birds.'

'I wish a friendly voice could read the "Phaedo" to me once more.'

'The voice was mortal, the words are immortal, you will hear them again.'

'Shall I ever hear again the sounds of Mozart's Requiem, my beloved Schubert and the titan chords of Beethoven?'

'It was only an echo from Heaven you overheard.'

'I am ready. Strike, friend!'

'I am not going to strike. I am going to put you to sleep.'

'Shall I dream?'

'Yes, it is all a dream.'

'Shall I awake?'

No answer came to my question.

* * *

'Who are you, beautiful boy? Are you Hypnos, the Angel of Sleep?'

He stood there close by my side with flower-crowned locks and dream-heavy forehead, beautiful as the Genius of Love.

'I am his brother, born of the same Mother Night. Thanatos is my name. I am the Angel of Death. It is thy life that is flickering out in the light of the torch I tread under my foot.'

* * *

I dreamt I saw an old man staggering wearily along on his lonely road. Now and then he looked upwards as if in search of someone to show him the way. Now and then he sank down on his knees as if he had no more strength to struggle on. Already the fields and forests, the rivers and the seas lay under his feet, and soon even the snow-capped mountains disappeared in the mist of the vanishing earth. Onwards, upwards went his way. Storm-driven clouds lifted him on their mighty shoulders and carried him with vertiginous speed through the vastness of the infinite, beckoning stars led him nearer and nearer to the land that knows of no night, no death. He stood at last before the Gates of Heaven riveted with golden hinges to the adamantine rock. The gates were closed. Was it an eternity, was it a day, was it a minute he knelt on the threshold hoping against hope to be let in? Suddenly, moved by invisible hands, the mighty doors swung wide open to let pass a floating form with the wings of an angel and the still face of a sleeping child. He sprang to his feet and with the audacity of despair he stole in through the gates just as they were closing before him.

'Who art thou, daring intruder?' a stern voice called out. A tall figure, robed in a white mantle, the golden key in his hands, stood before me.

'Keeper of the Gates of Heaven, holy St. Peter, I beseech Thee, let me stay!'

St. Peter glanced rapidly at my credentials, the scanty records of my life on earth.

'It looks bad,' said St. Peter. 'Very bad. How did you come here, I am sure there must be some mistake. . . .'

He stopped abruptly as a tiny messenger angel alighted swiftly in front of us. Folding his purple wings he adjusted his short tunic of gossamer and petals of roses, all glistening with morning dew. His little legs were bare and rosy like the rose petals, on his tiny feet were golden sandals. Cocked on one side of his curly head he wore a fairy cap of tulips and lilies of the valley. His eyes were full of sunglitter and his lips were full of joy. In his small hands he held an illuminated missal, which he presented to St. Peter with a smiling air of importance.

'They always turn to me when they are in trouble,' frowned St. Peter as he read the missal. 'When all is well, they pay no heed to my warnings. Tell them,' he said to the messenger angel, 'tell them I am coming at once, tell them to answer no questions till I am with them.'

The messenger angel lifted his rosy finger to his tulip cap, unfolded his purple wings and flew away swift as a bird and singing like one.

St. Peter looked perplexedly at me with his scrutinizing eyes. Turning to an aged Archangel who, leaning on his drawn sword, stood on guard by the golden curtain, St. Peter said pointing towards me:

'Let him await my return here. He is audacious and cunning, his tongue is smooth, see that he does not loosen yours. We all have our weaknesses, I know which is yours. There is something strange about his spirit, I cannot even understand how he came here. For all I know he may belong to that same tribe which allured you away from Heaven to follow Lucifer and caused your fall. Be on your guard, be silent, be vigilant!'

He was gone. I looked at the aged Archangel, and the aged Archangel looked at me. I thought it wiser to say nothing, but I watched him from the corner of my eye. Presently I saw him unbuckle his sword belt and with great precaution put his sword against a column of lapis-lazuli. He looked quite relieved. His old face was so kind, his eyes were so mild that I felt sure he was all for peace like myself.

'Venerable Archangel,' I said timidly, 'shall I have to wait long for St. Peter?'

'I heard the trumpets sounding in the Hall of Judgment,' said the Archangel, 'they are judging two cardinals who have summoned St. Peter to assist them in their defence. No, I do not think you will have to wait for long,' he added with a chuckle, 'as a rule not even St. Ignatius, the sharpest lawyer in Heaven, succeeds in wriggling them through. The Public Prosecutor is more than a match for him. He was a monk called Savonarola whom they burned at the stake.

'God is the Supreme Judge and not man,' I said, 'and God is merciful.'

'Yes, God is the Supreme Judge and God is merciful,' repeated the Archangel. 'But God rules over countless worlds, far greater in splendour and wealth than the half-forgotten little star these two men came from.'

The Archangel took me by the hand and led me to the open archway. With awe-stricken eyes I saw thousands of luminous stars and planets, all pulsating with life and light, wending their predestined ways through the infinite.

'Do you see that tiny little speck, dim like the light of a tallow candle on the point of flickering out? That is the world these two men came from, crawling ants on a clod of earth.'

'God created their world and He created them,' said I.

'Yes, God created their world. He ordered the sun to melt the frozen bowels of their earth. He cleansed it with rivers and seas, He clad its rugged surface with forests and fields, He peopled it with friendly animals. The world was beautiful and all was well. Then on the last day He created Man. Maybe it would have been better had He rested the day before He created Man instead of the day after. I suppose you know how it all came about. One day a huge monkey maddened by hunger set to work with his horny hands to forge himself weapons to slay the other animals. What could the six-inch-long canines of the Machaerodus do against his sharpened flint, sharper than the fang of the sabre-toothed tiger? What could the sickle-like claws of the Ursus Spelaeus do against his tree branch, studded with thorns and twig-spikes and set with razor-edged shells? What could their wild strength do against his cunning, his snares, his pitfalls? So he grew up, a brutish Protanthropos slaying friends and foes, a fiend to all living things, a Satan among animals. Erect over his victims he raised his blood-stained banner of victory over the animal world, crowning himself king of creation. Selection straightened his facial angle and enlarged his brain-pan. His raucous cry of wrath and fear grew into articulate sounds and words. He learned to tame fire. Slowly he evolved into man. His cubs sucked the blood from the palpitating flesh of the animals he had slain, and fought among themselves like hungry wolflings for the marrowbones his formidable jaws had cracked and strewn about his cave. So they grew up, strong and fierce like himself, bent on prey, eager to attack and devour any living thing that crossed their path, even were it one of their own foster brothers. The forest trembled at their approach, the fear of man was born amongst the animals. Soon, infuriated by their lust for murder, they started slaying one another with their stone axes. The ferocious war began, the war which has never ceased.

'Anger shone in the eyes of the Lord, He repented having created man. And the Lord said:

' "I will destroy man from the face of the earth, corrupt as he is and full of violence."

'He ordered the fountains of the great deep to be broken up and the windows of Heaven to be opened to engulf man and the world he had polluted with blood and crime. Would that He had drowned them all! But in His faithful mercy He willed their world to emerge once more cleansed and purified by the waters of the Flood. The curse remained in the seed of the few of the doomed race He had suffered to remain in the Ark. The murder began again, the never-ceasing war was let loose once more.

'God looked on with infinite patience, reluctant to strike, willing to the last to forgive. He even sent down His own Son to their wicked world to teach men mildness and love and to pray for them: you know what they did to Him. Hurling defiance against Heaven

343

they soon set their whole world ablaze with the flames of Hell. With Satanic cunning they forged themselves new weapons to murder each other. They harnessed death to swoop down upon their dwellings from the very sky, they polluted the life-giving air with the vapours of Hell. The thunderous roar of their battles shakes their whole earth. When the firmament is wrapped in night we up here can see the very light of their star shining red as if stained with blood and we can hear the moaning of their wounded. One of the angels who surround the throne of God has told me that the eyes of the Madonna are red with tears every mornng and that the wound in the side of Her Son has opened again.'

'But God Himself who is the God of mercy, how can He suffer these torments to go on ?' I asked. 'How can He listen impassive to these cries of anguish ?'

The aged Archangel looked around uneasily lest his answer might be overheard.

'God is old and weary,' he whispered as if awestruck by the sound of his own words, 'and His heart is grieved. Those who surround Him and watch over Him with their infinite love, have not the heart to disturb His rest with these never-ending tidings of horror and woe. Often He wakes up from His haunted slumber and asks what causes the roar of thunder that reaches His ears and the flashes of lurid light that pierce the darkness. And those around Him say that the thunder is the voice from His own storm-driven clouds and the flashes are the flashes of His own lightning. And His tired eyelids close again.'

'Better so, venerable Archangel, better so! For if His eyes had seen what I have seen and His ears had heard what I have heard, it would have repented the Lord once more that He had created man. Once more He would have ordered the fountains of the great deep to be broken up to destroy man. This time He would have drowned them all and left only the animals in the ark.'

'Beware of the wrath of God! Beware of the wrath of God!'

'I am not afraid of God. But I am afraid of those who once were men, of the stern prophets, of the Holy Fathers, of St. Peter, whose severe voice bade me await here his return.'

'I am rather afraid of St. Peter myself,' admitted the aged Archangel, 'you heard how he rebuked me for having been led astray by Lucifer. I have been forgiven by God Himself and suffered to return to His Heaven. Does St. Peter not know that to forgive means to forget ? You are right, the prophets are severe. But they are just, they were enlightened by God and they speak with His own voice. The Holy Fathers can only read the thoughts of another man by the dim light of mortal eyes, their voices are the voices of men.'

'No man knows another man. How can they judge what they do not know, what they do not understand? I wish St. Francis was among my judges, I have loved him my whole life and he knows me, he understands me.'

'St. Francis has never judged anybody, he has only forgiven like Christ Himself, who lays His hand in his as if He was his brother. St. Francis is not often seen in the Hall of Judgment where you soon will stand, he is not even much liked there. Many of the martyrs and saints are jealous of his holy stigmata, and more than one of the Peers of Heaven feel somewhat uncomfortable in their gorgeous mantles all embroidered with gold and precious stones, when "Il Poverello" appears amongst them in his torn and threadbare cassock, all in rags from wear and tear. The Madonna keeps on mending and patching it as well as she can, she says it is no good getting him a new cassock, for he would only give it away.'

'I wish I could see him, I long to ask him a question I have asked myself my whole life, if anybody can answer that question it is he. Maybe you, wise old Archangel, can tell me? Where do the souls of the friendly animals go to? Where is their Heaven? I should like to know because, because I have . . .'

I dared not say more.

' "In my father's house there are many mansions" said our Lord. God who has created the animals will see to that. Heaven is vast enough to shelter them also.

'Listen,' whispered the old Archangel, pointing his finger towards the open archway. 'Listen!'

A suave harmony, borne on strings of harps and sweet voices of children, reached my ears as I looked out over the gardens of Heaven, all fragrant with the scent of Elysian flowers.

'Lift thy eyes and see,' said the Archangel, reverently bending his head.

Ere my eyes had discerned the halo of pale gold round her head, my heart had recognized her. What an incomparable painter was he not, Sandro Botticelli! There she came just as he had so often painted her, so young, so pure, and yet with that tender watchfulness of motherhood in her eyes. Flower-crowned maidens with smiling lips and girlish eyes surrounded Her with eternal spring, tiny angels with folded wings of purple and gold held up Her mantle, others stretched a carpet of roses before Her feet. St. Clare,

345

the beloved of St. Francis, whispered in the Madonna's ear and it almost seemed to me as if the Mother of Christ had deigned to look at me for a moment as she passed by.

'Fear not,' said the Archangel softly, 'fear not, the Madonna has seen you, she will remember you in her prayers.

'St. Peter tarries,' said the Archangel, 'he is fighting a hard battle with Savonarola for the rescue of his cardinals.'

He lifted a corner of the golden curtain and glanced down the peristyle.

'Do you see that friendly spirit in his white robe and a flower stuck over his ear? I often have a little chat with him, he is beloved by us all here, he is as simple and innocent as a child. I often watch him with curiosity, he always walks about by himself picking up angels' feathers fallen on the ground, he has tied them into a sort of feather broom, and when he thinks nobody sees him he bends down to sweep a little star dust from the golden floor. He does not seem to know himself why he does it, he says he cannot help it. I wonder who he was in life. He came here not long ago, he may be able to tell you all you want to know about the Last Judgment.'

I looked at the white-robed spirit, it was my friend Arcangelo Fusco, the street sweeper from the Italian poor quarter in Paris! The same humble, guileless eyes, the same flower stuck over his ear, the rose he had offered with southern gallantry to the Countess the day I had taken her to present the dolls to the Salvatore children.

'Dear Arcangelo Fusco,' said I, stretching out my hands towards my friend, 'I never doubted you would come here.'

He looked at me with serene indifference as if he did not know me.

'Arcangelo Fusco, don't you recognize me, don't you remember me? Don't you remember how tenderly you nursed night and day Salvatore's children when they had diphtheria, how you sold your Sunday clothes to pay for the coffin when the eldest child died, the little girl you loved so?'

A shadow of suffering passed over his face.

'I do not remember.'

'Ah! my friend! what a tremendous secret you are revealing to me with these words! What a load you are taking from my heart! You do not remember! But how is it that I remember?'

'Perhaps you are not really dead, perhaps you are only dreaming you are dead.'

'I have been a dreamer my whole life, if this is a dream it is the most wonderful of all.'

'Perhaps your memory was stronger than mine, strong enough to survive for a while the parting from the body. I do not know, I do not understand, it is all too deep for me. I do not ask any questions.'

'That is why you are here, my friend. But tell me, Arcangelo Fusco, does nobody up here remember his life on earth?'

'They say not, they say only those who go to Hell remember, that is why it is called Hell.'

'But tell me at least, Arcangelo Fusco, was the trial hard, were the judges severe?'

'They looked rather severe at first, I was beginning to tremble all over, I was afraid they were going to ask me for particulars about the Neapolitan shoemaker who had taken my wife away from me and whom I had stabbed with his own knife. But luckily they did not want to know anything about the shoemaker. All they asked me was, if I had handled any gold and I said I had never had anything but coppers in my hands. They asked me if I had hoarded any goods or possessions of any kind, and I said I possessed nothing but the shirt I had died in in the hospital. They asked me nothing more and let me in. Then came an angel with a huge parcel in his hands.

' "Take off your old shirt and put on your Sunday clothes," said the angel. Would you believe it, it was my old Sunday clothes I had sold to pay the undertaker, all embroidered by the angels with pearls, you will see me wear them next Sunday if you are still here. Then came another angel with a big money-box in his hands.

' "Open it," said the angel, "it is all your savings, all the coppers you gave away to those as poor as yourself. All you give away on earth is saved for you in Heaven, all you keep is lost."

'Would you believe it, there was not a single copper in the money-box, all my coppers had been turned into gold.

'I say,' he added in a whisper lest the Archangel should hear us, 'I do not know who you are but you look rather badly off, do not take it amiss if I just tell you that you are welcome to anything you like from the money-box. I said to the angel I did not know what to do with all this money, and the angel told me to give it to the first beggar I should meet.'

'Would that I had followed your example, Arcangelo Fusco, and I should not be as badly off as I am to-day. Alas! I did not give away my Sunday clothes, that is why I am all in rags now. Indeed it is a great relief to me that they did not ask you for particulars about the Neapolitan shoemaker you dispatched to another world.

God knows how many shoemakers' lives I might have been made to answer for, I who have been a doctor for over thirty years!'

The golden curtain was drawn aside by invisible hands and an angel stood before us.

'Your time has come to appear before your judges,' said the old Archangel. 'Be humble and be silent, above all be silent! Remember it was speech that brought about my fall, so it will bring about yours if you loosen your tongue.'

'I say,' whispered Arcangelo Fusco, blinking cunningly at me. 'I think you'd better take no unnecessary risks. If I were you I wouldn't say anything about the other shoemakers you spoke about. I didn't say anything about my shoemaker since they didn't ask me about him. After all perhaps they never knew anything about him – chi lo sa?'

The angel took me by the hand and led me down the peristyle to the Hall of Judgment, vast as the Hall of Osiris with columns of jasper and opal and capitals of golden lotus flowers and shafts of sunbeams supporting its mighty vault all strewn with the stars of Heaven.

I lifted my head and I saw myriads of martyrs and saints in their white robes, hermits, anchorites and stylites, their wild features scorched by the Nubian sun, naked cenobites with their emaciated bodies covered by a fell of hair, stern-eyed prophets, their long beards spread over their chests, holy apostles with palm branches in their hands, patriarchs and Fathers of all lands and all creeds, a few popes in their glittering tiaras and a couple of cardinals in their red robes. Seated in a semicircle in front of me sat my judges, stern and impassible.

'It looks bad,' said St. Peter, handing them my credentials, 'very bad!'

St. Ignatius, the Grand Inquisitor, rose from his seat and spoke:

'His life is sullied with heinous sins, his soul is dark, his heart is impure. As a Christian and as a saint I ask for his damnation, may the devils torment his body and soul through all eternity.'

A murmur of assent echoed through the Hall. I lifted my head and looked at my judges. They all looked back at me in stern silence. I bent my head and said nothing, I remembered the warning of the old Archangel to be silent, and besides I did not know what to say. Suddenly I noticed far away in the background a small saint nodding frantically at me. Presently I saw him timidly making his way among the bigger saints to where I stood near the door.

348

'I know you well,' said the little saint with a friendly glance in his gentle eyes, 'I saw you coming,' and putting his finger to his lips, he added in a whisper, 'I also saw your faithful friend trotting at your heels.'

'Who are you, kind father?' I whispered back.

'I am St. Rocco, the patron saint of the dogs,' announced the little saint, 'I wish I could help you but I am rather a small saint here, they won't listen to what I say,' he whispered with a furtive glance towards the prophets and the holy fathers.

'He was an unbeliever,' St. Ignatius went on. 'A blasphemous scoffer, a liar, an impostor, an enchanter full of black magic, a fornicator . . .'

Several of the old prophets cocked their ears attentively.

'He was young and ardent,' pleaded St. Paul, 'it is better to . . .

'Old age did not improve him,' muttered a hermit.

'He loved children,' said St. John.

'He loved their mothers too,' growled a Patriarch in his beard.

'He was a hard-working doctor,' said St. Luke, the Beloved Physician.

'Heaven is full of his patients and so is Hell, I am told,' retorted St. Dominic.

'He has had the audacity to bring his dog with him, he is sitting waiting for his master outside the Gates of Heaven,' announced St. Peter.

'He will not have to wait for his master for long,' hissed St. Ignatius.

'A dog at the Gates of Heaven!' ejaculated a grim-looking old prophet in a furious voice.

'Who is that?' I whispered to the patron saint of the dogs.

'For God's sake don't say anything, remember the warning of the Archangel. I believe it is Habakkuk.'

'If Habakkuk is amongst my judges I am lost in any case, "il est capable de tout " said Voltaire.'

'A dog at the Gates of Heaven,' roared Habakkuk, 'a dog, an unclean beast!'

It was too much for me.

'He is not an unclean beast,' I shouted back, glaring angrily at Habakkuk, 'he was created by the same God who created you and me. If there is a Heaven for us, there must also be a Heaven for the animals, though you grim old prophets, so fierce and stalwart in your holiness, have forgotten all about them. So for the matter of that did you, Holy Apostles,' I went on losing my head more and more. 'Or why did you omit in your Holy scriptures to record a single saying of our Lord in defence of our dumb brethren?'

'The Holy Church to which I belonged on earth has never taken any interest in the animals,' interrupted St. Anastasius, 'nor do we wish to hear anything about them in Heaven. Blasphemous fool, you had better think of your own soul instead of theirs, your own wicked soul about to return to the darkness from whence it came.'

'My soul came from Heaven and not from the Hell you have let loose on earth. I do not believe in your Hell.'

'You soon will believe in it,' wheezed the Grand Inquisitor, his eyeballs reflecting invisible flames.

'The wrath of God is upon him, he is mad, he is mad!' called out a voice.

A cry of terror rang through the Hall of Judgment:

'Lucifer! Lucifer! Satan is amongst us!'

Moses rose from his seat, gigantic and fierce, his Ten Commandments in his sinewy hands and flashes of lightning in his eyes.

'How angry he looks,' I whispered awestruck to the patron saint of the dogs.

'He is always angry,' the little saint whispered back in terror.

'Let no more be said about this spirit,' thundered Moses. 'The voice I have heard is a voice from the smoking lips of Satan. Man or demon, away from here! Jehovah, God of Israel, put forth Thy hand to smite him down! Burn his flesh and dry up the blood in his veins! Break all his bones! Cut him off from Heaven and earth and send him back to the Hell from whence he came!'

'To Hell! To Hell!' echoed through the Hall of Judgment.

I tried to speak but no sound came from my lips. My heart froze, I felt abandoned by God and man.

'I will look after the dog if it comes to the worst,' whispered the little saint at my side.

Suddenly through the awful silence I thought I heard the twitter of birds. A little garden warbler alighted fearlessly on my shoulder and sang in my ear:

'You saved the life of my grandmother, my aunt and my three brothers and sisters from torture and death by the hand of man on that rocky island. Welcome! Welcome!'

At the same moment a skylark picked at my finger and twittered to me:

'I met a flycatcher in Lapland who told me that when you were a boy you mended the wing of one of his ancestors and warmed his frozen body near your heart, and as you opened your hand to set him free you kissed him and said: "God-speed little brother! God-speed little brother!" Welcome! Welcome!'

'Help me little brother! Help me little brother!'

'I will try, I will try,' sang the skylark as he unfolded his wings and flew away with a trill of joy, 'I will trrrrrry!'

My eyes followed the skylark as he flew away towards the line of blue hills I could just see through the Gothic archway. How well I knew those hills from the paintings of Fra Angelico! The same silver-grey olive-trees, the same sombre cypresses standing out against the soft evening sky. I heard the bells of Assisi ringing the Angelus and there he came, the pale Umbrian saint, slowly descending the winding hill path with brother Leo and brother Leonardo at his side. Swift-winged birds fluttered and sang round his head, others fed from his outstretched hands, others nestled fearlessly among the folds of his cassock. St. Francis stood still by my side and looked at my judges with his wonderful eyes, those eyes that neither God nor man nor beast could meet with anger in theirs.

Moses sank down in his seat letting fall his Ten Commandments.

'Always he,' he murmured bitterly. 'Always he, the frail dreamer with his flock of birds and his following of beggars and outcasts. So frail and yet strong enough to stay Thy avenging hand, O Lord! Art Thou then not Jehovah, the jealous God, who descended in fire and smoke on Mount Sinai and made the people of Israel tremble with awe? Was it not Thy anger that bade me stretch forth my avenging rod to smite every herb in the field and break every tree that all men and beasts should die? Was it not Thy voice that spake in my Ten Commandments? Who will fear the flash of Thy lightning, O Lord! if the thunder of Thy wrath can be silenced by the twitter of a bird?'

My head sank on St. Francis' shoulder.

I was dead, and I did not know it.